Multimodal Treatment Approach

FIBROMYALGIA

MOHIT RANA

ABSTRACT

Background: Fibromyalgia (FM) is described as a common chronic musculoskeletal pain disorder, characterized by the symptoms of widespread chronic pain associated with multiple tender points. Although there numerous treatment options are available for stabilizing the symptoms of FM yet there is dearth of tailored interventions specifically for affected individuals. Hence, present study was focused to determine the effectiveness of Integrated Physiotherapy Techniques combined with Pharmacotherapy and Cognitive Behavioral Therapy in patients with fibromyalgia.

Method: Ninety FM participants were selected based on the American College of Rheumatology 2010 criteria for fibromyalgia. Participants were randomly allocated into three groups with (n=30) in each group. Participants of Group 1 received pharmacotherapy along with Integrated Physical Therapy; Group 2 received Cognitive Behavioral Therapy along with Integrated Physical Therapy and of Group 3 received Integrated Physical Therapy. The intervention was given for the period of 12 weeks.

Outcome Measures. Primary outcome measures of the study was, Revised Fibromyalgia Impact Questionnaire and secondary outcome measures were Visual Analogue Scale, Beck Depression Index, Shortform-36 health survey, Pain Pressure Algometer, General Anxiety Disorder – 7.Baseline assessment was done at Day 0 and post intervention assessment was done at Day 30, Day 60 and Day 90. Data was analyzed with repeated measures ANOVA and Tukey's LSD test using SPSS version 22 with 95% CI and $p = 0.05$ level of significance.

Results: Within group statistical analysis revealed significant results with $p<0.05$ for primary and secondary outcome measures in all the groups. Between group comparison revealed significant difference between Group 2 and Group 3 for quality of life, pain, depression, physical and mental health and trigger point sensitivity and non significant difference for the general anxiety disorder scale -7 ($p>0.05$). After three months, a significance ($p < 0.05$) within-group improvement was noted in all three groups. The between group mean changes in all the outcome measures of Cognitive Behavioral Therapy along with Integrated Physical Therapy and Integrated Physical Therapy only groups showed significant results relative to the pharmacotherapy along with Integrated Physiotherapy techniques.

Conclusion: Cognitive behavioral therapy combined with Integrated Physiotherapy techniques was significant in reducing the severity of pain, depression, disability and improvement on the pain pressure threshold and quality of life in individuals affected with FM than other experimental groups.

CONTENTS

Title	Page No.
List of Tables	
List of Figures	
List of Abbreviations	
Chapter 1 Introduction	**1 – 6**
1.1 Need of the Study	4
1.2 Statement of the Problem	5
1.3 Aim of the Study	5
1.4 Objectives of the problem	5
1.5 Hypothesis	6
1.6 Limitations of the Study	6
1.7 Operational Definition	6
Chapter 2 Review of Literature	**7 – 66**
2.1 Search Strategies	7
2.2 Search Duration	7
2.3 Keywords	7
2.4 Level of Evidence	7
2.5 Epidemiology of Fibromyalgia	8
2.6 Sickness, Absenteeism, Medical cost, sedentary time and Physical activity in FM	10
2.7 Studies related to Pathophysiology of FM	13
2.8 Biomarkers and the other diagnostic procedure in FM	16
2.9 Studies related to FM associated with other condition	27
2.10 Studies related to symptoms of FM	29
2.11 Studies related to other symptoms of FM	35
2.12 Studies related to Tender points	38
2.13 Studies related to Pregabalin treatment	39
2.14 Studies related to Cognitive behavioral therapy (CBT)	42
2.15 Studies related to Integrated Physiotherapy Techniques	47

2.16 Studies related to other non-invasive treatments of fibromyalgia ... 52

2.17 Studies related to Complementary and Alternative Medicine (CAM) Therapies ... 57

Chapter 3 **Methodology** ... **67 – 81**

3.1 Research Design ... 67

3.2 Ethical Approval ... 67

3.3 Research Setting ... 67

3.4 Informed Consent ... 68

3.5 Study Population ... 68

3.6 Sample size and Sampling method ... 68

3.7 Sampling Criteria ... 68

3.7.1 Inclusion Criteria ... 68

3.7.2 Exclusion Criteria ... 69

3.8 Study Variables ... 69

3.8.1 Independent Variables ... 69

3.8.2 Dependent Variables ... 69

3.9 Materials / Instrumentation ... 69

3.10 Protocol ... 70

3.11 Outcome Measures ... 70

3.12 Procedure ... 72

Chapter 4 **Results** ... **82 – 252**

4.1 Baseline characteristics of study population ... 83

4.2 Role of pharmacotherapy along with integrated physiotherapy techniques (Group–I) in Fibromyalgia ... 89

4.3 Role of cognitive behavioral therapy along with Integrated Physiotherapy Techniques (Group-II) in Fibromyalgia ... 125

4.4 Role of Integrated Physiotherapy Techniques (Group-III) in Fibromyalgia ... 162

4.5 Identifying individual differences between all the three groups ... 200

Chapter 5 **Discussion** ... **253 – 262**

5.1 Role of PHAIPT, CBTAIPT and IPT on the quality of life in FM ... 255

5.2 Role of PHAIPT, CBTAIPT and IPT on depression in FM ... 256

	5.3 Role of PHAIPT, CBTAIPT and IPT on health status in FM	257
	5.4 Role of PHAIPT, CBTAIPT and IPT on anxiety in FM	257
	5.5 Role of PHAIPT, CBTAIPT and IPT on physical and mental health in FM	258
	5.6 Role of PHAIPT, CBTAIPT and IPT on the pain pressure sensitivity on painful sites in FM	259
	5.7 Effectiveness of experimental groups and its reasoning	260
Chapter 6	**Summary and Conclusion**	**263 – 264**
	References	**265 – 292**
	Appendices	**293 – 330**
Appendix – I	Ethical Approval Certificate	293
Appendix – II	Clinical Trial Registry - India (CTRI) Registration	294
Appendix – III	Consent Form	299
Appendix – IV	Sampling Calculation	301
Appendix – V	Fibromyaligia Impact Questionnaire (FIQR)	302
Appendix – VI	Beck Depression Inventory –II (BDI)	305
Appendix – VII	Generalized Anxiety Disorder (GAD) – 7	307
Appendix – VIII	SF-36 Health Survey	308
Appendix – IX	Home Program Exercises	313
Appendix – X	User Agreement FIQR	315
Appendix – XI	License Agreement SF-36v2 (OGSR)	320
Appendix – XII	Ethical Consideration	322
Appendix – XIII	Screening Form	323
Appendix – XIV	New Clinical Fibromyalgia Diagnostic Criteria	324
Appendix – XV	Assessment Form	325
Appendix – XVI	Data Collection Form	328
Appendix – XVII	Registration Letter	329
Appendix – XVIII	Fibromyalgia Flyer	330

LIST OF TABLES

S.No.	Title of the Table	Page No.
2.1	Centre of Evidence-Based Medicine: Levels of Evidence	7
4.1.1	Demographic characteristics of study population	83
4.1.2	Gender distribution of fibromyalgia patients in different interventional groups	85
4.1.3	Education level distribution of fibromyalgia patients in different interventional groups	86
4.1.4	Occupation distribution of fibromyalgia patients in different interventional groups	87
4.1.5	Marital status distribution of fibromyalgia patients in different interventional groups	88
4.2.1	Comparison of Revised Fibromyalgia Impact Questionnaire (FIQR) variable in group-1 from baseline to the third month.	89
4.2.1.1	Pair-wise comparison of Revised Fibromyalgia Impact Questionnaire (FIQR) variable in group-1 from Baseline to Third month at different time frame.	90
4.2.2	Comparison of Beck Depression Index (BDI) variable in group-1 from baseline to the third month.	90
4.2.2.1	Pair-wise comparison of Beck Depression Index (BDI) variable in group-1 from Baseline to Third month at different time frame.	91
4.2.3	Comparison of Visual Analogue Scale (VAS) variable in group-1 from baseline to the third month.	92
4.2.3.1	Pair-wise comparison of Visual Analogue Scale (VAS) variable in group-1 from Baseline to Third month at different time frame.	93
4.2.4	Comparison of General Anxiety Disorder (GAD-7) variable in group-1 from baseline to the third month.	93
4.2.4.1	Pair-wise comparison of General Anxiety Disorder (GAD-7) variable in group-1 from Baseline to Third month at different time frame.	94
4.2.5	Comparison of Short Form -36 Physical Component Summary (SF-36 PCS) variable in group-1 from baseline to the third month.	95
4.2.5.1	Pair-wise comparison of Short Form -36 Physical Component Summary (SF-36 PCS) variable in group-1 from Baseline to Third month at different time frame.	96

4.2.6   Comparison of Short Form -36 Mental Component Summary (SF-36 Mental variables in group-1 from baseline to the third month.   96

4.2.6.1   Pair-wise comparison of Short Form -36 Mentalcal Component Summary (SF-36 PCS) variable in group-1 from Baseline to Third month at different time frame.   97

4.2.7   Comparison of algometric measurement of widespread pain index points on Shoulder Girdle Left (SGL) variable in group-1 from baseline to third month.   98

4.2.7.1   Pair-wise comparison of algometric measurement of widespread pain index points on Shoulder Girdle Left (SGL) variable in group-1 from Baseline to Third month at different time frame.   99

4.2.8   Comparison of algometric measurement of widespread pain index points on Shoulder Girdle Right (SGR) variable in group-1 from baseline to third month.   99

4.2.8.1   Pair-wise comparison of algometric measurement of widespread pain index points on Shoulder Girdle Right (SGR) variable in group-1 from Baseline to Third month at different time frame.   100

4.2.9   Comparison of algometric measurement of widespread pain index points on Upper Arm Left (UAL) variable in group-1 from baseline to third month.   101

4.2.9.1   Pair-wise comparison of algometric measurement of widespread pain index points on Upper Arm Left (UAL) variable in group-1 from Baseline to Third month at different time frame.   102

4.2.10   Comparison of algometric measurement of widespread pain index points on Upper Arm Right (UAR) variable in group-1 from baseline to third month.   102

4.2.10.1   Pair-wise comparison of algometric measurement of widespread pain index points on Upper Arm Right (UAR) variable in group-1 from Baseline to Third month at different time frame.   103

4.2.11   Comparison of algometric measurement of widespread pain index points on Lower Arm Left (LAL) variable in group-1 from baseline to third month.   104

4.2.11.1   Pair-wise comparison of algometric measurement of widespread pain index points on Lower Arm Left (LAL) variable in group-1 from Baseline to Third month at different time frame.   105

4.2.12   Comparison of algometric measurement of widespread pain index points on Lower Arm Right (LAR) variable in group-1 from   105

baseline to third month.

4.2.12.1 Pair-wise comparison of algometric measurement of widespread pain index points on Lower Arm Right (LAR) variable in group-1 from Baseline to Third month at different time frame.   106

4.2.13 Comparison of algometric measurement of widespread pain index points on Hip Buttock Left (HBL) variable in group-1 from baseline to third month.   107

4.2.13.1 Pair-wise comparison of algometric measurement of widespread pain index points on Hip Buttock Left (HBL) variable in group-1 from Baseline to Third month at different time frame.   108

4.2.14 Comparison of algometric measurement of widespread pain index points on Hip Buttock Right (HBR) variable in group-1 from baseline to third month.   108

4.2.14.1 Pair-wise comparison of algometric measurement of widespread pain index points on Hip Buttock Right (HBR) variable in group-1 from Baseline to Third month at different time frame.   109

4.2.15 Comparison of algometric measurement of widespread pain index points on Upper Leg Left (ULL) variable in group-1 from baseline to third month.   110

4.2.15.1 Pair-wise comparison of algometric measurement of widespread pain index points on Hip Buttock Right (HBR) variable in group-1 from Baseline to Third month at different time frame.   111

4.2.16 Comparison of algometric measurement of widespread pain index points on Upper Leg Right (ULR) variable in group-1 from baseline to third month.   111

4.2.16.1 Pair-wise comparison of algometric measurement of widespread pain index points on Upper Leg Right (ULR) variable in group-1 from Baseline to Third month at different time frame.   112

4.2.17 Comparison of algometric measurement of widespread pain index points on Lower Leg Left (LLL) variable from in group-1 from baseline to third month.   113

4.2.17.1 Pair-wise comparison of algometric measurement of widespread pain index points on Lower Leg Left (LLL) variable in group-1 from Baseline to Third month at different time frame.   114

4.2.18 Comparison of algometric measurement of widespread pain index points on Lower Leg Right (LLR) variable in group-1 from baseline to third month.   114

4.2.18.1 Pair-wise comparison of algometric measurement of widespread 115
pain index points on Lower Leg Right (LLR) variable in group-1
from Baseline to Third month at different time frame.

4.2.19 Comparison of algometric measurement of widespread pain index 116
points on Jaw Left (JAWL) variable in group-1 from baseline to
third month.

4.2.19.1 Pair-wise comparison of algometric measurement of widespread 117
pain index points on Jaw Left (JAWL) variable in group-1 from
Baseline to Third month at different time frame.

4.2.20 Comparison of algometric measurement of widespread pain index 117
points on Chest variable in group-1 from baseline to third month.

4.2.20.1 Pair-wise comparison of algometric measurement of widespread 118
pain index points on Chest variable in group-1 from Baseline to
Third month at different time frame.

4.2.21 Comparison of algometric measurement of widespread pain index 119
points on Abdomen variable in group-1 from baseline to third
month.

4.2.21.1 Pair-wise comparison of algometric measurement of widespread 120
pain index points on Abdomen variable in group-1 from Baseline
to Third month at different time frame.

4.2.22 Comparison of algometric measurement of widespread pain index 120
points on Neck variable in group-1 from baseline to third month.

4.2.22.1 Pair-wise comparison of algometric measurement of widespread 121
pain index points on Neck variable in group-1 from Baseline to
Third month at different time frame.

4.2.23 Comparison of algometric measurement of widespread pain index 122
points on Upper Back (UB) variable in group-1 from baseline to
third month.

4.2.23.1 Pair-wise comparison of algometric measurement of widespread 123
pain index points on Upper Back (UB) variable in group-1 from
Baseline to Third month at different time frame.

4.2.24 Comparison of algometric measurement of widespread pain index 123
points on Lower Back (LB) variable in group-1 from baseline to
third month.

4.2.24.1 Pair-wise comparison of algometric measurement of widespread 124
pain index points on Lower Back (LB) variable in group-1 from
Baseline to Third month at different time frame.

4.3.1	Comparison of Revised Fibromyalgia Impact Questionnaire (FIQR) variable in group-2 from baseline to the third month.	126
4.3.1.1	Pair-wise comparison of Revised Fibromyalgia Impact Questionnaire (FIQR) variable in group-2 from Baseline to Third month at different time frame.	127
4.3.2	Comparison of Beck Depression Index (BDI) variable in group-2 from baseline to the third month.	127
4.3.2.1	Pair-wise comparison of Beck Depression Index (BDI) variable in group-2 from Baseline to Third month at different time frame.	128
4.3.3	Comparison of Visual Analogue Scale (VAS) variable in group-2 from baseline to the third month.	129
4.3.3.1	Pair-wise comparison of Visual Analogue Scale (VAS) variable in group-2 from Baseline to Third month at different time frame.	130
4.3.4	Comparison of General Anxiety Disorder (GAD-7) variable in group-2 from baseline to the third month.	130
4.3.4.1	Pair-wise comparison of General Anxiety Disorder (GAD-7) variable in group-2 from Baseline to Third month at different time frame.	131
4.3.5	Comparison of Short Form -36 Physical Component Summary (SF-36 PCS) variable in group-2 from baseline to the third month.	132
4.3.5.1	Pair-wise comparison of Short Form -36 Physical Component Summary (SF-36 PCS) variable in group-2 from Baseline to Third month at different time frame.	133
4.3.6	Comparison of Short Form -36 Mental Component Summary (SF-36 Mental variables in group-2 from baseline to the third month.	133
4.3.6.1	Pair-wise comparison of Short Form -36 Mentalcal Component Summary (SF-36 PCS) variable in group-2 from Baseline to Third month at different time frame.	134
4.3.7	Comparison of algometric measurement of widespread pain index points on Shoulder Girdle Left (SGL) variable in group-2 from baseline to third month.	135
4.3.7.1	Pair-wise comparison of algometric measurement of widespread pain index points on Shoulder Girdle Left (SGL) variable in group-2 from Baseline to Third month at different time frame.	136
4.3.8	Comparison of algometric measurement of widespread pain index points on Shoulder Girdle Right (SGR) variable in group-2 from	136

baseline to third month.

4.3.8.1   Pair-wise comparison of algometric measurement of widespread pain index points on Shoulder Girdle Right (SGR) variable in group-2 from Baseline to Third month at different time frame.   137

4.3.9   Comparison of algometric measurement of widespread pain index points on Upper Arm Left (UAL) variable in group-2 from baseline to third month.   138

4.3.9.1   Pair-wise comparison of algometric measurement of widespread pain index points on Upper Arm Left (UAL) variable in group-2 from Baseline to Third month at different time frame.   139

4.3.10   Comparison of algometric measurement of widespread pain index points on Upper Arm Right (UAR) variable in group-2 from baseline to third month.   139

4.3.10.1   Pair-wise comparison of algometric measurement of widespread pain index points on Upper Arm Right (UAR) variable in group-2 from Baseline to Third month at different time frame.   140

4.3.11   Comparison of algometric measurement of widespread pain index points on Lower Arm Left (LAL) variable in group-2 from baseline to third month.   141

4.3.11.1   Pair-wise comparison of algometric measurement of widespread pain index points on Lower Arm Left (LAL) variable in group-2 from Baseline to Third month at different time frame.   142

4.3.12   Comparison of algometric measurement of widespread pain index points on Lower Arm Right (LAR) variable in group-2 from baseline to third month.   142

4.3.12.1   Pair-wise comparison of algometric measurement of widespread pain index points on Lower Arm Right (LAR) variable in group-2 from Baseline to Third month at different time frame.   143

4.3.13   Comparison of algometric measurement of widespread pain index points on Hip Buttock Left (HBL) variable in group-2 from baseline to third month.   144

4.3.13.1   Pair-wise comparison of algometric measurement of widespread pain index points on Hip Buttock Left (HBL) variable in group-2 from Baseline to Third month at different time frame.   145

4.3.14   Comparison of algometric measurement of widespread pain index points on Hip Buttock Right (HBR) variable in group-2 from baseline to third month.   145

4.3.14.1 Pair-wise comparison of algometric measurement of widespread pain index points on Hip Buttock Right (HBR) variable in group-2 from Baseline to Third month at different time frame. 146

4.3.15 Comparison of algometric measurement of widespread pain index points on Upper Leg Left (ULL) variable in group-2 from baseline to third month. 147

4.3.15.1 Pair-wise comparison of algometric measurement of widespread pain index points on Hip Buttock Right (HBR) variable in group-2 from Baseline to Third month at different time frame. 148

4.3.16 Comparison of algometric measurement of widespread pain index points on Upper Leg Right (ULR) variable in group-2 from baseline to third month. 148

4.3.16.1 Pair-wise comparison of algometric measurement of widespread pain index points on Upper Leg Right (ULR) variable in group-2 from Baseline to Third month at different time frame. 149

4.3.17 Comparison of algometric measurement of widespread pain index points on Lower Leg Left (LLL) variable from in group-2 from baseline to third month. 150

4.3.17.1 Pair-wise comparison of algometric measurement of widespread pain index points on Lower Leg Left (LLL) variable in group-2 from Baseline to Third month at different time frame. 151

4.3.18 Comparison of algometric measurement of widespread pain index points on Lower Leg Right (LLR) variable in group-2 from baseline to third month. 151

4.3.18.1 Pair-wise comparison of algometric measurement of widespread pain index points on Lower Leg Right (LLR) variable in group-2 from Baseline to Third month at different time frame. 152

4.3.19 Comparison of algometric measurement of widespread pain index points on Jaw Left (JAWL) variable in group-2 from baseline to third month. 153

4.3.19.1 Pair-wise comparison of algometric measurement of widespread pain index points on Jaw Left (JAWL) variable in group-2 from Baseline to Third month at different time frame. 154

4.3.20 Comparison of algometric measurement of widespread pain index points on Jaw Right (JAWR) variable in group-2 from baseline to third month. 154

4.3.20.1 Pair-wise comparison of algometric measurement of widespread 155

pain index points on Jaw Right (JAWR) variable in group-2 from Baseline to Third month at different time frame.

4.3.21   Comparison of algometric measurement of widespread pain index   156
points on Chest variable in group-2 from baseline to third month.

4.3.21.1   Pair-wise comparison of algometric measurement of widespread   157
pain index points on Chest variable in group-2 from Baseline to Third month at different time frame.

4.3.22   Comparison of algometric measurement of widespread pain index   157
points on Neck variable in group-2 from baseline to third month.

4.3.22.1   Pair-wise comparison of algometric measurement of widespread   158
pain index points on Neck variable in group-2 from Baseline to Third month at different time frame.

4.3.23   Comparison of algometric measurement of widespread pain index   159
points on Upper Back (UB) variable in group-2 from baseline to third month.

4.3.23.1   Pair-wise comparison of algometric measurement of widespread   160
pain index points on Upper Back (UB) variable in group-2 from Baseline to Third month at different time frame.

4.3.24   Comparison of algometric measurement of widespread pain index   160
points on Lower Back (LB) variable in group-2 from baseline to third month.

4.3.24.1   Pair-wise comparison of algometric measurement of widespread   161
pain index points on Lower Back (LB) variable in group-2 from Baseline to Third month at different time frame.

4.4.1   Comparison of Revised Fibromyalgia Impact Questionnaire   162
(FIQR) variable in group-3 from baseline to the third month.

4.4.1.1   Pair-wise comparison of Revised Fibromyalgia Impact   163
Questionnaire (FIQR) variable in group-3 from Baseline to Third month at different time frame.

4.4.2   Comparison of Beck Depression Index (BDI) variable in group-3   164
from baseline to the third month.

4.4.2.1   Pair-wise comparison of Beck Depression Index (BDI) variable in   165
group-3 from Baseline to Third month at different time frame.

4.4.3   Comparison of Visual Analogue Scale (VAS) variable in group-3   165
from baseline to the third month.

4.4.3.1   Pair-wise comparison of Visual Analogue Scale (VAS) variable in   166 group-3 from Baseline to Third month at different time frame.

| 4.4.4 | Comparison of General Anxiety Disorder (GAD-7) variable in group-3 from baseline to the third month. | 167 |

| 4.4.4.1 | Pair-wise comparison of General Anxiety Disorder (GAD-7) variable in group-3 from Baseline to Third month at different time frame. | 168 |

| 4.4.5 | Comparison of Short Form -36 Physical Component Summary (SF-36 PCS) variable in group-3 from baseline to the third month. | 168 |

| 4.4.5.1 | Pair-wise comparison of Short Form -36 Physical Component Summary (SF-36 PCS) variable in group-3 from Baseline to Third month at different time frame. | 169 |

| 4.4.6 | Comparison of Short Form -36 Mental Component Summary (SF-36 Mental variables in group-3 from baseline to the third month. | 170 |

| 4.4.6.1 | Pair-wise comparison of Short Form -36 Mentalcal Component Summary (SF-36 PCS) variable in group-3 from Baseline to Third month at different time frame. | 171 |

| 4.4.7 | Comparison of algometric measurement of widespread pain index points on Shoulder Girdle Left (SGL) variable in group-3 from baseline to third month. | 171 |

| 4.4.7.1 | Pair-wise comparison of algometric measurement of widespread pain index points on Shoulder Girdle Left (SGL) variable in group-3 from Baseline to Third month at different time frame. | 172 |

| 4.4.8 | Comparison of algometric measurement of widespread pain index points on Shoulder Girdle Right (SGR) variable in group-3 from baseline to third month. | 173 |

| 4.4.8.1 | Pair-wise comparison of algometric measurement of widespread pain index points on Shoulder Girdle Right (SGR) variable in group-3 from Baseline to Third month at different time frame. | 174 |

| 4.4.9 | Comparison of algometric measurement of widespread pain index points on Upper Arm Left (UAL) variable in group-3 from baseline to third month. | 174 |

| 4.4.9.1 | Pair-wise comparison of algometric measurement of widespread pain index points on Upper Arm Left (UAL) variable in group-3 from Baseline to Third month at different time frame. | 175 |

| 4.4.10 | Comparison of algometric measurement of widespread pain index points on Upper Arm Right (UAR) variable in group-3 from baseline to third month. | 176 |

4.4.10.1 Pair-wise comparison of algometric measurement of widespread pain index points on Upper Arm Right (UAR) variable in group-3 from Baseline to Third month at different time frame.   177

4.4.11 Comparison of algometric measurement of widespread pain index points on Lower Arm Left (LAL) variable in group-3 from baseline to third month.   177

4.4.11.1 Pair-wise comparison of algometric measurement of widespread pain index points on Lower Arm Left (LAL) variable in group-3 from Baseline to Third month at different time frame.   178

4.4.12 Comparison of algometric measurement of widespread pain index points on Lower Arm Right (LAR) variable in group-3 from baseline to third month.   179

4.4.12.1 Pair-wise comparison of algometric measurement of widespread pain index points on Lower Arm Right (LAR) variable in group-3 from Baseline to Third month at different time frame.   180

4.4.13 Comparison of algometric measurement of widespread pain index points on Hip Buttock Left (HBL) variable in group-3 from baseline to third month.   180

4.4.13.1 Pair-wise comparison of algometric measurement of widespread pain index points on Hip Buttock Left (HBL) variable in group-3 from Baseline to Third month at different time frame.   181

4.4.14 Comparison of algometric measurement of widespread pain index points on Hip Buttock Right (HBR) variable in group-3 from baseline to third month.   182

4.4.14.1 Pair-wise comparison of algometric measurement of widespread pain index points on Hip Buttock Right (HBR) variable in group-3 from Baseline to Third month at different time frame.   183

4.4.15 Comparison of algometric measurement of widespread pain index points on Upper Leg Left (ULL) variable in group-3 from baseline to third month.   183

4.4.15.1 Pair-wise comparison of algometric measurement of widespread pain index points on Hip Buttock Right (HBR) variable in group-3 from Baseline to Third month at different time frame.   184

4.4.16 Comparison of algometric measurement of widespread pain index points on Upper Leg Right (ULR) variable in group-3 from baseline to third month.   185

4.4.16.1 Pair-wise comparison of algometric measurement of widespread   186

pain index points on Upper Leg Right (ULR) variable in group-3 from Baseline to Third month at different time frame.

4.4.17   Comparison of algometric measurement of widespread pain index points on Lower Leg Left (LLL) variable from in group-3 from baseline to third month.   186

4.4.17.1   Pair-wise comparison of algometric measurement of widespread pain index points on Lower Leg Left (LLL) variable in group-3 from Baseline to Third month at different time frame.   187

4.4.18   Comparison of algometric measurement of widespread pain index points on Lower Leg Right (LLR) variable in group-3 from baseline to third month.   188

4.4.18.1   Pair-wise comparison of algometric measurement of widespread pain index points on Lower Leg Right (LLR) variable in group-3 from Baseline to Third month at different time frame.   189

4.4.19   Comparison of algometric measurement of widespread pain index points on Jaw Left (JAWL) variable in group-3 from baseline to third month.   189

4.4.19.1   Pair-wise comparison of algometric measurement of widespread pain index points on Jaw Left (JAWL) variable in group-3 from Baseline to Third month at different time frame.   190

4.4.20   Comparison of algometric measurement of widespread pain index points on Jaw Right (JAWR) variable in group-3 from baseline to third month.   191

4.4.20.1   Pair-wise comparison of algometric measurement of widespread pain index points on Jaw Right (JAWR) variable in group-3 from Baseline to Third month at different time frame.   192

4.4.21   Comparison of algometric measurement of widespread pain index points on Chest variable in group-3 from baseline to third month.   192

4.4.21.1   Pair-wise comparison of algometric measurement of widespread pain index points on Chest variable in group-3 from Baseline to Third month at different time frame.   193

4.4.22   Comparison of algometric measurement of widespread pain index points on Abdomen variable in group-3 from baseline to third month.   194

4.4.22.1   Pair-wise comparison of algometric measurement of widespread pain index points on Abdomen variable in group-3 from Baseline to Third month at different time frame.   195

4.4.23	Comparison of algometric measurement of widespread pain index points on Neck variable in group-3 from baseline to third month.	195
4.4.23.1	Pair-wise comparison of algometric measurement of widespread pain index points on Neck variable in group-3 from Baseline to Third month at different time frame.	196
4.4.24	Comparison of algometric measurement of widespread pain index points on Upper Back (UB) variable in group-3 from baseline to third month.	197
4.4.24.1	Pair-wise comparison of algometric measurement of widespread pain index points on Upper Back (UB) variable in group-3 from Baseline to Third month at different time frame.	198
4.4.25	Comparison of algometric measurement of widespread pain index points on Lower Back (LB) variable in group-3 from baseline to third month.	198
4.4.25.1	Pair-wise comparison of algometric measurement of widespread pain index points on Lower Back (LB) variable in group-3 from Baseline to Third month at different time frame.	199
4.5.1	Comparison of Means of Revised Fibromyalgia Impact Questionnaire (FIQR) variable at the different time frame from baseline to third month.	201
4.5.1.1	Multiple comparisons of difference in means of improvement on Revised Fibromyalgia Impact Questionnaire (FIQR) among different interventional group.	202
4.5.2	Comparison of Means of Beck Depression Index (BDI) variable at the different time frame from baseline to third month.	203
4.5.2.1	Multiple comparisons of difference in means of improvement on Beck Depression Index (BDI) among different interventional group.	204
4.5.3	Comparison of Means of Visual Analogue Scale (VAS) variable at the different time frame from baseline to third month.	205
4.5.3.1	Multiple comparisons of difference in means of improvement on Visual Analogue Scale (VAS) among different interventional group.	206
4.5.4	Comparison of Means of General Anxiety Disorder (GAD-7) variable at the different time frame from baseline to third month.	207
4.5.4.1	Multiple comparisons of difference in means of improvement on General Anxiety Disorder (GAD-7) among different interventional	209

group.

4.5.5   Comparison of Means of Short Form -36 Physical Component   210
         Summary (SF-36 PCS) variable at the different time frame from
         baseline to third month.

4.5.5.1 Multiple comparisons of difference in means of improvement on   211
         Short Form -36 Physical Component Summary (SF-36 PCS)
         among different interventional group.

4.5.6   Comparison of Means of Short Form -36 Mental Component   212
         Summary (SF-36 MCS) variable at the different time frame from
         baseline to third month.

4.5.6.1 Multiple comparisons of difference in means of improvement on   213
         Short Form -36 Mental Component Summary (SF-36 MCS) among
         different interventional group.

4.5.7   Comparison of Means of Shoulder Girdle Left (SGL) variable on   214
         algometric measurement between the groups at the different time
         frame from baseline to third month.

4.5.7.1 Multiple comparisons of difference in means of improvement on   215
         algometric measurement of Shoulder Girdle Left (SGL) among
         different interventional group.

4.5.8   Comparison of Means of Shoulder Girdle Right (SGR) variable on   216
         algometric measurement between the groups at the different time
         frame from baseline to third month.

4.5.8.1 Multiple comparisons of difference in means of improvement on   217
         algometric measurement of Shoulder Girdle Right (SGR) among
         different interventional group.

4.5.9   Comparison of Means of Upper Arm Left (UAL) variable on   218
         algometric measurement between the groups at the different time
         frame from baseline to third month.

4.5.9.1 Multiple comparisons of difference in means of improvement on   219
         algometric measurement of Upper Arm Left (UAL) among
         different interventional group.

4.5.10   Comparison of Means of Upper Arm Right (UAR) variable on   220
         algometric measurement between the groups at the different time
         frame from baseline to third month.

4.5.10.1 Multiple comparisons of difference in means of improvement on   221
         algometric measurement of Upper Arm Right (UAR) among
         different interventional group.

4.5.11	Comparison of Means of Lower Arm Left (LAL) variable on algometric measurement between the groups at the different time frame from baseline to third month.	222
4.5.11.1	Multiple comparisons of difference in means of improvement on algometric measurement of Lower Arm Left (LAL) among different interventional group.	223
4.5.12	Comparison of Means of Lower Arm Right (LAR) variable on algometric measurement between the groups at the different time frame from baseline to third month.	224
4.5.12.1	Multiple comparisons of difference in means of improvement on algometric measurement of Lower Arm Right (LAR) among different interventional group.	225
4.5.13	Comparison of Means of Hip Buttock Left (HBL) variable on algometric measurement between the groups at the different time frame from baseline to third month.	226
4.5.13.1	Multiple comparisons of difference in means of improvement on algometric measurement of Hip Buttock Left (HBL) among different interventional group.	227
4.5.14	Comparison of Means of Hip Buttock Right (HBR) variable on algometric measurement between the groups at the different time frame from baseline to third month.	228
4.5.14.1	Multiple comparisons of difference in means of improvement on algometric measurement of Hip Buttock Right (HBR) among different interventional group.	229
4.5.15	Comparison of Means of Upper Leg Left (ULL) variable on algometric measurement between the groups at the different time frame from baseline to third month.	230
4.5.15.1	Multiple comparisons of difference in means of improvement on algometric measurement of Upper Leg Left (ULL) among different interventional group.	231
4.5.16	Comparison of Means of Upper Leg Right (ULR) variable on algometric measurement between the groups at the different time frame from baseline to third month.	232
4.5.16.1	Multiple comparisons of difference in means of improvement on algometric measurement of Upper Leg Right (ULR) among different interventional group.	233
4.5.17	Comparison of Means of Lower Leg Left (LLL) variable on	234

algometric measurement between the groups at the different time frame from baseline to third month.

4.5.17.1   Multiple comparisons of difference in means of improvement on algometric measurement of Lower Leg Left (LLL) among different interventional group.   235

4.5.18   Comparison of Means of Lower Leg Right (LLR) variable on algometric measurement between the groups at the different time frame from baseline to third month.   236

4.5.18.1   Multiple comparisons of difference in means of improvement on algometric measurement of Lower Leg Right (LLR) among different interventional group.   237

4.5.19   Comparison of Means of Jaw Left (JawL) variable on algometric measurement between the groups at the different time frame from baseline to third month.   238

4.5.19.1   Multiple comparisons of difference in means of improvement on algometric measurement of Jaw Left (JawL) among different interventional group.   239

4.5.20   Comparison of Means of Jaw Right (JawR) variable on algometric measurement between the groups at the different time frame from baseline to third month.   240

4.5.20.1   Multiple comparisons of difference in means of improvement on algometric measurement of Jaw Right (JawR) among different interventional group.   241

4.5.21   Comparison of Means of Chest variable on algometric measurement between the groups at the different time frame from baseline to third month.   242

4.5.21.1   Multiple comparisons of difference in means of improvement on algometric measurement of Chest variable among different interventional group.   243

4.5.22   Comparison of Means of Abdomen variable on algometric measurement between the groups at the different time frame from baseline to third month.   244

4.5.22.1   Multiple comparisons of difference in means of improvement on algometric measurement of Abdomen variable among different interventional group.   245

4.5.23   Comparison of Means of Neck variable on algometric measurement between the groups at the different time frame from   246

baseline to third month.

4.5.23.1   Multiple comparisons of difference in means of improvement on algometric measurement of Neck variable among different interventional group.   247

4.5.24   Comparison of Means of Upper Back (UB) variable on algometric measurement between the groups at the different time frame from baseline to third month.   248

4.5.24.1   Multiple comparisons of difference in means of improvement on algometric measurement of Upper Back (UB) variable among different interventional group.   249

4.5.25   Comparison of Means of Lower Back (LB) variable on algometric measurement between the groups at the different time frame from baseline to third month.   250

4.5.25.1   Multiple comparisons of difference in means of improvement on algometric measurement of Lower Back (LB) variable among different interventional group.   251

LIST OF FIGURES

S.No.	Title of Figures	Page No.
3.1	Flow chart of procedure followed in the study	70
3.2	Pressure algometer tool	71
3.3	Drug Pregabid (75 mg)	73
3.4	Cervical release (Starting position)	75
3.5	Cervical release (End position)	75
3.6	Cranial Base Release	77
3.7	Psoas Release	78
3.8	Sacral Release	78
3.9	Cross Hand Release	79
4.1.1	Mean Age distribution of all three groups.	84
4.1.2	Gender distribution of all three groups.	85
4.1.3	Distribution of subjects according to Education in different groups.	86
4.1.4	Distribution of subjects according to occupation in different groups.	87
4.1.5	Distribution of subjects according to marital status in different groups.	88
4.2.1	Mean and SD on algometer measurement of Revised Fibromyalgia Impact Questionnaire score from baseline to third month.	89
4.2.2	Mean and SD on algometer measurement of Beck Depression Index score from baseline to third month.	91
4.2.3	Mean and SD on algometer measurement of Visual Analogue Scale score from baseline to third month.	92
4.2.4	Mean and SD on algometer measurement of General Anxiety Disorder score from baseline to third month.	94
4.2.5	Mean and SD on algometer measurement of Short Form – 36 Physical Component summary score from baseline to third month.	95
4.2.6	Mean and SD on algometer measurement of Short Form – 36 Mental Component summary score from baseline to third month.	97
4.2.7	The Mean and SD on algometer measurement of shoulder girdle left side point from baseline to third month.	98
4.2.8	Mean and SD on algometer measurement of shoulder girdle right side point from baseline to third month.	100
4.2.9	The Mean and SD on algometer measurement of upper arm left side point from baseline to third month.	101

4.2.10 The Mean and SD on algometer measurement of upper arm right side point from baseline to third month. 103

4.2.11 The Mean and SD on algometer measurement of lower arm left side point from baseline to third month. 104

4.2.12 The Mean and SD on algometer measurement of lower arm right side point from baseline to third month. 106

4.2.13 The Mean and SD on algometer measurement of Hip Buttock Left side point from baseline to third month. 107

4.2.14 The Mean and SD on algometer measurement of Hip Buttock Right side point from baseline to third month. 109

4.2.15 The Mean and SD on algometer measurement of Upper Leg Right side point from baseline to third month. 110

4.2.16 The Mean and SD on algometer measurement of Upper Leg Right side point from baseline to third month. 112

4.2.17 The Mean and SD on algometer measurement of Lower Leg Left side point from baseline to third month. 113

4.2.18 The Mean and SD on algometer measurement of Lower Leg Right side point from baseline to third month. 115

4.2.19 The Mean and SD on algometer measurement of Jaw Left side point from baseline to third month. 116

4.2.20 The Mean and SD on algometer measurement of Chest point from baseline to third month. 118

4.2.21 The Mean and SD on algometer measurement of Abdomen point from baseline to third month. 119

4.2.22 The Mean and SD on algometer measurement of Neck point from baseline to third month. 121

4.2.23 The Mean and SD on algometer measurement of Upper Back point from baseline to third month. 122

4.2.24 The Mean and SD on algometer measurement of Lower Back point from baseline to third month. 124

4.3.1 Mean and SD on algometer measurement of Revised Fibromyalgia Impact Questionnaire score from baseline to third month. 126

4.3.2 Mean and SD on algometer measurement of Beck Depression Index score from baseline to third month. 128

4.3.3 Mean and SD on algometer measurement of Visual Analogue Scale score from baseline to third month. 129

4.3.4   Mean and SD on algometer measurement of General Anxiety Disorder Score from baseline to third month.   131

4.3.5   Mean and SD on algometer measurement of Short Form-36 Physical Component Summary score from baseline to third month.   132

4.3.6   Mean and SD on algometer measurement of Short Form-36 Mental Component Summary score from baseline to third month.   134

4.3.7   Mean and SD on algometer measurement of Shoulder Girdle Left from baseline to third month.   135

4.3.8   Mean and SD on algometer measurement of Shoulder Girdle Right from baseline to third month.   137

4.3.9   Mean and SD on algometer measurement of Upper Arm Left from baseline to third month.   138

4.3.10 Mean and SD on algometer measurement of Upper Arm Right from baseline to third month.   140

4.3.11 Mean and SD on algometer measurement of Lower Arm Left from baseline to third month.   141

4.3.12 Mean and SD on algometer measurement of Lower Arm Right from baseline to third month.   143

4.3.13 Mean and SD on algometer measurement of Hip Buttock Left from baseline to third month.   144

4.3.14 Mean and SD on algometer measurement of Hip Buttock Right from baseline to third month.   146

4.3.15 Mean and SD on algometer measurement of Upper Leg Left from baseline to third month.   147

4.3.16 Mean and SD on algometer measurement of Upper Leg Right from baseline to third month.   149

4.3.17 Mean and SD on algometer measurement of Lower Leg Left from baseline to third month.   150

4.3.18 Mean and SD on algometer measurement of Lower Leg Right from baseline to third month.   152

4.3.19 Mean and SD on algometer measurement of Jaw Left from baseline to third month.   153

4.3.20 Mean and SD on algometer measurement of Jaw Right from baseline to third month.   155

4.3.21 Mean and SD on algometer measurement of Chest point from baseline to third month.   156

4.3.22 Mean and SD on algometer measurement of Neck point from baseline to third month.   158

4.3.23 Mean and SD on algometer measurement of Upper Back point from baseline to third month.   159

4.3.24 Mean and SD on algometer measurement of Lower Back point from baseline to third month.   161

4.4.1 Mean and SD of Revised Fibromyalgia Impact Questionnaire score from baseline to third month.   163

4.4.2 Mean and SD of Beck Depression Index score from baseline to third month.   164

4.4.3 Mean and SD of Visual Analogue Scale score from baseline to third month.   166

4.4.4 Mean and SD of General Anxiety Disorder score from baseline to third month.   167

4.4.5 Mean and SD of Short Form – 36 Physical Component summary score from baseline to third month.   169

4.4.6 Mean and SD of Short Form – 36 Mental Component summary score from baseline to third month.   170

4.4.7 Mean and SD on algometer measurement of shoulder girdle left side point from baseline to third month.   172

4.4.8 Mean and SD on algometer measurement of Shoulder Girdle Right side point from baseline to third month.   173

4.4.9 Mean and SD on algometer measurement of upper arm left side point from baseline to third month.   175

4.4.10 Mean and SD on algometer measurement of Upper Arm Right side point from baseline to third month.   176

4.4.11 Mean and SD on algometer measurement of Lower Arm Left side point from baseline to third month.   178

4.4.12 Mean and SD on algometer measurement of Lower Arm Right side point from baseline to third month.   179

4.4.13 Mean and SD on algometer measurement of Hip Buttock Left [H (B) L] point from baseline to third month.   181

4.4.14 Mean and SD on algometer measurement of Hip Buttock Right [H (B) R] point from baseline to third month.   182

4.4.15 Mean and SD on algometer measurement of Upper Leg Left (ULL) point from baseline to third month.   184

4.4.16 Mean and SD on algometer measurement of Upper Leg Right (ULR)   185
point from baseline to third month.

4.4.17 Mean and SD on algometer measurement of Lower Leg Left (LLL)   187
point from baseline to third month.

4.4.18 Mean and SD on algometer measurement of Lower Leg Right (LLR)   188
point from baseline to third month.

4.4.19 Mean and SD on algometer measurement of Jaw Left (JAWL) point   190
from baseline to third month.

4.4.20 Mean and SD on algometer measurement of Jaw Right (JAWR)   191
point from baseline to third month.

4.4.21 Mean and SD on algometer measurement of Chest point from   193
baseline to third month.

4.4.22 Mean and SD on algometer measurement of abdomen point from   194
baseline to third month.

4.4.23 Mean and SD on algometer measurement of Neck point from   196
baseline to third month.

4.4.24 Mean and SD on algometer measurement of upper back point from   197
baseline to third month.

4.4.25 Mean and SD on algometer measurement of lower back point from   199
baseline to third month.

4.5.1 Means Scores of Revised Fibromyalgia Impact Questionnaire from   202
baseline to third month between group 1, 2 and 3.

4.5.2 Mean Scores of Beck Depression Index from baseline to third month   204
between group 1, 2 and 3.

4.5.3 Mean Scores of Visual Analogue Scale from baseline to third month   206
between group 1, 2 and 3.

4.5.4 Mean Scores of General Anxiety Disorder Scale from baseline to   208
third month between group 1, 2 and 3.

4.5.5 Mean Scores of Short Form -36 Physical Component Summary from   211
baseline to third month between group 1, 2 and 3.

4.5.6 Mean Scores of Short Form -36 Mental Component Summary from   213
baseline to third month between group 1, 2 and 3.

4.5.7 Mean Scores of Algometric measurement of Shoulder Girdle Left   215
tender point from baseline to third month between group 1, 2 and 3.

4.5.8 Mean Scores of Algometric measurement of Shoulder Girdle Right   217
tender point from baseline to third month between group 1, 2 and 3.

4.5.9   Mean Scores of Algometric measurement of Upper Arm Left tender point from baseline to third month between group 1, 2 and 3.   219

4.5.10   Mean Scores of Algometric measurement of Upper Arm Right tender point from baseline to third month between group 1, 2 and 3.   221

4.5.11   Mean Scores of Algometric measurement of Lower Arm Left tender point from baseline to third month between group 1, 2 and 3.   223

4.5.12   Mean Scores of Algometric measurement of Lower Arm Right tender point from baseline to third month between group 1, 2 and 3.   225

4.5.13   Mean Scores of Algometric measurement of Hip (Buttock) Left tender point from baseline to third month between group 1, 2 and 3.   227

4.5.14   Mean Scores of Algometric measurement of Hip (Buttock) Right tender point from baseline to third month between group 1, 2 and 3.   229

4.5.15   Mean Scores of Algometric measurement of Upper Leg Left tender point from baseline to third month between group 1, 2 and 3.   231

4.5.16   Mean Scores of Algometric measurement of Upper Leg Right tender point from baseline to third month between group 1, 2 and 3.   233

4.5.17   Mean Scores of Algometric measurement of Lower Leg Left tender point from baseline to third month between group 1, 2 and 3.   235

4.5.18   Mean Scores of Algometric measurement of Lower Leg Right tender point from baseline to third month between group 1, 2 and 3.   237

4.5.19   Mean Scores of Algometric measurement of Jaw Left tender point from baseline to third month between group 1, 2 and 3.   239

4.5.20   Mean Scores of Algometric measurement of Jaw Right tender point from baseline to third month between group 1, 2 and 3.   241

4.5.21   Mean Scores of Algometric measurement of Chest tender point from baseline to third month between group 1, 2 and 3.   243

4.5.22   Mean Scores of Algometric measurement of Abdomen tender point from baseline to third month between group 1, 2 and 3.   245

4.5.23   Mean Scores of Algometric measurement of Neck tender point from baseline to third month between group 1, 2 and 3.   247

4.5.24   Mean Scores of Algometric measurement of Upper Back tender point from baseline to third month between group 1, 2 and 3.   249

4.5.25   Mean Scores of Algometric measurement of Lower Back tender point from baseline to third month between group 1, 2 and 3.   251

LIST OF ABBREVIATIONS

6MWT	Six-Minute Walk Test
ABC	Activities-Specific Balance Confidence Scale
ACR	American College of Rheumatology
AMED	Allied and Complementary Medicine
AP	Attention-Placebo
AS	Ankylosing Spondylitis
ASA	Affective Self-Awareness
BAI	Beck Anxiety Inventory
BDI	Beck Depression Index
BEST	Balance Evaluation Systems Test
BFI	Brief Fatigue Inventory
BMCS	Blood Mononuclear Cells
BMI	Body Mass Index
CAM	Complementary and Alternative Medicine
CBT	Cognitive Behavioral Therapy
CBTAIPT	Cognitive Behavioral Therapy and Integrated Physiotherapy Techniques
CES-D	Center for Epidemiological Studies Depression Scale
CFS	Chronic Fatigue Syndrome
CLBP	Chronic Low Back Pain
CMSI	Complex Medical Symptom Inventory
COMT	Catechol-O-Methyltransferase
CPFRC	Chronic Pain and Fatigue Research Centre
CPSE	Chronic Pain Self-Efficacy Scale
CPT	Cold Pressor Test
CS	Conditioning Stimulus
CV	Conduction Velocity
CWP	Widespread Chronic Pain
DCS	Diffuse Correlation Spectroscopy
DLPFC	Dorso-Lateral Prefrontal Cortex
DMN	Default Mode Network
DNA	Deoxyribonucleic Acid
DTF	Deep Transverse Friction

DTFM	Deep Transverse Friction Massage
EAN	Executive Attention Network
FDA	Food and Drug Administration
FI	Fatigue Index
FIM	Functional Independence Measure
FIQ	Fibromyalgia Impact Questionnaire
FM	Fibromyalgia
fMRI	functional Magnetic Resonance Imaging
FMS	Fibromyalgia Syndrome
FSH	Follicle Stimulating Hormone
GAD	General Anxiety Disorder scale
GCPS	Graded Chronic Pain Scale
HAQ	Health Assessment Questionnaire
HLA-DR	Human Leucocyte Antigen D-Related
HM	Hypermobility
H-MRS	Proton Magnetic Resonance Spectroscopy
HP	Heart Period
HPG	Hypothalamic-Pituitary-Gonadal
HRQoL	Health-Related Quality of Life
HRV	Heart Rate Variability
HTTLPR	Human-serotonin Transporter Long Polymorphism
HVs	Healthy volunteers
IBS	Irritable Bowel Syndrome
IC	Insular Cortex
ICA	Independent Component Analysis
IEC	Institutional Ethical Committee
IPT	Integrated Physiotherapy Techniques
IPT	Integrated Physical therapy Techniques
IPT	Integrated Physiotherapy Techniques
JPFS	Juvenile Primary Fibromyalgia Syndrome
kFIQ	Korean Fibromyalgia Impact Questionnaire
LFESSQ	London Fibromyalgia Epidemiologic Study Screening Questionnaire
LH	Luteinizing Hormone
MANTIS	Manuals of Alternative and Natural Therapy Index System

MASQ	Multiple Abilities Self-Report Questionnaire
MB	Masochistic Behavior
MBT	Mind-Body Therapy
MCC	Mid-Cingulate Cortex
MDD	Major Depressive Disorder
MDF	Median Spectral Frequency
MEAP	Met-Enkephalin-Arg -Phe
MeSH	Medical Subject Headings
MFI	Multidimensional Fatigue Inventory
MFI	Multidimensional Fatigue Inventory
MFR	Myofascial Release
MINI	Mini International Neuropsychiatric Interview
MMRT	Massage-Myofascial Release Therapy
MOS	Medical Outcomes Study Sleep Scale
MRI	Magnetic Resonance Imaging
MTPS	Myofascial trigger points
MVN	Medial Visual Network
MVPA	Moderate to Vigorous Physical Activity
NC	Healthy Controls
NFR	Nociceptive Flexion Reflex
NIRS	Near-Infrared Diffuse Optical Spectroscopies
NK	Natural Killer
NP	Neuropathic pain
NW	Nordic Walking
OA	Osteoarthritis
OBT	Operant Behavioral Therapy
OPRM1	Mu-Opioid Receptor
OTG	Operant Treatment Group
PA	Physical Activity
PBMC	Peripheral Blood Mononuclear Cells
PEDro	Physiotherapy Evidence Database
PGIC	Global Patient Impression of Change
PGWB	Psychological General Wellbeing Index
PHAIPT	Pharmacotherapy and Integrated Physiotherapy Techniques

POP	Position of Participants
POT	Position of Therapist
PPT	Pain Pressure Threshold
PsA	Psoriatic arthritis
PSG	Polysomnography
PTG	Physical Therapy Group
PYD	Pyridostigmine
RA	Rheumatoid Arthritis
RCT	Randomized Controlled Trials
RPS	Regional Pain Score
SAP	Systolic Arterial Pressure
SEMG	Surface Electromyography
SF-36	Short-Form health survey -36
SMA	Supplementary Motor Area
SMWT	Six Minute Walking Test
SOT	Sensory Organization Test
SS	Symptom Severity
SSS	Symptom Severity Scale
STPI	State-Trait Personality Inventory
TAU	Treatment-As-Usual
tDCS	transcranial Direct Current Stimulation
TdT	Terminal de-oxynucleotidyl Transferase
TMS	Transcranial Magnetic Stimulation
TS	Test Stimuli
US	United States
VAS	Visual Analogue Scale
VBM	Voxel-Based Morphometric
VNS	Vagus Nerve Stimulation
WPI	Widespread Pain Index
WPI	Widespread Pain Index

Fibromyalgia (FM) is defined as widespread chronic pain for more than three months and the presence of tender points in all the four quadrants of the body. It is a multidimensional disorder that is unpredictable in its course (Sarzi-Puttini *et al.*, 2008), and the management of this condition is a challenge for the patient and health provider (Sumpton and Moulin 2008). The rate of prevalence varies according to the geographical area, so the overall incidence of FM has been studied. The estimated global prevalence of FM in Europe was 4.7% of widespread chronic pain and was 2.9% when stronger pain and fatigue criteria were simultaneously used (Branco *et al.*, 2009). It affects 4% of the United States (US) population, approximately 6 -10 million Americans (Lawrence *et al.*, 2008; Lindell *et al.*, 2000), with strong female predominance between the ages of 20 and 50 (Reiffenberg and Amundson, 1996). The precise incidence of this disorder in India is scarce.

Chronic pain in FM is of muscle origin, in a constant state of pain; pain does no longer fulfill a protective function but represents a pathological condition with devastating effects on quality of life (Eccleston & Crombez, 1999). There is strong evidence that the potential mechanisms of the patho-physiology of FM may be due to central sensitization, abnormalities of descending inhibitory pain pathways, neurotransmitter abnormalities, and co-morbid psychiatric conditions increasingly recognized as being relevant to the development of fibromyalgia (Bennet, 2005). However, plasma muscle enzyme levels, electromyographic studies, and muscle biopsies have been reported as completely normal (Spaeth and Briley, 2009). Because of the complexity of its cause, patients with FM often experience several other symptoms include tenderness, stiffness, mood disturbances (e.g. depression and anxiety), cognitive difficulties (e.g. trouble concentrating, forgetfulness, and disorganized thinking). There is believable support to link fibromyalgia and depression; the concurrence of depressive symptoms in FM is approximately 40% (Gracely *et al.*, 2012).

Depression is under-diagnosed in medical settings and is a frequently reported symptom which is often difficult for general practitioners to recognize (Henriques*et al.*, 2009) and is associated with increased morbidity with a variable psychopathological presentation (Yates, 2007). The lifetime prevalence rate of major depressive disorders in the general population is 10% to 25% for women and from 5% to 12% for men (Kessler *et al.*, 2005). The FM and depression co-occur and share the same pathophysiology, about 74% of FM patients report at least one Major Depressive Disorder (MDD) episode in their lifetime (Arnold *et al.*, 2006). Depression is known to worsen FM symptom severity, including pain, functional impairment, sleep quality, and quality of life (Patten *et al.*, 2005; Nicholl *et al.*, 2009). Patients often feel incapable of performing necessary daily life activities such as walking, going upstairs, or lifting objects (Bennett *et al.*, 2005; Cymet, 2003). Additionally, tension-type headache/ migraine, interstitial cystitis or painful bladder syndrome, chronic prostitis or prostodynia, temporo-mandibular disorder, and chronic pelvic pain (Ablin & Clauw, 2009) associated with FM. There are so many diagnostic tests are available to rule out the condition, but, none of those diagnostic tests have sensitivity to prove the FM disorder.

The recent classification of the American College of Rheumatology (ACR) criteria for the diagnosis of Fibromyalgia Syndrome (FMS) includes the presence of pain in all four body quadrants in combination with excess tenderness to manual palpation in at least 11 of 18 muscle-tendon sites, in the absence of clinically demonstrable peripheral nociceptive causes (Wolfe *et al.*, 1990). Also, extra-pain symptoms are a significant symptom of fibromyalgia (Clauw, 2003), but there is no emphasis on extra-pain symptoms in the 1990 ACR classification criteria. Currently, the Fibromyalgia Impact Questionnaire (FIQ) and Visual Analogue Scale (VAS) for pain taken into account for diagnosis, and there is a follow-up observation for the assessment of extra-pain symptoms. Still, detailed agreement or treatment guidelines are insufficient.

The ACR criteria also suggested new preliminary classification criteria. The 2010 ACR primary classification criteria diagnose fibromyalgia as the sum of the Widespread Pain Index (WPI) and total Symptom Severity (SS) being more than a specific score, continuing symptoms for more than three months, and all three criteria without disease-related to symptoms being satisfied. These criteria do not include a tender point test, and the patients are required to indicate the location and severity of pain as well as the extra-pain symptoms. Besides, the WPI and SS have numerical values, so objective diagnosis and follow-up observations are possible (Wolfe *et al.*, 2010). The vital role in the treatment approach of FM may consist of reduction of other pain symptoms, improvement of central sensitization, and depression.

Bennett (2005) described the most effective interventions of FM in descending order by rest, heat modalities, prescription pain medications, prescription antidepressants, prescription sleep medications, prayer, and massage. The United States (US) Food and Drug Administration (FDA) approved medication for the management of FM, including Pregabalin, Duloxetine, and Milnacipran (Arnold *et al.*, 2012). Pregabalin was the first drug to be approved by the FDA for the treatment of FM and has shown to improve pain, sleep, and quality of life but to be ineffective against depression (Boomershine, 2010). In FM, prescription of medication alone is not generally sufficient for the treatment of fibromyalgia, because the restoration of physical and emotional functioning, as well as the quality of life improvement, are also essential factors to be considered. Therefore, to conquer the FM symptoms, researches have to focus on the non-pharmacological treatment also.

The other Non-pharmacological treatments showing beneficial effects in relieving some symptoms of FM include cognitive behavioral therapy, exercise (strength and flexibility training), and complementary and alternative medicine, i.e., Osteopathic manipulations, Dry needling, Acupuncture, Low power Laser Therapy, and Balneotherapy. Similarly, numerous other studies have documented on the management of FM like Spa therapy (Fraioli *et al.*, 2013), Internet Enhanced Management (Williams *et al.*, 2010), Repeated Intrathecal Antidepressant (Nishiyori *et al.*, 2011), Transcranial Magnetic Stimulation (Tzabazis *et al.*, 2013), Low-Level Laser therapy (De Carvalho *et al.*, 2012), Hydrotherapy (Perraton *et al.*, 2009), Craniosacral Therapy (Mataran-Penarrocha *et al.*, 2011), Diet (Donaldson *et al.*, 2001), Yoga (Curtis *et al.*, 2011), Exercise (Busch *et al.*, 2011), Affective Cognitive Behavioral Treatment (Woolfolk *et al.*, 2012), Hypnosis (Grondahl and Rosvold, 2008), Guided imagery (Menzies *et al.*, 2006), Acupuncture (Vas *et al.*, 2011) and Myofascial Release (Castro-Sanchez *et al.*, 2011).

Cognitive Behavioral Therapy (CBT) programs have developed to provide patients with chronic pain the opportunity to reassess their beliefs about the relationship between pain and functioning and to experience that spontaneous safety behavior, which may be adaptive in acute episodes of pain (Keefe *et al.*, 2004; Cedraschi *et al.*, 2004). Indeed, a recent meta-analysis of randomized controlled trials of these treatments in adults reported a beneficial effects on pain and mood (Eccleston *et al.*, 2009).

Integrated Physical therapy Techniques (IPT) are a combination of two or more therapeutic techniques used to treat any disorder. Castro-Sanchez *et al.* (2011) reported that Massage-Myofascial Release Therapy (MMRT) improved pain, anxiety, quality of sleep, depression, and quality of life in patients with fibromyalgia. Myofascial Release (MFR) has classified as a combined direct and indirect manual technique, which applies the principles of biomechanical loading of soft tissue and the neural reflex modifications by stimulation of mechano-receptors in the fascia (Greenman, 1996; Remvig *et al.*, 2008). It represents a widely employed manual technique specific for fascial tissues, to reduce adhesions, restore and optimize fascia sliding mobility in both acute and chronic conditions (Barnes, 1996; Sucher, 1993; Walton 2008). Some studies have shown the efficacy of MFR to decrease pain, improve posture, and quality of life (Lukban, 2001; Radjieski *et al.*, 1998).

Deep Transverse Friction (DTF) massage is a technique used by James Cyriax and Gillean Russell to affect musculoskeletal structures of ligament, tendon, and muscle to provide therapeutic movement over a small area (Prentice, 2002). DTF is a specific type of connective tissue massage applied precisely to the soft tissue structures (Stasinopoulos and Johnson, 2004) to stretch and mobilize the myofascial trigger points and its associated taut bands (Hong *et al.*, 1993). The technique applied at right angles to the fibers comprising the tissue containing the lesion in a relaxed and shortened position (Boyling and Palastanga, 1994).

Most of the clinical studies on FM conducted in developed countries; studies in emerging countries or under-assisted populations are scarce. Several researchers demonstrated the personal effects of their therapeutic techniques. Till now, there is no single treatment which provides a complete cure of FM patients. Each patient has a different constellation of symptoms resulting in different responses to therapeutic interventions. A specific intervention will not work for every patient, though there are no disagreements on existing suggestions for the multidisciplinary approach in clinical practice for the management of fibromyalgia.

1.1   Need of the Study

Fibromyalgia is a multidimensional condition in which muscle pain, insomnia, inability to concentrate; depression and anxiety are the predominant symptoms. The earlier researches documented the possible treatment procedures like prescription of medications, non-pharmacological treatments, complimentary and alternate medicines.

All the investigations either concentrated on reducing the widespread muscle pain component or the psychosocial (depression and anxiety) aspects of the FM patients. The authors of the present study unable to locate studies in the literature about multidisciplinary approach in the management of all the symptoms of FM. However, to fulfill the dearth of research for effective management an interdisciplinary approach is necessary to resolve the widespread musculoskeletal pain sensitivity, psychosocial environment and quality of life. Thus, the study has been proposed.

1.2 Statement of the Problem

There have been considerable researches focused on the powerful treatment effects on FM condition like conventional treatment, pharmacotherapy, cognitive behavioral therapy and soft tissue releases. Further research is needed to evaluate whether the addition of pregabalin drug or CBT along with integrated physiotherapy techniques is more effective in the treatment of fibromyalgia?

This clinical trial attempt to promote early recovery from the musculoskeletal pain sensitivity and to improve physical and psychosocial status of FM condition.

1.3 Aim of the Study

To determine the effectiveness of Integrated Physiotherapy Techniques combined with medication and Cognitive Behavioral Therapy in patients with fibromyalgia.

1.4 Objectives of the Study

To find out the effect of integrated physiotherapy techniques alone and in combination with pregabalin drug and cognitive behavioral therapy in patients with fibromyalgia

i. On reduction of pain as measured through the Visual Analogue Scale (VAS).

ii. On the quality of life as measured through the Revised Fibromyalgia Impact Questionnaire (FIQR).

iii. On depression, as measured through the Beck Depression Index – II (BDI-II).

iv. On physical and mental health, as measured through short-form health survey (SF-36).

v. On anxiety, as measured through the General Anxiety Disorder scale (GAD-7).

vi. On trigger point sensitivity, as measured through the algometer tool.

1.5   Hypothesis

H_1. The integrated physiotherapy techniques combined with Pregabalin will be more effective in patients with fibromyalgia on VAS, FIQR, BDI, SF-36, GAD-7 and PPT.

H_2. The integrated physiotherapy techniques combined with cognitive behavioral therapy will show better improvement in patients of fibromyalgia than integrated physiotherapy techniques alone on VAS, FIQR, BDI, SF-36, GAD-7 and PPT.

H_3. Integrated physiotherapy techniques alone will have more impact in patients of fibromyalgia than the integrated physiotherapy techniques combined with Pregabalin on VAS, FIQR, BDI, SF-36, GAD-7 and PPT.

1.6   Limitations of the study

1. The subjects included in the study were recruited according to the ACR 2010 diagnostic criteria of fibromyalgia only.
2. Participants with age 18-50 years were only included in the study.
3. The biomarker outcome measures not included.
4. The subjects in pharmacotherapy group received 150 mg only.

1.7   Operational Definition

- **Integrated physical therapy techniques** (IPT) – In the present study the IPT is defined as the combination of moist heat, ultrasound therapy, deep transverse friction, Myofascial release, and exercises. In the present study IPT was used individually as a treatment protocol and combination along with Pregabalin drug and Cognitive behavioral therapy.

- **Cognitive behavioral therapy** is a psychotherapy which involves a process of teaching, coaching, and reinforcing positive behaviors and it helps people to identify cognitive patterns or thoughts and emotions that are linked with behaviors.

2.1 Search Strategies

Comprehensive literature in the English language were identified by searching through databases and search engines like MEDLINE, Physiotherapy Evidence Database (PEDro), Science Direct, Research gate, Cochrane Central Library, Google Scholar.

2.2 Search Duration

The study limited from January 1990 to July 2018. Free full-text articles collected from each database and search engine.

2.3 Keywords

Searching for studies in English language using the Medical subject headings (MeSH) terms like Prevalence, Incidence, Symptoms, Diagnosis, treatment of fibromyalgia, Fibromyalgia Impact Questionnaire, Beck Depression Index in fibromyalgia, General Anxiety Disorder Scale, SF-36 Health Survey, ACR Criteria for fibromyalgia, Pain Pressure Algometry.

2.4 Level of Evidence

Articles used in this review graded independently following the criteria described by the Centre of Evidence-Based Medicine. Oxford Centre, United Kingdom (Table 2.1 below).

Table 2.1: Centre of Evidence-Based Medicine: "Levels of Evidence 1"

Level	Definition
1a*	Systematic reviews of randomized controlled trials
1b*	Individual randomized controlled trials
2a*	Systematic reviews of Cohort studies
2b*	Different Cohort studies or low quality randomized controlled trials
3a*	Systematic reviews of case-control studies
3b	Individual case-control studies
4	Case series, Poorly designed cohort or case-control studies
5	Animal and bench research, expert opinion

* Authors have used level 1a, 1b, 2a, 2b, and 3a in review of literature

2.5   Epidemiology of Fibromyalgia

Epidemiology is the branch of medicine which deals with the incidence, distribution, and possible control of diseases and other factors relating to health. Fibromyalgia is the second most common condition seen in rheumatology practices. As same as the prevalence, the FM condition has the characteristics of widespread symptoms, mostly the affected population is heterogeneous in regard to symptom reporting. According to a published report through an internet survey in the year 2009, the manifestation, health care utilization, work, and physical data were available for 2,182 female responders (Wilson *et al.*, 2009). To assess the consequence of FM on the patient's lives, a qualitative study conducted by Arnold *et al.* (2008) in which six focus group sessions with 48 women diagnosed with fibromyalgia to elicit concepts and ideas. Fibromyalgia patients identified symptom domains that had the most significant impact on their quality of life, including pain, sleep disturbance, fatigue, depression, anxiety, and cognitive impairment. Patients reported disrupted relationships with family and friends, social isolation, reduced activities of daily living and leisure activities, avoidance of physical activity, and loss of career or inability to advance in careers or education. Fibromyalgia had a substantial negative impact on social and occupational function.

Reisine and Colleagues (2008) assessed the baseline employment status, which influences health outcomes adjusting for other baseline factors among women with FM over five years. Two hundred eighty-seven female FM patients from a national sample of rheumatologists were interviewed by phone at baseline and annually for four years. The authors summarized to say that the employed women with FM have better health status at baseline and maintain that advantage over time. But they found that employment does not seem to provide a protective health benefit. In a cross-sectional study, the authors (Palstam *et al.*, 2012) try to investigate which aspects of health differ between working women with FM and nonworking women with FM. This study had an enrolment of 129 women in it, and the authors categorized the women as working and nonworking. The authors mentioned that the working women with FM reported better health than nonworking women with FM in terms of pain, fatigue, stiffness, depression, disease-specific health status, and physical aspects of quality of life, which represent body functions and overall health status. However, they equally impaired in tests of physical capacity. Moderate pain levels were compatible with work, while severe pain appeared to compromise work. Fatigue was better tolerated, as women scoring critical levels of fatigue worked.

A survey carried out in patients with FM by Noller and Sprott (2003), to examine their general health status and work incapacity (disability-pension status), over an observation period of two-year, in this study the authors included 48 patients diagnosed with FM according to the American College of Rheumatology (ACR) criteria. The FM patients showed no improvement in pain, despite the many various treatments received over the two years. The increase in general satisfaction over the observation period believed to be the result of patient instruction and education about the disease.

The economic hardship and daily financial worries on daily pain among women with a chronic musculoskeletal condition were studied. The authors Rios and Zautra (2011), reported a study with 250 women affected with osteoarthritis (N=105), Fibromyalgia (N=46), or both (N=99). Financial stress was associated not only with greater exposure to daily financial worries but also with greater susceptibility to pain on days when everyday economic concerns experienced.

In a retrospective factor analysis of hair minerals in female patients with FM in Ajou University hospital at the Department of rheumatology and Department of family practice and community health from March to August 2010 was conducted. The authors Kim *et al.* (2011) compared a healthy reference group hair minerals with the female patients with fibromyalgia. Total Forty-four female patients diagnosed with fibromyalgia according to the ACR criteria were enrolled. The authors concluded lower concentrations of calcium, magnesium, iron, and manganese in the hair of female patients with fibromyalgia than of controls, even after adjustment of potential confounders

The United Kingdom (UK) general practice research database investigated the incidence of symptoms of fatigue at primary care from 1990 to 2001. Gallagher *et al.* (2004) recorded all the manifestations of exhaustion; the prevalence of fibromyalgia increased from less than 1 per 100,000 to 35 per 100,000. However, they found no consistent change in the incidence of all recorded symptoms of fatigue, with an average of 1503 per 100,000, equivalent to 1.5% per year. Chronic Fatigue Syndrome (CFS) / Myalgic Encephalomyelitis (ME) and fibromyalgia were rarely diagnosed in children and were uncommon in the elderly. Therefore, all symptoms and diagnoses were more common in heterogeneous populations. Generally, the overall incidence of fatigue diagnoses has fallen, and which has raised on the incidence rates of the specific diagnoses of CFS/ME and fibromyalgia. The estimated regional data from the Japan epidemiological surveillance in population studies in 2003 was up-to 1.66% following by internet surveillance in 2011 showed 2.04%. According to the Japanese FM database, the authors Nishioka *et al.* in 2004 estimated that the prevalence of FM, reaching 40% in women age 30 to 50 years old.

In a 2011 study by Perrot, the FM prevalence in the French metropolitan population studied; the entire national territory used, based on a multi-step sampling analysis, the data was collected by widespread screening, and a trained specialist has confirmed the condition. Patients above 18 years of age were contacted by telephone using the LFES Questionnaire and included in the study. The author discussed about 1.6% of the rate of prevalence calculated in the French population supported the figures of European literature published data.

A Sweden study explored the prevalence of fibromyalgia and chronic widespread musculoskeletal pain in a general population using the 1990 criteria of the American College of Rheumatology. The authors Lindell and Colleagues (2000) assessed all the participants with the structured interview and clinical examination, number of tender-point, and pain threshold. Participants with suspected chronic widespread pain recruited from a previously defined cohort containing 2425 men and women aged 20-74 years. Of these, 303 subjects identified and included. Two hundred two individualfs invited, and 147 agreed to participate. Authors concluded that fibromyalgia and chronic widespread musculoskeletal pain appeared to be comparatively rare conditions in the south-west of Sweden.

2.6 Sickness, Absenteeism, Medical cost, sedentary time and Physical activity in FM

Cost utilization in FM is a global burden to the affected individuals. Knight *et al.* (2013) included two separate, cross-sectional, observational studies of subjects with FM (one in the US and one in France and Germany). The authors evaluated and compared 442 subjects (203 US, 70 France, 169 Germany) health resource use (HRU) and associated costs related to FM in routine clinical practice across the US, France, and Germany. Patient out-of-pocket costs and lost productivity were collected via subject self-report. Values assigned to HRU based on standard algorithms. Direct and indirect damages were evaluated and compared by simple linear regression. The authors highlighted the substantial global economic burden of FM in the US, France, and Germany. Indirect costs characterized a significant proportion of the total costs, particularly in Europe. Comparisons between the three countries demonstrate differences in HRU, with significantly higher straight prices in the US compared with France and Germany.

The impact of FM severity on patients' symptoms, health-related quality of life (HRQoL), and productivity evaluated in the United States Schaefer *et al.* (2011) recruited 203 FM subjects from twenty physician centers. The author result reported that FM imposes a considerable humanistic burden on patients in the United States, and leads to extensive productivity loss, despite treatment. This burden is superior among subjects with worse FM severity.

The utilization of complementary and alternative medical (CAM) therapy may lower the insurance coverage of chronically ill patients. To admit the above sentence, the Lind *et al.* (2010) compared health care expenditures between insured patients with back pain, fibromyalgia syndrome, or menopause symptoms. The CAM providers group matched with the No-CAM provider's group based on age group, gender, index medical condition, overall disease burden, and prior-year expenditures. The analysis showed the equal Insurance coverage for both conventional and CAM providers. After minimizing the selection bias, the report indicates that among insured patients with back pain, fibromyalgia, and menopause symptoms, by matching patients who use CAM providers to those who do not, those who use CAM will have lower insurance expenditures than those who do not use CAM.

Linder *et al.* (2009) conducted a descriptive study to gain knowledge of fibromyalgia (FM) patients on long-term sick leave individuals from social insurance offices and the department of psychiatry, orthopedic surgery, and rehabilitation medicine included. Ninety-two women diagnosed with FM showed reduced sleep. The authors concluded that FM patients did not meet more criteria for personality disorder than patients with the other bodily pain conditions. The majority of FM patients experienced disabilities in the mobility and domestic-life areas.

Similarly, a prospective cohort study of the risk of absence due to sickness among employees examined in individuals with fibromyalgia. Kivimaki*et al.* (2007)

examined the 1-year follow-up of recorded and certified absence due to illness after a survey of chronic diseases among 34,100 Finnish public sector employees (27,360 women and 6740 men) aged 17–65 years at baseline in 2000–2002. The employees with fibromyalgia and for others have documented a total of 20,224 days of absence due to sickness for the 644 employees and 4,54,816 days, respectively. Of those with fibromyalgia, 67% had co-occurring chronic conditions such as osteoarthritis, rheumatoid arthritis, depression, or other psychiatric disorders. Fibromyalgia is associated with a substantially increased risk of medically certified absence due to sickness that is not accounted for by co-existing osteoarthritis, rheumatoid arthritis, or psychiatric disorders.

Across-sectional and retrospective study analyzed health care and non-health care resource utilization under routine medical practice in a primary care rating claims database and to calculate the incremental average cost per patient per year of fibromyalgia syndrome (FMS). The authors, Sicras-Mainer *et al.* (2009), conducted a 12-month study using computerized medical records from a health provider database. The results of the study reported that patients with FMS were associated with considerably higher annual total costs in the primary care setting compared with the reference population.

In the same way, the cost of illness of fibromyalgia, chronic low back pain (CLBP), and ankylosing spondylitis (AS) compared to well being. Boonen*et al.* (2005) compared three randomized trials completed a cost diary, comprising direct medical and non-medical resource utilization and inability to perform paid and unpaid work. The cost utilization data in 70 patients with fibromyalgia, 110 with chronic low back pain, and 111 with AS were analyzed. The authors discussed fibromyalgia and CLBP as both had higher cost utilization than AS, mainly because of the cost of formal and informal care, aids and adaptations, and workdays lost.

Ruiz *et al.* (2013) conducted a cross-sectional study on objectively measured sedentary time and physical activity in women with fibromyalgia in Spain. They mentioned a total of 94 women diagnosed with fibromyalgia who did not have other severe somatic or psychiatric disorders, or other diseases that prevent physical loading, able to ambulate and to communicate and capable and willing to provide informed consent included. The authors reported that women spent, on average, 10 min less on

Moderate to Vigorous Physical Activity (MVPA) and 22 min less on sedentary behaviors during weekends compared with weekdays.

To manipulating pain modulation and determining relationships to both Physical Activity (PA) and sustained sedentary behavior, Ellingson*et al.* (2012) conducted their work on eleven women with FM. Accelerometer and MRI were the two outcome measures used in this study. All the participants underwent functional magnetic resonance imaging of heat, administered alone, and during distracting cognitive tasks. For a sedentary time, significant negative relationships observed in areas involved in both pain modulation and the sensory-discriminative aspects of pain, including the Dorso-Lateral Prefrontal Cortex (DLPFC), thalamus and superior frontal and pre and postcentralgyri. The authors suggested that physical activity and sedentary behaviors are associated with central nervous system regulation of pain in FM.

To illustrate the school absences in adolescents with Juvenile Primary Fibromyalgia Syndrome (JPFS), Kashikar-Zuck*et al.* (2010) conducted a survey to describe the relationship between school absenteeism, pain, psychiatric symptoms, and maternal pain history. One hundred and two adolescents with JPFS were studied. Completed measures of anxiety and depressive symptoms and completed a psychiatric interview. Information from the parents obtained about the adolescents' school absences, type of schooling, and parental pain history. School attendance reports were obtained directly from schools. Above 12% of adolescents with JPFS were homeschooled. On average, about 2.9 days and more than three days per month of school missing noted in those enrolled in regular school. The authors also reported that Pain and maternal pain history were not related to school absenteeism. However, depressive symptoms were significantly associated with school absences.

2.7   Studies related to Pathophysiology of FM

Understanding the pathophysiology and its associated disorders may assist the health providers in implementing definitive treatment to the patients. There are different factors which are responsible for the disordered physiological processes of FM condition like environmental factors, genetic factors, psychological factors, abnormalities in the neuroendocrine, and autonomic nervous system. Most of the risk factors have similar characteristics of FM.

A review attempted by Gupta and Silman (2004) to reconcile the dichotomy that exists in the literature to fibromyalgia, in that it is considered either a bodily response to psychological stress or a distinct organically based syndrome. Specifically, the hypothesis explored is that one or more abnormalities can explain the link between chronic stress and the subsequent development of fibromyalgia in neuroendocrine function. There are several such abnormalities recognized that both occur as a result of chronic stress and observe in fibromyalgia. Whether such defects have an etiologic role remains uncertain but should be testable by well-designed prospective studies

The 1990 and 2010 ACR criteria were compared for the diagnosis and assessment of FM and to analyze the correlation and agreement Kim *et al.* (2012), conducted on 98 FM patients. The patients had diffuse whole body pain for three months or more together with 11 or more tender points according to the 1990 ACR classification criteria. And patients who did not satisfy the 11 tender points but were suspected of fibromyalgia in clinical examination and had a Fibromyalgia impact questionnaire (FIQ) of 40 or more included. The authors agreed that the ACR preliminary diagnostic criteria for FM with the 1990 ACR criteria during the disease course. The first measures were a more sensitive method than the 1990 rules. Besides, the 2010 standards might have advantages since it is easy to assess the physical and psychological symptoms and can be quantified.

Weather plays an essential role in the chronic musculo-skeletal and arthritic pain to examine the association between fibromyalgia pain and climate to determine the nature of their interrelationship, Fors, and Sexton (2002) studied the daily pain ratings of 55 female patients previously diagnosed with fibromyalgia. The Visual Analogue Scales (VAS) over 28 days recorded. The results of the study reported that a group of patients with less chronic fibromyalgia might be weather sensitive.

A report by Guedj and Weinberger (1990), also conducted a one-month prospective study on 62 rheumatic patients, of which, 16 with rheumatoid arthritis (RA), 24 with osteoarthritis (OA), 11 with inflammatory arthritis, 11 with fibromyalgia joint pain-swelling. The authors compared everyday activity with changes in daily weather conditions. Most of the studies accepted that weather changes increased arthritic symptoms, and low temperatures may increase the thickness of the synovial fluid inside the joints. The study also explained that women were more sensitive to weather than men (62% vs. 37%). These results support the belief of most rheumatic patients that weather conditions significantly influence their day to day symptoms.

A similar report has been documented by Wilbarger *et al.* (2011), on the sensory sensitivities to non-noxious sensory stimuli in daily life in patients with fibromyalgia (FM). A total of eighty-three participants included in this descriptive study, twenty-seven women individuals with FM compared with twenty-eight women with rheumatoid arthritis (RA) and twenty-eight healthy pain-free women (controls). The authors concluded, according to the self-report measure, that women with FM have increased sensory sensitivities to both tactile and non-somatic sensory stimuli in the environment and could experience more stress-related to sensory conditions in daily life.

In 2006, Buskila and Puttinireported that genetic and environmental factors might play a role in the etiopathology of fibromyalgia syndrome (FMS) and other related syndromes. According to this study, the family history of FMS was more prevalent. The authors showed evidence that the role of polymorphisms of genes in the endocrinal systems in the etiology of FMS. These polymorphisms are not specific for FMS and are associated with other functional somatic disorders and depression. They suggested that more prospective studies in larger cohorts of patients conveyed for a better understanding of the role of genetics in FMS and other related conditions. To accomplish the previous suggestion, Finan*et al.* (2010) conducted a study on genetic influences on the dynamics of pain and affected in FM. Forty-six female patients were studied to determine the variation in the Catechol-O-Methyltransferase (COMT), and mu-opioid receptor (OPRM1) genes are associated with pain-related positive affective regulation in fibromyalgia (FM). All the participants completed an electronic diary that included daily assessments of positive affect and pain. A Multilevel modeling utilized to analyze Between- and within-person data. The author concluded that together, the findings offer ample reason to investigate further the contribution of the catecholamine and opioid systems, and their associated genomic variants, to the still poorly understood experience of FM.

Carvalho *et al.* (2008) conducted a Brazilian study to state that the genetic factors in FM help to identify patients with a differently altered frequency of immune cells. They evaluated endocrine and immunological features of distinct subsets of Seventy-five FM patients. Subjects recruited those who are meeting the ACR criteria and 27 healthy age-matched controls. The groups divided according to Human serotonin transporter Long Polymorphism (5-HTTLPR) genotyping as the L group (patients who expressed only the long allele) and the S group (patients with at least one short allele). Salivary cortisol levels, the absolute number of leucocyte counts, natural killer (NK) cells, and activated T and B lymphocytes evaluated. The results of this study showed decreased cortisol levels, more intense in the L group, increased all B lymphocytes subsets, and reduced CD4, CD25 T lymphocytes. The L group had increased CD4 CD25 activated T lymphocytes, while the S group displayed elevated CD4 human leucocyte antigen D-related (HLA-DR) activated T lymphocytes and decreased NK cells. The authors proved that genetic factors help to identify FM individuals with differentially altered frequencies of immune cells.

The mechanism of pain perception from the baroreceptors to the spinal cord, the spinal cord to the brain, has established previously. Bradly (2009)reported the contribution of biological, genetic, and environmental factors to the pathophysiology of fibromyalgia. The pain symptoms of fibromyalgia may be due to alterations in the central processing of sensory input, along with aberrations in the endogenous inhibition of pain; Genetic research has shown familial aggregation of fibromyalgia and other related disorders such as major depressive disorder. The dysfunctional pain processing has the contribution to combined exposure of physical or psychosocial stressors, as well as abnormal biologic responses in the ANS and neuroendocrine responses.

In another randomized controlled trial (RCT) by Malt *et al.* (2002) studied the variance in pain in ninety women with fibromyalgia. A combined model, including neuroendocrine and autonomic factors, would give the most sparing explanation of variation in pain. Fibromyalgia patients may have reduced reactivity in the central sympathetic system or perturbations in the sympathetic-parasympathetic balance. The authors concluded that to explain the perceived pain in FM, and it is necessary to understand the bio-psychosocial model including psychological factors as well as factors related to perturbations of the autonomic nervous system and hypothalamic-pituitary-adrenal axis as compared to psychological factors alone

2.8   Biomarkers and the other diagnostic procedure in FM

The previous researches highlighted some of the biochemical, metabolic, and immunoregulatory abnormalities associated with fibromyalgia. A cohort study conducted by Feng *et al.* (2013). The authors performed a complete exome sequencing on a subset of FMS patients. Out of 150 nuclear families (trios), DNA from 19 probands subjected to complete exome sequencing. Two nonsense mutations, W32X in C11orf40 and Q100X in ZNF77 among 150 FMS trios, had a significantly elevated frequency of transmission to affected probands (p = 0.026 and p = 0.032, respectively) and were present in a subset of 13% and 11% of FMS patients, respectively. The subgroup with the C11orf40 mutation had elevated plasma levels of the inflammatory cytokines, MCP-1 and IP-10, compared with unaffected controls or FMS patients with the wild-type allele. Similarly, patients with the ZNF77 mutation have elevated levels of the inflammatory cytokine, IL-12, compared with controls or patients with the wild type allele. The authors of this study results strongly implicate a provocative basis for FMS, as well as specific cytokine dysregulation, in at least 35% of FMS.

In another study, Hernandez *et al.* (2010) measured the movement levels of pro-inflammatory cytokines to determine the influence of BMI on these levels in FM patients and healthy volunteers (HVs). Authors found significant differences in BMI levels between FM patients (26.40 ± 4.46) and HVs (23.64 ±3.45) and significant increase in IL-6 in FM patients (16.28 ± 8.13 vs 0.92 ± 0.32 pg/ml) (P < 0.001). IL- 1β and TNF-α decreased in FM patients compared with HVs. The authors concluded that FM patients of BMI as a covariate of pro-inflammatory cytokines levels showed that serum TNF-α and IL-6 levels are independent of BMI.

In another experimental study by Behm*et al.* (2012) determined whether cytokine production by immune cells altered in FM patients by comparing the cellular responses to mitogenic activators of stimulated blood mononuclear cells of a large number of patients with FM to those of healthy matched individuals. The authors recruited 110 patients with the clinical diagnosis of FM and 91 healthy donors. Twenty-eight mL of blood obtained from patients and healthy volunteers after obtaining their consent for research. Blood was withdrawn in four 7 mL tubes containing 0.081 mL of 15% K EDTA solution by Venipuncture. Plasma and peripheral blood mononuclear cells (PBMC) obtained from 110 patients with the clinical diagnosis of FM and 91 healthy donors. Parallel samples of PBMC cultured overnight in medium alone or the presence of mitotic activators, PHA or PMA, in combination with ionomycin medication. The cytokine responses to mitogenic activators of PBMC isolated from patients with FM were significantly lower than those of healthy individuals, implying that cell-mediated immunity impaired in FM patients.

Another study mentioned by Sprott*et al.* (2004) determined whether there is evidence of increased DNA fragmentation and ultrastructural changes in muscle tissue of patients with fibromyalgia (FM) compared with healthy controls. Muscle tissues from 10 community residents with FM and ten age and sex-matched healthy controls were examined "blindly" for the presence of DNA fragmentation by two different methods: terminal de-oxynucleotidyltransferase (TdT) staining (TUNEL) and the FragEL-Klenow DNA fragmentation detection kit. To conclude, the authors stated that the ultra-structural changes suggested that patients with FM characterized by abnormalities in muscle tissue that include increased DNA fragmentation and changes in the number and size of mitochondria. These cellular changes are not signs of apoptosis. Persistent focal contractions in muscle may contribute to ultra-structural tissue abnormalities as well as to the induction and long duration of nociceptive transmission from muscle to the central nervous system.

The gray matter volumes of brain areas associated with pain-related areas of FM patients identified by functional brain imaging investigated by Robinson *et al.* (2011), Using voxel-based morphometric (VBM) analysis of magnetic resonance brain images, they compared 19 pain-related brain areas of 14 female patients with FM and 11 healthy controls (NC). The authors found that FM patients had significantly less gray matter volumes than NC in three brain regions, including the anterior and mid-cingulate, as well as mid-insular cortices. Notably, the authors detailed that FM patients neither demonstrated global gray matter atrophy nor gray matter changes associated with depression. They provided evidence for decreased gray matter volumes in many pain linked brain areas in FM.

Authors Pujol and Colleagues (2009) conducted a study on twenty-seven female subjects to characterize the brain response to painful pressure in fibromyalgia patients through functional MRI by generating activation maps adjusted for the duration of brain responses. The sample included nine fibromyalgia patients and two groups of nine healthy subjects who received 4 kg/cm 2 of pressure on the thumb by a specially designed hydraulic device. Nine additional control subjects received 6.8 kg/cm 2 to match the patients for the severity of perceived pain. The authors suggested that data-driven fMRI assessments may complement conventional neuro-imaging for characterizing pain responses and that enhancement of brain activation in fibromyalgia patients may be particularly relevant in emotion-related regions.

Shang *et al.* (2012) used two experimental protocol to investigate the blood flow muscle responses, thirty-two post-menopausal women with and without FM analyzed and evaluated through the near-infrared diffuse optical source to evaluate muscle blood flow, blood oxygen, and oxygen metabolism during fatiguing leg exercise and arm arterial cuff occlusion. The authors in this study suggested an alteration of muscle oxygen utilization in the FM population and the potential of using combined near-infrared diffuse optical spectroscopies (NIRS) or near-infrared diffuse correlation spectroscopy (DCS) to evaluate tissue oxygen and flow kinetics in skeletal muscle comprehensively.

The abnormalities of the hypothalamic-pituitary-gonadal (HPG) axis and cortisol concentrations in young women with primary FM evaluated. Also determine whether depression, fatigue, and sleep disturbance affect these hormones, Gur*et al.* (2004) conducted an experimental study on 63 women with FM and which compared with 38 matched healthy controls. FSH, luteinizing hormone (LH), oestradiol, progesterone, prolactin, and cortisol concentrations were the outcome measures. The authors suggested that in young women with FM, a low cortisol concentration, HPG axis hormones are healthy, except for LH levels in patients with high depression rates and with sleep disturbance. Fatigue, depression rate, sleep disturbance and mean age of the study group may affect cortisol levels, or cortisol may be a biological factor that contributes to fatigue chronicity, a depressive state and sleep disturbance.

Harris *et al.* (2009) study hypothesized that increased levels of insular Glutamate (Glu) would be present in FM patients and that the concentration of this molecule is comparing the pain report. 19 FM patients and 14 age and sex-matched pain-free controls underwent pressure stimuli on the subject's thumbnail using a stimulation device. All the subjects' pressure pain examined at rest through a proton magnetic resonance spectroscopy (H-MRS) session wherein the right anterior and right posterior insula observed. The authors of this study accepted that enhanced glutamate neurotransmission resulting from higher concentrations of Glu within the posterior insula might play a role in the abnormal physiology of FM and other central pain augmentation syndromes. However, Harris (2010) reported, it is unknown if elevated Glu is acting at the synapse. Investigations are needed to investigate the molecular action of Glu in FM and to investigate these findings during treatment that modulates glutamate neurotransmission.

In a quantitative study, Alvarez- Bulla *et al.* (2008) measured urinary cortisol levels for a sample of 47 women aged 29 to 64 years (mean age 53 years), diagnosed with FM 2–3 years previously, and compared the results with those for a control sample of 58 healthy women of a similar age. Samples of 24-hour urine were appropriately collected, and levels of urinary cortisol were measured using the fluorescence polarization immunoassay method. Authors confirm that women with FM have significantly lower urinary cortisol levels than healthy women. But at the same time, Information on 24-hour urine cortisol levels does not constitute useful information in itself but may be valuable when combined with other clinical tests usually performed to diagnose FM. Although a dysfunctional hypothalamic-pituitary-adrenal axis can lead to decreased sensitivity and resiliency in the stress system, it does not necessarily affect baseline cortisol levels, so 24-hour urinary cortisol levels alone cannot evaluate FM.

The relationship between the quality of life of the FMS patient and indexes of the cardiovascular autonomic control as estimated from spontaneous fluctuations of heart period (HP) and systolic arterial pressure (SAP) evaluated by Zamuner*et al.* (2017). Thirty-five women with FMS (age: 48.8±8.9 years; body mass index: 29.3±4.3 Kg/m2) included in this study. The ECG, invasive finger blood pressure, and respiratory activity continuously recorded during 15 minutes at rest in supine position (REST) and orthostatic position during active standing (STAND). The lower the degree of cardiac baroreflex involvement during STAND in women with FMS, the higher the impact of FMS on the quality of life, thus the authors suggesting that Granger causality analysis might be clinically helpful in assessing the state of the FMS patient.

An experimental study on 150 individuals conducted toevaluate muscle modifications by surface electromyography (SEMG) analysis in FM women concerning a sample of healthy controls and to investigate the relationships between SEMG parameters and the clinical aspects of the disease by Bazzichi*et al.* (2009). SEMG was recorded in 100 FM women (48.10 ± 11.96 years) and 50 healthy women (48.60 ± 11.18 years), from the tibialis anterior and the distal part of vastusmedialis muscle during isometric contraction. The authors found some exciting muscle modifications in FM patients concerning healthy controls regarding median spectral frequency (MDF), conduction velocity (CV), and fatigue index (FI) values, which resulted significantly lower in FM. Patients might have different fiber recruitment or possible atrophy of type II fibers suggesting that they are not able to reach muscle relaxation.

The mechanism(s) of nociceptive dysfunction and potential roles of opioid neurotransmitters in the chronic pain syndromes of fibromyalgia and chronic low back pain on 30 individuals studied by Baraniuk*et al.* (2004), History and physical examinations, tender point examinations, and questionnaires used to identify 14 fibromyalgia, ten chronic low back pain, and six healthy control subjects. Lumbar punctures executed in all the patients: Met-enkephalin-Arg -Phe (MEAP) and harmful stimuli immuno-reactive materials measured in the CSF radioimmunoassays. Fibromyalgia and low back pain groups had significantly higher MEAP than the healthy control group. The conclusion made by the authors that Fibromyalgia distinguished by higher cerebrospinal fluid MEAP, systemic complaints, and manual tender points; average SF-36 scores; and lower pain thresholds compared to the low back pain and healthy groups. MEAP and systemic pain thresholds inversely correlated in LBP subjects. Central nervous system opioid dysfunction may contribute to pain in fibromyalgia.

A six-year prospective study of a cohort of patients with FM was conducted by Baumgartner *et al.* (2004) to examine the long term prognosis in patients with fibromyalgia (FM). Forty-five of seventy patients who had participated in a three-week trial six years earlier completed again the same questionnaires used previously. Pain scale, sleep quality, morning stiffness, number of analgesic tablets taken during the past week, patients'evaluation of their health, a functional limitations questionnaire, the regional pain score (RPS), and the psychological general wellbeing index (PGWB), a generic quality of life questionnaire re-evaluated. Most of the symptoms had remained stable. The pain had increased, but some aspects of quality of life had improved over time. The symptoms of FM persisted over the six years, but patients appeared better able to cope with them.

Ceko*et al.* (2012) focused on the experimental evidence related to FM symptoms and connect these perceptual and cognitive signs to abnormalities observed in the brains of FM patients. Neuroimaging studies support the neurophysical evidence of altered pain perception and inhibition. Researchers reported it augmented sensory processing in pain-related areas, which, together with gray matter decreases and neurochemical abnormalities in areas related to pain modulation. Working memory suggests that cognitive disturbances could be related to brain alterations. Thus, altered levels of neurotransmitters involved in sleep regulation link disordered sleep to neurochemical abnormalities.

The Left Ventricular (LV) function assessed in patients with fibromyalgia (FM) with chronic emotional and physical stress. Cho *et al.* (2010) conducted a study on thirty consecutive postmenopausal women (mean age, 48±8 years) satisfying the criteria for FM with atypical chest pain and 20 age-matched healthy controls using standard and 2dimensional strain (2DS) echocardiography. Each individual underwent a clinical examination also during the survey, FIQ, Beck Depression Index (BDI), Brief Fatigue Inventory, and echocardiographic evaluation assessed. Conclusively it was stated that the Global and segmental LV strains were negatively associated with fatigue, tender point count, and FIQ score. However, there was no significant association between depression and LV strain.

A twenty-five-year follow-up of the Adventist health study conducted by Choi *et al.* (2010).to investigate the association between incident self-reported FM and prior somatic diseases, lifestyle factors, and health behaviors among 3,136 women who participated in two cohort studies 25–26 years apart (the Adventist Health Study 1 and 2). One hundred thirty-six women reported a diagnosis of FM during 25 years of follow-up, giving a period incidence of 43/1,000 or 1.72/1000 per year. In this study the authors found a history of hyperemesis gravidarum was associated with FM with OR of 1.32 (95% CI: 0.75–2.32) and 1.73 (95% CI: 0.99–3.03), (p[trend]<0.05), respectively, for some or all pregnancies versus none. A positive association with smoking was also found with OR of 2.37 (95% CI: 1.33–4.23) forever smokers versus never smokers. No significant association was found with number of surgeries, history of peptic ulcers, or taking medications to control various symptoms.

A case-control and correlational study comparing 65 patients and 45 healthy controls were carried by Cordero *et al.* (2011), to examine lipid oxidative degradation blood mononuclear cells (BMCs) and plasma, as a marker of oxidative damage, and its association to clinical symptoms in Fibromyalgia (FM) patients. Fibromyalgia Impact Questionnaire (FIQ), Visual Analogues Scales (VAS), and the BeckDepression Inventory (BDI) evaluated as clinical parameters. Oxidative stress was determined by measuring LPO in BMCs and plasma. The authors found increased LPO levels in BMCs and plasma from FM patients as compared to normal control (P<0.001). A significant correlation between LPO in BMCs and clinical parameters was observed (r = 0.584, P<0.001 for VAS; r = 0.823, P<0.001 for FIQ total score; and r = 0.875, P<0.01 for depression in the BDI). They also found a positive correlation between LPO in plasma and clinical symptoms (r = 0.452, P<0.001 for VAS; r = 0.578, P<0.001 for FIQ total score; and r = 0.579, P<0.001 for depression in the BDI). Partial correlation analysis controlling for age and BMI, and sex, showed that both LPO in cells and plasma were independently associated with clinical symptoms. However, LPO in cells, but not LPO in plasma, was independently associated with clinical symptoms when controlling for depression (BDI scores. The authors suggested a role for oxidative stress in the pathophysiology of fibromyalgia and that LPO in BMCs rather than LPO in plasma is better associated with clinical symptoms in FM.

Three hundred thirty-eight children with a mean age of 11.5 years enrolled in a study by Gedalia*et al.* (1993) to test the hypothesis that joint hypermobility may play a part in the pathogenesis of pain in fibromyalgia. The schoolchildren from one public school in Beer-Sheva, Israel, were examined for the coexistence of joint hypermobility and fibromyalgia. The Carter and Bird method of joint hypermobility utilized. In conclusion, the authors suggest that there is a strong association between joint hypermobility and fibromyalgia in schoolchildren. Joint hypermobility may play a part in the pathogenesis of pain in fibromyalgia.

Neural correlates of executive function investigated in 18 FM patients and 14 age-matched HCs during a simple go/no-go task (response inhibition). At the same time, they underwent functional magnetic resonance imaging (fMRI). The authors Glass *et al.* (2011) drawn the samples from a registry of individuals diagnosed with FM who had previously indicated an interest in participating in clinical research within the Chronic Pain and Fatigue Research Centre (CPFRC) at the University of Michigan. Total seven outcome measures assessed viz. clinical pain, Center for Epidemiological Studies Depression Scale (CES-D), State-Trait Personality Inventory (STPI) for anxiety, Complex Medical Symptom Inventory (CMSI), Multidimensional Fatigue Inventory (MFI), Medical Outcomes Study Sleep Scale (MOS Sleep Scale), and Multiple Abilities Self-Report Questionnaire (MASQ) for cognitive difficulty. The fMRI revealed that FM patients had lower activation in the right pre-motor cortex, supplementary motor area (SMA), mid-cingulate cortex (MCC), putamen, and, after controlling for anxiety, in the right insular cortex (IC) and right inferior frontal gyrus (IFG). Authors hypothesized that response -inhibition and pain perception may rely on partially overlapping networks and that in chronic pain, patient's resources taken up by pain processing may not be available for executive functioning tasks such as response inhibition.

Gormsen *et al.* (2010) carried a study on thirty neuropathic pain (NP) patients, 28 patients with fibromyalgia (FM), and 26 pain-free age- and gender-matched controls and examined for mental distress (self-rated Symptom Checklist-92), depression (doctor-rated Hamilton Depression Scale and self-rated Major Depression Inventory) and anxiety (doctor-rated Hamilton Anxiety Scale and self-rated Anxiety Inventory). Only a few chronic pain patients meet the diagnostic criteria for depression (NP 3.3%, FM 7.1%), and associations between pain and mental symptoms only found in the FM group despite similar pain intensities. The author findings suggested that different mechanisms are responsible for the development of mood disorders in the two patient groups.

The arterial stiffness in FM patients using pulse wave velocity (PWV) investigated and analyzed to determine whether arterial stiffness was affected by the clinical parameters of FM. Lee *et al.* (2011), recruited 108 female FM patients (51.5±8.9 years) without any known cardiovascular diseases and 76 healthy female controls (50.1±8.9 years). VAS, Korean Fibromyalgia Impact questionnaire (kFIQ), the Beck Depression Inventory (BDI) scale, and Brief Fatigue Inventory (BFI) scale, was utilized to assess the various symptoms of FM. Arterial stiffness evaluated by measuring brachial-ankle (ba) PWVs using an automatic waveform analyzer. The participants further divided into two subgroups based on the FIQ score. The authors concluded that patients with FM showed significantly increased arterial stiffness, suggesting a pathophysiologic link between FM and endothelial dysfunction.

Napadow *et al.* (2010) investigated the degree of connectivity between multiple brain networks in FM, as well as how activity in these networks correlates with spontaneous pain. Resting functional magnetic resonance imaging (fMRI) data in FM patients (n=18) and age-matched healthy controls (HC, n=18) were analyzed using dual regression independent component analysis (ICA). Authors evaluated intrinsic, or resting, connectivity in multiple brain networks: the default mode network (DMN), the executive attention network (EAN), and the medial visual network (MVN), with the MVN serving as a negative control. Spontaneous pain levels also covaried with intrinsic connectivity. In conclusion, the authors indicated that resting brain activity within multiple networks is associated with spontaneous clinical pain in FM—the

Heterogeneity of psychophysiological stress responses in fibromyalgia syndrome patients studied by Thieme& Turk (2005). The authors recruited ninety female FMS patients and thirty age and sex-matched HCs. A physician examines the laboratory measures and evaluation of tender points.

EMG activity recorded from the left and right m. trapezius, according to the positioning recommended by Fridlund and Cacioppo, and BP measured with a photoplethysmographic device on the fourth digit of the left hand. The authors identified four Neuro-physiological response patterns. 63.3% of HCs showed increased muscle tension and stable cardiovascular responses; 34.8% of FMS patients showed a pattern of increased sympathetic blood vessel reactivity; steady sweat gland activity, and reduced muscular response; 12.2% of FMS patients. And, in contrast, 46.7% of FMS patients showed a pattern of para-sympathetic vasomotor reactivity and decreased sweat gland activity as well as strong response. The result of this study supports the heterogeneity of the mechanism involved in FMS.

In an attempt to investigate to what the subjective estimation of pain alters extent cortical reactivity, researchers Pollok *et al.* (2010) conducted a study on 30 subjects (10 subjects with masochistic behavior (MB) and 20 control subjects) matched to age, gender, and handedness. Non-painful electrical pulses activating the tactile afferents of the superficial branch of the radial nerve of the right hand were applied as test stimuli (TS) 500 ms after a conditioning stimulus (CS). CS was either electrical stimuli at the same location and intensity as the TS or slightly painful nociceptive cutaneous laser stimulation applied to the dorsum of the right hand.

The results implied altered cortical reactivity of the primary somatosensory cortex in FMS patients and MB, possibly reflecting differences in the individual pain experience.

In an experimental study by Mcloughlin*et al.* (2011) to determine whether physical activity was predictive of brain responses to experimental pain in FM using fMRI. Thirty-four participants (n=16 FM; n=18 Control) completed self-report and accelerometer measures of physical activity and underwent fMRI of painful heat stimuli. Each participant received seven temperatures (whole degree increments between 43 and 49 °C) twice, in random order, and rated the intensity and unpleasantness of each stimulus. Heat stimuli delivered for 8 seconds each, with 1-minute inter-stimulus intervals. The authors reported that greater physical activity was significantly (p<0.05) associated with decreased pain ratings to repeated heat stimuli for FM patients. Also, they suggested an association between measures of physical activity and central nervous system processing of pain.

Different nocturnal Heart Rate Variability (HRV) parameters as potential FM biomarkers and seek a correlation between HRV parameters and diverse FM symptoms, Lerma *et al.* (2011) conducted a study on 22 women suffering from FM and 22 age-matched controls. All participants used a Holter monitor over 24 hours while undertaking their routine activities during the day and while sleeping at their homes at night. The results reported by the researchers that Nocturnal SDNN of less than 114 ms had the greatest predictive value to set apart patients from controls with an odds ratio of 13.6 (95% confidence interval: 3.9 to 47.8). In patients, decreased nighttime HRV markers indicative of sympathetic predominance had significant correlations with several FM symptoms: SDSD associated with pain intensity ($r = -0.65$, $P<0.001$). SDNN correlated with constipation ($r = -0.53$, $P<0.001$), and mean NN with depression ($r = -0.53$, $P<0.001$). The authors concluded that the Nocturnal HRV indices indicative of sympathetic predominance are significantly different in FM women when compared to healthy individuals. In FM patients, these HRV parameters correlated with several symptoms, including pain severity.

Ross *et al.* (2010) hypothesized that serum cytokine levels and FM symptom severity would be higher in FM patients with inadequate growth hormone response to exhaustive exercise compared to those without growth hormone response. Outpatients with FM (n = 165) underwent a Modified Balke Treadmill Protocol and GH response to a thorough workout measured in peripheral blood samples. The authors suggested that an inadequate growth hormone response to exercise may be associated with increased levels of blood cytokines and pain severity in FM patients.

Menzies and Lyon (2010) synthesized the results of research studies focused on the relationship between cytokines and FMS and among cytokines and core symptoms of FMS. Literature supports the for relationships among FMS symptoms and cytokines; however, there are discrepant findings related to whether pro- and anti-inflammatory cytokines are elevated or reduced in persons with FMS and whether or not their levels correlate with the core symptoms of this disorder. Although the use of cytokine biomarkers must be considered exploratory at this time due to the lack of consistent empirical findings, bio-behavioral research focused on understanding the relationship of FMS with cytokines may lead to a better understanding of this complex syndrome.

This knowledge may ultimately contribute to the development of interventions for symptom management that address not only the symptom manifestation but also a biological mediator of symptoms.

Forty FM women with a mean age of fifty-four studied. Morf*et al.* (2004) tested all items within five weeks by the same investigators, using two noninvasive methods, laser fluxmetry, and capillary microscopy. The data reported that FM patients had fewer capillaries in the nail fold (P< 0.001) and significantly more capillary dilatations (P < 0.05) and irregular formations (P < 0.01) than the healthy controls. Interestingly, the peripheral blood flow in FM patients was much less (P < 0.001) than in healthy controls but did not differ from that of SSc patients (P = 0.73).The authors suggested that functional disturbances of micro-circulation are present in FM patients and that morphological abnormalities may also influence their microcirculation.

Martinez conducted a randomized pilot study–Lavin *et al.* (2002), to define if fibromyalgia patients have norepinephrine-evoked pain. Twenty FM patients and two age/sex-matched control groups, 20 rheumatoid arthritis patients, and 20 healthy controls recruited. Ten micrograms of norepinephrine diluted in 0.1 ml of saline solution injected in a forearm. The contrasting substance, 0.1 ml of the saline solution alone, was inserted in the opposite forearm. Norepinephrine-evoked pain diagnosed when norepinephrine injection-induced more significant pain than placebo injection. The authors reported that the Norepinephrine-evoked pain seen in 80 % of FM patients. This finding supports the hypothesis that fibromyalgia may be a sympathetically maintained pain syndrome.

2.9   Studies related to FM associated with other condition

A pilot study on the high frequency of FM in patients with Psoriatic arthritis conducted by Magrey*et al.* (2013). Thirty-four PsA patients and 44 controls fulfilled the inclusion criteria. The frequency of FMS was determined using the London Fibromyalgia Epidemiologic Study Screening Questionnaire (LFESSQ) and Symptoms Intensity scale (SIs). FMS was present in 53.33% of PsA patients compared to 4.54% of the controls (*P* < 0.001), based on LFESSQ. 37.50% of PsA had FMS compared to 6.66% of controls (*P* < 0.001) based on SIs. The authors concluded that FMS associated pain and fatigue are significantly more frequent in patients with PsA compared to controls.

In 2011, Vincent *et al.* explored whether pain and other fibromyalgia symptoms are worse among women who had undergone the surgical removal of the uterus with or without an ovariectomy versus those who had not. The authors recruited 813 women who seen at the Fibromyalgia Treatment Program at a tertiary medical center between 2001 and 2004 and who completed the Fibromyalgia Impact Questionnaire (FIQ) and Short Form-36 Health Survey (SF-36) at initial evaluation. Researchers reported that the Total FIQ scores from women who had a hysterectomy were higher (worse symptoms) than those who had not (58.1 vs. 56.4, P =0.002). FIQ subscale scores of pain (P = 0.003), fatigue (P = 0.030), stiffness (P = 0.035), and depression (P = 0.008) were also worse in women who had had a hysterectomy. Similar to the FIQ, SF-36 physical component scores were worse in women who had a hysterectomy (P = 0.045). Toward the conclusion, pain and other fibromyalgia symptom severity were worse in women who had surgical removal of the uterus with or without an ovariectomy.

Sperber*et al.* (2011) recruited seventy-five women to determine the diagnostic validity of new symptom-based criteria in patients with FMS and IBS using the American College of Rheumatology (ACR) criteria as a gold standard. The study participants consisted of women with FMS (n = 30), IBS (n = 27) and controls (n = 28). Compared to the ACR, the sensitivity of the new criteria was 82.9%, specificity 96.0%, positive predictive value 93.5%, and negative predictive value 88.9%. Besides, new criteria were useful for the diagnosis of FMS among the subjects with IBS. The authors suggested that the new symptom-based diagnostic criteria for the diagnosis of FMS can utilized in large-scale clinical and epidemiological co-morbidity studies, in which physical examination is unfeasible. Gastroenterologists are investigating the effects of co-morbid. FMS in IBS patients can use these new criteria with confidence.

Educate the gastro-enterologist about the common pathogenesis and clinical implications of IBS and FM conducted by Kim (2011), and tender point prevalence is around 2% in the general population and up to 20% among rheumatology outpatients. However, the prevalence of FM in patients with IBS is approximately 32.5% (26%-65%), and the prevalence of IBS in patients with FM is around 48% (32%-77%). The high incidence of non-GI co-morbidities in IBS suggests that there might be common patho-physiological mechanisms in IBS. The co-morbidities such as abnormal pain sensitivity and descending pain inhibition, autonomic nervous system dysregulation, brain-gut axis dysfunction, immune dysfunction, and abnormalities in the levels of serotonin or its receptor. Also, psychosocial factors, including psychological stress, emotional stress, and emotional, physical, or sexual abuse, are trigger factors in both IBS and FM.

Okifuji*et al.* (2009) investigated the associations between obesity and fibromyalgia syndrome (FMS). Thirty-eight FMS patients included in this study. This study provided preliminary evidence suggesting that obesity plays a role in FMS-related dysfunction. In continuance to this, Okifuji (2010), evaluated the relationships between FMS and obesity in the multiple FMS-related domains: hyperalgesia, symptoms, physical abilities, and sleep. A total of 215 FMS patients completed a set of self-report inventories to assess FMS-related symptoms and underwent the tender point (TP) examination, physical performance testing, and seven day home sleep assessment. The results confirmed that obesity is a prevalent co-morbidity of FMS that may contribute to the severity of the problem. Potential mechanisms underlying the relationship discussed. Approximately 50% of patients were obese, and an additional 30% were overweight. Furthermore, the authors found that obesity in FMS was associated with higher pain sensitivity, more mediocre sleep quality, and reduced physical strength and flexibility.

2.10   Studies related to symptoms of FM

The hallmark symptoms used to identify FM are widespread chronic pain, fatigue, and sleep disturbances (Arnold *et al.*, 2011). A review conducted to clarify the association between pain and sleep in fibromyalgia by Keskindag and Karaaziz (2017). Electronic databases searched to identify the eligible articles, including PsycINFO, the Cochrane database for systematic reviews, PubMed, EMBASE, and Ovid. Sixteen quantitative studies fulfilled the inclusion criteria. According to the results, increased pain in fibromyalgia associated with reduced sleep quality, efficiency, and duration and increased sleep disturbance and onset latency and total wake time.

The mechanical, spatial summation of pain (MSSP) determined by Staud*et al.* (2007), the authors recruited twelve healthy controls (NC) and eleven FM subjects. MSSP testing consisted of 5sec suprathreshold pressure-pain stimulations of forearm muscles by up to three identical probes (separated by 4cm or 8cm). The stimulated areas ranged between 0.79cm and 2.37cm. Muscle stimuli elicited more MSSP when separated by 8cm than 4cm, and this finding was not different between NC and FM subjects. Thus, mechanisms of MSSP were similar for both FM and NC subjects. The vital role of MSSP for pain encoding suggests that decreasing pain in some muscle areas by local anesthetics or other means may improve the overall clinical pain of FM patients.

The authors Malin & Littlejohn (2012) examined personality traits in young women with FM, to seek associations with vital psychological processes and clinical symptoms. Twenty-seven women with FM and twenty-nine age-matched female healthy controls [HC] completed a series of questionnaires examining FM symptoms, personality, and psychological variables. The researchers confirmed that the personality trait of neuroticism significantly associates with the critical FM characteristics of pain, sleep, fatigue, and confusion, as well as the common co-morbidities of depression, anxiety, and stress. Personality appears to be an essential modulator of FM clinical symptoms.

The brain responses associated with Temporal summation of "second pain" (TSSP) compared in eleven healthy participants and thirteen fibromyalgia (FM) patients by Staud*et al.* in 2008. The volume-of-interest analysis used to assess TSSP-related brain activation. All participants underwent fMRI-scanning during repetitive heat pulses at 0.33 Hz and 0.17 Hz to the right foot. The stimulus temperatures necessary to evoke equivalent levels of TSSP and corresponding brain activity were less in FM patients. These results suggested that enhanced neural mechanisms of TSSP in FM are reflected in all pain-related brain areas, including posterior thalamus, and are not the result of selective enhancement at cortical levels.

Staud *et al.* (2009) studied the role of peripheral tissue impulse input in the initiation and maintenance of FM. Fifty female FM subjects tested the effects of trapezius muscle (TrapM) tender point injections with 1% lidocaine on local pain thresholds as well as on remote heat hyperalgesia at the forearm. Lidocaine injections increased local pain-thresholds and decreased slight secondary heat sensitivity in FM patients emphasizing the vital role of peripheral impulse input in maintaining central sensitivity in chronic pain syndrome, similar to other persistent pain conditions like irritable bowel syndrome and complex regional pain syndrome.

Paul-Savoie *et al.* (2012) recruited fifty FM patients and Thirty-nine healthy controls (HC) to determine the clinical correlates of experimentally-induced pain perception in FM. Thermal pain thresholds and tolerance were higher in HC compared to FM patients. Anxiety, depression, sleep, and FM symptoms measured with questionnaires or interview-type scales. Experimental pain testing consisted of two tonic heat pain stimulations separated by a 2-minute cold pressor test (CPT). Thermal pain thresholds and tolerance were higher in HC compared to FM patients. Pain ratings during the CPT were lower in HC relative to FM patients. ICPM efficacy was stronger in HC compared to FM patients. Finally, sleep quality was the only factor significantly related to ICPM efficiency.

Ting *et al.* (2012) attended an observational study to examine the role of benign joint hypermobility (HM) in the pain experience in Juvenile FM. Any differences in self-reported pain intensity and physiologic pain sensitivity between Juvenile FM patients with and without joint HM measured. One hundred thirty-one adolescent patients with Juvenile FM recruited from four pediatric musculoskeletal clinics completed a daily visual analog scale (VAS) pain rating for one week and underwent a standardized 18-count tender point (TP) threshold assessment. The authors found that the presence of HM among adolescent patients with Juvenile FM appears to be associated with enhanced physiologic pain sensitivity, but not self-report of clinical pain.

Wagner *et al.* (2012) conducted a cross-sectional, Internet-based survey to assess the burden of sleep difficulty symptoms on HRQoL among patients with FM. The authors included data from the 2009 National Health and Wellness Survey (N=75,000) of the adult US population. The prevalence of sleep difficulty symptoms among patients with FM (n=2,196) compared with matched controls (n=2,194), identified using propensity-score matching. Sleep difficulty symptoms were independently associated with clinically meaningful decrements in mental and Physical Health-Related Quality of Life (HRQoL). These results highlighted the treatment of sleep difficulty symptoms among the FM population might be necessary.

In an experimental study, Staud*et al.* (2012) aimed to develop practical tests of primary (mechanical) and secondary (heat) hyperalgesia that also strongly predict clinical pain intensity in patients with chronic musculoskeletal pain disorders. Thirty-six individuals with FM, 24 with local musculoskeletal pain, and 23 healthy controls underwent testing of mechanical and heat hyperalgesia at the shoulders and hands. In this study, the authors emphasize the critical contributions of peripheral and central factors to both local and widespread chronic pain. Overall, measures of mechanical and heat hyperalgesia in combination with tender point and negative affect provided powerful predictors of clinical pain intensity in chronic musculoskeletal pain patients that can readily use in clinical practice and trials.

Seventy-five patients with FMS completed a seven day home assessment protocol to evaluate the concordance between the subjective and objective methods of sleep assessment in patients with fibromyalgia (FMS) and to delineate factors associated with discrepancy between the two sleep assessment methods. Author Okifuji (2011) measured the restless sleep, difficulty falling asleep, and fatigue. The author made a discussion that the mis-estimation of sleep appears common in FMS patients, mainly when their sleep quality is poor.

Silverman *et al.* (2010) recruited 129 individuals with 18 years of age with a clinician-confirmed diagnosis ofFM $\geq$ 3 months and a current pain rating >2 on a 0-10 numeric rating scale (NRS). To evaluate whether patient self-reported severity of FM is associated with severity of pain and sleep interference and the presence of core co-morbidities. The authors found that pain, functional disability, and fatigue severity were ranked as the top three criteria by the highest proportion of physicians when evaluating FM severity. The researchers concluded a higher self-reported FM severity; patients have more significant pain and sleep interference as well as increased frequency of core co-morbidities.

Thirty women with FMS with a complaint of inadequate sleep, which could contribute to common symptoms including sleepiness, fatigue, or pain studied by Chervin*et al.* (2009), Three nights of polysomnography; Multiple Sleep Latency Tests to assess sleepiness; testing of auditory arousal thresholds during non-REM stage 2 and stage 4 sleep; overnight assessment of urinary free-cortisol; and analysis of 24-hour heart rate variability measured. On the second night of polysomnography, women with FMS in comparison to controls showed more stage shifts (p=0.04) but did not differ significantly on any other standard polysomnographic measure or the Multiple Sleep Latency Tests. The authors concluded that HRV analyses showed more promise, as they suggested both increased sympathetic activity and decreased complexity of autonomic nervous system function in FMS.

In another study, Stutts*et al.* (2009) examined the patient-centered success criteria of individuals with facial pain (FP) or fibromyalgia (FM). 53 FP (46 women, seven men) patients and 52 FM (49 women, three men) individuals who completed the Patient-Centered Outcomes (PCO) Questionnaire were participated in this study. FM participants reported high levels of pain, fatigue, distress, and interference. FP participants' ratings of these domains were significantly lower for pain, fatigue, grief, and interference. These results demonstrate the high expectations of individuals with chronic pain regarding treatments of their symptoms. Healthcare providers should incorporate these expectations into their treatment plans and discuss realistic treatment goals with their pain populations.

A one-year follow-up of fibromyalgia patients was conducted by Bigatti *et al.* (2013) to examination of sleep, pain, depression, and physical functioning. Six hundred patients diagnosed with fibromyalgia recruited according to the American College of Rheumatology criteria, and 492 completed the 1-year assessment. They highlighted the high prevalence of sleep problems in this population and suggested that they play a critical role in exacerbating FMS symptoms.

The association between a current major depressive episode and temperament traits investigated by Santos *et al.* (2011) recruited 69 adult female patients with fibromyalgia assessed with the Temperament and Character Inventory. Psychiatric diagnoses assessed with the Mini-International Neuro-psychiatric Interview severity of depressive symptomatology with the Beck Depression Inventory, and anxiety symptom with the IDATE-state and pain intensity with a visual analog scale. The authors result explained that a current major depressive episode diagnosed in 28 (40.5%) of the patients. The results highlighted specific features of depression in fibromyalgia subjects and may prove crucial for enhancing the diagnosis and prognosis of depression in fibromyalgia patients.

Togo *et al.* (2008) evaluated polysomnograms of chronic fatigue syndrome (CFS) patients with and without fibromyalgia to determine whether patients in either group had elevated rates of sleep-disturbed breathing (obstructive sleep apnea or upper airway resistance syndrome) or periodic leg movement disorder. The authors also determined whether feelings of unrefreshing sleep were associated with differences in sleep architecture from normal. The sleep structures and subjective scores compared on visual analog scales for sleepiness and fatigue in CFS patients with or without coexisting fibromyalgia (n = 12 and 14, respectively) with 26 healthy subjects. The possible result from the study indicated that CFS patients had significant differences in polysomnographic findings from healthy controls and felt sleepier and more fatigued than controls after a night's sleep. Subjects complaints this difference was due neither to diagnosable sleep disorders nor to coexisting fibromyalgia but primarily to a decrease in the length of periods of uninterrupted sleep in the patients with more sleepiness in the morning than on the night before. This sleep disruption may explain the overwhelming fatigue, report of unrefreshing sleep, and pain in this subgroup of patients.

The role of sleep examined by Anderson *et al.* (2012), the authors hypothesized that measures of sleep would increase the predictive ability of the clinical pain model. Actions of usual pain, the spatial extent of pain, negative mood, and pain after sensation taken from 74 adults with fibromyalgia. Objective (actiFigure) and subjective (diary) measures of sleep duration and nightly wake time also obtained from the participants over 14 days. None of the sleep variables produces significant predictors of clinical pain. Results replicate previous research and suggest that the spatial extent of hurt, pain after-sensation, and negative mood play essential roles in clinical illness. Still, sleep disturbance did not aid in its prediction.

A cross-sectional study was done by Ericson *et al.* (2013), to explore in which contexts ratings of multiple dimensions of fatigue are useful in fibromyalgia, and to compare multidimensional fatigue between women with fibromyalgia and healthy women. The Multidimensional Fatigue Inventory (MFI-20), comprising five subscales of fatigue, as compared with the 1-dimensional subscale of fatigue from the Fibromyalgia Impact Questionnaire (FIQ) in 133 women with fibromyalgia (mean age 46 years; standard deviation 8.6), in association with socio-demographic and health-related aspects and analyses of explanatory variables of severe fatigue. The patients also compared with 158 healthy women (mean age 45 years; standard deviation 9.1) for scores on MFI-20 and FIQ fatigue. The authors found that the dimensions of exhaustion, assessed by the MFI-20, appear to be valuable in studies of employment, pain intensity, sleep, distress, and physical function in women with fibromyalgia. The patients reported higher levels on all fatigue dimensions in comparison with healthy women.

Twenty-one age-matched women were studied by Norregaard *et al.* (1994), to determine the extent of voluntary muscle strength and endurance due to lack of exertion in FM patients. All examined by the twitch interpolation technique was used to assess the degree of central activation and estimate the "true" quadriceps muscle strength in patients with fibromyalgia and age and sex-matched controls. Subjects performed an endurance test consisting of repetitive contractions at 50% of estimated "true" muscle strength of four seconds duration followed by a six-second rest until exhaustion, or maximally for 40 minutes. Twitch decline and increases in mean rectified EMG used as objective markers of fatigue. A reduction of the estimated muscle strength per area unit of about 35% found in patients with fibromyalgia. Thus, it might be secondary to physical inactivity or neuroendocrine factors. The authors concluded that no differences in changes in the neurophysiological indices associated with fatigue found between the two groups.

Humphrey *et al.* (2010) conducted qualitative research to understand better aspects of fatigue that might be unique to FM as well as the impact it has on patients' lives. Open-ended interviews were conducted with 40 individuals with FM (US [n = 20], Germany [n = 10] and France [n = 10]). The key elements of fatigue in FM includes: an overwhelming feeling of tiredness (n = 17, 42.5%), not relieved by resting/sleeping (n = 15, 37.5%), not proportional to effort exerted (n = 25, 62.5%), associated with a feeling of weakness/heaviness (n = 20, 50%), interferes with motivation (n = 22, 55%), interferes withdesiredactivities (n = 27, 67.5%), prolongs tasks (n = 15, 37.5%), and makes it difficult to concentrate (n = 21, 52.5%), think clearly (n = 12, 30%) or remember things (n = 9, 22.5%). The authors concluded that the majority of individuals with FM who participated in this study experience fatigue and describe it as more severe than normal tiredness.

2.11 Studies related to other symptoms of FM

To update the previous results, De Tomassoet al. (2011) assessed the prevalence of fibromyalgia (FM) syndrome in migraine and tension-type headache. A consecutive sample of 1,123 patients screened. Frequency of FM in the main groups and types of primary headaches; discriminating factor for FM co-morbidity derived from headache frequency and duration, age, anxiety, depression, headache disability, allodynia, pericranial tenderness, fatigue, quality of life and sleep, and the probability of FM membership in groups assessed. FM was present in 174 among a total of 889 included patients. Headache frequency, anxiety, pericranial tenderness, poor sleep quality, and physical disability were the best discriminating variables for FM co-morbidity, with 81.2% sensitivity.

Kassam and Patten estimated the prevalence of depression in 2006. Subjects were reporting that they had been diagnosed with fibromyalgia by a health professional.

The logistic regression models predicting labor force participation also examined. The authors demonstrated that the annual prevalence of major depression was three times higher in subjects with fibromyalgia. Fibromyalgia and major depression commonly co-occur and may be related to each other at a pathophysiological level.

The working memory between FM patients and healthy subjects was assessed by Seo*et al.* (2012) with the use of functional Magnetic Resonance Imaging (MRI). Nineteen FM patients and 22 healthy subjects performed an n-back memory task during an MRI scan. Their results suggested that the working memory deficit found in FM patients may be attributable to differences in neural activation of the frontoparietal memory network and may result from both pain itself and depression and anxiety associated with pain.

A survey study was conducted by Kashikar-Zuck*et al.* (2008)to assessthe prevalence of mood, anxiety, and behavioral disorders in a clinical sample of children and adolescents with juvenile primary fibromyalgia syndrome (JPFS) and assess the relationship between psychiatric disorders and JPFS symptom severity. The study enrolled 76 children and adolescents diagnosed with JPFS (ages 11 to 18 y) in pediatric rheumatology clinics at four hospitals in the Midwest. A high prevalence of anxiety disorders in patients with JPFS, and the presence of anxiety disorder is associated with poorer physician-rated functioning was noted through pain and global physician rating scale and psychiatric interview.

A Cross-sectional observational study was performed in Spain by Perez-de-Heredia-Torres*et al.* (2017). to compare the sensory organization of balance control and balance strategies between women with fibromyalgia (FM) and healthy women; and to investigate which sensory component, that is, vestibular, visual, or somatosensory, is the most affected in FM. In addition to determine the associations between the functional independence measure (FIM) and balance responses in FM. Twenty women with FM and 20 matched healthy women enrolled in the study. The sensory organization test (SOT) used to determine postural sway and balance during six different conditions with subjects in a standing position. The authors found that women with FM exhibited balance deficiencies and used different strategies for maintaining their balance in standing, which was associated with a negative impact on functional independence.

In 2009, Jones *et al.* resolved whether FM patients differ from matched healthy controls in clinical tests of balance ability and fall frequency. The authors administered the Balance Evaluation Systems Test (BESTest), rated their balance confidence with the Activities-Specific Balance Confidence Scale (ABC), and reported the number of falls in the last six months on 34 FM patients and 32 age-matched controls. Fibromyalgia patients scored poor balance control. FM patients said a total of 37 falls during the previous six months compared to 6 falls in healthy controls. The conclusion suggested that FM may affect peripheral and central mechanisms of postural control. Further objective study is needed to identify the relative contributions of neural and musculo-skeletal impairments to postural stability in FM, thus providing clinicians with exercise prescriptions that maximize postural stability.

The dynamic posturography has been studied by Jones *et al.* (2011) to determine whether FM patients, compared to age-matched healthy controls (HCs), have differences in dynamic posturography, including sensory, motor, and limits of stability and to determine whether postural instability is associated with strength, proprioception and lower-extremity myofascial trigger points (MTPs). The authors evaluated FM symptoms and physical function, dyscognition; balance confidence; and medication use. Also, they evaluated self-reported falls over the past six months. Twenty-five FM patients and twenty-seven HCs (combined mean age ± standard deviation (SD): 48.6 ± 9.7 years) completed testing. Comparison was done on computerized dynamic posturography testing and completed the Fibromyalgia Impact Questionnaire-Revised (FIQR) and balance and fall questionnaires of the middle-aged FM patients. The authors reported the results that middle-aged FM patients have consistent objective sensory deficits on dynamic posturography, despite having a regular clinical neurological examination.

A review of 37 studies of FM conducted by Hoffman and Dukes (2008) that measured health status with the 36-item Medical Outcomes Study, Short-Form Health Survey (SF-36), or the 12-item Short-Form Health Survey (SF-12). To describe how the health status profile of people with fibromyalgia (FM) compares to that of people in the general population and patients with other health conditions. FM groups scored significantly lower than the pain condition groups mentioned above on domains of bodily pain and vitality. Health status impairments in pain and energy are consistent with the core features of FM. In conclusion, the authors explained that people with FM had an overall health status burden that was greater in magnitude compared to people with other specific pain conditions that widely accepted as impairing.

The long-term outcomes of a pediatric sample of clinically referred JPFS patients and their matched healthy controls assessed by Kashikar-Zuck*et al.* (2010). Forty-eight youths participants (current mean age=19 years) diagnosed with JPFS in childhood or adolescence and 43 healthy controls matched in age, gender, and race. The average length of follow-up was 3.67 years (range 2–6 years). Participants completed online (web-based) self-report questionnaires about current pain and physical symptoms, health status, anxiety, depressive symptoms, and current and past treatments. The authors demonstrated that symptoms of FM appear to be chronic in a majority of clinically referred JPFS patients, and the associated physical and emotional impairment can also be persistent.

2.12 Studies related to Tender points

Tender points on the various body parts are one of the hallmarks of fibromyalgia, which produces local tenderness on palpation and produces widespread pain in all quadrants of the body. Smythe was the first in the recent literature, in 1972 who pointed out that the presence of so-called tender points was a diagnostic criterion for fibrositis/fibromyalgia. According to Smythe, local tenderness at palpation at 12 of 14 specified sites had to be present in case of fibromyalgia (Campbell *et al.*, 1983).

To investigate whether the overall spontaneous FM pain pattern can be represented by local and referred pain from active MTPs located in different muscles, Ge*et al.* (2011), recorded a spontaneous pain pattern in 30 FM patients and 30 healthy subjects served as controls. Only women between the ages of 18-70 were recruited. Pincer and flat palpation was administered for the identification of MTRs by eliciting a local twitch response and a subjective response to the local or referred pain over the area of palpation, suggesting that fibromyalgia pain is composed mainly of pain arising from muscle pain and spasm. The authors concluded that targeting active MTPs and related perpetuating factors may be an essential strategy in FM pain control.

A survey was conducted by Wolfe (1997), to investigate the relationship between measures of pain threshold and symptoms of distress to determine if fibromyalgia is a discrete construct/ disorder in the rheumatology center. The survey conducted from 1993 to 1996. A total of 627 patients underwent tender point and dolorimetry examinations. Fatigue, sleepdisturbance, anxiety, depression, global severity, pain, functional disability, and rheumatology distress index measured as outcome measures. The authors reported that tender points are linearly related to fibromyalgia variables and distress, and there is no discrete improvement or perturbation of fibromyalgia or distress variables associated with very high levels of tender points.

Croft *et al.* (1996), ina two-stage cross-sectional survey, investigated that fibromyalgia represents one end of a spectrum in which there is a more general association between musculoskeletal pain and tender points. One hundred seventy-seven individuals selected from a population-based screening survey for musculoskeletal pain. There were moderately active associations between the reported presence of pain in a body segment and the presence of a tender point within that segment. The authors demonstrated that the association between tender points and pain not restricted to the clinically defined subgroup with widespread chronic pain. The widespread pain and tender points have previously linked with distress; this might reflect lesser degrees or earlier phases of the somatization of trouble.

In another study, Croft *et al.* in 1994, conducted a cross-sectional two-stage survey to determine the relation between tender points, complaints of pain, and symptoms of depression, fatigue, and sleep quality in the general population. The examination of tender points and pain assessed through an initial questionnaire. Based on pain complaints, a total of 250 individuals selected for testing of tender points; 177 individuals subsequently participated. Pain, depression, fatigue, and difficulty with sleeping assessed as outcome measures. In this study, females had higher median tender points (six) than males (three), authors concluded that tender point's pain is separately associated with fatigue and depression. Sleep problems are associated with tender points, although future studies are needed to establish whether they generate tenderness.

2.13   Studies related to Pregabalin treatment

Pregabalin was the first drug approved for FMS management and, as an anti-convulsant, differs from the other authorized agents that are antidepressants. Pregabalin inhibits presynaptic excitatory neurotransmitter release by blocking α δ calcium channels (Boomershine, 2012). The authors denoted a three-part series on approved medications for managing fibromyalgia syndrome (FMS) reviews pregabalin (Lyrica).

Five randomized, placebo-controlled trials have demonstrated pregabalin reduces pain and improves sleep and health-related quality of life in FMS patients. While indicated, dosing is 300–450 mg divided twice daily, initial dosing of 25–50 mg at night recommended owing to side effects including sleepiness, dizziness, and cognitive dysfunction. Since side effects such as weight gain and peripheral edema are dose-related, up-titration in weekly increments based on tolerability and therapeutic response recommended. Pregabalin may worsen sedation when combined with central nervous system depressants. Pregabalin-treated patients should be monitored for the emergence or worsening of depression, suicidal thoughts, or behavior. Pregabalin, in combination with the other approved medications, maybe synergistic in treating FMS.

Another study conducted in 2014 by Ohta*et al.*, the authors evaluated the efficacy and safety of pregabalin in Japanese patients with fibromyalgia at 44 centers. Patients aged over 18 years were randomized to receive pregabalin, starting at 150 mg/day and increasing to a maintenance dose of 300 or 450 mg/day, or placebo, for 15 weeks. A total of 498 patients (89% female) were randomized to receive either pregabalin (n = 250) or placebo (n = 248). This trial demonstrated that pregabalin, at doses of up to 450 mg/day, was effective for the symptomatic relief of pain in Japanese patients with fibromyalgia. Pregabalin also improved measures of sleep and functioning and was well tolerated.

The effectiveness of amitriptyline and pregabalin compared to the symptoms of fibromyalgia patients. The authors, Acet *et al.* (2017), recruited 71 female patients aged more than 18 years were studied. The patients evaluated at the start of treatment and the end of 12 weeks. Significant improvement observed in both groups after 12 weeks of treatment ($p < 0.05$). Percent change in Leeds Assessment of Neuropathic Symptoms and Signs was more considerable in the pregabalin group compared with the amitriptyline group. Tender point pressure pain thresholds and total myalgic score improved significantly in both groups ($p < 0.05$); however higher percentage change in these parameters was achieved in the amitriptyline group when compared with the pregabalin group ($p < 0.05$).

The Clinical utility, safety, and efficacy of pregabalin in the treatment of fibromyalgia were studied. Bhusal *et al.* (2016) reported that pregabalin, an anti-convulsant and α-2-Δ subunit receptor ligand, is one of the anchor drugs approved by the US Food and Drug Administration for the treatment of fibromyalgia. The effects of pregabalin in fibromyalgia pain has evaluated in most of the studies; these studies hint towards a meaningful benefit on sleep, functioning, quality of life, and work productivity. Pregabalin is cost-saving with long-term use, and its low-costs profile is comparable in fibromyalgia. In the present era of limited therapeutic options, pregabalin undoubtedly retains its role as one of the cardinal drugs used in the treatment of fibromyalgia.

A 15-week, randomized, double-blind, placebo-controlled study conducted by Arnold *et al.* (2016). 6-month open-label safety trial of flexible-dose pregabalin (75–450 mg/day) for the treatment of adolescents (12–17 years) with FM. One hundred seven subjects were randomized to treatment (54 pregabalin, 53 placebos), and 80 completed the study (44 pregabalin, 36 placebos). The authors reported that pregabalin did not significantly improve the mean pain score in adolescents with FM. There were significant improvements in secondary outcomes measuring pain and impression of change.

The efficacy of combining milnacipran to pregabalin in patients with fibromyalgia who have experienced an incomplete response to pregabalin evaluated the safety and tolerability. Mease*et al.* (2013) recruited 364 patients; all subjects received pregabalin 300 or 450 mg/day during a 4 to 12-week run-in period. Out of this, 184 patients received an added dose of milnacipran 100 mg/day. Patient Global Impression of Severity score of at least four and Global Patient Impression of Change (PGIC) score assessed. The percentage of PGIC responders was significantly higher with milnacipran added to pregabalin (46.4%) than with pregabalin alone (20.8%; $p < 0.001$). Mean improvement from randomization in weekly recall VAS. Pain scores were more excellent in patients receiving milnacipran added to pregabalin (-20.77) than in patients receiving pregabalin alone (-6.43; $p < 0.001$). The authors concluded that adding milnacipran to pregabalin improved global status, pain, and other symptoms in patients with fibromyalgia with an incomplete response to pregabalin treatment.

One retrospective cohort design used to examine the main reasons for inpatient or outpatient visits after initiating duloxetine or pregabalin. The authors Zhao *et al.* (2012) recruited according to a previous study in 2006 (3711 duloxetine patients and 4111 pregabalin patients) between the age of 18–64 years. 12-month continuous enrollment before and after initiation identified. Patients with fibromyalgia who initiated duloxetine or pregabalin, duloxetine patients had significantly lower health care costs over the 12-month post-index period. The leading reasons for inpatient or outpatient visits were also somewhat different.

Calandre *et al.* (2011) conducted a two-phase, 24-week, open-label uncontrolled study on trazodone plus pregabalin combination in the treatment of fibromyalgia. Trazodone medication, flexibly dosed (50-300 mg/day), was administered to 66 fibromyalgia patients during 12 weeks; 41 patients received pregabalin drug, also flexibly dosed (75-450 mg/day), added to trazodone treatment for an additional 12-week period. Treatment with trazodone significantly improved global fibromyalgia severity, sleep quality, and depression, as well as pain interference with daily activities, although without showing a direct effect on bodily pain. After pregabalin combination, additional and significant improvements seen on fibromyalgia severity, depression, and pain interference with daily activities, and a decrease in physical pain were also apparent.

2.14   Studies related to Cognitive behavioral therapy (CBT)

Cognitive-behavioral therapy is a form of psychological treatment used to treat depression and anxiety disorder and patients with severe mental illness. Lifestyle-oriented non-pharmacological treatments for fibromyalgia was thoroughly studied by Friedberg *et al.* (2012). These interventions are intended to facilitate enduring improvement in pain and functional status. Lifestyle-oriented treatments include patient education, aerobic or other physical exercises, and CBT. These interventions in FM can be delivered in medical or behavioral health care settings by trained professionals, through patient-oriented treatment manuals, or via remote-access technologies. Non-pharmacological treatments, in particular exercise and CBT, have yielded effect sizes and cost-benefit ratios comparable to medications.

Bernardy *et al.* (2013), conducted a systematic review of CBT for fibromyalgia.Twenty-three studies with 24 study arms with CBTs included. A total of 2031 patients were involved; 1073 patients in CBT groups and 958 patients in control groups. Only two studies were without any risk of bias. The GRADE quality of evidence of the studies was low. CBTs were superior to controls in reducing pain at the end of treatment by 0.5 points on a scale of 0 to 10 and by 0.6 points at long-term follow-up (median six months); in reducing negative mood at end of treatment by 0.7 points on a scale of 0 to 10 and by 1.3 points at long-term follow-up (median six months); and in reducing disability at end of treatment by 0.7 points on a scale of 0 to

10 and at long-term follow-up (median six months) by 1.2 points. There was no statistically significant difference in dropout rates for any reason between CBTs and controls (risk ratio (RR) 0.94; 95% CI 0.65 to 1.35). They concluded that CBTs provided a small incremental benefit over control interventions in reducing pain, negative mood, and disability at the end of treatment and long-term follow-up. The dropout rates due to any reason did not differ between CBTs and controls.

A randomized controlled trial conducted to assess the efficacy of an individually administered form of cognitive-behavioral treatment for fibromyalgia. Woolfolk *et al.* (2012) recruited 76 patients diagnosed with fibromyalgia obtained randomly and assigned to either the experimental treatment (affective-cognitive behavioral therapy (ACBT), ten individual sessions, one per week) administered concurrently with treatment-as-usual (TAU) or to an unaugmented treatment-as-usual condition. The Hollingson four-factor index was employed to measure participants' socioeconomic status, VAS, Medical Outcomes Study SF-36 Physical Functioning Scale, the Chronic Pain Self-Efficacy Scale (CPSE), the Beck Depression Inventory (BDI), and the Beck Anxiety Inventory (BAI) were the assessed outcome measures. The result indicated that the patients receiving the experimental treatment reported less pain and overall better functioning than control patients, both at post-treatment (3 months after the baseline assessment) and at follow-up (9 months after the baseline assessment).

Kashikar-Zuck *et al.* (2012) conducted a single-blind, randomized controlled clinical trial on Cognitive Behavioral Therapy for the Treatment of Juvenile Fibromyalgia. The primary purpose of the test, whether cognitive–behavioral therapy (CBT) was superior to fibromyalgia (FM) education in reducing functional disability, pain, and symptoms of depression in juvenile FMS. One hundred fourteen adolescents received eight weekly individual sessions with a therapist and two booster sessions. Assessments were conducted at baseline, immediately following the 8-week treatment phase, and at a 6-month follow-up. They reported that CBT was significantly superior to FM education in reducing the primary outcome of functional disability, reduction in symptoms of depression, and pain in adolescents with juvenile FMS.

A randomized, controlled trial conducted by Alda *et al.* in 2011, the effectiveness of CBT and the medication compared with Treatment as usual at the primary care level for the treatment of pain. One hundred sixty-nine fibromyalgia patients were studied. After Six-month of intervention, they reported that CBT significantly decreased global PC, increasing pain acceptance, improving global function based on the Fibromyalgia Impact Questionnaire (FIQ), and quality of life based on the European Quality of Life Scale in FM.

A pilot study evaluated the effects of CBT on the nociceptive flexion reflex (NFR) threshold, an objective measure of spinal sensation of pain transmission. The authors Ang *et al.* (2011) included 32 Female fibromyalgia patients; they were randomized to 6 weekly sessions of telephone-delivered CBT or usual care (UC). Assessments included the NFR threshold and the completion of web-based self-administered clinical measures. The authors reported that the UC group exhibited longitudinal decreases in both the stimulation level and pain associated with the NFR threshold; those receiving CBT required more intense stimulation to elicit the NFR as well as rated that stimulation as less painful than at baseline.

The efficacy of Cognitive Behavioral Therapy for Insomnia in Patients with Chronic Pain studied 199 subjects by Jungquist *et al.* (2010). They included three studies to assess insomnia in chronic pain conditions. In this randomized, single-blind trial, Mini International Neuropsychiatric Interview (MINI), and urine toxicology were used to rule out acute psychiatric and addiction problems. The subjects underwent one night of polysomnography (PSG) to rule out sleep disorders other than insomnia. The pain was assessed through the McGill pain index. The authors reported the results that the insomnia was independently associated with the perceived impact of pain on daily functioning and life satisfaction and that these effects were reversed with the sleep continuity improvements that occurred in the subjects treated with CBT-I.

Another randomized controlled trial evaluated by Hsu *et al.* (2010) to sustain pain reduction through affective self-awareness (ASA) in fibromyalgia. Forty-five women with fibromyalgia were randomized to a manualized ASA intervention (n=24) or a wait-list control (n=21). The intervention began with a one-time physician consultation, followed by three weekly, 2-h group sessions based upon a mind-body model of pain. The pain severity was measured through the Brief Pain Inventory, and tender-point threshold and physical function (SF-36 Physical Component Summary) was the secondary measure utilized in the study. The authors concluded that affective self-awareness intervention improved pain, tenderness, and self-reported physical function for at least six months in women with fibromyalgia compared to a wait-list control.

A nationwide telephone survey was administered to determine whether physical therapists incorporate CBT techniques when treating older patients with chronic pain, ascertained their interest in and barriers to using CBT, and identified participant-related factors associated with interest in CBT. The authors Beissener *et al.* (2009) included one hundred fifty-two members of the Geriatrics and Orthopedics sections of the American Physical Therapy Association who completed the survey. Barriers to use of CBT included a lack of knowledge of and skill in the techniques, reimbursement concerns, and time constraints. Practice type and the interaction of the percentage of patients with pain and educational degree of the physical therapist were independently associated with provider interest. Although only a minority of physical therapists reported the use of some CBT techniques when treating older patients with chronic pain, their interest in incorporating these techniques into practice is substantial.

Thieme *et al.* (2006) focused on the evaluation of the effects of operant behavioral (OBT) and cognitive-behavioral (CBT) treatments for fibromyalgia syndrome (FMS). One hundred and twenty-five patients who fulfilled the American College of Rheumatology criteria for FMS obtained and randomly assigned to OBT, CBT, or an attention-placebo (AP) treatment that consisted of discussions of FMS-related problems. Physical functioning, pain, affective distress, and cognitive and behavioral variables are conducted until 12 months post-treatment. Patients receiving the OBT or CBT reported a significant reduction in pain intensity post-treatment. Besides, the CBT group recorded statistically significant improvements in cognitive and affective variables, and the OBT group demonstrated statistically significant improvements in physical functioning and behavioral variables compared with AP. The AP group reported no significant improvement but deterioration in the outcome variables. The post-treatment effects for the OBT and CBT groups sustained at both the 6- and 12-month follow-ups.

Similarly, a controlled study on the Operant behavioral treatment of fibromyalgia was investigated by Thieme *et al.* (2003). Total Sixty-one patients who fulfilled the American College of Rheumatology criteria for FMS are randomly assigned to the operant pain treatment group or a standardized medical program with an emphasis on physical therapy. Pain assessments were performed before, immediately after, six months after, and 15 months after treatment. The Operant treatment group (OTG) patients reported a significant and stable reduction in pain intensity, interference, solicitous behavior of the spouse, medication, pain behaviors, number of doctor visits, and days at a hospital as well as an increase in sleeping time. Sixty-five percent of the OTG compared with none of the patients in the Physical Therapy Group (PTG) showed clinically significant improvement.These results suggested that operant pain treatment provided in an inpatient setting is an effective treatment for FMS. In contrast, a purely somatically oriented program may lead to a deterioration of the pain problem.

In 2002, William *et al.* studied theSustained improvement in physical functional status was the primary goal of a brief, six-session cognitive-behavioral therapy (CBT) protocol for fibromyalgia (FM). One hundred forty-five patients with FM were randomly assigned to either standard medical care that included pharmacological management of symptoms and suggestions for aerobic fitness, or the same standard medical treatment plus six sessions of CBT. The Medical Outcome Study Short Form-36 Physical Component Score and McGill ratings of pain were included. Outcomes were treated dichotomously using a pre-established criterion for clinically significant success based upon the reliability of change index from baseline to one-year post-treatment. Twenty-five percent of the patients receiving CBT were able to achieve clinically meaningful levels of long term improvement in physical functioning. In contrast, only 12% of the patients receiving standard care achieved the same level of refinement.

Hadhazy *et al.* (2000) conducted a systematic review to assess the effectiveness of mind-body therapy (MBT) for fibromyalgia syndrome (FM). Thirteen trials involving 802 subjects were included. Seven trials received a high methodological score. There is moderate evidence that MBT plus exercise (MBT+E) is more effective than waiting list/treatment as usual (for self-efficacy and quality of life); limited evidence that MBT+E is more effective than education/attention control; inconclusive for other outcomes.

Another systematic review and meta-analysis of randomized controlled trials of cognitive behavior therapy and behavior therapy for chronic pain in adults, excluding headache, was conducted by Morley *et al.* (1999). Thirty-three papers from which 25 trials suitable for meta-analysis were identified. The effectiveness of cognitive-behavioral treatments with the waiting list control and alternative treatment control conditions were compared. The measurements of pain domains representing significant facets. Comparison with alternative active treatments revealed that cognitive-behavioral therapies produced significantly more substantial changes for the fields of the pain experience, cognitive coping, and appraisal (positive coping measures) and reduced behavioral expression of pain. The authors concluded that active psychological treatments based on the principle of cognitive-behavioral therapy are effective.

2.15 Studies related to Integrated Physiotherapy Techniques

The soft tissue releases, along with rehabilitation exercises, play an integral part in avoiding the recurrence in chronic conditions like FM. In a systematic review with meta-analysis by Sosa Reina *et al.* (2017) summarized the evidence on the effectiveness of therapeutic exercise in Fibromyalgia Syndrome. Studies retrieved from the Cochrane Plus, PEDro, and Pubmed databases were systematically reviewed. The authors provide strong evidence that the aerobic and muscle-strengthening exercises are the most effective way of reducing pain and improving global well-being in people with fibromyalgia and that stretching and aerobic exercises increase health-related quality of life. Also, combined use produces the biggest beneficial effect on symptoms of depression.

The acute effects of physical exercise on the serum insulin-like growth factor system in women with fibromyalgia were studied by Mannerkorpi *et al.* (2017). Forty-nine individuals included in this randomized controlled study. The authors proved that fifteen minutes of bicycling at moderate intensity was sufficient to acutely mobilize S-IGF-1 in women with FM similarly to healthy controls despite higher score of fatigue and pain. In contrast, Glascow *et al.* (2017) investigated the effects of resistance exercise training (RET) on disease impact, pain catastrophizing, and autonomic modulation in women with FM. Thirty-seven women with FM (n=26) and healthy control women (HC: n=9), aged 19-65 years, were compared at rest. The authors demonstrated that the disease impact was significantly reduced, and there were no significant changes in autonomic modulation after the RET intervention.

In a longitudinal study, Bjersing *et al.* (2017) evaluated the role of metabolic factors in lean, overweight, and obese women during resistance exercise, concerning symptom severity and muscle strength in women with FM. Forty-three women participated in supervised progressive resistance exercise twice weekly for 15-weeks. The authors found that the individualized resistance exercise in lean patients with FM produced changes in IGF-1 and leptin, reduced pain, fatigue, and improved muscular strength. In overweight and obese women, FM markers of metabolic signaling and clinical symptoms were unchanged, but strength has been improved in the upper limb. In adding together; Bjersing *et al.* (2013) examined the effects of exercise on fatigue in lean, overweight, and obese FM patients. 48 FM patients (median 52 years) exercised for 15 weeks. The Exercise reduced fatigue in all FM patients; this effect achieved earlier in lean patients. Baseline levels of resistin in both serum and CSF associated negatively with fatigue. Resistin increased after the exercise period, which correlated with decreased fatigue. Changes in IGF-1 indicate similar long-term effects in obese patients. This study shows reduced fatigue after moderate exercise in FM and suggests the involvement of IGF-1 and resistin in these beneficial effects.

Passive body heating on the sleep patterns of patients with fibromyalgia was assessed on six menopausal women by Silva *et al.* (2013). All women underwent passive immersion in a warm bath at a temperature of $36 \pm 1°C$ for 15 sessions of 30 minutes each for three weeks. Their sleep patterns were assessed by polysomnography, and the Core body temperature was evaluated by a thermistor pill at pre-intervention, on the first day, the last day of the intervention (chronic), and three weeks after the end of the intervention (follow-up). The results of the author showed a significant reduction in sleep latency, rapid eye movement sleep latency, and slow-wave sleep was significantly reduced inthe chronic and acute conditions compared with baseline. Sleep efficiency was significantly increased duringthe chronic disease, and the awakening index was decreased at the chronic and follow-up time points relativeto the baseline values. They reported that passive body heating had a positive effect on the sleep patterns of women with fibromyalgia.

Similarly, Lofgren and Norrbrink (2009) compared the effects of portable superficial warmth with transcutaneous electrical nerve stimulation on pain in patients with fibromyalgia. Thirty-two patients with fibromyalgia included. After instruction, the patients treated themselves using a portable device providing superficial warmth (42°C) or a transcutaneous electrical nerve stimulation apparatus. After three weeks, the patients rated pain intensity on a 0–100 numerical rating scale before and after each treatment, and after six weeks, patients were questioned concerning therapy preference. The authors detailed that sensory stimulation with superficial warmth or transcutaneous electrical nerve stimulation yielded comparable temporary pain reduction in patients with fibromyalgia.

The effectiveness of Positional Release Therapy and Deep Transverse Friction Massage on gluteus medius Trigger Point was compared by Doley *et al.* (2013) examined the effectiveness of Positional Release Therapy and Deep Transverse Friction Massage on gluteus medius Trigger Point. Thirty subjects randomly recruited from the hospitals and community centers in Dehradun and Guwahati. The pressure pain threshold assessed through Algometer. The author summarized that deep, transverse friction massage was proven a better choice of treatment in improving pain threshold in subjects with gluteus medius trigger point.

A meta-analysis of the randomized controlled trial was done by Kelly *et al.* (2011) to determine the efficacy and effectiveness of exercise on Tender Points in Adults with Fibromyalgia. The studies published in any language between January 1, 1980, and January 1, 2008, were included. Using random-effects models and 95% of confidence interval, a significant reduction of TPs was observed based on per-protocol analyses (8 studies representing 322 participants) but not intention-to-treat analyses (5 studies representing 338 participants) (per-protocol, g, -0.68, 95% CI, -1.16, -0.20; intention-to-treat, g, -0.24, 95% CI, -0.62, 0.15). Changes were equivalent to relative reductions of 10.9% and 6.9%, respectively, for per-protocol and intention-to-treat analyses. The authors concluded that exercise is efficacious for reducing TPs in women with FM. Also, Bush *et al.* (2011) support that aerobic and strength training to improve physical fitness and function, reduce fibromyalgia symptoms, and improve quality of life. However, other forms of exercise (e.g., tai chi, yoga, Nordic walking, vibration techniques) and lifestyle physical activity also have been investigated to determine their effects.

In another systematic review with meta-analysis by Kelly *et al.* (2010) was determined the exercise and global well-being in community-dwelling adults with fibromyalgia. Studies derived from six electronic sources. One thousand twenty-five studies screened, 7 representing five per-protocol and five intention-to-treat outcomes in 473 (280 exercises, 193 control), primarily female (99%) participants 18-73 years of age included. The authors suggested that exercise improves global well-being in community-dwelling women with fibromyalgia.

The Benefits of Massage-Myofascial Release Therapy on Pain, Anxiety, Quality of Sleep, Depression, and Quality of Life in Patients with Fibromyalgia. Castro-Sanchez *et al.* (2011) randomized Seventy-four fibromyalgia patients to experimental (massage-myofascial release therapy) and placebo (sham treatment with disconnected magnotherapy device) groups. The intervention period was 20 weeks. After six months post-intervention, the authors suggested that the Myofascial release techniques improved pain and quality of life in patients with fibromyalgia. Further, a randomized, placebo-controlled trial by Castro-Sanchez *et al.* (2011) studied the effects of myofascial release techniques on pain, physical function, and postural stability in patients with fibromyalgia. Eighty-six patients with fibromyalgia syndrome were received treatments for 20 weeks. The experimental group underwent ten myofascial release modalities, and the placebo group received sham short-wave and ultrasound electrotherapy. The estimated result outcomes are with number of tender points, pain, postural stability, physical function, clinical severity, and global clinical assessment of improvement. After the follow-up of one year, the authors suggested that myofascial release techniques can be a complementary therapy for pain symptoms, physical function, and clinical severity but do not improve postural stability in patients with fibromyalgia syndrome.

Eighty-four minimally active adults with FM were randomized to either lifestyle physical activity (LPA) or an FM education control (FME) group. The authors Fontaine *et al.* (2010) evaluated the effects of accumulating at least 30 minutes of self-selected LPA on perceived physical function, pain, fatigue, body mass index, depression, tenderness, and the six-minute walk test in adults with FM. The study proved that the accumulating 30 minutes of LPA throughout the day produces clinically relevant changes in perceived physical function and pain in previously minimally active adults with FM.

A double-blind placebo-controlled study was conducted by Ayr and Etkinliyi (2010) to investigate the effectiveness of ultrasound therapy in cervical myofascial pain syndrome (MPS). Fifty-five patients with cervical MPS were divided and included in this study. Ultrasound diathermy (n = 28) was implemented over three trigger points bilaterally for 8 minutes (min) once a day for 15 days over three weeks, and the same treatment protocol given in another group (n = 27), but the ultrasound instrument was switched off during applications. All patients performed daily isometric exercise and stretching exercises for the cervical region. Improvement in the Neck Disability Index and pain and physical abilities subgroups of Nottingham Health Profile was better in the ultrasound diathermy group. Based on the results, ultrasound therapy showed effective management of cervical MPS.

Remvig *et al.* (2008) assessed the current state of scientific knowledge about myofascial release, a noninvasive manual treatment technique, and to identify the reliability of diagnostic tests for Myofascial dysfunction and efficacy of the treatment. Twenty-three items identified in the literature search. No studies found with which to determine the authenticity of the diagnostic method, and the authors unable to reach any conclusion on the diagnostic criteria and methods or any efficacy of myofascial release. A case study on the effects of MFR as a manual therapy technique in the treatment of idiopathic scoliosis studied by Lebauer *et al.* (2008). One 18-year-old female subject underwent six weeks of MFR treatment consisting of two sessions each week for 60 min. The item improved with pain levels, trunk rotation, posture, quality of life, and pulmonary function. The author suggested for further investigation on using MFR, as a useful manual therapy treatment for idiopathic scoliosis.

In 2008, Jones *et al.* (2008) evaluated the clinical effectiveness of 6 months of Pyridostigmine (PYD) and group exercise on FM symptoms. FM patients were randomized to 1 of the following four groups: PYD plus exercise, PYD plus diet recall but no exercise, placebo plus exercise, and placebo plus diet recall but no training. One hundred sixty-five FM patients completed baseline measurements; 154 (93.3%) completed the study. Their reports proved that PYD did improve anxiety and sleep, and exercise improved fatigue and fitness. They speculated that PYD might have enhanced vagal tone, thus benefiting sleep and stress.

A randomized controlled trial on the cardiovascular fitness exercise in people with fibromyalgia evaluated in 134 patients. The authors Richards and Scott (2002) divided the subjects into graded aerobic exercise (active treatment) and relaxation and flexibility (control treatment). Subjects self-assessment of improvement, tender point count, the impact of condition measured by fibromyalgia impact questionnaire, and short-form McGill pain questionnaire. People in the exercise group are very much better at three months, and the benefits were maintained or improved at one year follow up. Furthermore, they had more significant reductions in tender point counts and scores on the fibromyalgia impact questionnaire.

An observer-blinded study was administered by the authors Ramsay *et al.* (2000) on the supervised and unsupervised aerobic exercises in the treatment of patients with fibromyalgia. The researchers included 74 subjects to a 12-week exercise class program with home exercises. Subjects pain score, and the quality of life measured through the VAS and Health Assessment Questionnaire (HAQ). They demonstrated no benefit over a single physiotherapy session with home exercises in the treatment of pain in patients with fibromyalgia, and their result showed some significant advantage in psychological well being in the exercise class group and perhaps a slowing of functional deterioration.

The effect of treatment with ultrasound, massage, and exercises on myofascial trigger-points (MTrP) in the neck and shoulder was examined in 1998 by Gam *et al*. The outcome measures were pain at rest and on daily function, analgesic usage, global preference and index of MTrP. The long-term effect of treatment and control groups was assessed after six months using a questionnaire. Fifty-six patients were randomized to ultrasound, massage, and exercise (20), sham-ultrasound, massage, and training (18), and control group (18). The duration of the study was six weeks. Treatment was given twice a week from the second to the fifth week. The authors found no difference between groups given ultrasound or sham ultrasound, and they concluded that the US provides no pain with reduction. Still, massage and exercise reduces the number and intensity of MTrP. The impact of this reduction on neck and shoulder pain is weak.

2.16 Studies related to other non-invasive treatments of fibromyalgia

The other conservative treatment, such as exercises, hydrotherapy, and stimulation, are equally effective in the management of FM. The widespread, deep pain of FMS can be a consequence of chronic psychological stress with autonomic dysregulation. Pressure acts centrally to facilitate pain and performs at the edge, via sympathetic vasoconstriction, to establish painful muscular ischemia. Also, stress interacts reciprocally with systems of control over depression, meditation, and sleep, developing FMS as a multiple-system disorder. Thus, weight and the ischemic pain it generates are fundamental to the multiple confusions of FMS and a therapeutic procedure that attenuates stress and peripheral vasoconstriction should be highly beneficial for FMS. Vierck (2012) explained that physical exercise had shown to counteract peripheral vasoconstriction and to mitigate anxiety, depression, and fatigue and improve meditation and sleep quality. Thus, activity can interrupt the reciprocal interactions between psychological stress and each of the multiple-system disorders of FMS. The vast literature supporting these conclusions indicates that exercise should be considered strongly as a first-line approach to FMS therapy.

Bjersing *et al.* (2012) examined changes in serum IGF-1, cerebrospinal fluid, neuro-peptides, and cytokines during aerobic exercise in FM patients. Forty-nine patients (median age, 52 years) with FM included. Patients participated in blood tests before and after 15 weeks of aerobic exercise. The authors found that the baseline level of serum-free IGF-1 did not change during the high or low intensity of aerobic exercise. Changes in IGF-1 correlated positively with a variation in CSF substance P (SP), neuropeptide Y (NPY), and pain threshold. They indicated a beneficial role of IGF-1 during exercise in FM.

A systematic review synthesized the effects of exercise therapy (ET) on pain and physical function for patients with MSCs. They have integrated the evidence from systematic reviews on, Besides, the authors Hagen *et al.* (2012) provided evidence for the effect of ET on disease pathogenesis, and whether particular components of exercise programs are associated with the size of the treatment effects to explored. Nine reviews, comprising a total of 224 trials and 24,059 patients with Fibromyalgia, low back pain, neck pain, and shoulder pain. Also, four specific musculoskeletal diseases: osteoarthritis, rheumatoid arthritis, ankylosing spondylitis, and osteoporosis included. They identified nine reviews, comprising a total of 224 trials and 24,059 patients. Also, one report addressing the effect of exercise on pathogenesis included. Overall, the authors found substantial evidence supporting ET in the management of MSCs, but there were significant differences in the level of research. They concluded empirical evidence that ET has beneficial clinical effects for most MSCs. Except for osteoporosis, there seems to be a gap in the understanding of how ET influences disease mechanisms.

In 2001, Hakkinen *et al.* investigated the effects of 21 weeks' progressive strength training on nerves and muscle function and individually perceived symptoms in premenopausal women with fibromyalgia. Twenty-one women with FM randomly assigned to experimental (FM_T) or control (FM_C) groups. Twelve healthy women served as training controls (H_T). The FM_T and H_T groups carried out progressive strength training twice a week for 21 weeks. They concluded that the strength training data indicated comparable trainability of the neuro-muscular system of women with FM and healthy women. Progressive strength training can safely be used in the treatment of FM to decrease the impact of the syndrome on the neuromuscular system, perceived symptoms, and functional capacity.

53

A randomized, controlled trial of a treatment program based on self-management, using pool exercise and education in patients with fibromyalgia, was evaluated in 2004 by Cedraschi and Colleagues. A total of 164 patients with FM allocated to an immediate 6-week program (n = 84) or a waiting list control group (n = 80) completed the program and six months follow up examinations. The questionnaires included the Fibromyalgia Impact Questionnaire (FIQ), Psychological General Well-Being (PGWB) index, regional pain score diagrams, and patient satisfaction measures. They suggested that the program would improve the participants' quality of life and satisfaction with treatment as well as decrease the functional and symptomatic consequences of FM, as compared with a control group.

A systematic review summarized the components of hydrotherapy programs used in randomized controlled trials for FM. Data relating to the elements of hydrotherapy programs (exercise type, duration, frequency and intensity, environmental factors, and service delivery) were analyzed. The authors Perraton *et al.* (2009) included eleven randomized controlled trials in this review. Overall, the quality of the tests was excellent. Aerobic exercise featured in all 11 trials and the majority of hydrotherapy programs included either a strengthening or flexibility component. Considerable variability noted in both the environmental elements of hydrotherapy programs and service delivery. The authors concluded that the treatment duration of 60 minutes, frequency of three sessions per week, and an intensity equivalent to 60%–80% maximum heart rate were the most commonly reported exercise components. Exercise appears to be the most crucial component of an effective hydrotherapy program for FMS, particularly when considering mental health-related outcomes.

Another randomized controlled trial conducted by Gusi and Carus (2008), they assessed the cost-utility of adding an aquatic exercise program to the usual care of women with fibromyalgia. Thirty-three participants randomly assigned to the experimental group or a control group. The intervention in the experimental group consisted of a 1-h, supervised, water-based exercise session three times per week for eight months. The primary outcome measures were the health care costs and the number of quality-adjusted life-years (QALYs) using the time trade-off elicitation technique from the EuroQol EQ-5D instrument. The authors concluded that the addition of an aquatic exercise program to the usual care regime for fibromyalgia in women is cost-effective in terms of both health care costs and societal costs.

Lange *et al.* (2011) evaluated the safety and tolerability of vagus nerve stimulation (VNS) as well as to determine preliminary measures of efficacy in patients with treatment-resistant FM. Fourteen patients implanted with the VNS stimulator, 12 completed the initial 3-month study of VNS; 11 returned for follow-up visits 5, 8, and 11 months after the start of stimulation. They concluded that Side effects and tolerability were similar to those found in disorders currently treated with VNS. Preliminary outcome measures suggested that VNS may be a useful adjunct treatment for FM patients resistant to conventional therapeutic management, but further research is required to understand its actual role in the treatment of FM.

A randomized, double-blinded controlled trial performed by Riberto *et al.* (2011). The authors aimed to test whether active transcranial direct current stimulation (tDCS) coupled with multidisciplinary rehabilitation, as compared with sham tDCS, combined with interdisciplinary rehabilitation, is associated with significant clinical gains in fibromyalgia. Twenty-three patients were randomized to receive weekly sessions of a multidisciplinary rehabilitation approach combined with sham or anodal tDCS of M1. Patients were evaluated for pain with VAS and quality of life with SF-36, fibromyalgia pain questionnaire, and health assessment questionnaire by a blinded rater before and after the four months of rehabilitation. The results reported by the authors that active tDCS was associated with superior results in one domain (SF-36 pain domain), the lack of significance in the other fields do not fully support this strategy (weekly tDCS) combined with a multidisciplinary approach.

A randomized control pilot study on Transcranial Magnetic Stimulation (TMS) conducted by Short *et al.* (2011), the authors suggested that the application of TMS to the prefrontal cortex can cause changes in acute pain perception. Several weeks of daily left prefrontal TMS has shown to treat depression. Twenty patients with fibromyalgia recruited based on ACR criteria and randomized them to receive 4000 pulses at 10Hz TMS (n=10), or sham TMS (n=10) treatment for ten sessions over two weeks along with their standard medications, which were fixed and stable for at least four weeks before starting sessions. Daily pain, mood and activity. Blinded raters assessed anxiety, mood, functional status, and tender points weekly with the Brief Pain Inventory, Hamilton Depression Rating Scale, and Fibromyalgia Impact Questionnaire recorded. At two weeks treatment Patients who received active TMS had a low 29% (statistically significant) reduction in pain symptoms and depression in comparison to their baseline score. The authors explained that TMS was well tolerated, with few side effects. Further studies that address study limitations are needed to determine whether daily prefrontal TMS may be an active, durable, and clinically useful treatment for fibromyalgia symptoms.

Mannerkorpi and Colleagues (2010) recruited 67 women with FM to investigate the effects of moderate-to-high intensity Nordic walking (NW) on functional capacity and pain. All the subjects are randomized either to moderate-to-high intensity Nordic Walking or to a control group engaging in supervised low-intensity walking. The primary outcomes were the six-minute walk test (6MWT) and the Fibromyalgia Impact Questionnaire Pain Scale (FIQ Pain). Exercise heart rate in a sub-maximal ergometer bicycle test, the FIQ Physical (activity limitations), and the FIQ total score were the secondary outcomes. Moderate-to-high intensity aerobic exercise using Nordic walking twice a week for 15 weeks found to be a feasible mode of practice, resulting in improved functional capacity and a decreased level of activity limitations. Pain severity did not change over time during the exercise period.

A randomized parallel design experiment was conducted by Volz *et al.* (2013) to test whether different sensory, behavioral tasks induce significant effects in pain processing and whether these changes correlate with cortical plasticity. The authors included forty healthy right-handed males. Three various sensory tasks, including learning tasks with and without visual feedback and simple somatosensory input, tested on pressure pain threshold and motor cortex quickly excited using Transcranial Magnetic Stimulation (TMS). Sensory tasks induced hand-specific pain modulation effects. They increased pain thresholds of the left hand (which was the target to the sensory functions) and decreased them in the right side. TMS showed that sensory input decreased cortical excitability, as indexed by reduced MEP amplitudes and increased SICI. The authors found significant somatosensory learning on the visual feedback task alone. However, there was a significant change in pain thresholds suggest that analgesic effects of sensory tasks are not primarily associated with motor cortical neural mechanisms. Thus, implying that sub-cortical neural circuits and spinal cord are involved with the observed results. Identifying the neural mechanisms of somatosensory stimulation on pain may open novel possibilities for combining different targeted therapies for pain control.

2.17 Studies related to Complementary and Alternative Medicine (CAM) Therapies

Complementary and Alternative medicine is a group of diverse medical and health care systems, which include medications such as Ayurvedic and traditional Chinese medicine. Also include a wide range of other forms of therapy, like acupuncture, plant extracts and oils, biofeedback, chiropractic medicine, diet therapy, herbalism, homeopathy, hypnosis, massage therapy, meditation, nutritional therapy, osteopathic manipulative therapy, qigong, massage to the reflex areas, reiki, tai chi, and yoga. Dogru *et al.* (2017) investigated the effect ofvitamin D therapy on quality of life in patients with fibromyalgia. The authors included seventy patients diagnosed with fibromyalgia and 65 age- and sex-matched controls in the study. Patients grouped as deficient (<20 mg/mL), inadequate (20-30 mg/mL), and sufficient (>30 mg/mL) according to the levels of vitamin D. Vitamin D replacement was performed for patients with deficiencies and inadequacies. Fibromyalgia impact questionnaire (FIQ), Arizona Sexual Experience Scale (ASEX), Beck Depression Inventory (BDI), Visual Analog Scale (VAS) and Short Form-36 (SF-36) utilized as assessment tools at baseline and after the end of Vitamin D administration. The vitamin D replacement therapy, shown statistically significant differences in the FIQ, BDI, VAS, and SF-36 compared with pre-treatment. The authors confirmed that Vitamin D deficiency seems to linked to the pathogenesis of fibromyalgia, and the inclusion of Vitamin D supplementation may improve the QOL in patients with fibromyalgia.

Meta-analysis tried by Makrani *et al.* in 2017 to combine the conflicting results of the primary studies compared with control groups regarding the serum concentration of vitamin D. Keywords were searched in PubMed, Science Direct, Scopus, Cochrane, and Google scholar and primary studies were selected. After screening, the risk of bias in the selected studies and also the heterogeneity between the initial results using Cochrane (Q) and I-squared (I2) indices investigated. Twelve eligible studies included in the meta-analysis, 851 cases compared with 862 controls. The standardized mean difference of Vitamin D between the two groups was −0.56 (95% confidence interval: −1.05, −0.08). The authors of this meta-analysis showed lower levels of vitamin D serum in patients with fibromyalgia that of control group.

Another meta-analysis of observational study was conducted by Hsiao *et al.* (2015) to determine whether hypovitaminosis D was independently associated with widespread chronic pain (CWP). Published studies up to November 2014 comparing the prevalence of hypovitaminosis D and serum vitamin D levels between participants with and without CWP searched on the Electronic databases. Twelve studies included comprising 1,854 patients with CWP. The patient group showed a significantly higher risk of hypovitaminosis D than the control group. The authors concluded that there was a positive crude association between hypovitaminosis D and CWP, and the association was likely to remain after adjusting confounding factors. The use of a cut-off value of hypovitaminosis D (8 – 10 ng/mL) could better define the population with and without CWP. The authors suggested that future follow-up studies are warranted to explain the causal relationship between hypovitaminosis D and CWP.

A double-blinded randomized controlled trial involving two groups of FMS patients, one receiving EMG biofeedback and the other sham biofeedback, was carried out by Babu *et al.* (2014), to evaluate the efficacy of electromyography (EMG) biofeedback to reduce pain in patients with FMS. Visual Analog Scale (VAS), Fibromyalgia Impact Questionnaire (FIQ), and Six Minute walking test (SMWT) were measured at baseline and after six days of treatment. After using biofeedback, the mean VAS scores and the mean number of tender points found to be 3 out of 10 and 6 out of 18, respectively. Subjective analysis from both groups showed improvement in physical and psychological domains. The authors of this study concluded that Biofeedback, as a treatment modality, reduces pain in patients with FMS, along with increases in FIQ, SMWT, and the number of tender points.

Fraioli *et al.* (2013) conducted a systemic review regarding spa therapy in the treatment of FM intending to determine whether balneotherapy with mineral waters and mineral-water containing mud is useful in the management of fibromyalgia. Articles publishedbetween 2000 and 2012 searched through many databases. A total of seven studies retrieved in this systematic review, with a total of 142 patients, received balneotherapy, and 129 were controls. The authors confirmed that spa therapy could improve the symptoms of fibromyalgia, including pain, depression, and minor symptoms.

In 2012, Bardal *et al.* investigated the upper limb position control during sustained isometric contractions in patients with FM and healthy controls (HCs). Fifteen female FM patients and 13 HCs asked to keep a fixed upper limb position during sustained elbow flexion and shoulder abduction, respectively. Accelerations of the dominant upper limb recorded, with variance (SD of mean place) and power spectrum analysis used to characterize limb position control. Normalized power of the acceleration signal extracted for three frequency bands: 1–3 Hz, 4–7 Hz, and 8–12 Hz. Their results were consistent for all load conditions and both elbow flexion and shoulder abduction, and the authors concluded that FM patients exhibit an altered neuromuscular strategy for upper limb position control compared to HCs. The predominance of low-frequency limb oscillations among FM patients may indicate a sensory deficit.

One hundred sixty-two female patients diagnosed with fibromyalgia and depression included to study the effects of sleep and touch therapy, followed by music and plant extracts and oils by Dermibag and Erci (2012). After the interventions, it observed that the depression levels in the touch-music-aroma therapy group showed a more considerable decrease than in the sleep-music-aroma therapy group and control groups. Symptoms such as restless sleep, headache, morning fatigue, exhaustion, and feeling like crying and bowel complaints were also significantly reduced. They suggested that nurses providing healthcare to FMS patients should also offer these patients aromatherapy, sleep, music, and touch therapies.

Boehm *et al.* (2012) conducted a study on the effectiveness of yoga interventions for fatigue conducted through systematic review and meta-analysis. PubMed / Medline searched until January 2012 for controlled clinical studies. Data and the methodological quality assessed through two reviewers. Nineteen clinical studies (total n = 948) included, and the participants who have cancer, multiple sclerosis, dialysis, chronic pancreatitis, fibromyalgia, asthma, or were healthy. Overall, the author concluded that the effects of yoga interventions on fatigue were only small, particularly in cancer patients. Although yoga is generally a safe therapeutic intervention and valid to attenuate other health-related symptoms, this meta-analysis was not able to define the powerful effect of yoga on patients suffering from fatigue.

A randomized controlled trial of qigong compared with a wait-list control group in fibromyalgia studied by Lynch *et al.* (2012). One hundred participants randomly assigned to immediate or delayed practice groups, with the delayed group receiving training at the end of the control period. Qigong training (level 1 ChaoyiFanhuan Qigong, CFQ), given over three half-days, was followed by weekly review/practice sessions for eight weeks; participants also asked to practice at home for 45 to 60 minutes per day for this interval. The authors reported the results that both the immediate and delayed treatment groups demonstrated significant improvements in pain, impact, sleep, physical function, and mental function when compared to the wait-list/usual care control group at eight weeks, with benefits extending beyond this time. They demonstrated that CFQ, a particular form of qigong, provides long-term benefits in several core domains in fibromyalgia.

A modified 8-form Yang-style Tai chi program, compared to an education control, was studied. The authors Mist *et al.* in 2012 investigated that 10-form Tai Chi yields symptomatic benefit in patients with fibromyalgia (FM). Participants met in small groups twice weekly for 90 minutes over 12 weeks. The primary endpoint was symptom reduction and improvement in self-report physical function, as measured by the Fibromyalgia Impact Questionnaire (FIQ), from baseline to 12 weeks. Secondary endpoints included pain severity and interference [Brief Pain Inventory (BPI)], sleep (Pittsburg Sleep Inventory), self-efficacy, and functional mobility. After treatment, the authors concluded that Tai chi appears to be a safe and effective mind/body exercise treatment that could be used as an adjunctive modality in FM patients for both symptom reduction and functional mobility improvement.

Similarly, Romero-Zurita *et al.* (2012) analyzed the effects of Tai-Chi training in women with fibromyalgia (FM). Thirty-two women with FM attended to Tai-Chi intervention three sessions weekly for 28 weeks. FIQ and the SF-36 Health survey utilized as outcome measures. The result of this study showed improvements in pain threshold, total number of tender points, and algometer score. They suggested that a 28-week Tai-Chi intervention showed improvements in pain, functional capacity, symptomatology, and psychological outcomes in female FM patients.

The complementary and alternative medicine (CAM) intervention for fibromyalgia (FM) was reviewed systematically by Terhost and Schneider (2012).

Electronic Database searches included the Cochrane Library, PubMed, PsycINFO, Cumulative Index to Nursing and Allied Health, Natural Medicines Comprehensive Database, Manuals of Alternative and Natural Therapy Index System (MANTIS), Index for Chiropractic Literature, and Allied and Complementary Medicine (AMED. Sixty studies met inclusion criteria and rated by two reviewers; 18 rated as good quality; 20 moderate quality; 18 low quality; and four deficient quality. Synthesis of information for CAM categories represented by more than five studies revealed that balneotherapy and mind-body therapies were effective in treating FM pain. In conclusion, the authors described that only Two CAM categories showed the most promising findings, balneotherapy, and mind-body therapies. Most of the other CAM categories showed a trend favoring the treatment group. It appears that several CAM therapies show some preliminary treatment effect for FM pain, but more extensive trials that are more adequately powered are needed.

Another study on complementary and alternative medicine (CAM) performed by the authors Wahner- Roeder *et al.* (2009). Fifty patients randomly assigned to daily soy or placebo (casein) shakes for six weeks. However, twenty-eight patients completed the study. The results revealed no benefit of soy compared with the placebo. Shakes that contain soy and shakes that contain casein, when combined with a multidisciplinary fibromyalgia treatment program, provide a decrease in fibromyalgia symptoms. The authors suggested that separation between the effects of soy and casein (control) shakes did not favor the intervention.

Wright *et al.* (2012) recruited fifty-three women with FM who were randomized to an eight week RCT of 2 hours weekly supervised group yoga and mindfulness or waitlisted control. Yoga and mindfulness consisted of gentle poses, meditation, breathing exercises, yoga-based coping instructions. The researchers studied whether the central hypothesis of the study is that yoga practiced with concurrent substantive mindfulness will reduce pain-related fear, increase pain acceptance and pressure pain thresholds, resulting in long-term adherence. The Yoga intervention compared to wait-listed controls. The authors concluded that more significant improvements on standardized measures of FM symptoms and functioning (Revised Fibromyalgia Impact Questionnaire, FIQR), including pain, pain pressure thresholds, fatigue, mood, pain catastrophizing, acceptance, and other coping strategies in FM.

The acupuncture and simulated acupuncture effects compared in patients with fibromyalgia. The authors Vinjamury *et al.* (2012) recruited fifty fibromyalgia patients and randomized into two groups based on predetermined eligibility criteria. However, thirty-nine participants only completed the experienced study acupuncturists provided real or simulated acupuncture two to three times per week to complete ten sessions within four to six weeks. Fibromyalgia Impact Questionnaire (FIQ), Multidimensional Pain Inventory (MPI), Composite Physical Function Scale (CPF) and 30-second chair stand were used to determine the improvements in pain, physical function, and lower body strength, respectively. Data were collected at baseline, at the end of the fifth treatment, at the end of the tenth treatment, and six-month follow up. The authors summarized that a fixed point acupuncture protocol as adopted and shown no better than simulated acupuncture in relieving pain or improving overall functionality in fibromyalgia patients. Further trials that utilize individualized treatments recommended with larger sample sizes.

An experimental, double-blind longitudinal clinical trial was conducted on Craniosacral therapy to assess the depression, anxiety, and quality of life in fibromyalgia patients with painful symptoms. The authors Mataran-Penarrocha *et al.* (2011), recruited eighty-four patients diagnosed with fibromyalgia randomly assigned to an intervention group (craniosacral therapy) or placebo group (simulated treatment with disconnected ultrasound). The treatment period was 25 weeks. At the 1-year follow-up, State anxiety and trait anxiety, pain, quality of life, and Pittsburgh sleep quality index were significantly higher compared to the placebo group. Authors concluded that approaching fibromyalgia utilizing craniosacral therapy contributes to improving anxiety and quality of life levels in these patients.

A single-blind, randomized trial conducted by Wang *et al.* (2010). Theclassic Yang-style tai chi as compared with a control intervention consisting of wellness education and stretching for the treatment of fibromyalgia. All the subjects underwent 60 minutes session, twice a week for 12 weeks. The primary outcome measures were the Fibromyalgia Impact Questionnaire (FIQ) score, and the secondary measures were the 36-Item Short-Form Health Survey (SF-36). All assessments were repeated at 24 weeks to test the durability of the response. Sixty-six participants were included and randomly assigned to the 33 in the tai chi group had clinically essential improvements in the FIQ total score and quality of life. They concluded that Tai chi might be a useful treatment for fibromyalgia and merits long-term study in larger study populations.

Temporomandibular joint pain in FM and widespread pain was assessed by Velly *et al.* (2010) at Minneapolis/ St. Paul area, USA. Four hundred eighty-five participants recruited through media advertisements and local dentists received examinations and completed the Graded Chronic Pain Scale (GCPS) at baseline and in 18th months. Baseline widespread pain ($P=0.04$) and depression (5.30, $P=0.005$) were associated with the onset of clinically significant pain (GCPS II-IV) within 18 months after baseline. The persistence of clinically considerable pain was related to fibromyalgia ($P=0.02$) and depression ($P=0.02$). These results indicated that these centrally generated pain conditions play a role in the onset and persistence of clinically significant TMJD.

A multidisciplinary part-time daycare intervention was assessed by Kroese *et al.* (2009) to examine the feasibility and long-term results in FM patients. One hundred and five patients diagnosed with FM assessed through FIQ and quality of life (EuroQol-5 D [EQ-5 D] until nine months after completion. The program consisted of Sociotherapy, physiotherapy, psychotherapy, and creative arts therapy. After the 12-week program, statistically significant improvement seen in both FIQ and EQ-5D. The authors concluded that the 12week multidisciplinary part-time daycare intervention with five aftercare meetings for FM patients is feasible, and it indicated that it could lead to sustained improvement in functional status and quality of life.

In a Japan study, Itoh and Kitakoji (2010) evaluated the effects of acupuncture on pain and quality of life (QoL) in FM patients. Sixteen patients (13 women and three men aged 25-63 years) suffering from FM randomized into two groups: group A received five acupuncture treatments after the control period of five weeks, and group B received ten acupuncture treatments once a week. The treatment session continued for 30 minutes, and the subjective measurement analyzed through VAS and FIQ scores. After the fifth week, pain intensity in group B decreased, and QoL improved compared to group A. The authors suggested that acupuncture treatment is useful to relieve pain for FM patients in terms of QoL and FIQ. However, Martin-Sanchez *et al.* (2009) conducted a review to evaluate the effectiveness of acupuncture as a treatment for fibromyalgia. Electronic databases like PubMed; The Cochrane Library (CENTRAL);

EMBASE; CINAHL; and Pascal Biomed searched till January 2008. This review covered a total of 6 studies (323 subjects). No statistically significant differences observed in terms of pain intensity or withdrawals. The authors found that no evidence of benefit resulting from acupuncture versus placebo, as a treatment for fibromyalgia.

A double-blinded, randomized controlled trial in Geneva, Switzerland, was conducted by Deluze *et al.* (1992) to determine the efficacy of electroacupuncture in patients with fibromyalgia. Seventy patients (54 women) referred to the division of physical medicine and rehabilitation. All the patients included after fulfilling the criteria defined by the American College of Rheumatology. The Pain threshold, number of analgesic tablets used, regional pain score, pain recorded on visual analog scale, sleep quality, and morning stiffness measured. The authors concluded that Electro-acupuncture is effective in relieving symptoms of fibromyalgia.

A pilot study was performed by Grondahl and Rosvold (2008) to evaluate the effect of a standardized hypnosis treatment used in general practice for patients with widespread chronic pain (CWP). Sixteen patients randomized into a treatment group or a control group. Seven patients in the treatment group completed the program. After the control period, five of the patients in the control group also received treatment, making a total of 12 patients having completed the treatment sessions. The intervention group went through a standardized hypnosis treatment with ten consecutive therapeutic sessions once a week, each lasting for about 30 minutes, focusing on ego-strengthening, relaxation, releasing muscular tension, and increasing self-efficacy. The researchers indicated that hypnosis treatment might have a positive effect on pain and quality of life for patients with chronic muscular pain.

Donaldson *et al.* (2001) tested thirty people to evaluate whether a mostly raw vegetarian diet, pure vegetarian diet would significantly improve fibromyalgia symptoms. Thirty people participated in this dietary intervention, mainly using fresh, pure vegetarian food. The food consisted of raw fruits, salads, carrot juice, tubers, grain products, nuts, seeds, and a dehydrated barley grass juice product. The fibromyalgia impact questionnaire (FIQ), SF-36 health survey, a quality of life survey (QOLS), and physical performance measurements recorded. Twenty subjects returned surveys at the beginning, end, and either 2 or 4 months of intervention; 3 subjects lost to follow-up. The authors concluded that dietary intervention shows that many fibromyalgia subjects can be helped by a mostly raw vegetarian diet.

A prospective study was conducted on the efficacy and the adverse effects of intravenous lignocaine therapy in fibromyalgia by Raphael *et al.* (2002). The authors recruited 106 FM patients. Serial infusions of intravenous lignocaine given for six consecutive days. They were started at 5 mg/kg minus 100 mg and increased by 50 mg per day to 5 mg/kg plus 150 mg, provided the maximum was no higher than 550 mg. The authors found two significant (pulmonary edema and supraventricular tachycardia), and 42 minor sideeffects reported. None had long-term sequelae. The commonest were hypotension (17 cases). Pain and a range of psychosocial measures (on single 11-point scales) improved significantly after treatment. There was no effect of the treatment on work status. The average duration of pain relief after the 6-day course of treatment was 11.5 ± 6.5 weeks. They concluded that Intravenous lignocaine appears to be both safe and of benefit in improving pain and quality of life for patients with fibromyalgia.

In a pilot study, Cuatrecasas *et al.* (2007) investigated the efficacy and safety of low dose GH as an adjunct to standard therapy in the treatment of severe, prolonged, and well-treated fibromyalgia patients with low IGF-1 levels. Twenty-four patients were enrolled. They found that adding a daily GH dose to the standard therapy in a subset of severe fibromyalgia patients with low IGF-1 serum levels reduced the mean number of tender points. There was a prompt response to GH administration, with most patients showing improvement within the first months in most of the outcomes. The concomitant administration of GH and standard therapy well-tolerated and no patients discontinued their study due to adverse events.

Roptrotherapy, a new myofascial release method introduced by Farasyn (2009) that consists of deep cross-friction massage with the aid of a myofascial T bar (roptron). The intervention of roptrotherapy consists of a 30-minute session, total, of deep-friction massage with the assistance of a myofascial T bar, the treatment bars made of bronze, an inert material to skin. The advantages of bronze over wooden or plastic fabrication is that the resulting pressure bars are more comfortable to use by hand and contribute to the compression force by their weight (0.8 kg), resulting in less fatigue for the therapist. The work is performed by the therapist within the threshold of tolerable pain, applying a compressive force of $5 - 10$ kg/cm2 on each of the myofascial trigger points found.

Summary of literature review

Fibromyalgia is a widespread musculoskeletal disorder widely found in age between 25-50 years. The analysis suggested the previously incorporated studies fail to decrease all the symptoms of FM. There is a need to educate the different manifestations of fibromyalgia (chronic muscular pain and its associated depression) in the community. The previous studies showed various treatment techniques like Pharmacotherapy, cognitive-behavioral therapies, exercise therapy, massage, positional release therapy, deep, transverse friction, hot packs, serotonin uptake, electromyography feedback, resistance and aerobic exercises, yoga, growth hormone therapy, therapy with plant extracts and oils, raw vegetarian diet, roptrotherapy, SpA, treatment with water, hypnosis, acupuncture, vagus nerve stimulation, Qigong therapy, Nordic walking, tai chi, intravenous lignocaine infusions, tDCS, TMS, manual lymphatic drainage. However, evidence shows the treatment procedures explained about the special effects, and most of these treatments recovered some of the symptoms of FM. The recent methods mostly recommend the combination of treatment procedures that may concentrate on the psychosocial components of FM symptoms.

The purpose of this Chapter is to describe the research design and research setting of the present study, explain the sample selection, and describe the procedure of data collection by using the outcome measures and assessing predictor variables for the present study. An explanation of the statistical procedures used to analyze the data has also been provided.

3.1 Research Design

The Randomized Controlled Trials (RCT) is mainly the firm way of leading whether a cause-effect relationship exists among the intervention and the outcome (Kendall, 2003). The clinical trials is one in which the participants receive some kind of intervention, such as a new medicine or therapeutic techniques. In the present RCT, all the participants were randomly assigned to one of the three intervention groups. Stattreks.com generated a table of three-digit random numbers. Each group was assigned 40 numerals in no systematic order or relationship, and a simple random sampling method was used to select the subject by the raffle method. The three different groups received three different types of interventions are i) Pharmacotherapy along with Integrated Physiotherapy Techniques (PHAIPT), 2) Cognitive Behavioral Therapy along with Integrated Physiotherapy Techniques (CBTAIPT), and Integrated Physiotherapy Techniques (IPT) alone in patients with Fibromyalgia.

3.2 Ethical Approval and Clinical Registration

Approval to conduct the present study was obtained from the Instituitional Ethical Committee (IEC) of Punjabi University Patiala with reference No. 143/DLS/HG dated 22/05/2014 (Annexure - I). The study was registered in Clinical Trials Registry-India (ctri.gov.in) Ref. No: Trial REF/2015/01/008265 (Annexure-II).

3.3 Research Setting

The study was conducted at the various out-patient physiotherapy departments and associated clinics of Sardar Bhagwan Singh University, Balawala, Dehradun District, Uttarakhand, India.

- Prayas healthcare, East Canal road, Dehradun District, Uttarakhand, India.
- College out-patient Department, Balawala, Dehradun District, Uttarakhand, India.
- Bala Pritam Hospital, Patel Nagar, Dehradun District, Uttarakhand, India.

The data was also collected from the following centres and hospital.

- Manuals Physiotherapy clinic, Nehru colony, Dehradun District, Uttarakhand, India.
- Out-patient Department, Gianilal Hospital, Near Leela Bhawan, Patiala District, Punjab, India
- Department of Psychiatry, Mahant Indiresh Hospital, Patel Nagar, Dehradun District, Uttarakhand, India.

3.4   Informed Consent

A written informed consent for participation was obtained from each subject before the inclusion in the commencement of the study (Annexure-III).

3.5   Study Population

The study population consisted of adults with symptomatic Fibromyalgia condition, age ranging between 18-50 years from Dehradun District, Uttarakhand and Patiala District, Punjab.

3.6   Sample size and Sampling method

The present study has 90 participants in total. 30 participants were equally allocated in three groups. Group 1 (PHAIPT), Group 2 (CBTAIPT), Group 3 (IPT alone). All the participants were selected randomly using a randomization list generated by the computer. The participants were asked to pick up a chit paper with concealed numbers (raffle method). Once a figure was picked up, this number further correlated to the generated list for group allocation. The formula used to calculate the sample size (Annexure-IV).

3.7   Sampling Criteria

Participants were selected based on the following selection criteria

3.7.1   Inclusion Criteria

- Heterogeneous population between the ages 18 – 50 years.
- Individuals who fulfilled the ACR criteria (2010).
  - Symptoms have been present at a similar level for at least 3 months.
  - Widespread pain index (WPI) $\geq 7/19$ and symptom severity (SS) score ≥ 5 or WPI 3-6 and SS scale ≥ 9.
  - The patient does not have a disorder that would otherwise explain the pain.
- Pain level must be ≥ 4 on 10 point visual analogue scale.

- Pain on digital palpation (4 Kg/cm^2 applied over 4 seconds) over the specified tender points on pressure algometer.

3.7.2 Exclusion Criteria

- Symptoms of vertigo and dizziness.
- Spinal surgery or fractures for the past 1 year.
- Any Skin conditions affecting the implementation of protocol.
- Known evidence of spinal pathology (such as, spinal canal stenosis, fractures, nerve root pain, infection, cervical rib).
- Contraindications to general exercise (e.g. Breathlessness, decreased pulse rate).
- Leg length inequality.

3.8 Study Variables

3.8.1 Independent Variables

- Pharmacotherapy (Drug pregabalin) protocol
- Cognitive behavioral therapy protocol
- Integrated physiotherapy protocol

3.8.2 Dependent Variables

- Revised fibromyalgia impact questionnaire
- Visual analogue scale
- Beck depressive inventory
- Pressure algometry
- SF-36 Health survey
- General Anxiety Disorder (GAD) -7 scale

3.9 Materials / Instrumentation

- Visual analogue scale (reliability: 0.98)
- Beck depressive inventory (reliability: 0.88)
- Fibromyalgia impact questionnaire (reliability: 0.82)
- General Anxiety Disorder (GAD) -7 (reliability: 0.83)
- SF-36 (reliability: 0.80)
- Pressure algometry (reliability: 0.96)
- Ultrasound Machine
- Treatment couch
- Chair/surgical stool

3.10 Protocol

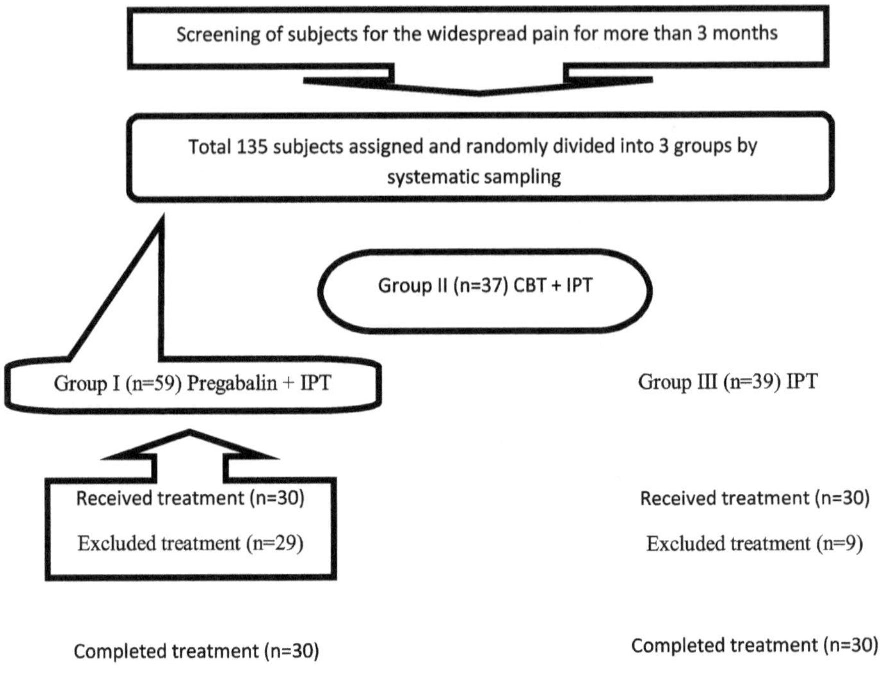

Figure 3.1: Procedure followed in the study

3.11 Outcome Measures

3.11.1 Primary Outcome Measures: Fibromyalgia Impact Questionnaire (FIQ) is a patient reported instrument used to assess FM to measure both physical and psychological symptoms of FM Syndrome (Silverman *et al.*, 2010). The FIQR is a 21-item self-administered questionnaire. All items are measured in visual analogue scales with 11 boxes discreetly scoring from 0 to 10 (Bennet *et al.*, 2009). The three FIQR domains, symptoms showed adequate test-retest reliability (ICC = 0.81), as well as function (ICC = 0.73). However, overall impact performed somewhat lower (ICC = 0.51, 95% CI = 0.36 to 0.63), the test-retest reliability of the FIQR total score evaluated with the ICC was 0.82 (Salgueiro *et al.*, 2013) (Annexure - V).

3.11.2 Secondary Outcome Measures

3.11.2.1 The Visual Analog Scale (VAS) is the most commonly known and used for measurement of pain. The scale consists of a straight line of a specified length (100 mm) with verbal descriptors at each end. The line may be horizontal or vertical, no pain is on one end of the line and worst pain is on the other end of the line. The reliability of visual analogue scale is high (ICC= 0.98) for pain (Bijur, 2001).

3.11.2.2 Pressure Algometer "Force Gauge Model" (Baseline Instruments, New York, USA) was used to measure the pain sensitivity by determining the pressure pain threshold using a pressure transducer probe. Pressure threshold is referred to as the minimum pressure (force) that induces pain or discomfort. Studies have demonstrated the reliability and validity of the pressure algometer as an index of myofascial trigger point sensitivity r = 0.94- 0.98 (Fischer 1987).

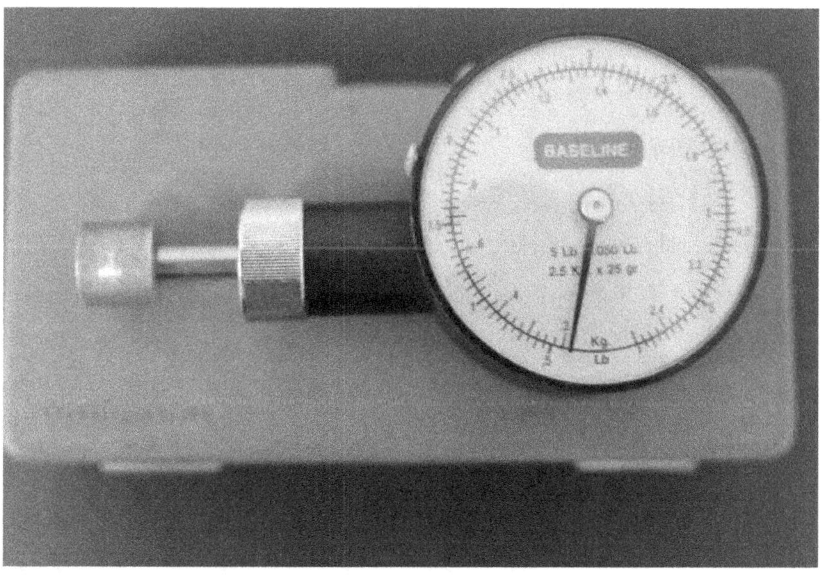

Figure 3.2: Pressure Algometer

3.11.2.3 Beck Depression Inventory (BDI), a self-applied 21-item questionnaire that used to assess a wide spectrum of depressive symptoms. It focuses on the cognitive components of depression, which represent around 50% of the total questionnaire score. Out of the 21 items, 15 refer to ecological-cognitive symptoms and 6 to somatic-vegetative symptoms; each item has four response options in order of increasing symptom severity (Bonilla 2004). The aim of the questionnaire is to quantify symptoms rather than yield a diagnosis. The total questionnaire score ranges from 0 to 63 points, and the usual classifications are as follows: no depression: 0–9 points; mild depression: 10–18 points; moderate depression: 19–29 points; severe depression: ≥30 points. The reliability of the BDI is 0.65–0.72 and the Chronbach's alpha coefficient is 0.82 (Lasa *et al.*, 2000) (Annexure - VI)

3.11.2.4 The Generalized Anxiety Disorder (GAD) -7 has seven items, which measures severity of various signs of generalized anxiety disorder. The internal consistency of the GAD-7 was excellent (cronbach α = .92). Test-retest reliability was 0.83 (Spitzer *et al.*, 2006) (Annexure - VII).

3.11.2.5 SF-36 health survey is a patient reported survey of patient health. It yields an 8 scale profile of functional health and well being scores as well as psychometrically-based physical and health summary measure and a preference based health utility index. The median reliability co-efficients for each of eight scales was equal or greater than 0.80 (McHorney *et al.*, 1993) (Annexure - VIII).

3.12 Procedure

Ninety participants with age 18- 50 years were selected based on selection criteria and randomly divided into three groups.

Group I Participants received a Pregabalin drug and integrated physiotherapy technique (PHAIPT).

Group II Participants received Cognitive behavioral therapy and integrated physiotherapy technique (CBTAIPT).

Group III Participants received an Integrated Physiotherapy Technique (IPT) only.

All three groups were assessed for the pain status, Depression, Anxiety and Quality of life and pressure threshold by visual analogue Scale, revised fibromyalgia impact questionnaire, Beck Depression Index, SF-36 and pressure algometer. These parameters were assessed at the baseline of the program and on Day 30, Day 60, and Day 90.

Group I participants received 150 mg oral dosage of Pregabalin (Pregabid) daily. The researcher administered the drug was prescribed by a psychiatrist and the integrated Physiotherapy techniques on a thrice a week for three months (Figure 3.1).

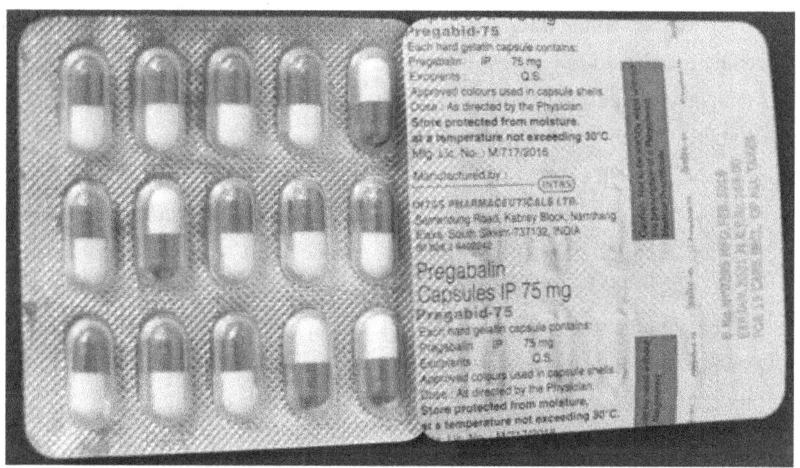

Figure 3.3: Drug Pregabid (75 mg)

Group II received 90-minute cognitive Behavioral therapy which was administered by a clinical psychologist, the CBT group includes nine standard CBT sessions and one specific session on Pain Catastrophising (PC)] for ten weeks. The duration of the intervention is 10 to 12 weeks. The program is structured as follows. *Session 1:* The connection between stress and pain. *Session 2:* Identification of automated thoughts. *Session 3:* Evaluation of automated views. *Session 4:* Questioning the automatic thoughts and constructing alternatives. *Session 5:* Nuclear beliefs. *Session 6:* Nuclear ideas on pain. *Session 7:* Changing coping mechanisms. *Session 8:* coping with ruminations, obsessions, and worrying. *Session 9:* Expressive writing. *Session 10:* Assertive communication.

Session 8 is the additional PC session that begins after the coping session. This session is directed primarily at participants who show high rumination. Participants were instructed to write a story regarding the worst possible scenario for the future based on their greatest fear. This story should stress aspects that generate the most considerable amount of malaise (for example, 'How do you see yourself in this situation?', 'What do you think?', 'How do you feel?' and so forth). The story was audio recorded for a subsequent presentation to the patient. Patients were instructed to listen to this story for 30 to 60 minutes until it no longer causes anxiety. In general, this process takes between 10 and 15 sessions and the integrated Physiotherapy techniques on a thrice-weekly basis for three months.

Participants in all the groups received the Integrated Physiotherapy Technique weekly thrice for three months.

Group III the Integrated Physiotherapy Technique (IPT) alone which consist of administration of hot packs, ultrasound, myofascial release, deep transverse friction followed by an exercise regime. The duration of the treatment was 1 hour to 1 ½ hours and the program was structured as follows.

Moist heat Pack / Hot Pack

The hydro-collator unit is a stainless steel tank in which silica gel packs or Bentonite crystal packs were heated to provide moist heat to the painful area of the body. These packs were stored in thermostatically controlled water in the unit at a temperature between 70^0C and 80^0C (Tanita, 2010). It can be left on continuously as long as there is enough water in the tank. The moist heat has been administered before the soft tissue release over the pain point for 10 minutes continuously.

Ultrasound Therapy

The Ultrasound (US) treatment wass given circularly over the area of 2 x the size of the transducer (Ultrasound head) with a frequency of 3 MHZ in a continuous mode, and a dose of 1.5 W/Cm^2 delivered at each tender point. The duration of the US treatment was 3 minutes of 3 sessions/week for four weeks.

Deep friction massage

Deep friction massage was performed through the therapist's fingers perpendicular to the exact site of the lesion, with the depth of friction tolerable to the patient. The duration of the treatment was 5 minutes / sessions with total of 3 sessions for 12 weeks.

Myofascial release technique

Myofascial release technique (Cervical release, Cranial Base Release, Psoas Release, Sacrum release, Cross Hand Release) was applied over the point of restriction for 3minutes. Each tender area received a sustained hold of 60-180 seconds.

Cervical release (Platysma Spread)

- **Position of Participants (POP):** Supine lying
- **Position of Therapist (POT):** sitting on the chair at the head end of the Treatment couch.
- **Procedure:** the therapist placed one hand at the base of the occiput, apply gentle traction towards the therapist, the other hand will release the cervical fascia in various position [neutral (at the sterna level), 30^0 (middle finger at the level of nipple), 60^0 (middle finger at the level of the axilla), 90^0 (thenar eminence at the level of the shoulder)]. Each position was holded for at least 1 minutes.
- **Note:** Each technique has been performed 3 repetitions per visit.

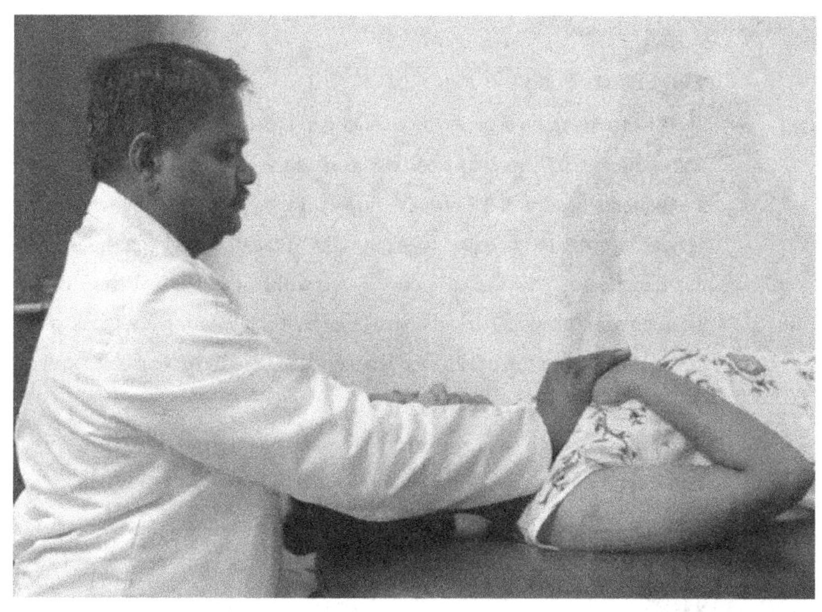

Figure 3.4: Cervical Release (Starting Position)

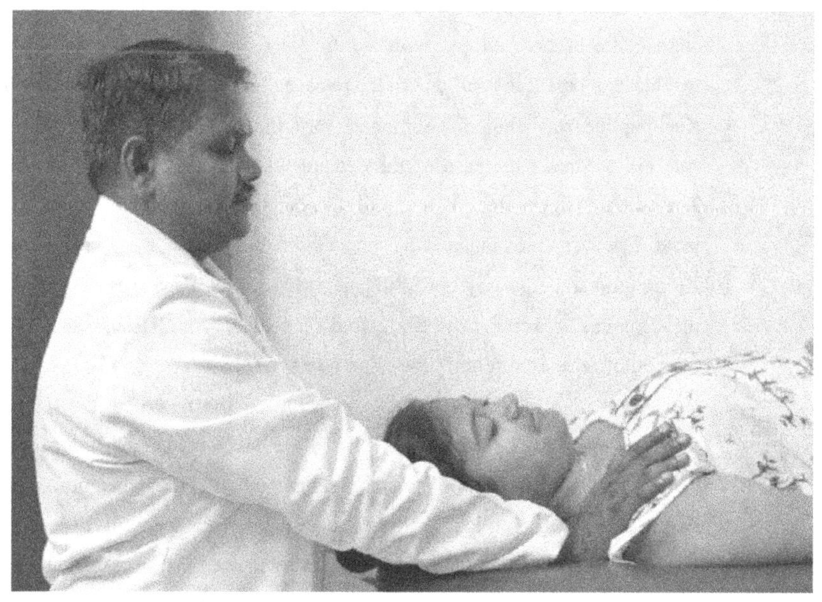

Figure 3.5: Cervical Release (End Position)

Cranial Base Release

- **POP:** Supine lying
- **POT:** sitting on the chair at the head end of the Treatment couch.
- **Procedure:** the therapist placed the hand at the base of the occiput, be sure that the patients head will eventually drop into the hand; Rest the back of hand on the table, use traction equal to the weight of the patients head, hold and weight for the release; When release occurs, we will feel the full weight of the patient head on your hands.; The final stroke is performed with both hands at the same time, ending with the heel of the hands just under the curve of his skull with the fingers extended along the neck.
- The fingers of each hand should straddle the spinous process of the cervical spine and slowly pull cephalad until reaching the firmness of the occipital ridge. Then move the fingers caudad (towards the feet). The fingers should slip in to the occipital space between the occipital ridge and the spinous process of C-2 (axis).
- Elevate the cranium slowly towards the ceiling by bending the MCP joints to 90 degrees, keeping the hands next to each other; use the pressure of the pads of ring and middle fingers of hand.
- Hold it in that position for a few minutes until the feel of Myofascial structures soften, like butter melting. Wait a little longer to allow the atlas to shift or wobble as it balances itself due to the releasing of the Myofascial structures.
- Keeping the ring fingers pointing toward the ceiling and pushing the atlas anteriorly, contact the base of the occiput with the middle and index fingers. They act as "trigger fingers" and pull the occiput in a circular motion toward the table. This further disengages the suboccipital area.
- At the third stage, slowly open the hands without releasing the pressure. Cradle the occipital area and then gently pull cephalad. The pressure should be in ounces for releases of dural tube as far away as the sacrum.
- **Variation:** The hands are firmly supported on the treatment table. Without moving the hands, flex the fingers at the Metacarpophalangeal joints until the fingertips are supporting the patients head at the base of the Occiput; As the soft tissues release, the cervical lordosis straightens and the chin will tuck as capital extension increases; Maintain the vertical stretch and push the knuckles forward toward the patients feet, when the knuckles are forward of the fingertips, allow the fingers to flex. Pull the patients head back toward the therapist.

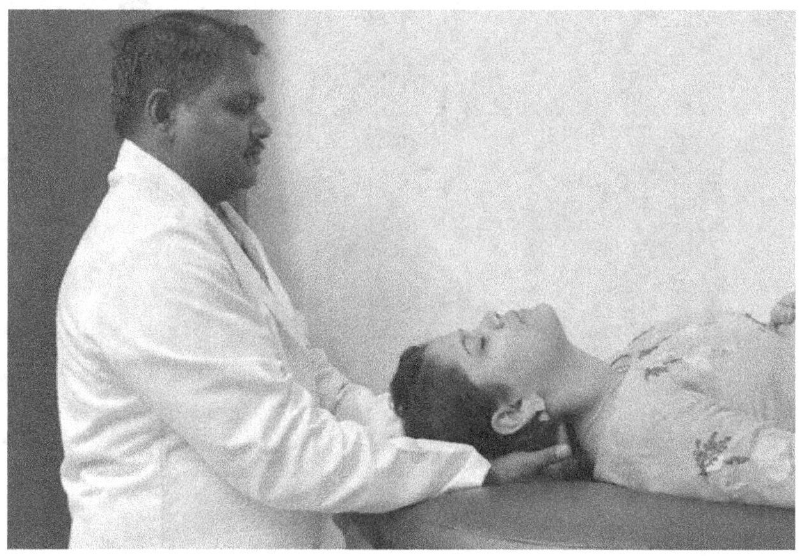

Figure 3.6: Cranial Base Release

Psoas Release

- **POP:** Supine with knees flexed and the foot is supported on the table.
- **POT:** Standing beside the patient hip joint level.
- **Technique:** Draw an imaginary line between the umbilicus and the ASIS; The oblique lines are the working lines for the release; The vertical line denotes the lateral margin of rectus abdominis; Use the fingers to make contact on this line about halfway between the ASIS and the edge of the rectus abdominis; Sink in a medial/posterior line and uses a transverse stroking technique. Engage the first layer of restriction and wait. Once the release occurs, sink to the next layer and continue to treat as appropriate.

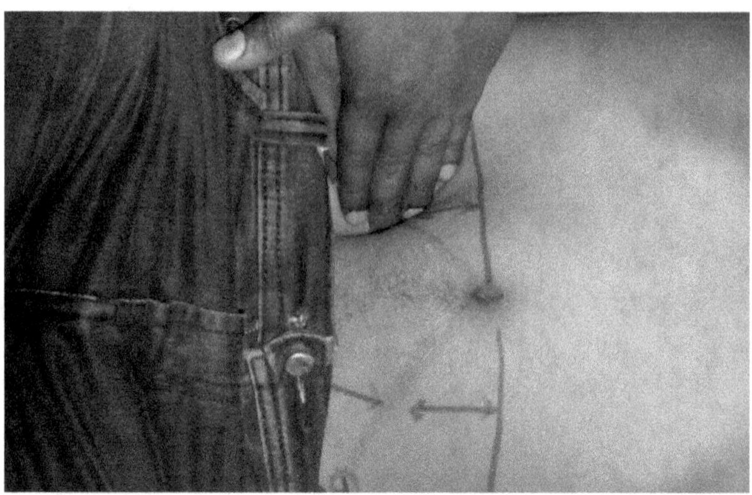

Figure 3.7: Psoas Release

Sacrum release

- **POP:** Supine with both the knees in extension.

- **POT:** Standing beside the patient hip joint level.

- **Procedure:** one hand under the sacrum and the other hand above the pubic symphysis and apply gross hand stretch between sacrum and abdomen. Move the upper hand to either ASIS. Sacro-Iliac: One hand under the sacrum and the other hand over the both ASIS and apply slow compression.

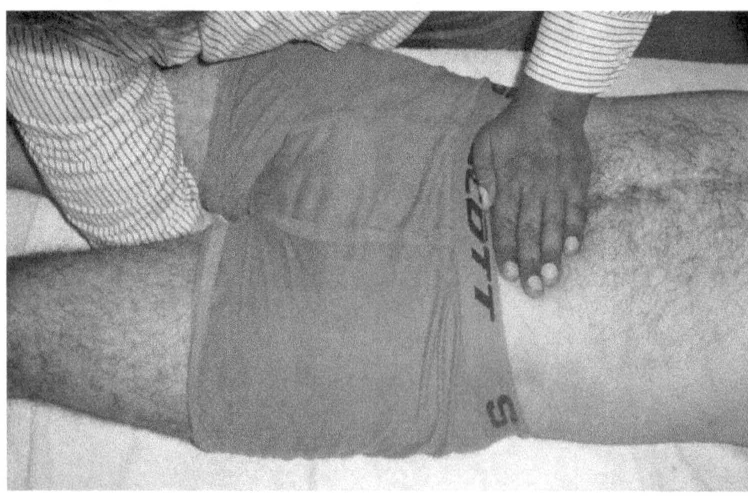

Figure 3.8: Sacral Release

Cross Hand Release

- **POP:** prone lying position.
- **POT:** Standing beside the patient hip joint level.
- **Procedure:** Lay the hands on the area to be stretched, crossed the arms over to form a fulcrum, weight comfortable over the area; Sink into the tissues until therapist encounter a barrier, then begin to move the hands in opposite directions, without sliding on the surface; Hold and wait for 60-120 seconds; Continue the treatment up to 3-6 minutes, going through the barriers as they release.

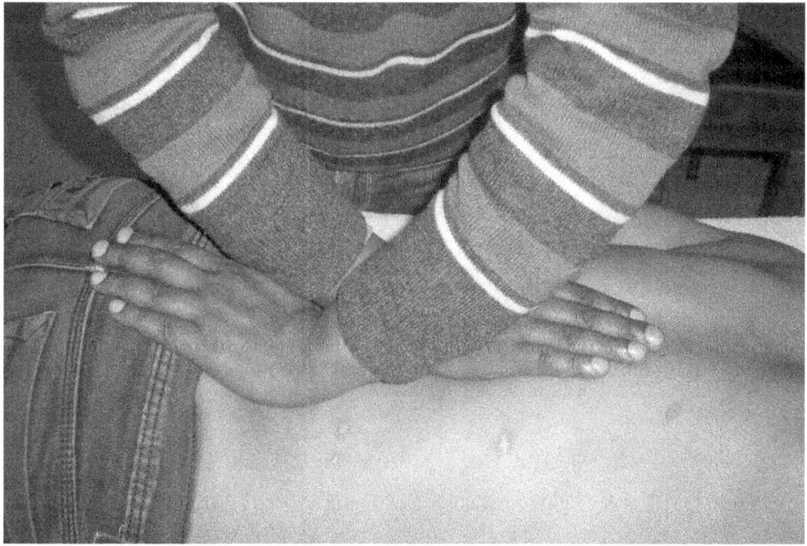

Figure 3.9: Cross Hand Release

Home program exercises

Home program exercises include stretching exercises to upper trapezius, levator scapulae, and pectoral muscles along with isometric neck exercises (Chin tuck-in) and the lower abdomen in-drawing (pelvic neutral) to maintain posture. For the first time, the patient should perform all the tasks under the supervision of a physiotherapist. The frequency of the exercise was of 5days / week, with duration of 15 – 20 minutes. Diaphragmatic breathing exercises were continued throughout the procedure to relax the patients. (Appendix – IX).

Data Analysis

Microsoft Excel was used to describe the Mean and Standard Deviation (SD) of Age in all three groups.

Percentage method was used to describe the demoFigureic data along with the characteristics of gender, educational level, current occupation, and marital status.

IBM SPSS v25 software was utilized for the analysis.

The primary outcome measure tool for the study was revised fibromyalgia impact questionnaire, to measure the differences between the different time frame viz. baseline, first month, second month, and third month repeated measures ANOVA was used.

The secondary outcome measure (objective tool) for the pain pressure threshold was pressure algometer, to measure the differences between the different time frame viz. baseline, first month, second month, and third month repeated measures ANOVA was used.

The secondary outcome measure (subjective tool) for the study was beck depression index, general anxiety disorder – 7 scale, visual analogue scale, and short form health survey – 36, to measure the differences between the different time frame viz. baseline, first month, second month, and third month repeated measures ANOVA was used.

One way ANOVA was used to compare the differences between the groups. Post Hoc (Tukey HSD) test was applied to differentiate the individual differences in all three groups.

Description of Statistical Method

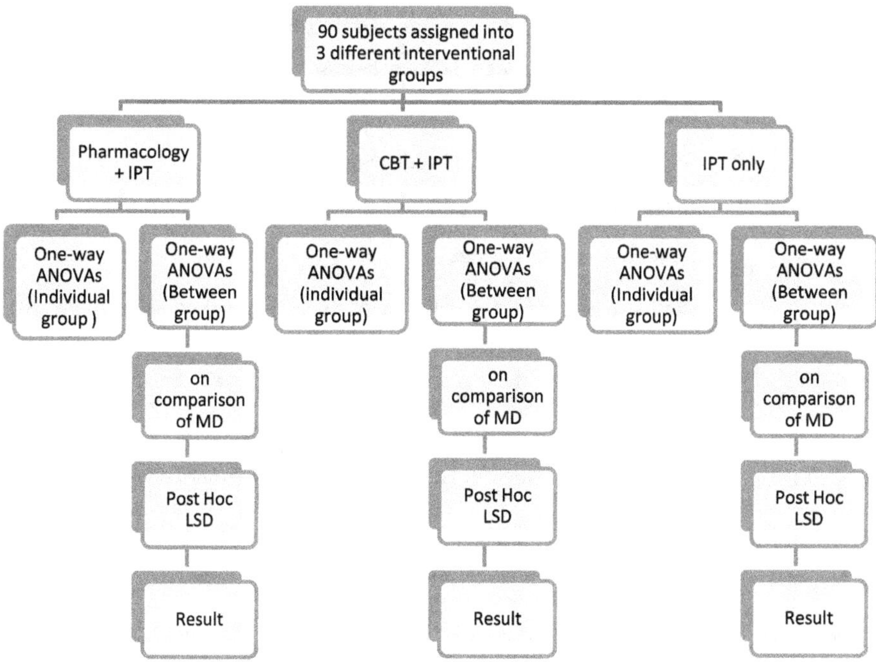

This Chapter interprets the data with descriptive and inferential statistical method. The method of descriptive statistics has been used to describe the subject's demoFigureic and clinical characteristics whereas the method of inferential statistics has been used to determine the efficacy of various interventions in treatment of FM. The findings of descriptive and inferential statistics are obtainable in the form of pie chart, histograms and tables wherever necessary. The results are represented under following headings.

4.1   Baseline characteristics of study population

4.2   Role of pharmacotherapy along with integrated physiotherapy techniques (Group–I) in Fibromyalgia.

4.3   Role of cognitive behavioral therapy along with Integrated Physiotherapy Techniques (Group-II) in Fibromyalgia.

4.4   Role of Integrated Physiotherapy Techniques (Group-III) in Fibromyalgia.

4.5   Identifying individual differences between all the three groups.

4.1   Baseline characteristics of study population

According to the treatment Protocol the study population divided into three groups. Each group comprises 30 subjects. Descriptive statistics has been used to describe demographic characteristics of study population. The means with standard deviation for Age and the percentage method were used to describe other characters like gender, Education level, Occupation; marital status has been showed in table 4.1.1.

Table 4.1.1: Demographic characteristics of study population

Demographic Characteristics		Number of participants (Percentages)		
		Pharmacotherapy	CBT	IPT
		Mean ± SD	Mean ± SD	Mean ± SD
Age		37.6 ± 8.5	33.5 ± 8.3	38.4 ± 9.4
Demographic Characteristics		Number (Percentage)	Number (Percentage)	Number (Percentage)
Gender	Male	03 (10.0)	11(36.7)	06 (20.0)
	Female	27 (90.0)	19(63.3)	24 (80.0)
Education level	No education	03 (10.0)	00	01 (3.3)
	Elementary	03 (10.0)	00	05 (16.7)
	Secondary	09 (30.0)	03 (10.0)	09 (30.0)
	Undergraduate	09 (30.0)	20 (66.7)	11 (36.7)
	Post-graduate	06 (20.0)	07 (13.3)	04 (13.3)
Current occupation	No occupation	17 (56.7)	08 (26.7)	12 (40.0)
	Student	00	07 (13.3)	03 (10.0)
	School / Office assistant	05 (16.7)	03 (10.0)	07 (13.3)
	Business	02 (6.7)	05 (16.7)	03 (10.0)
	Professor / Teacher	04 (13.3)	05 (16.7)	01 (3.3)
	NCC / Police	00	02 (6.7)	01 (3.3)
	Bank Worker	01 (3.3)	00	01 (3.3)
	NGO	00	00	01 (3.3)
	Politician	00	00	01 (3.3)
	HR	01 (3.3)	00	00
Marital status	Married	26 (86.7)	23 (76.7)	22 (73.3)
	Unmarried	03 (10.0)	07 (13.3)	08 (26.7)
	Divorced	01 (3.3)	00	00

Table 4.1.1 depicts that the subjects Mean and standard deviation of Age (37.6 ± 8.5, 33.5 ± 8.3, 38.4 ± 9.4); the number of subjects according to gender (M = 3: F = 27; M = 11: F = 19; M = 6: F = 24); the educational level from first group to third group [No education (3,0,1), Elementary (3,0,5), Secondary (9,3,9), Undergraduate (9,20,11), Post-Graduate (6,7,4)]; current occupation [Employed (13,22,18) and Unemployed (17,8,12)] and marital status (married (26,23,22), Unmarried (3,7,8), Divorced (1,0,0)] for group 1, group 2, and group 3 respectively.

The demographic characteristics reveal that the fibromyalgia condition is a female predominance condition and mostly affected population falls between the age group of 25 – 48 years. Also it affects the well educated (undergraduate), married subjects with occupation are highly prevalent to this condition.

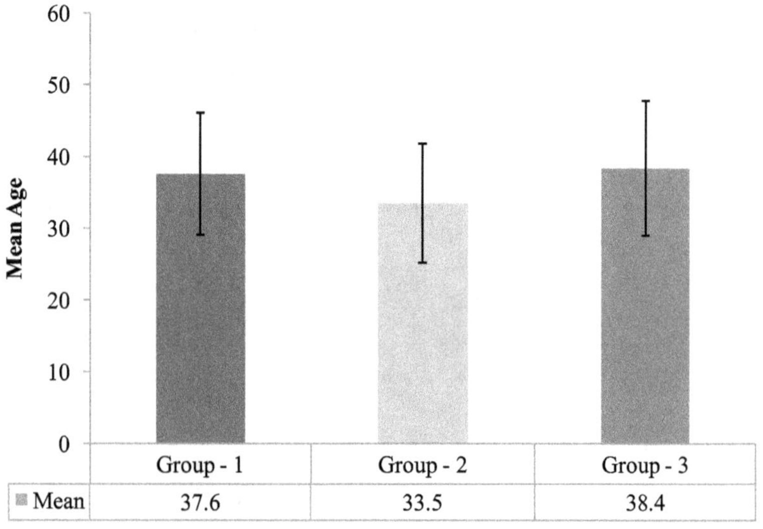

Figure 4.1.1 represents the Mean Age distribution of all three groups from the table no. 4.1.1.

Table 4.1.2: **Gender distribution of Fibromyalgia patients in different interventional groups**

S.No.	Groups	Male	Female
1.	Pharmacotherapy and IPT	03	27
2.	CBT and IPT	11	19
3.	IPT alone	06	24
	Total	**20 (22%)**	**70 (78%)**

Table 4.1.2 presents the number of males and females who participated in different interventional groups. There were 3 males and 27 females in pharmacotherapy along with IPT group, 11 males and 19 females in cognitive behavioral therapy along with IPT group and 6 males and 24 females in IPT alone group. Figure 4.1.2 displays the total percentage of males and females of the study population.

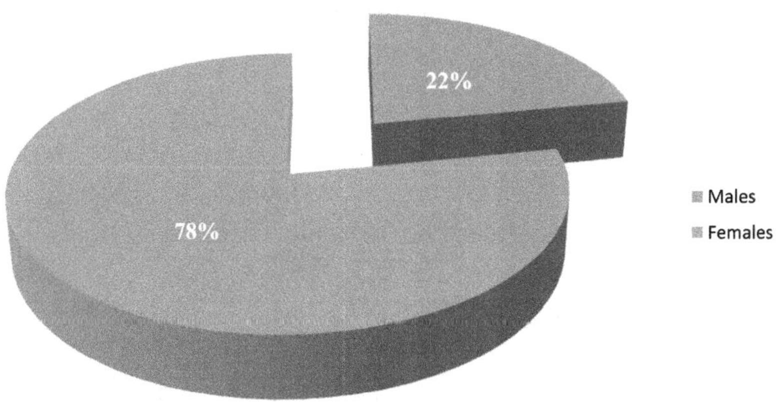

Figure 4.1.2: Percentage of males and females distribution of all participated subjects

Table 4.1.3:   Education level distribution of Fibromyalgia patients in different interventional groups

S.No.	Educational Level	Pharmacotherapy and IPT	CBT and IPT	IPT alone	Total
1.	No Education	3	0	1	4 (4%)
2.	Elementary	3	0	5	8 (9%)
3.	Secondary	9	3	9	21(24%)
4.	Undergraduate	9	20	11	40 (44%)
5.	Postgraduate	6	7	4	17 (19%)

Table 4.1.3 presents the educational levels of subjects who participated in different interventional groups. There were 3 with no education, 3 in elementary, 9 in secondary, 9 with undergraduate and 6 with postgraduate levels in pharmacotherapy along with IPT group, 3 in secondary, 20 in undergraduate and 7 with postgraduate level in cognitive behavioral therapy along with IPT group and 1 with no education, 5 in elementary, 9 in secondary, 11 with undergraduate and 4 with postgraduate levels in IPT alone group. Figure 4.1.3 displays the total percentage of educational level of the study population.

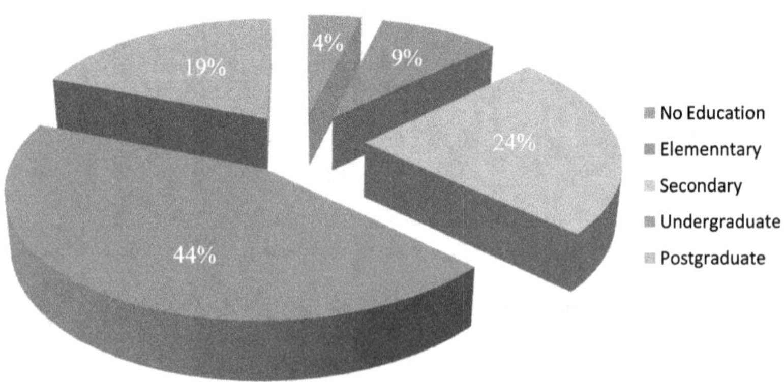

Figure 4.1.3: Percentage of educational level distribution of all participated subjects

Table 4.1.4: **Occupation distribution of Fibromyalgia patients in different interventional groups**

S.No.	Groups	Unemployed	Employed
1.	Pharmacotherapy and IPT	17	13
2.	CBT and IPT	15	15
3.	IPT alone	15	15
Total		**47 (52%)**	**43 (48%)**

Table 4.1.4 presents the number of unemployed and employed subjects who participated in different interventional groups. There were 17 unemployed and 13 employed in pharmacotherapy along with IPT group, 15 unemployed and 15 employed in cognitive behavioral therapy along with IPT group and 15 unemployed and 15 in IPT alone group. Figure 4.1.2 displays the total percentage of males and females of the study population.

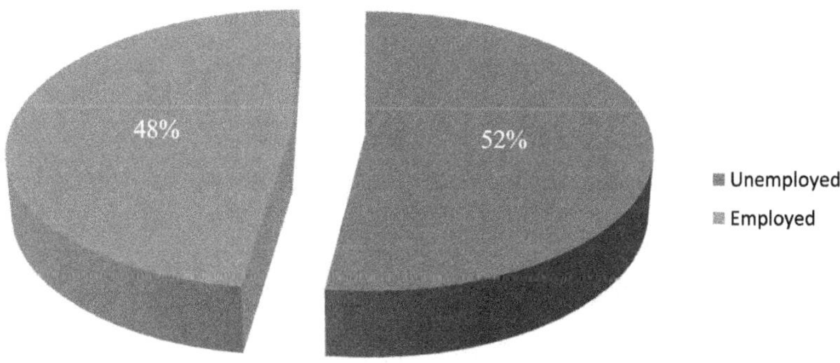

Figure 4.1.4: Distribution of subjects according to occupation in different groups

Table 4.1.5: **Marietal status distribution of Fibromyalgia patients in different interventional groups**

S.No.	Groups	Married	Unmarried	Divorced
1.	Pharmacotherapy and IPT	26	3	1
2.	CBT and IPT	23	7	0
3.	IPT alone	22	8	0
	Total	**71 (79%)**	**18 (20%)**	**1(1%)**

Table 4.1.4 presents the number of married, unmarried and divorced subjects who participated in different interventional groups. There were 26 married, 3 unmarried and 1 divorced in pharmacotherapy along with IPT group, 23 married, and 7 unmarried in cognitive behavioral therapy along with IPT group and 22 married, and 8 unmarried in IPT alone group. Figure 4.1.5 displays the total percentage of males and females of the study population.

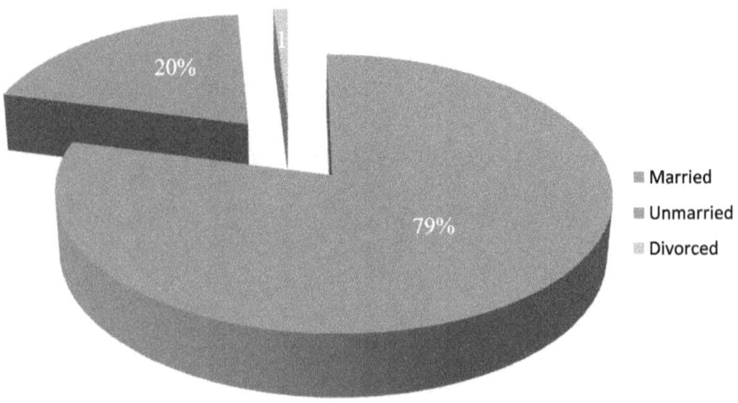

Figure 4.1.5: Percentage of marietal status of subjects in different interventional groups

4.2 Role of pharmacotherapy along with integrated physiotherapy techniques (Group – I) in Fibromyalgia

As per study protocol, the experimental group-I (n = 30) received 150 mg pregabalin drug continuously for three months and integrated physiotherapy techniques on alternate days for three month which is followed by home programme of neck exercises and stretches regime. The role of pregabalin drug and integrated physiotherapy techniques was evaluated from pre-intervention (baseline), in-between intervention (2nd and 3rd months) and post intervention (3 months). Analysis of Variance (ANOVA) was used for this purpose.

Table 4.2.1: Comparison of Revised Fibromyalgia Impact Questionnaire (FIQR) variable within the group-I from Baseline to Third month

Variable	n	Mean ± SD	SE	df	F	P
FIQR (B)		51.84 ± 11.54	2.10			
FIQR (1)	30	42.86 ± 12.91	2.35	3	69.75	< 0.01*
FIQR (2)		35.32 ± 13.75	2.51			
FIQR (3)		30.18 ± 13.14	2.40			
FIQR = Revised Fibromyalgia Questionnaire; **n** = Number of participants; **SD** = Standard Deviation; **SE** = Standard Error; **df** = differential frequency; **F** = Mean of the within group variances; * = The Mean score is significant at the 0.05 level.						

Table 4.2.1 depicts the Mean and Standard Deviation within the group for Revised Fibromyalgia Impact Questionnaire at baseline (51.84 ± 11.54), 1st month (42.86 ± 12.91), 2nd month (35.32 ± 13.75), and 3rd month (30.18 ± 13.14) in PHAIPT group. The result showed significant difference (F = 69.75, P < 0.01).

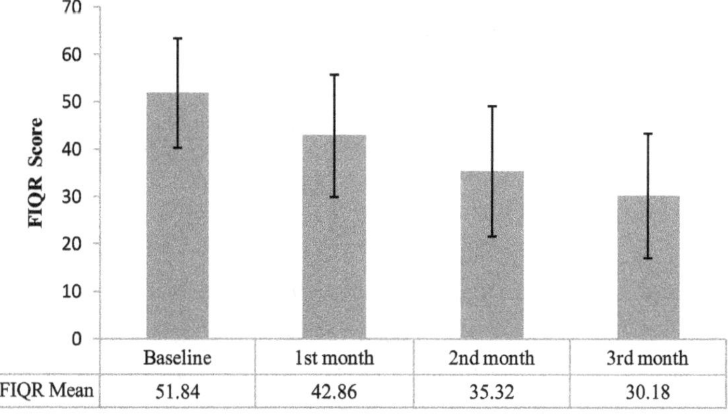

Figure 4.2.1: The Mean improvement of Revised Fibromyalgia Impact Questionnaire score from baseline to third month

Table 4.2.1.1: Pair-wise comparison of Revised Fibromyalgia Impact Questionnaire (FIQR) variable from baseline to third month at different time frame

Time frame	n	Mean difference	Standard Error	P	95% CI [b]	
					Lower bound	Upper bound
Baseline – 1 month		8.97[*]	1.38	< 0.01	6.13	11.81
1 month – 2 month	30	16.52[*]	1.81	< 0.01	12.81	20.23
2 month – 3 month		21.65[*]	2.06	< 0.01	17.42	25.88

n = number of participants, CI = Confidence Interval
[*] The Mean Difference is significant at the 0.05 level.
b. Adjustment for multiple comparisons: Least Significant Difference (equivalent to no adjustments).

Table 4.2.1.1 showing the pair-wise comparison of Revised Fibromyalgia Impact Questionnaire score Mean Difference (MD) and Standard Error (SE) on different time frame at baseline to 1st month (MD = 8.97; SE = 1.38; p < 0.01), 1st month – 2nd month (MD = 16.52; SE = 1.81; p < 0.01), and 2nd – 3rd month (MD = 21.65; SE = 2.06; P < 0.01) the result showing statistical significance (p < 0.01).

Table 4.2.2: Comparison of Beck Depression Index (BDI) variable within the group-I from Baseline to Third month

Variable	n	Mean ± SD	SE	df	F	P
BDI (B)		34.63 ± 12.68	2.31			
BDI (1)	30	29.93 ± 11.70	2.13	3	35.65	< 0.01*
BDI (2)		24.50 ± 12.67	2.31			
BDI (3)		20.93 ± 11.18	2.04			

BDI = Beck Depression Index; **n** = Number of participants; **SD** = Standard Deviation; **SE** = Standard Error; **df** = differential frequency; **F** = Mean of the within group variances; * = The Mean score is significant at the 0.05 level.

Table 4.2.2 depicts the Mean and Standard Deviation for Beck Depression Index at baseline (34.63 ± 12.68), 1st month (29.93 ± 11.70), 2nd month (24.50 ± 12.67), and 3rd month (20.93 ± 11.18) in PHAIPT group. The result showed significant difference (F = 35.65, p < 0.01).

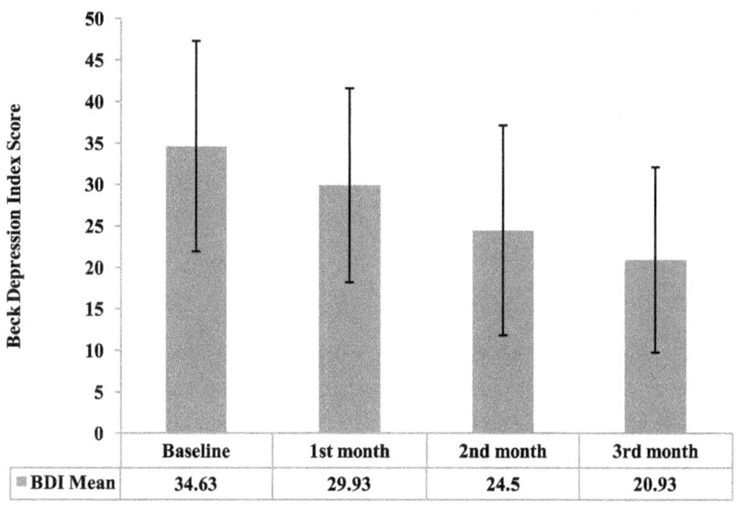

Figure 4.2.2: The Mean and SD of Beck Depression Index score from baseline to third month.

Table 4.2.2.1: Pair-wise comparison of Beck Depression Index (BDI) variable from Baseline to Third month at different time frame

Time frame	n	Mean difference	Standard Error	P	95% CI [b]	
					Lower bound	Upper bound
Baseline – 1 month		4.70*	1.31	**< 0.01**	2.00	7.39
1 month – 2 month	30	10.13*	1.67	**< 0.01**	6.70	13.56
2 month – 3 month		13.70*	1.88	**< 0.01**	9.83	17.56

n = number of participants, CI = Confidence Interval

*= The Mean Difference is significant at the 0.05 level.

b. Adjustment for multiple comparisons: Least Significant Difference (equivalent to no adjustments).

Table 4.2.2.1 showing the pair-wise comparison of Beck Depression Index Mean Difference (MD) and Standard Error (SE) on different time frame at baseline to 1st month (MD = 4.70; SE = 1.31; p = 0.01), 1st month – 2nd month (MD = 10.13; SE = 1.67; p < 0.01), and 2nd – 3rd month (MD = 13.70; SE = 1.88; P < 0.01) the result showing statistical significance (p < 0.01).

Table 4.2.3: **Comparison of Visual Analogue Scale (VAS) variable within the group-I from Baseline to Third month**

Variable	n	Mean ± SD	SE	df	F	P
VAS (B)		7.90 ± 1.37	0.25			
VAS (1)	30	5.27 ± 1.83	0.33	3	149.52	< 0.01*
VAS (2)		3.83 ± 2.19	0.40			
VAS (3)		3.10 ± 2.10	0.38			
VAS = Visual Analogue Scale; **n** = Number of participants; **SD** = Standard Deviation; **SE** = Standard Error; **df** = differential frequency; **F** = Mean of the within group variances; * = The Mean score is significant at the 0.05 level.						

Table 4.2.3 depicts the Mean and Standard Deviation for Visual Analogue Scale at baseline (7.90 ± 1.37), 1st month (5.27 ± 1.83), 2nd month (3.83 ± 2.19), and 3rd month (3.10 ± 2.10) in PHAIPT group. The result showed significant difference (F = 149.52, p < 0.01).

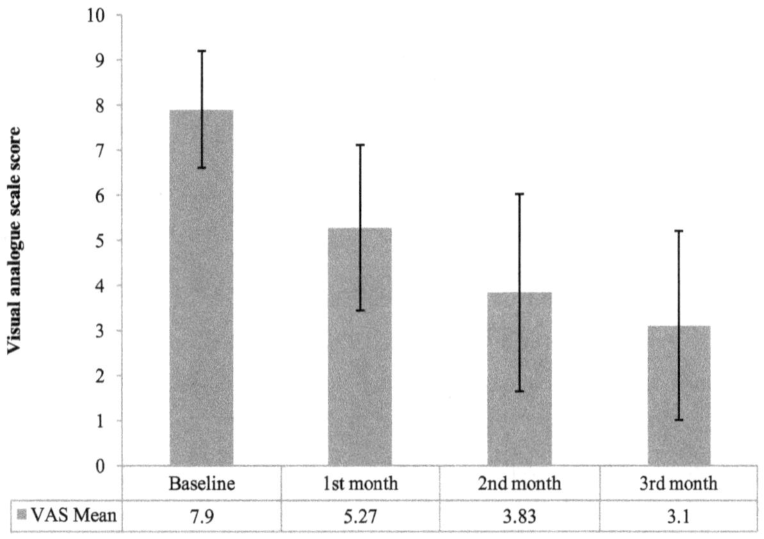

Figure 4.2.3: The Mean and SD of Visual Analogue Scale score from baseline to third month

Table 4.2.3.1: Pair-wise comparison of Visual Analogue Scale (VAS) variable from Baseline to Third month at different time frame

Time frame	n	Mean difference	Standard Error	P	95% CI [b]	
					Lower bound	Upper bound
Baseline – 1 month		2.63[*]	0.232	< 0.01	2.15	3.10
1 month – 2 month	30	4.06[*]	0.303	< 0.01	3.44	4.68
2 month – 3 month		4.80[*]	0.301	< 0.01	4.18	5.41
Based on estimated marginal Means n = number of participants, CI = Confidence Interval [*] = The Mean Difference is significant at the 0.05 level. b. Adjustment for multiple comparisons: Least Significant Difference (equivalent to no adjustments).						

Table 4.2.3.1 showing the pair-wise comparison of Visual Analogue Scale Mean Difference (MD) and Standard Error (SE) on different time frame at baseline to 1st month (MD = 2.63; SE = 0.23; p < 0.01), 1st month – 2nd month (MD = 4.06; SE = 0.30; p < 0.01), and 2nd – 3rd month (MD = 4.80; SE = 0.30; P < 0.01) the result showing statistical significance (p < 0.01).

Table 4.2.4: Comparison of General Anxiety Disorder (GAD) variable within the group-1 from Baseline to Third month

Variable	n	Mean ± SD	SE	df	F	P
GAD (B)		15.53 ± 3.19	0.58			
GAD (1)	30	13.63 ± 4.20	0.78	3	24.88	< 0.01*
GAD (2)		11.60 ± 4.85	0.88			
GAD (3)		10.37 ± 4.56	0.83			
GAD = General Anxiety Disorder Scale; n = Number of participants; SD = Standard Deviation; SE = Standard Error; df = differential frequency; F = Mean of the within group variances; * = The Mean Difference is significant at the 0.05 level.						

Table 4.2.4 depicts the Mean and Standard Deviation for General Anxiety Disorder scale at baseline (15.53 ± 3.19), 1st month (13.63 ± 4.20), 2nd month (11.60 ± 4.85), and 3rd month (10.37 ± 4.56) in PHAIPT group. The result showed significant difference (F = 24.88, p < 0.01).

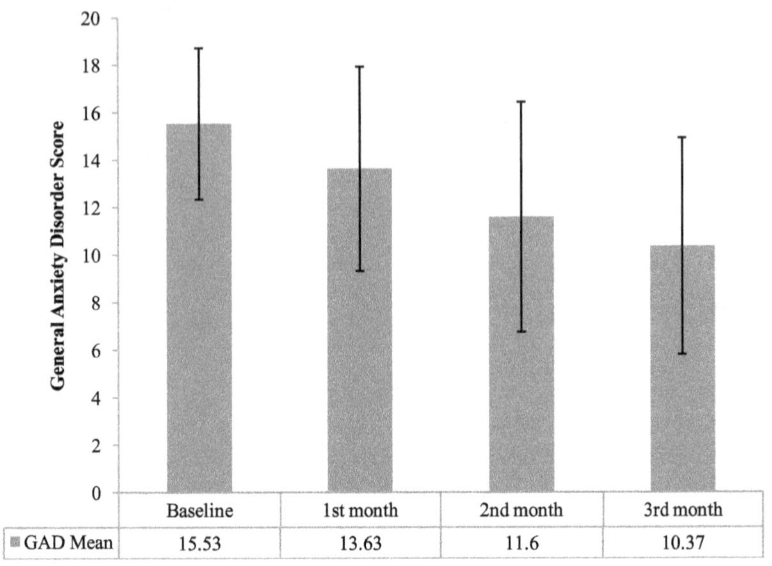

	Baseline	1st month	2nd month	3rd month
▦ GAD Mean	15.53	13.63	11.6	10.37

Figure 4.2.4: The Mean and SD of General Anxiety Disorder score from baseline to third month

Table 4.2.4.1: Pair-wise comparison of General Anxiety Disorder (GAD) variable from Baseline to Third month at different time frame

Time frame	n	Mean difference	Standard Error	P	95% CI [b]	
					Lower bound	Upper bound
Baseline – 1 month		1.90[*]	0.56	< 0.01	0.74	3.05
1 month – 2 month	30	3.93[*]	0.77	< 0.01	2.34	5.51
2 month – 3 month		5.16[*]	0.69	< 0.01	3.74	6.59

n = number of participants, CI = Confidence Interval

[*] = The Mean Difference is significant at the 0.05 level.

b. Adjustment for multiple comparisons: Least Significant Difference (equivalent to no adjustments).

Table 4.2.4.1 showing the pair-wise comparison of General Anxiety Disorder Mean Difference (MD) and Standard Error (SE) on different time frame at baseline to 1st month (MD = 1.90; SE = 0.56; p < 0.01), 1st month – 2nd month (MD = 3.93; SE = 0.77; p < 0.01), and 2nd – 3rd month (MD = 5.16; SE = 0.69; P < 0.01) the result showing statistical significance (p < 0.01).

Table 4.2.5:   Comparison of Short Form-36 health survey Physical Component Summary (SF-36 PCS) variable within the group-I from Baseline to Third month

Variable	n	Mean ± SD	SE	df	F	P
SF-36 PCS (B)		28.84 ± 14.80	2.70			
SF-36 PCS (1)	30	39.65 ± 22.77	4.15	3	29.75	< 0.01*
SF-36 PCS (2)		51.23 ± 26.56	4.85			
SF-36 PCS (3)		59.37 ± 25.85	4.72			
SF-36 PCS = Short Form-36 Physical Component Summary; **n** = Number of participants; **SD** = Standard Deviation; **SE** = Standard Error; **df** = differential frequency; **F** = Mean of the within group variances. * = The Mean score is significant at the 0.05 level.						

Table 4.2.5 depicts the Mean and Standard Deviation for Short Form-36 Physical Component Summary at baseline (28.84 ± 14.80), 1st month (39.65 ± 22.77), 2nd month (51.23 ± 26.56), and 3rd month (59.37 ± 25.85) in PHAIPT group. The result showed significant difference (F = 29.75, p < 0.01).

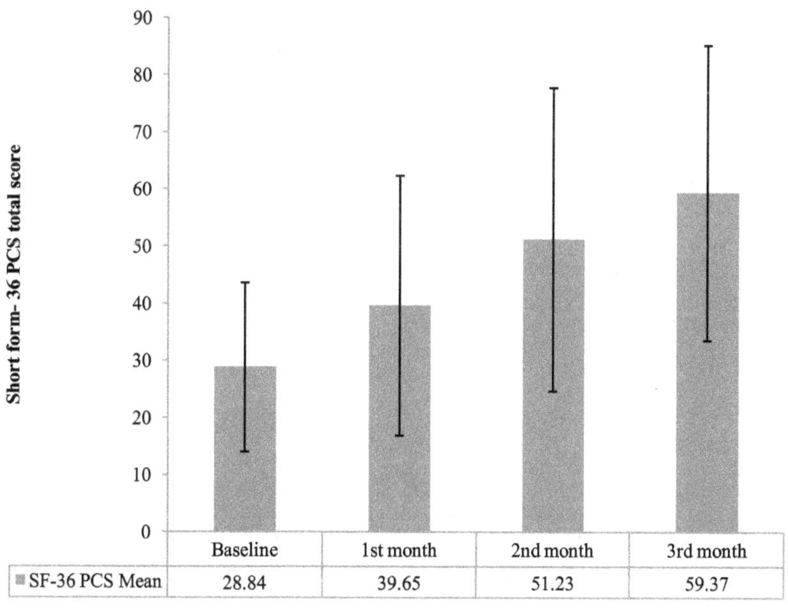

Figure 4.2.5: The Mean and SD of Short Form – 36 Physical Component summary score from baseline to third month

Table 4.2.5.1: Pair-wise comparison of Short Form-36 health survey Physical Component Summary (SF-36 PCS) variable from Baseline to Third month at different time frame

Time frame	n	Mean difference	Standard Error	P	95% CI [b]	
					Lower bound	Upper bound
Baseline – 1 month		10.80[*]	3.19	< 0.01	17.34	4.26
1 month – 2 month	30	22.39[*]	4.23	< 0.01	31.25	13.52
2 month – 3 month		30.53[*]	4.10	< 0.01	38.92	22.14

Based on estimated marginal Means

n = number of participants, CI = Confidence Interval

[*] = The Mean Difference is significant at the 0.05 level.

b. Adjustment for multiple comparisons: Least Significant Difference (equivalent to no adjustments).

Table 4.2.5.1 showing the pair-wise comparison of Short Form-36 Physical Component Summary within the PHAIPTgroup Mean Difference (MD) and Standard Error (SE) on different time frame at baseline to 1st month (MD = 10.80; SE = 3.19; p < 0.01), 1st month – 2nd month (MD = 22.39; SE = 4.23; p < 0.01), and 2nd – 3rd month (MD = 30.53; SE = 4.10; P < 0.01) the result showing statistical significance (p < 0.01).

Table 4.2.6: Comparison of Short Form-36 health survey Mental Component Summary (SF-36 MCS) variable within the group-I from Baseline to Third month

Variable	n	Mean ± SD	SE	df	F	P
SF-36 MCS (B)		33.54 ± 14.55	2.65			
SF-36 MCS (1)	30	44.27 ± 20.98	3.83	3	31.24	< 0.01*
SF-36 MCS (2)		52.71 ± 23.93	4.26			
SF-36 MCS (3)		60.44 ± 23.02	4.20			

SF-36 MCS = Short Form-36 Mental Component Summary; n = Number of participants; SD = Standard Deviation; SE = Standard Error; df = differential frequency; F = Mean of the within group variances. * = The Mean score is significant at the 0.05 level.

Table 4.2.6 depicts the Mean and Standard Deviation for Short Form-36 Mental Component Summary at baseline (33.54 ± 14.55), 1st month (44.27 ± 20.98), 2nd month (52.71 ± 23.93), and 3rd month (60.44 ± 23.02) in PHAIPT group. The result showed significant difference (F = 31.24, p < 0.01).

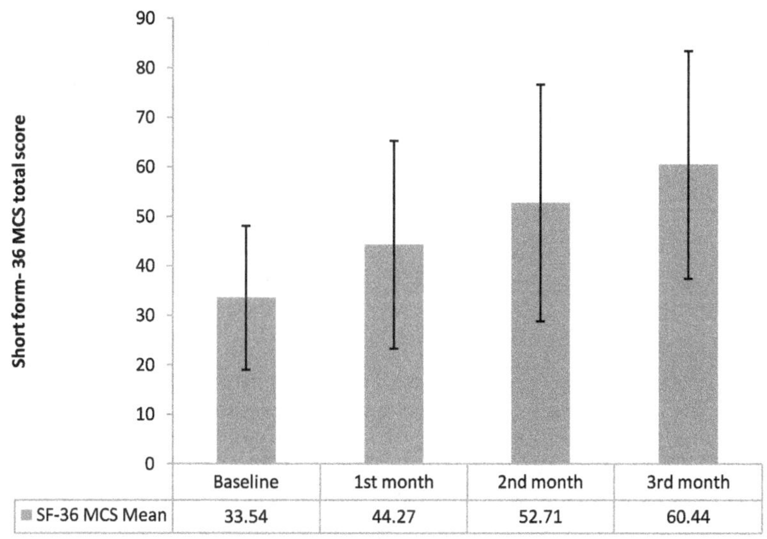

Figure 4.2.6: The Mean and SD of Short Form – 36 Mental Component summary score from baseline to third month

Table 4.2.6.1: Pair-wise comparison of Sort Form-36 health Survey Mental Component Summary (SF-36 MCS) variable from Baseline to Third month at different time frame

Time frame	n	Mean difference	Standard Error	P	95% CI [b]	
					Lower bound	Upper bound
Baseline – 1 month		10.72[*]	2.99	< 0.01	16.84	4.60
1 month – 2 month	30	19.16[*]	3.30	< 0.01	25.91	12.41
2 month – 3 month		26.89[*]	3.25	< 0.01	33.54	20.24
n = number of participants, CI = Confidence Interval						
[*] = The Mean Difference is significant at the 0.05 level.						
b. Adjustment for multiple comparisons: Least Significant Difference (equivalent to no adjustments).						

Table 4.2.6.1 showing the pair-wise comparison of Short Form-36 Mental Component Summary within the PHAIPTgroup Mean Difference (MD) and Standard Error (SE) on different time frame at baseline to 1st month (MD = 10.72; SE = 2.99; p < 0.01), 1st month – 2nd month (MD = 19.16; SE = 3.30; p < 0.01), and 2nd – 3rd month (MD = 26.89; SE = 3.25; P < 0.01) the result showing statistical significance (p < 0.01).

Table 4.2.7: Comparison of algometric measurement of widespread pain index points on Shoulder Girdle Left (Left) variable within the group-I from Baseline to Third month

Variable	n	Mean ± SD	SE	df	F	P
SGL (B)		1.05 ± 0.42	0.07			
SGL (1)	30	1.52 ± 0.53	0.09	3	173.80	< 0.01*
SGL (2)		2.03 ± 0.55	0.10			
SGL (3)		2.54 ± 0.65	0.12			

SGL = Shoulder Girdle Left; **n** = Number of participants; **SD** = Standard Deviation; **SE** = Standard Error; **df** = differential frequency; **F** = Mean of the within group variances. * = The Mean score is significant at the 0.05 level.

Table 4.2.7 depicts the comparison of Mean and Standard Deviation within the group for pain pressure threshold of shoulder girdle left side point on algometer at Baseline (1.05 ± 0.42), 1st month (1.52 ± 0.53), 2nd Month (2.03 ± 0.55), and 3rd month (2.54 ± 0.65) in PHAIPT group. The result showed significant difference (F = 173.80, p < 0.01).

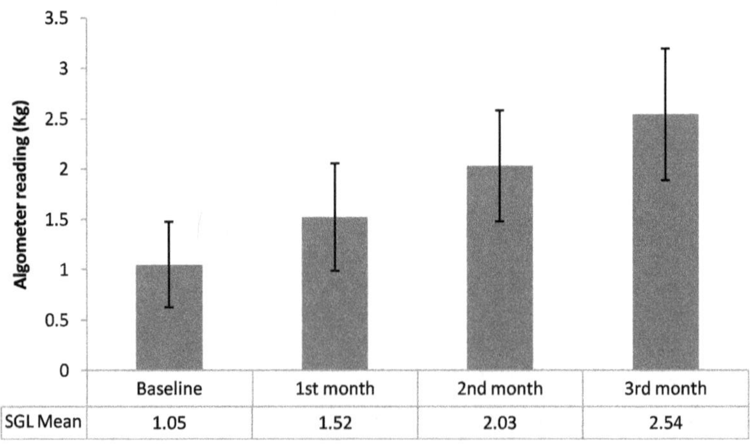

Figure 4.2.7: The Mean and SD on algometer measurement in shoulder girdle left side point

Table 4.2.7.1: Pair-wise comparison of algometric measurement of widespread pain index points on Shoulder Girdle Left (SGL) variable from Baseline to Third month at different time frame

Time frame	n	Mean difference	Standard Error	P	95% CI [b]	
					Lower bound	Upper bound
Baseline – 1 month		0.47*	0.05	< 0.01	0.58	0.37
1 month – 2 month	30	0.98*	0.07	< 0.01	1.12	0.84
2 month – 3 month		1.49*	0.09	< 0.01	1.68	1.30

n = number of participants, CI = Confidence Interval
* = The Mean Difference is significant at the 0.05 level.
b. Adjustment for multiple comparisons: Least Significant Difference (equivalent to no adjustments).

Table 4.2.7.1 showing the pair-wise comparison of estimated marginal Mean s of pain pressure threshold of Shoulder Girdle Left point on algometer within the PHAIPTgroup; The Mean Difference (MD) and Standard Error (SE) on different time frame at baseline to 1st month (MD = 0.47; SE = 0.05), 1st month – 2nd month (MD = 0.98; SE = 0.07), and 2nd – 3rd month (MD = 1.49; SE = 0.09) the result showing statistical significance (p < 0.01).

Table 4.2.8: Comparison of algometric measurement of widespread pain index points on Shoulder Girdle Right (SGR) variable within the group-I from Baseline to Third month

Variable	n	Mean ± SD	SE	df	F	P
SGR (B)		1.11 ± 0.48	0.08			
SGR (1)	30	1.60 ± 0.54	0.09	3	172.82	< 0.01*
SGR (2)		2.08 ± 0.63	0.11			
SGR (3)		2.49 ± 0.64	0.11			

SGR = Shoulder Girdle Right; **n** = Number of participants; **SD** = Standard Deviation; **SE** = Standard Error; **df** = differential frequency; **F** = Mean of the within group variances; * = The Mean score is significant at the 0.05 level.

Table 4.2.8 depicts the Mean and Standard Deviation for pain pressure threshold of shoulder girdle right side point on algometer at Baseline (1.11 ± 0.48), 1st month (1.60 ± 0.54), 2nd Month (2.08 ± 0.63), and 3rd month (2.49 ± 0.64) in PHAIPT group. The result showed significant difference (F = 172.82, p < 0.01).

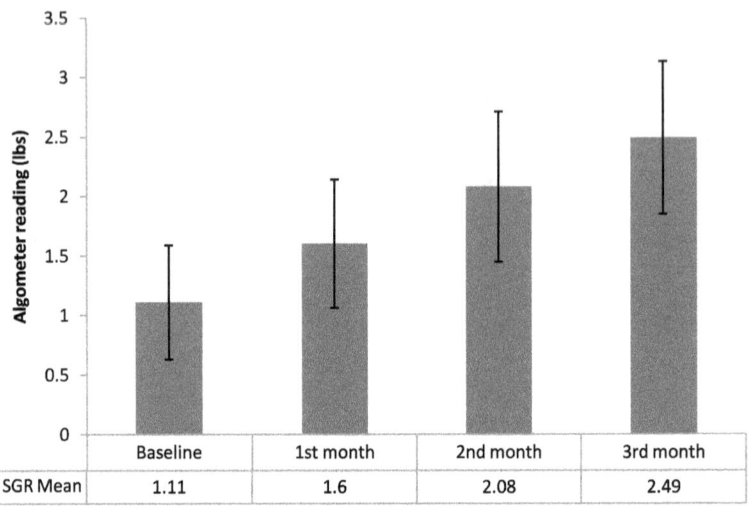

Figure 4.2.8: The Mean and SD of pain pressure threshold value on algometer in shoulder girdle right side point.

Table 4.2.8.1: Pair-wise comparison of algometric measurement of widespread pain index points on Shoulder Girdle Right (SGR) variable from Baseline to Third month at different time frame

Time frame	n	Mean difference	Standard Error	P	95% CI [b]	
					Lower bound	Upper bound
Baseline – 1 month		0.49[*]	0.05	< 0.01	0.61	0.37
1 month – 2 month	30	0.97[*]	0.08	< 0.01	1.13	0.80
2 month – 3 month		1.38[*]	0.09	< 0.01	1.56	1.19

n = number of participants, CI = Confidence Interval

* = The Mean Difference is significant at the 0.05 level.

b. Adjustment for multiple comparisons: Least Significant Difference (equivalent to no adjustments).

Table 4.2.8.1 showing the pair-wise comparison of estimated marginal Mean s of pain pressure threshold of Shoulder Girdle Right point on algometer within the PHAIPTgroup; The Mean Difference (MD) and Standard Error (SE) on different time frame at baseline to 1st month (MD = 0.49; SE = 0.05), 1st month – 2nd month (MD = 0.97; SE = 0.08), and 2nd – 3rd month (MD = 1.38; SE = 0.09) the result showing statistical significance (p < 0.01).

Table 4.2.9: Comparison of algometric measurement of widespread pain index points on Upper Arm Left (UAL) variable within the group-I from Baseline to Third month

Variable	n	Mean ± SD	SE	df	F	P
UAL (B)		0.25 ± 0.44	0.08			
UAL (1)	30	0.39 ± 0.68	0.12	3	8.52	< 0.05*
UAL (2)		0.55 ± 0.97	0.17			
UAL (3)		0.67 ± 1.16	0.21			
UAL = Upper Arm Left; **n** = Number of participants; **SD** = Standard Deviation; **SE** = Standard Error; **df** = differential frequency; **F** = Mean of the within group variances. * = The Mean score is significant at the < 0.05 level.						

Table 4.2.9 depicts the Mean and Standard Deviation for pain pressure threshold of upper arm left side point on algometer at Baseline (0.25 ± 0.44), 1st month (0.39 ± 0.68), 2nd Month (0.55 ± 0.97), and 3rd month (0.67 ± 1.16) in PHAIPT group. The result showed significant difference (F = 8.52, p < 0.05).

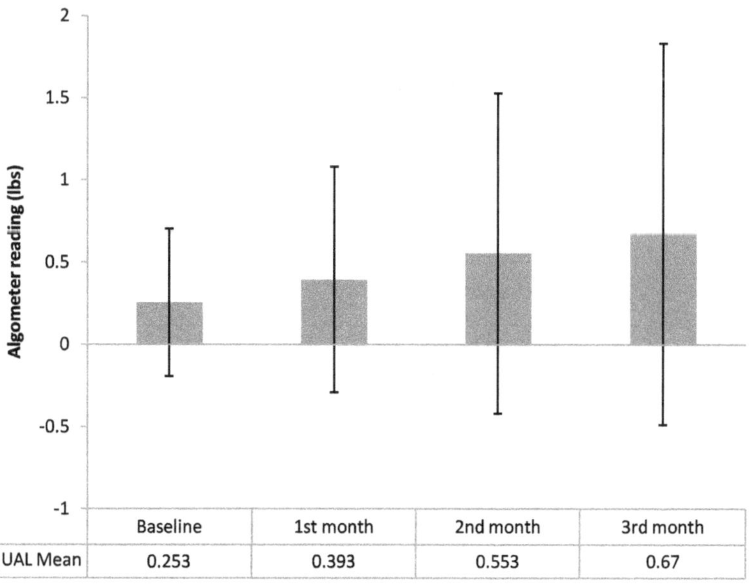

Figure 4.2.9: The Mean and SD on algometer measurement in upper arm left side point

Table 4.2.9.1: Pair-wise comparison of algometric measurement of widespread pain index points on Upper Arm Left (UAL) variable from Baseline to Third month at different time frame

Time frame	n	Mean difference	Standard Error	P	95% CI [b]	
					Lower bound	Upper bound
Baseline – 1 month		0.14*	0.04	< 0 .01	0.23	0.04
1 month – 2 month	30	0.30*	0.10	< 0 .01	0.51	0.08
2 month – 3 month		0.41*	0.13	< 0.01	0.69	0.13

n = number of participants, CI = Confidence Interval

* = The Mean Difference is significant at the 0.05 level.

b. Adjustment for multiple comparisons: Least Significant Difference (equivalent to no adjustments).

Table 4.2.9.1 showing the pair-wise comparison of estimated marginal Means of pain pressure threshold of Upper Arm Left point on algometer within the PHAIPTgroup; The Mean Difference (MD) and Standard Error (SE) on different time frame at baseline to 1st month (MD = 0.14; SE = 0.04; p < 0.01), 1st month – 2nd month (MD = 0.30; SE = 0.10; p = < 0.01), and 2nd – 3rd month (MD = 0.41; SE = 0.13; P < 0.01) the result showing statistical significance ($p < 0.05$).

Table 4.2.10: Comparison of algometric measurement of widespread pain index points on Upper Arm Right (UAR) variable within the group-I from Baseline to Third month

Variable	N	Mean ± SD	SE	df	F	P
UAR (B)		0.20 ± 0.44	0.08			
UAR (1)	30	0.30 ± 0.64	0.11	3	6.68	< 0.05*
UAR (2)		0.43 ± 0.89	0.16			
UAR (3)		0.51 ± 1.06	0.19			

UAR = Upper Arm Right; n = Number of participants; SD = Standard Deviation;

SE = Standard Error; df = differential frequency; F = Mean of the within group variances.

* = The Mean score is significant at the < 0.05 level.

Table 4.2.10 depicts the Mean and Standard Deviation for pain pressure threshold of upper arm right side point on algometer at Baseline (0.20 ± 0.44), 1st month (0.30 ± 0.64), 2nd Month (0.43 ± 0.89), and 3rd month (0.51 ± 1.06) in PHAIPT group. The result showed significant difference (F = 6.68, p < 0.05).

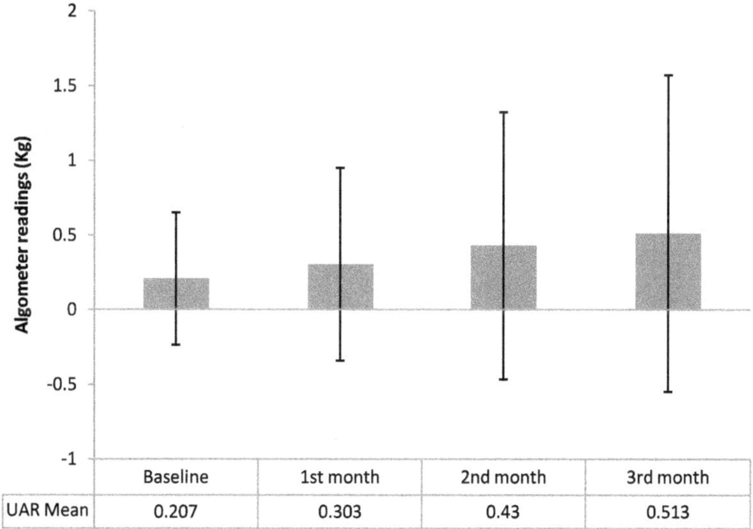

Figure 4.2.10: The Mean and SD on algometer measurement in upper arm right side point

Table 4.2.10.1: Pair-wise comparison of algometric measurement of widespread pain index points on Upper Arm Right (UAR) variable from Baseline to Third month at different time frame

Time frame	N	Mean difference	Standard Error	P	95% CI [b]	
					Lower bound	Upper bound
Baseline – 1 month		0.09*	0.03	0.01	0.17	0.01
1 month – 2 month	30	0.22*	0.08	0.01	0.39	0.04
2 month – 3 month		0.30*	0.11	0.01	0.54	0.06

n = number of participants, CI = Confidence Interval

* = The Mean Difference is significant at the 0.05 level.

b. Adjustment for multiple comparisons: Least Significant Difference (equivalent to no adjustments).

Table 4.2.10.1 showing the pair-wise comparison of estimated marginal Means of pain pressure threshold of Upper Arm Right point on algometer within the PHAIPTgroup; The Mean Difference (MD) and Standard Error (SE) on different time frame at baseline to 1st month (MD = 0.09; SE = 0.03; p = 0.01), 1st month – 2nd month (MD = 0.22; SE = 0.08; p = 0.01), and 2nd – 3rd month (MD = 0.30; SE = 0.11; P = 0.01) the result showing statistical significance (p < 0.05).

Table 4.2.11: Comparison of algometric measurement of widespread pain index points on Lower Arm Left (LAL) variable within the group-I from Baseline to Third month

Variable	n	Mean ± SD	SE	Df	F	P
LAL (B)		0.14 ± 0.47	0.08			
LAL (1)	30	0.17 ± 0.55	0.10	3	3.09	> 0.05#
LAL (2)		0.21 ± 0.67	0.12			
LAL (3)		0.26 ± 0.82	0.15			

LAL = Lower Arm Left; **n** = Number of participants; **SD** = Standard Deviation; **SE** = Standard Error; **df** = differential frequency; **F** = Mean of the within group variances; # = The Mean score is Non-significant at the 0.05 level.

Table 4.2.11 depicts the Mean and Standard Deviation for pain pressure threshold of lower arm left side point on algometer at Baseline (0.14 ± 0.47), 1st month (0.17 ± 0.55), 2nd Month (0.21 ± 0.67), and 3rd month (0.26 ± 0.82) in PHAIPT group. The result showed significant difference (F = 3.09, p > 0.05).

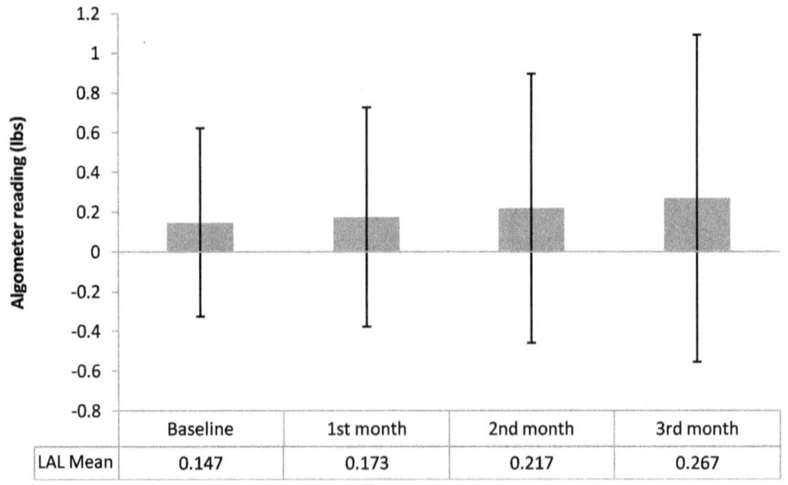

Figure 4.2.11: The Mean and SD on algometer measurement in lower arm left side point

Table 4.2.11.1: Pair-wise comparison of algometric measurement of widespread pain index points on Upper Arm Right (UAR) variable from Baseline to Third month at different time frame

Time frame	N	Mean difference	Standard Error	P	95% CI [b]	
					Lower bound	Upper bound
Baseline – 1 month		$0.02^{\#}$	0.01	0.08	0.05	0.00
1 month – 2 month	30	$0.07^{\#}$	0.04	0.09	0.15	0.01
2 month – 3 month		$0.12^{\#}$	0.06	0.08	0.25	0.01

n = number of participants, CI = Confidence Interval
#. The Mean Difference is non-significant at the 0.05 level.
b. Adjustment for multiple comparisons: Least Significant Difference (equivalent to no adjustments).

Table 4.2.11.1 showing the pair-wise comparison of estimated marginal Mean s of pain pressure threshold of Lower Arm Left point on algometer within the PHAIPTgroup; The Mean Difference (MD) and Standard Error (SE) on different time frame at baseline to 1st month (MD = 0.02; SE = 0.01; p = 0.08), 1st month – 2nd month (MD = 0.07; SE = 0.04; p = 0.09), and 2nd – 3rd month (MD = 0.12; SE = 0.06; P = 0.08) the result showing statistical non-significance (p > 0.05).

Table 4.2.12: Comparison of algometric measurement of widespread pain index points on Lower Arm Right (LAR) variable within the group-I from Baseline to Third month

Variable	n	Mean ± SD	SE	df	F	P
LAR (B)		0.07 ± 0.27	0.05			
LAR (1)	30	0.11 ± 0.45	0.08	3	1.97	$> 0.05^{\#}$
LAR (2)		0.14 ± 0.55	0.10			
LAR (3)		0.19 ± 0.74	0.13			

LAR = Lower Arm Right; n = Number of participants; SD = Standard Deviation; SE = Standard Error; df = differential frequency; F = Mean of the within group variances; # = The Mean score is Non-significant at the 0.05 level.

Table 4.2.12 depicts the Mean and Standard Deviation for pain pressure threshold of lower arm right side point on algometer at Baseline (0.07 ± 0.27), 1st month (0.11 ± 0.45), 2nd Month (0.14 ± 0.55), and 3rd month (0.19 ± 0.74) in PHAIPT group. The result showed significant difference (F = 1.97, p > 0.05).

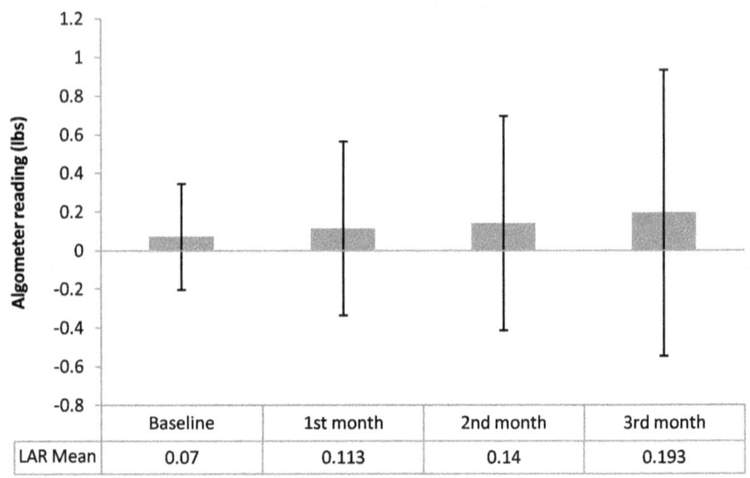

	Baseline	1st month	2nd month	3rd month
LAR Mean	0.07	0.113	0.14	0.193

Figure 4.2.12: The Mean and SD on algometer measurement in lower arm right side point

Table 4.2.12.1: Pair-wise comparison of algometric measurement of widespread pain index points on Lower Arm Right (LAR) variable from Baseline to Third month at different time frame

Time frame	N	Mean difference	Standard Error	P	95% CI [b]	
					Lower bound	Upper bound
Baseline – 1 month		0.04[#]	0.03	0.19	0.11	0.02
1 month – 2 month	30	0.07[#]	0.05	0.18	0.17	0.03
2 month – 3 month		0.12[#]	0.08	0.16	0.29	0.05

n = number of participants, CI = Confidence Interval

[#]. The Mean Difference is non-significant at the 0.05 level.

b. Adjustment for multiple comparisons: Least Significant Difference (equivalent to no adjustments).

Table 4.2.12.1 showing the pair-wise comparison of estimated marginal Means of pain pressure threshold of Lower Arm Right point on algometer within the PHAIPTgroup; The Mean Difference (MD) and Standard Error (SE) on different time frame at baseline to 1st month (MD = 0.04; SE = 0.03; p = 0.19), 1st month – 2nd month (MD = 0.07; SE = 0.05; p = 0.18), and 2nd – 3rd month (MD = 0.12; SE = 0.08; P = 0.16) the result showing statistical non -significance (p > 0.05).

Table 4.2.13: Comparison of algometric measurement of widespread pain index points on Hip Buttock Left (HBL) variable within the group-I from Baseline to Third month

Variable	n	Mean ± SD	SE	df	F	P
HBL (B)		1.23 ± 0.86	0.15			
HBL (1)	30	1.64 ± 1.05	0.19	3	63.60	< 0.01*
HBL (2)		1.95 ± 1.18	0.21			
HBL (3)		2.30 ± 1.38	0.25			

HBL = Hip Buttock Left; **n** = Number of participants; **SD** = Standard Deviation; **SE** = Standard Error; **df** = differential frequency; **F** = Mean of the within group variances. * = The Mean score is significant at the 0.05 level.

Table 4.2.13 depicts the Mean and Standard Deviation for pain pressure threshold of hip buttock left side point on algometer at baseline (1.23 ± 0.86), 1st month (1.64 ± 1.05), 2nd month (1.95 ± 1.18), and 3rd month (2.30 ± 1.38) in PHAIPT group. The result showed significant difference (F = 63.60, p < 0.01).

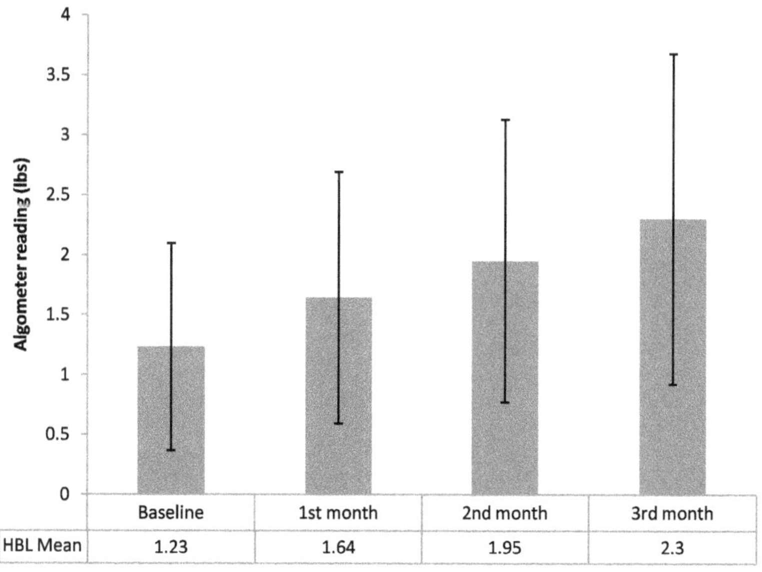

Figure 4.2.13: The Mean and SD on algometer measurement in Hip Buttock Left side point

Table 4.2.13.1: Pair-wise comparison of algometric measurement of widespread pain index points on Hip Buttock Left (HBL) variable from Baseline to Third month at different time frame

Time frame	n	Mean difference	Standard Error	P	95% CI [b]	
					Lower bound	Upper bound
Baseline – 1 month		0.41[*]	0.06	< 0.01	0.54	0.28
1 month – 2 month	30	0.72[*]	0.09	< 0.01	0.90	0.53
2 month – 3 month		1.06[*]	0.12	< 0.01	1.31	0.81

Based on estimated marginal Mean s
n = number of participants, CI = Confidence Interval
[*] = The Mean Difference is significant at the 0.05 level.
b. Adjustment for multiple comparisons: Least Significant Difference (equivalent to no adjustments).

Table 4.2.13.1 showing the pair-wise comparison of estimated marginal Means of pain pressure threshold of Hip Buttock Left point on algometer within the PHAIPTgroup; The Mean Difference (MD) and Standard Error (SE) on different time frame at baseline to 1st month (MD = 0.41; SE = 0.06; p = < 0.01), 1st month – 2nd month (MD = 0.72; SE = 0.09; p = < 0.01), and 2nd – 3rd month (MD = 1.06; SE = 0.12; P = < 0.01) the result showing statistical significance (p < 0.01).

Table 4.2.14: Comparison of algometric measurement of widespread pain index points on Hip Buttock Right (HBR) variable within the group-I from Baseline to Third month

Variable	n	Mean ± SD	SE	df	F	P
HBR (B)		1.17 ± 0.91	0.16			
HBR (1)	30	1.53 ± 1.09	0.20	3	49.82	< 0.01*
HBR (2)		1.81 ± 1.24	0.22			
HBR (3)		2.13 ± 1.48	0.27			

HBR = Hip Buttock Right; **n** = Number of participants; **SD** = Standard Deviation; **SE** = Standard Error; **df** = differential frequency; **F** = Mean of the within group variances; Significance = < 0.01. * = The Mean score is significant at the 0.05 level.

Table 4.2.14 depicts the Mean and Standard Deviation for pain pressure threshold of hip buttock right side point on algometer at baseline (1.17 ± 0.91), 1st month (1.53 ± 1.09), 2nd month (1.81 ± 1.24), and 3rd month (2.13 ± 1.48) in PHAIPT group. The result showed significant difference (F = 49.82, p < 0.01).

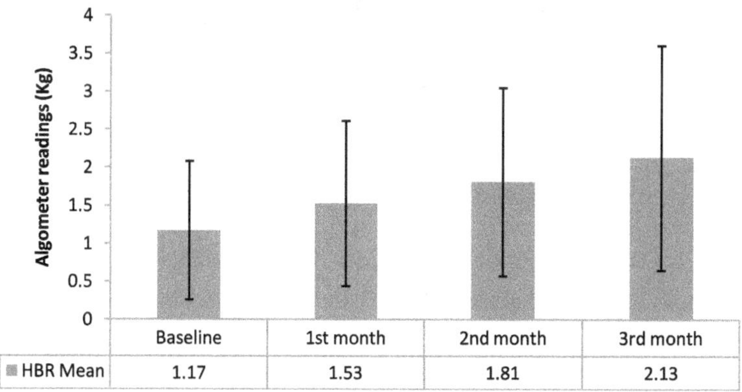

	Baseline	1st month	2nd month	3rd month
▤ HBR Mean	1.17	1.53	1.81	2.13

Figure 4.2.14: The Mean and SD on algometer measurement in Hip Buttock Right side point

Table 4.2.14.1: Pair-wise comparison of algometric measurement of widespread pain index points on Hip Buttock Right (HBR) variable from Baseline to Third month at different time frame

Time frame	n	Mean difference	Standard Error	P	95% CI [b]	
					Lower bound	Upper bound
Baseline – 1 month	30	0.36[*]	0.05	< 0.01	0.47	0.25
1 month – 2 month		0.64[*]	0.08	< 0.01	0.81	0.46
2 month – 3 month		1.95[*]	0.12	< 0.01	1.21	0.69
n = number of participants, CI = Confidence Interval						
[*] = The Mean Difference is significant at the 0.05 level.						
b. Adjustment for multiple comparisons: Least Significant Difference (equivalent to no adjustments).						

Table **4.2.14.1** showing the pair-wise comparison of estimated marginal Means of pain pressure threshold of Hip Buttock Right point on algometer within the PHAIPT group; The Mean Difference (MD) and Standard Error (SE) on different time frame at baseline to 1st month (MD = 0.36; SE = 0.05; p = < 0.01), 1st month – 2nd month (MD = 0.64; SE = 0.08; p = < 0.01), and 2nd – 3rd month (MD = 1.95; SE = 0.12; P = < 0.01) the result showing statistical significance (p < 0.01).

Table 4.2.15: Comparison of algometric measurement of widespread pain index points on Upper Leg Left (ULL) variable within the group-I from Baseline to Third month

Variable	n	Mean ± SD	SE	df	F	P
ULL (B)		0.08 ± 0.33	0.06			
ULL (1)	30	0.10 ± 0.39	0.07	3	2.04	> 0.05[#]
ULL (2)		0.13 ± 0.50	0.09			
ULL (3)		0.14 ± 0.54	0.10			

ULL = Upper Leg Left; **n** = Number of participants; **SD** = Standard Deviation; **SE** = Standard Error; **df** = differential frequency; **F** = Mean of the within group variances; # = The Mean score is Non-significant at the 0.05 level.

Table 4.2.15 depicts the Mean and Standard Deviation for pain pressure threshold of upper limb left side point on algometer at baseline (0.08 ± 0.33), 1st month (0.10 ± 0.39), 2nd month (0.13 ± 0.50), and 3rd month (0.14 ± 0.54) in PHAIPT group. The result showed non-significant difference (F = 2.04, p > 0.05).

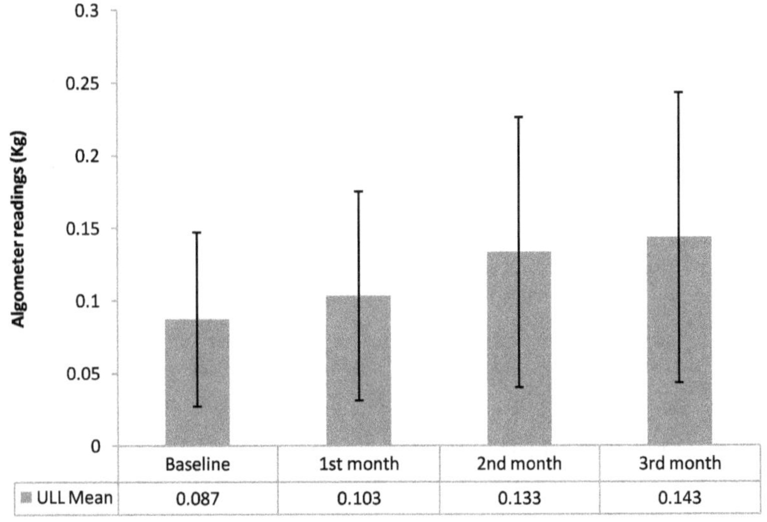

Figure 4.2.15: The Mean and SD on algometer measurement in Upper Leg Right side point

Table 4.2.15.1: Pair-wise comparison of algometric measurement of widespread pain index points on Upper Leg Left (ULL) variable from Baseline to Third month at different time frame

Time frame	n	Mean difference	Standard Error	P	95% CI [b]	
					Lower bound	Upper bound
Baseline – 1 month		0.01[#]	0.01	0. 16	0.04	0.00
1 month – 2 month	30	0.04[#]	0.03	0. 16	0.11	0.02
2 month – 3 month		0.05[#]	0.39	0. 16	0.13	0.02

n = number of participants, CI = Confidence Interval

[#]. The Mean Difference is non-significant at the 0.05 level.

b. Adjustment for multiple comparisons: Least Significant Difference (equivalent to no adjustments).

Table 4.2.15.1 showing the pair-wise comparison of estimated marginal Mean s of pain pressure threshold of Upper Leg Left point on algometer within the PHAIPT group; The Mean Difference (MD) and Standard Error (SE) on different time frame at baseline to 1st month (MD = 0.01; SE = 0.01; p = 0.16), 1st month – 2nd month (MD = 0.04; SE = 0.03; p = 0.16), and 2nd – 3rd month (MD = 0.05; SE = 0.39; P = 0.16) the result showing statistical significance (p > 0.05).

Table 4.2.16: Comparison of algometric measurement of widespread pain index points on Upper Leg Right (ULR) variable within the group-I from Baseline to Third month

Variable	n	Mean ± SD	SE	df	F	P
ULR (B)		0.10 ± 0.41	0.07			
ULR (1)	30	0.13 ± 0.50	0.09	3	1.94	> 0.05[#]
ULR (2)		0.15 ± 0.60	0.11			
ULR (3)		0.18 ± 0.71	0.13			

ULR = Upper Leg Right; **n** = Number of participants; **SD** = Standard Deviation; **SE** = Standard Error; **df** = differential frequency; **F** = Mean of the within group variances; # = The Mean score is Non-significant at the 0.05 level.

Table 4.2.16 depicts the Mean and Standard Deviation for pain pressure threshold of upper limb right side point on algometer at baseline (0.10 ± 0.41), 1st month (0.13 ± 0.50), 2nd month (0.15 ± 0.60), and 3rd month (0.18 ± 0.71) in PHAIPT group. The result showed non-significant difference (F = 1.94, p > 0.05).

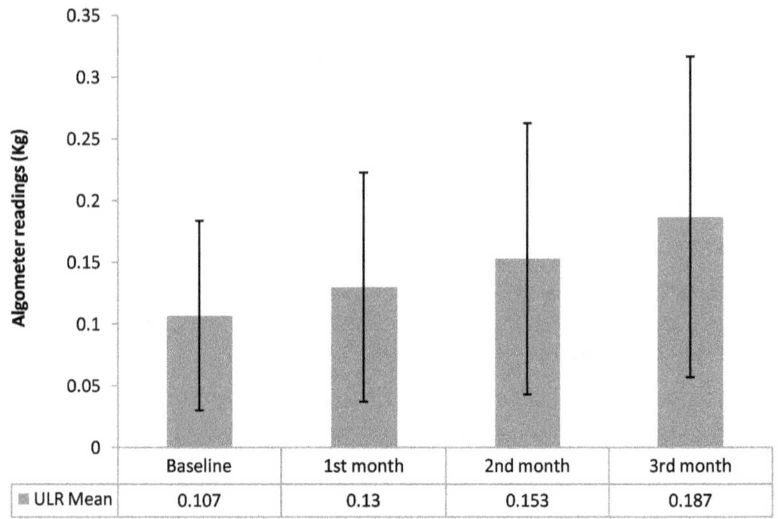

	Baseline	1st month	2nd month	3rd month
■ ULR Mean	0.107	0.13	0.153	0.187

Figure 4.2.16: The Mean and SD on algometer measurement in Upper Leg Right side point

Table 4.2.16.1: Pair-wise comparison of algometric measurement of widespread pain index points on Upper Leg Right (ULR) variable from Baseline to Third month at different time frame

Time frame	N	Mean difference	Standard Error	P	95% CI [b]	
					Lower bound	Upper bound
Baseline – 1 month		$0.02^{\#}$	0.01	0.16	0.05	0.01
1 month – 2 month	30	$0.04^{\#}$	0.03	0.17	0.11	0.02
2 month – 3 month		$0.08^{\#}$	0.05	0.16	0.19	0.03

n = number of participants, CI = Confidence Interval

[#]. The Mean Difference is non-significant at the 0.05 level.

b. Adjustment for multiple comparisons: Least Significant Difference (equivalent to no adjustments).

Table 4.2.16.1 showing the pair-wise comparison of estimated marginal Mean s of pain pressure threshold of Upper Leg Right point on algometer within the PHAIPT group; The Mean Difference (MD) and Standard Error (SE) on different time frame at baseline to 1st month (MD = 0.02; SE = 0.01; p = 0.16), 1st month – 2nd month (MD = 0.04; SE = 0.03; p = 0.17), and 2nd – 3rd month (MD = 0.08; SE = 0.05; P = 0.16) the result showing statistical significance (p > 0.05).

Table 4.2.17: Comparison of algometric measurement of widespread pain index points on Lower Leg Left (LLL) variable within the group-I from Baseline to Third month

Variable	n	Mean ± SD	SE	df	F	P
LLL (B)		0.43 ± 0.85	0.15			
LLL (1)	30	0.51 ± 0.02	0.18	3	6.99	< 0.05*
LLL (2)		0.63 ± 1.23	0.22			
LLL (3)		0.71 ± 1.34	0.24			
LLL = Lower Leg Left; **n** = Number of participants; **SD** = Standard Deviation; **SE** = Standard Error; **df** = differential frequency; **F** = Mean of the within group variances; * = The Mean score is significant at the < 0.05 level.						

Table 4.2.17 depicts the Mean and Standard Deviation for pain pressure threshold of lower leg left side point on algometer at baseline (0.43 ± 0.85), 1st month (0.51 ± 0.02), 2nd month (0.63 ± 1.23) and 3rd month (0.71 ± 1.34) in PHAIPT group. The result showed significant difference (F = 6.99, p < 0.05).

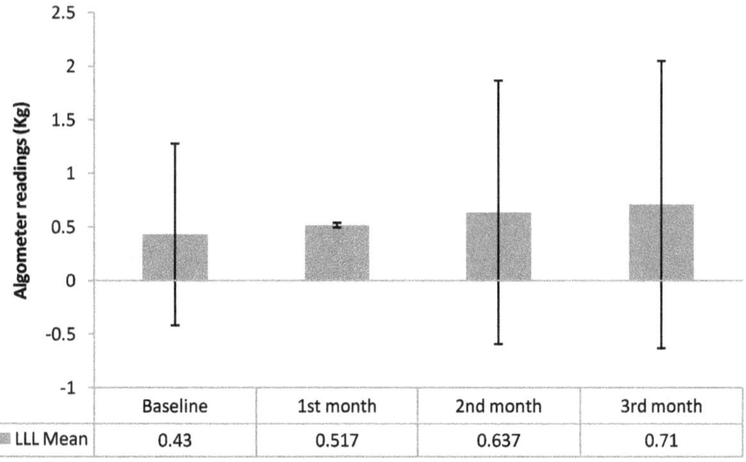

Figure 4.2.17: The Mean and SD on algometer measurement in Lower Leg Left side point

Table 4.2.17.1: Pair-wise comparison of algometric measurement of widespread pain index points on Lower Leg Left (LLL) variable from Baseline to Third month at different time frame

Time frame	n	Mean difference	Standard Error	P	95% CI [b]	
					Lower bound	Upper bound
Baseline – 1 month		0.08[*]	0.03	0.01	0.15	0.02
1 month – 2 month	30	0.20[*]	0.08	0.01	0.37	0.04
2 month – 3 month		0.28[*]	0.09	< 0.01	0.48	0.07
n = number of participants, CI = Confidence Interval						
[*] = The Mean Difference is significant at the 0.05 level.						
b. Adjustment for multiple comparisons: Least Significant Difference (equivalent to no adjustments).						

Table 4.2.17.1 showing the pair-wise comparison of estimated marginal Mean s of pain pressure threshold of Lower Leg Left point on algometer within the PHAIPT group; The Mean Difference (MD) and Standard Error (SE) on different time frame at baseline to 1st month (MD = 0.08; SE = 0.03; p = < 0.01), 1st month – 2nd month (MD = 0.20; SE = 0.08; p = < 0.01), and 2nd – 3rd month (MD = 0.28; SE = 0.09; P = < 0.01) the result showing statistical significance (p < 0.05).

Table 4.2.18: Comparison of algometric measurement of widespread pain index points on Lower Leg Right (LLR) variable within the group-I from Baseline to Third month

Variable	n	Mean ± SD	SE	df	F	P
LLR (B)		0.32 ± 0.68	0.12			
LLR (1)	30	0.43 ± 0.90	0.16	3	6.28	< 0.05*
LLR (2)		0.52 ± 1.09	0.20			
LLR (3)		0.57 ± 1.19	0.21			
LLR = Lower Leg Right; n = Number of participants; SD = Standard Deviation;						
SE = Standard Error; df = differential frequency; F = Mean of the within group variances;						
* = The Mean score is significant at the < 0.05 level.						

Table 4.2.18 depicts the Mean and Standard Deviation for pain pressure threshold of lower limb right side point on algometer at baseline (0.32 ± 0.68), 1st month (0.43 ± 0.90), 2nd month (0.52 ± 1.09), and 3rd month (0.57 ± 1.19) in PHAIPT group. The result showed significant difference (F = 6.28, p < 0.05).

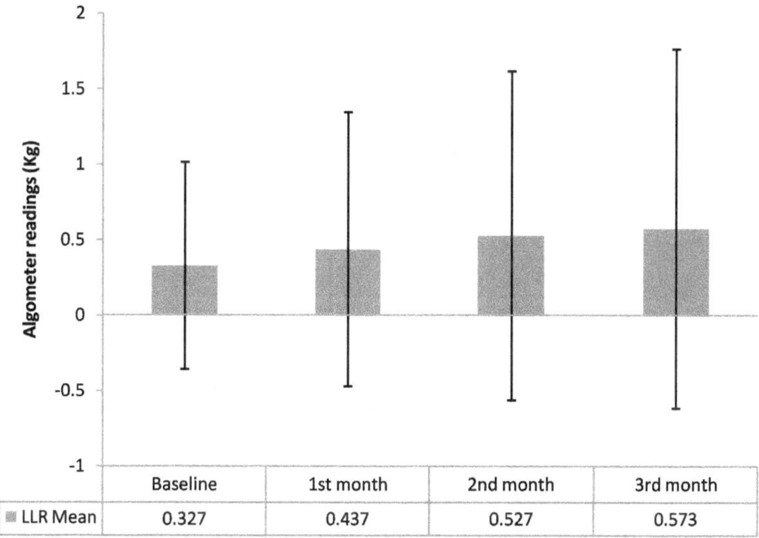

	Baseline	1st month	2nd month	3rd month
LLR Mean	0.327	0.437	0.527	0.573

Figure 4.2.18: The Mean and SD on algometer measurement in Lower Leg Right side point

Table 4.2.18.1: Pair-wise comparison of algometric measurement of widespread pain index points on Lower Leg Right (LLR) variable from Baseline to Third month at different time frame

Time frame	n	Mean difference	Standard Error	P	95% CI [b]	
					Lower bound	Upper bound
Baseline – 1 month		0.11*	0.04	0.01	0.20	0.02
1 month – 2 month	30	0.20*	0.07	0.01	0.36	0.04
2 month – 3 month		0.24*	0.09	0.01	0.44	0.04
n = number of participants, CI = Confidence Interval						
* = The Mean Difference is significant at the 0.05 level.						
b. Adjustment for multiple comparisons: Least Significant Difference (equivalent to no adjustments).						

Table 4.2.18.1 showing the pair-wise comparison of estimated marginal Mean s of pain pressure threshold of Lower Leg Right point on algometer within the PHAIPT group; The Mean Difference (MD) and Standard Error (SE) on different time frame at baseline to 1st month (MD = 0.11; SE = 0.04; p = < 0.01), 1st month – 2nd month (MD = 0.20; SE = 0.07; p = < 0.01), and 2nd – 3rd month (MD = 0.24; SE = 0.09; P = < 0.01) the result showing statistical significance (p < 0.05).

Table 4.2.19: Comparison of algometric measurement of widespread pain index points on Jaw Left (JAWL) variable within the group-I from Baseline to Third month

Variable	n	Mean ± SD	SE	Df	F	P
JAWL (B)		0.02 ± 0.14	0.02			
JAWL (1)	30	0.04 ± 0.23	0.04	3	1.00	> 0.05$^{\#}$
JAWL (2)		0.06 ± 0.36	0.06			
JAWL (3)		0.08 ± 0.43	0.08			
JAWL = JAW Left; **n** = Number of participants; **SD** = Standard Deviation; **SE** = Standard Error; **df** = differential frequency; **F** = Mean of the within group variances; # = The Mean score is Non-significant at the 0.05 level.						

Table 4.2.19 depicts the Mean and Standard Deviation for pain pressure threshold of jaw left side point on algometer at baseline (0.02 ± 0.14), 1st month (0.04 ± 0.23), 2nd month (0.06 ± 0.36), and 3rd month (0.08 ± 0.43) in PHAIPT group. The result showed non-significant difference (F = 1.00, p > 0.05).

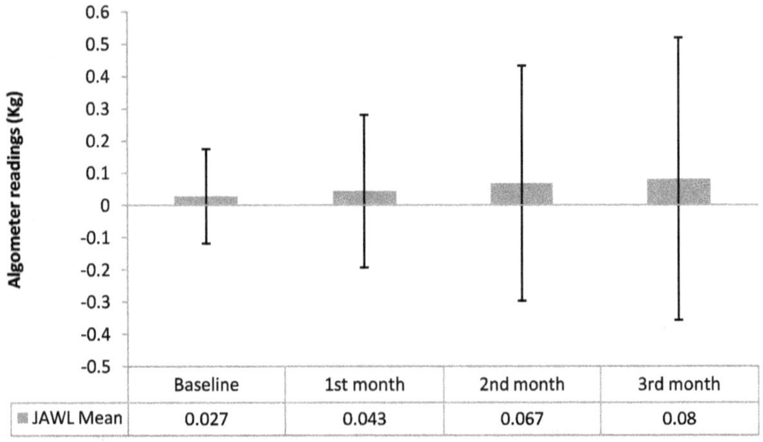

Figure 4.2.19: The Mean and SD on algometer measurement in Jaw Left side point

Table 4.2.19.1: Pair-wise comparison of algometric measurement of widespread pain index point on Jaw Left (JAWL) variable from Baseline to Third month at different time frame

Time frame	N	Mean difference	Standard Error	P	95% CI [b]	
					Lower bound	Upper bound
Baseline – 1 month		0.01#	0.01	0.32	0.05	0.01
1 month – 2 month	30	0.04#	0.04	0.32	0.12	0.04
2 month – 3 month		0.05#	0.05	0.32	0.16	0.05

n = number of participants, CI = Confidence Interval

= The Mean Difference is non-significant at the 0.05 level.

b. Adjustment for multiple comparisons: Least Significant Difference (equivalent to no adjustments).

Table 4.2.19.1 showing the pair-wise comparison of estimated marginal Mean s of pain pressure threshold of Chest point on algometer within the PHAIPT group; The Mean Difference (MD) and Standard Error (SE) on different time frame at baseline to 1st month (MD = 0.01; SE = 0.01; p = 0.32), 1st month – 2nd month (MD = 0.04; SE = 0.04; p = 0.32), and 2nd – 3rd month (MD = 0.28; SE = 0.09; P = 0.32) the result showing statistical significance (p > 0.05).

Table 4.2.20: Comparison of algometric measurement of widespread pain index points on Chest variable within the group-I from Baseline to Third month

Variable	n	Mean ± SD	SE	Df	F	P
CHEST (B)		0.13 ± 0.35	0.06			
CHEST (1)	30	0.27 ± 0.67	0.12	3	5.02	0.05*
CHEST (2)		0.36 ± 0.83	0.15			
CHEST (3)		0.43 ± 0.98	0.17			

n = Number of participants; SD = Standard Deviation; SE = Standard Error; df = differential frequency; F = Mean of the within group variances; * = The Mean score is significant at the 0.05 level.

Table 4.2.20 depicts the Mean and Standard Deviation for pain pressure threshold of chest point on algometer at baseline (0.13 ± 0.35), 1st month (0.27 ± 0.67), 2nd month (0.36 ± 0.83), and 3rd month (0.43 ± 0.98) in PHAIPT group. The result showed significant difference (F = 5.02, p = 0.05).

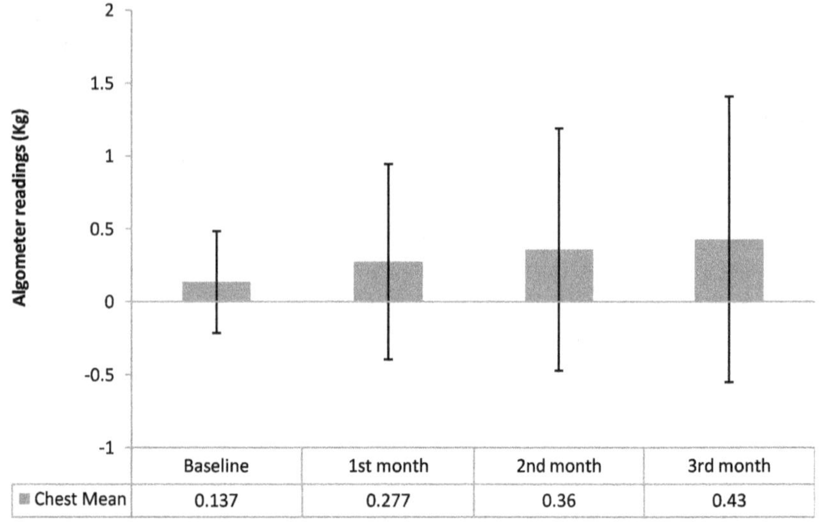

	Baseline	1st month	2nd month	3rd month
▪ Chest Mean	0.137	0.277	0.36	0.43

Figure 4.2.20: The Mean and SD on algometer measurement in Chest point

Table 4.2.20.1: Pair-wise comparison of algometric measurement of widespread pain index points on Chest variable from Baseline to Third month at different time frame

Time frame	n	Mean difference	Standard Error	P	95% CI [b]	
					Lower bound	Upper bound
Baseline – 1 month		0.14[*]	0.07	0.05	0.28	0.00
1 month – 2 month	30	0.22[*]	0.09	0.03	0.42	0.02
2 month – 3 month		0.29[*]	0.12	0.02	0.54	0.04

n = number of participants, CI = Confidence Interval

[*] The Mean Difference is significant at the 0.05 level.

b. Adjustment for multiple comparisons: Least Significant Difference (equivalent to no adjustments).

Table 4.2.20.1 showing the pair-wise comparison of estimated marginal Means of pain pressure threshold of Chest point on algometer within the PHAIPT group; The Mean Difference (MD) and Standard Error (SE) on different time frame at baseline to 1st month (MD = 0.14; SE = 0.07; p = 0.05), 1st month – 2nd month (MD = 0.22; SE = 0.09; p = 0.03), and 2nd – 3rd month (MD = 0.29; SE = 0.12; P = 0.02) the result showing statistical significance (p = 0.05).

Table 4.2.21: Comparison of algometric measurement of widespread pain index points on Abdomen variable within the group-I from Baseline to Third month

Variable	n	Mean ± SD	SE	df	F	P
ABDOMEN (B)		0.14 ± 0.45	0.08			
ABDOMEN (1)	30	0.18 ± 0.56	0.10	3	2.69	> 0.05$^{\#}$
ABDOMEN (2)		0.23 ± 0.74	0.13			
ABDOMEN (3)		0.26 ± 0.81	0.14			

n = Number of participants; **SD** = Standard Deviation; **SE** = Standard Error; **df** = differential frequency; **F** = Mean of the within group variances; # = The Mean score is Non-significant at the 0.05 level.

Table 4.2.21 depicts the Mean and Standard Deviation for pain pressure threshold of abdomen point on algometer at baseline (0.14 ± 0.45), 1st month (0.18 ± 0.56), 2nd month (0.23 ± 0.74), and 3rd month (0.26 ± 0.81) in PHAIPT group. The result showed non-significant difference (F = 2.69, p > 0.05).

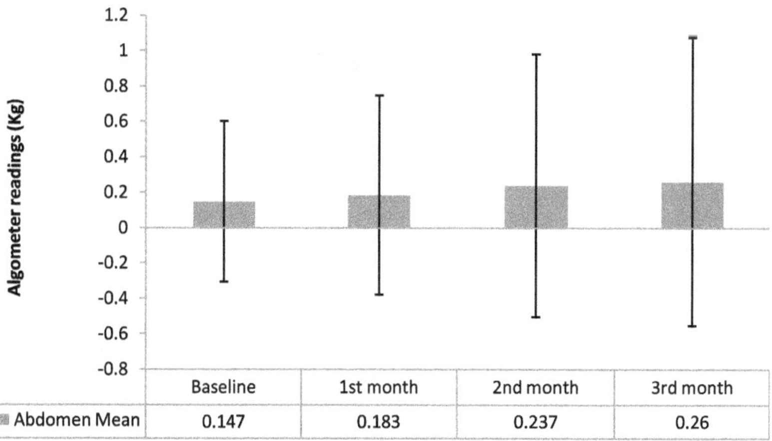

Figure 4.2.21: The Mean and SD on algometer measurement in Abdomen point

Table 4.2.21.1: Pair-wise comparison of algometric measurement of widespread pain index points on Abdomen variable from Baseline to Third month at different time frame

Time frame	n	Mean difference	Standard Error	P	95% CI [b]	
					Lower bound	Upper bound
Baseline – 1 month		0.03[#]	0.02	0.11	0.08	0.01
1 month – 2 month	30	0.09[#]	0.05	0.11	0.20	0.02
2 month – 3 month		0.11[#]	0.06	0.10	0.25	0.02

n = number of participants, CI = Confidence Interval

[#]. The Mean Difference is non-significant at the 0.05 level.

b. Adjustment for multiple comparisons: Least Significant Difference (equivalent to no adjustments).

Table 4.2.21.1 showing the pair-wise comparison of estimated marginal Mean s of pain pressure threshold of Abdomen point on algometer within the PHAIPTgroup; The Mean Difference (MD) and Standard Error (SE) on different time frame at baseline to 1st month (MD = 0.03; SE = 0.02; p = 0.11), 1st month – 2nd month (MD = 0.09; SE = 0.05; p = 0.11), and 2nd – 3rd month (MD = 0.11; SE = 0.06; P = 0.10) the result showing statistical non-significance (p > 0.05).

Table 4.2.22: Comparison of algometric measurement of widespread pain index points on Neck variable within the group-I from Baseline to Third month

Variable	n	Mean ± SD	SE	df	F	P
NECK (B)		1.10 ± 0.59	0.10			
NECK (1)	30	1.63 ± 0.66	0.12	3	103.5	< 0.01*
NECK (2)		2.02 ± 0.73	0.13			
NECK (3)		2.52 ± 0.88	0.16			

n = Number of participants; **SD** = Standard Deviation; **SE** = Standard Error; **df** = differential frequency; **F** = Mean of the within group variances; Significance = < 0.01. * = The Mean score is significant at the 0.05 level.

Table 4.2.22 depicts the Mean and Standard Deviation for pain pressure threshold of neck point on algometer at baseline (1.10 ± 0.59), 1st month (1.63 ± 0.66), 2nd month (2.02 ± 0.73) and 3rd month (2.52 ± 0.88) in PHAIPT group. The result showed significant difference (F = 103.5, p < 0.01).

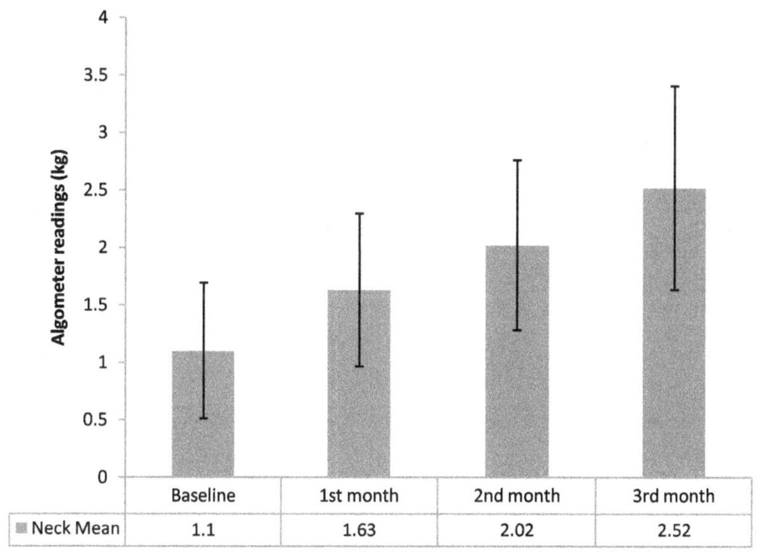

Figure 4.2.22: The Mean and SD on algometer measurement in Neck point

Table 4.2.22.1: Pair-wise comparison of algometric measurement of widespread pain index points on Neck variable from Baseline to Third month at different time frame

Time frame	n	Mean difference	Standard Error	P	95% CI [b]	
					Lower bound	Upper bound
Baseline – 1 month		0.53[*]	0.07	< 0.01	0.67	0.38
1 month – 2 month	30	0.91[*]	0.09	< 0.01	1.10	0.72
2 month – 3 month		1.41[*]	0.13	< 0.01	1.68	1.14

n = number of participants, CI = Confidence Interval

[*] = The Mean Difference is significant at the 0.05 level.

b. Adjustment for multiple comparisons: Least Significant Difference (equivalent to no adjustments).

Table 4.2.22.1 showing the pair-wise comparison of estimated marginal Mean s of pain pressure threshold of Neck point on algometer within the PHAIPT group; The Mean Difference (MD) and Standard Error (SE) on different time frame at baseline to 1st month (MD = 0.53; SE = 0.07; p < 0.01), 1st month – 2nd month (MD = 0.91; SE = 0.09; p < 0.01), and 2nd – 3rd month (MD = 1.41; SE = 0.13; P < 0.01) the result showing statistical significance (p < 0.01).

Table 4.2.23: Comparison of algometric measurement of widespread pain index points on Upper Back (UB) variable within the group-I from Baseline to Third month

Variable	N	Mean ± SD	SE	df	F	P
UB (B)		0.96 ± 0.69	0.12			
UB (1)	30	1.45 ± 0.82	0.15	3	64.07	< 0.01*
UB (2)		2.82 ± 1.00	0.18			
UB (3)		2.20 ± 1.23	0.22			

UB = Upper Back; **n** = Number of participants; **SD** = Standard Deviation; **SE** = Standard Error; **df** = differential frequency; **F** = Mean of the within group variances; * = The Mean score is significant at the 0.05 level.

Table 4.2.23 depicts the Mean and Standard Deviation for pain pressure threshold of upper back point on algometer at baseline (0.96 ± 0.69), 1st month (1.45 ± 0.82), 2nd month (2.82 ± 1.00), and 3rd month (2.20 ± 1.23) in PHAIPT group. The result showed significant difference (F = 64.07, p < 0.01).

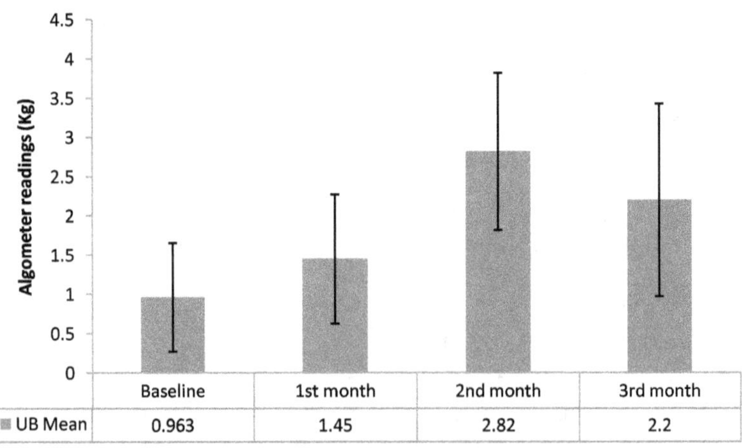

Figure 4.2.23: The Mean and SD on algometer measurement in Upper Back point

Table 4.2.23.1: Pair-wise comparison of algometric measurement of widespread pain index points on Upper Back (UB) variable from Baseline to Third month at different time frame

Time frame	N	Mean difference	Standard Error	P	95% CI [b]	
					Lower bound	Upper bound
Baseline – 1 month		0.49*	0.07	< 0.01	0.63	0.34
1 month – 2 month	30	0.86*	0.10	< 0.01	1.07	0.64
2 month – 3 month		1.23*	0.14	< 0.01	1.52	0.95

n = number of participants, CI = Confidence Interval

*= The Mean Difference is significant at the 0.05 level.

b. Adjustment for multiple comparisons: Least Significant Difference (equivalent to no adjustments).

Table 4.2.23.1 showing the pair-wise comparison of estimated marginal Mean s of pain pressure threshold of upper back point on algometer within the PHAIPT group; The Mean Difference (MD) and Standard Error (SE) on different time frame at baseline to 1st month (MD = -0.49; SE = 0.07; p < 0.01), 1st month – 2nd month (MD = 0.86; SE = 0.10; p < 0.01), and 2nd – 3rd month (MD = 1.23; SE = 0.14; P < 0.01). The result showing statistical significance (p < 0.01).

Table 4.2.24: Comparison of algometric measurement of widespread pain index points on Lower (LB) variable within the group-I from Baseline to Third month

Variable	N	Mean ± SD	SE	df	F	P
LB (B)		1.067 ± 0.8180	0.149			
LB (1)	30	1.523 ± 0.1041	0.202	3	42.960	< 0.01*
LB (2)		1.840 ± 1.3281	0.242			
LB (3)		2.093 ± 1.4730	0.269			

LB = Lower Back; **n** = Number of participants; **SD** = Standard Deviation; **SE** = Standard Error; **df** = differential frequency; **F** = Mean of the within group variances; * = The Mean score is significant at the 0.05 level.

Table 4.2.24 depicts the Mean and Standard Deviation for pain pressure threshold of lower back point on algometer at baseline (1.067 ± 0.8180), 1st month (1.523 ± 0.1041), 2nd month (1.840 ± 1.3281), and 3rd month (2.093 ± 1.4730) in PHAIPT group. The result showed significant difference (F = 42.960, p < 0.001).

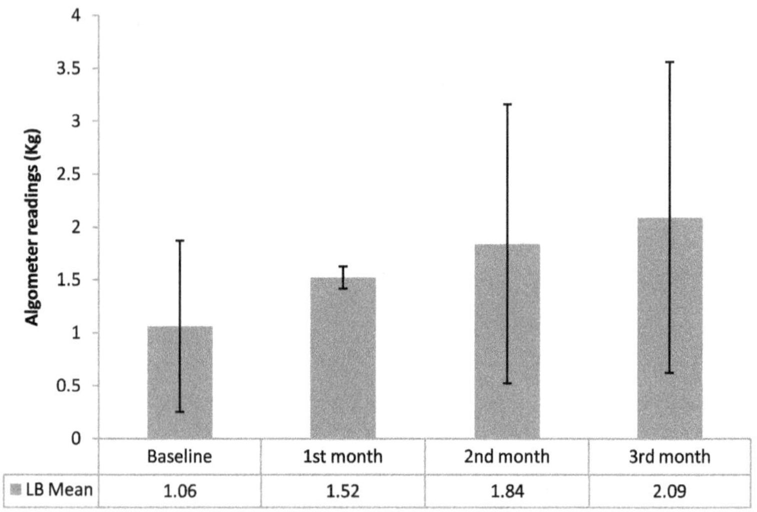

Figure 4.2.24: The Mean and SD on algometer measurement in Lower Back point

Table 4.2.24.1: Pair-wise comparison of algometric measurement of widespread pain index point on Lower Leg Left (ULL) variable from Baseline to Third month at different time frame

Time frame	n	Mean difference	Standard Error	P	95% CI [b] Lower bound	Upper bound
Baseline – 1 month		0.45[*]	0.08	< 0.01	0.62	0.28
1 month – 2 month	30	0.77[*]	0.12	< 0.01	1.02	0.52
2 month – 3 month		1.02[*]	0.15	< 0.01	1.33	0.72

n = number of participants, CI = Confidence Interval

[*] = The Mean Difference is significant at the 0.05 level.

b. Adjustment for multiple comparisons: Least Significant Difference (equivalent to no adjustments).

Table 4.2.24.1 showing the pair-wise comparison of estimated marginal Mean's of pain pressure threshold of lower back point on algometer within the PHAIPT group; the Mean Difference (MD) and Standard Error (SE) on different time frame at baseline to 1st month (MD = 0.45; SE = 0.08; p < 0.01), 1st month – 2nd month (MD = 0.77; SE = 0.12; p < 0.01), and 2nd – 3rd month (MD = 1.02; SE = 0.15; P < 0.01) the result showing statistical significance (p < 0.01).

Summary of the result of Pharmacotherapy along with Integrated Physiotherapy Techniques group

The primary outcome measure FIQR revealed significant results within the group PHAIPT(p < 0.05), also other variables showed significant results on beck depression index, visual analog scale, general anxiety disorder, and short-form – 36 health survey. Furthermore, on most of the variables of widespread pain index measured by algometer for the pain pressure threshold over the shoulder girdle left, shoulder girdle right, upper arm left, upper arm right, hip buttock left, hip buttock right, lower leg left, lower leg right, chest, neck, upper back, and lower back over the tender points shown significant (p < 0.05) results. However, some of the variables demonstrated non-significant results (p > 0.05) viz. lower arm left, lower arm right, upper leg left, upper leg right, jaw left, and abdomen. Thus, it signifies that PHAIPT was effective in improving the quality of life, physical and mental health, reduction of pain, anxiety, depression, and the trigger point sensitivity.

4.3 Role of cognitive behavioral therapy along with Integrated Physiotherapy Techniques (Group-II) in Fibromyalgia

As per the study protocol, the experimental group-II (n=30) received cognitive behavioral therapy along with Integrated Physiotherapy Techniques. The total duration of intervention was similar to experimental group 1. Analysis of Variance (ANOVA) was used to compare the study variable at different level of intervention. So as to examine the role of cognitive behavioral therapy along with Integrated Physiotherapy Techniques in patients with fibromyalgia.

Table 4.3.1: Comparison of Revised Fibromyalgia Impact Questionnaire (FIQR) variable within the group-2 from Baseline to Third month

Variable	N	Mean ± SD	SE	df	F	P
FIQR (B)		51.98 ± 12.26	2.23			
FIQR (1)	30	36.93 ± 11.66	2.13	3	155.6	< 0.01*
FIQR (2)		27.54 ± 8.72	1.59			
FIQR (3)		21.80 ± 6.26	1.14			

FIQR = Revised Fibromyalgia Impact Questionnaire; **n** = Number of participants; **SD** = Standard Deviation; **SE** = Standard Error; **df** = differential frequency; **F** = Mean of the within group variances. * = The Mean score is significant at the 0.05 level.

Table 4.3.1 depicts the Mean and standard deviation for Revised Fibromyalgia Impact Questionnaire at baseline (51.98 ± 12.26), 1st month (36.93 ± 11.66), 2nd month (27.54 ± 8.72), and 3rd month (21.80 ± 6.26) in CBTAIPT group. The result showed significant difference (F = 155.6, p ≤ 0.01).

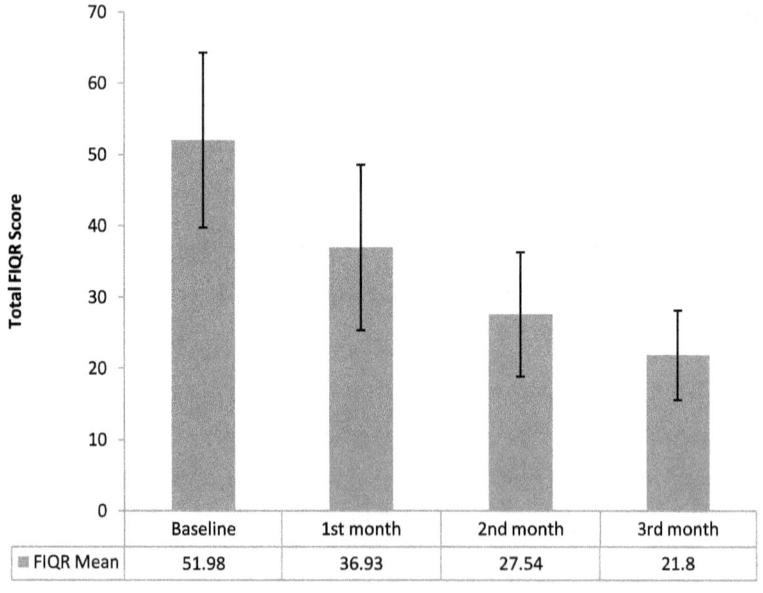

Figure 4.3.1: The Mean and SD of Revised Fibromyalgia Impact Questionnaire score from baseline to third month

Table 4.3.1.1: Pair-wise comparison of Revised Fibromyalgia Impact Questionnaire (FIQR) variable from Baseline to Third month at different time frame

Time frame	n	Mean difference	Standard Error	P	95% CI [b]	
					Lower bound	Upper bound
Baseline – 1 month		15.05*	1.02	< 0.01	12.95	17.15
1 month – 2 month	30	24.34*	1.65	< 0.01	21.06	27.82
2 month – 3 month		30.18*	1.95	< 0.01	26.17	34.18

Based on estimated marginal means

n = number of participants, CI = Confidence Interval

*= The mean difference is significant at the 0.05 level.

b. Adjustment for multiple comparisons: Least Significant Difference (equivalent to no adjustments).

Table 4.3.1.1 showing the pair-wise comparison of Revised Fibromyalgia Impact Questionnaire score Mean Difference (MD) and Standard Error (SE) on different time frame at baseline to 1st month (MD = 15.05; SE = 1.02; $p \leq 0.01$), 1st month – 2nd month (MD = 24.34; SE = 1.65; $p \leq 0.01$), and 2nd – 3rd month (MD = 30.18; SE = 1.95; $P \leq 0.01$) the result showing statistical significance ($p \leq 0.05$).

Table 4.3.2: Comparison of Beck Depression Index (BDI) variable within the group-2 from Baseline to Third month

Variable	N	Mean ± SD	SE	df	F	P
BDI (B)		31.37 ± 13.01	2.37			
BDI (1)	30	24.60 ± 12.79	2.33	3	80.92	< 0.01*
BDI (2)		16.07 ± 9.00	1.64			
BDI (3)		12.17 ± 7.58	1.38			

BDI = Beck Depression Index; **n** = Number of participants; **SD** = Standard Deviation; **SE** = Standard Error; **df** = differential frequency; **F** = Mean of the within group variances. * = The Mean score is significant at the 0.05 level.

Table 4.3.2 depicts the mean and standard deviation for Beck Depression Index at baseline (31.37 ± 13.01), 1st month (24.60 ± 12.79), 2nd month (16.07 ± 9.00), and 3rd month (12.17 ± 7.58) in CBTAIPT group. The result showed significant difference (F = 80.92, $p \leq 0.01$).

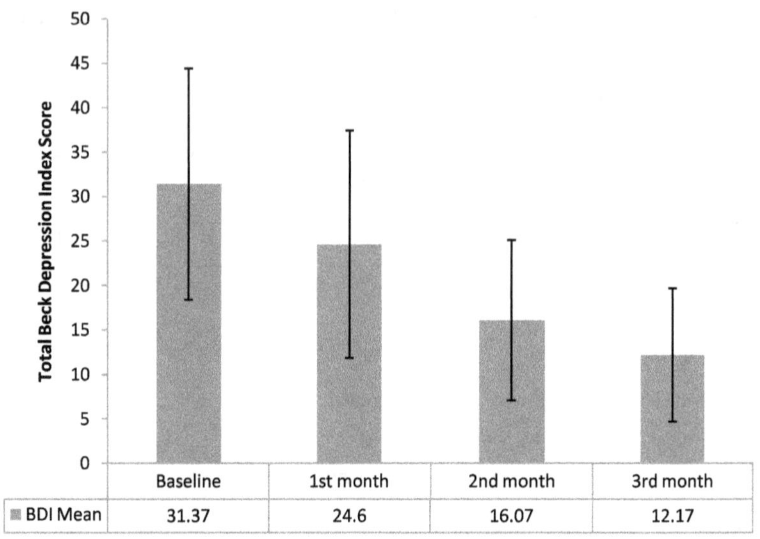

Figure 4.3.2: The Mean and SD of Beck Depression Index score from baseline to third month

Table 4.3.2.1: Pair-wise comparison of Beck Depression Index (BDI) variable from Baseline to Third month at different time frame

Time frame	n	Mean difference	Standard Error	P	95% CI [b]	
					Lower bound	Upper bound
Baseline – 1 month		6.76[*]	0.97	< 0.01	4.77	8.75
1 month – 2 month	30	15.30[*]	1.36	< 0.01	12.51	18.08
2 month – 3 month		19.20[*]	1.78	< 0.01	15.54	22.85

n = number of participants, CI = Confidence Interval

[*] The mean difference is significant at the 0.05 level.

b. Adjustment for multiple comparisons: Least Significant Difference (equivalent to no adjustments).

Table 4.3.2.1 showing the pair-wise comparison of Mean Difference (MD) and Standard Error (SE) on different time frame at baseline to 1st month (MD = 6.76; SE = 0.97; p ≤ 0.01), 1st month – 2nd month (MD = 15.30; SE = 1.36; p ≤ 0.01), and 2nd – 3rd month (MD = 19.20; SE = 1.78; P ≤ 0.01) the result showing statistical significance (p ≤ 0.01).

Table 4.3.3: Comparison of Visual Analogue Scale (VAS) variable within the group-2 from Baseline to Third month

Variable	n	Mean ± SD	SE	df	F	P
VAS (B)		8.43 ± 1.19	0.21			
VAS (1)	30	5.17 ± 1.68	0.30	3	317.7	< 0.01*
VAS (2)		3.10 ± 1.76	0.32			
VAS (3)		2.07 ± 1.43	0.26			

VAS = Visual Analogue Scale; **n** = Number of participants; **SD** = Standard Deviation; **SE** = Standard Error; **df** = differential frequency; **F** = Mean of the within group variances. * = The Mean score is significant at the 0.05 level.

Table 4.3.3 depicts the mean and standard deviation for Visual Analogue Scale at baseline (8.43 ± 1.19), 1st month (5.17 ± 1.68), 2nd month (3.10 ± 1.76), and 3rd month (2.07 ± 1.43) in CBTAIPT group. The result showed significant difference ($F = 317.7$, $p \leq 0.01$).

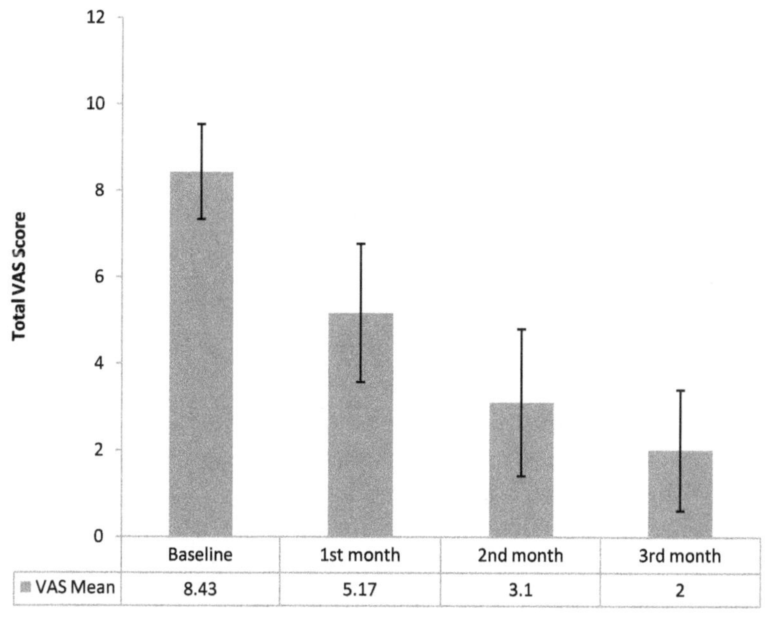

Figure 4.3.3: The Mean and SD of Visual Analogue Scale score from baseline to third month

Table 4.3.3.1: Pair-wise comparison of Visual Analogue Scale (VAS) variable from Baseline to Third month at different time frame

Time frame	n	Mean difference	Standard Error	P	95% CI [b]	
					Lower bound	Upper bound
Baseline – 1 month		3.26[*]	0.21	< 0.01	2.81	3.71
1 month – 2 month	30	5.33[*]	0.26	< 0.01	4.79	5.87
2 month – 3 month		6.36[*]	0.21	< 0.01	5.93	6.80

Based on estimated marginal means

n = number of participants, CI = Confidence Interval

[*] The mean difference is significant at the 0.05 level.

b. Adjustment for multiple comparisons: Least Significant Difference (equivalent to no adjustments).

Table 4.3.3.1 showing the pair-wise comparison of Mean Difference (MD) and Standard Error (SE) on different time frame at baseline to 1st month (MD = 3.26; SE = 0.21; $p \leq 0.01$), 1st month – 2nd month (MD = 5.33; SE = 0.26; $p \leq 0.01$), and 2nd – 3rd month (MD = 6.36; SE = 0.21; $P \leq 0.01$) the result showing statistical significance ($p \leq 0.01$).

Table 4.3.4: Comparison of General Anxiety Disorder (GAD-7) variable within the group-2 from Baseline to Third month

Variable	n	Mean ± SD	SE	df	F	P
GAD - 7 (B)		15.33 ± 4.09	0.74			
GAD - 7 (1)	30	12.23 ± 4.28	0.78	3	42.01	< 0.01*
GAD - 7 (2)		10.53 ± 4.59	0.84			
GAD - 7 (3)		9.17 ± 3.79	0.69			

GAD - 7 = General Anxiety Disorder – 7 Scale; **n** = Number of participants; **SD** = Standard Deviation; **SE** = Standard Error; **df** = differential frequency; **F** = Mean of the within group variances. * = The Mean score is significant at the 0.05 level.

Table 4.3.4 depicts the mean and standard deviation for General Anxiety Disorder at baseline (15.33 ± 4.09), 1st month (12.23 ± 4.28), 2nd month (10.53 ± 4.59), and 3rd month (9.17 ± 3.79) in CBTAIPT group. The result showed significant difference (F = 42.01, $p \leq 0.01$).

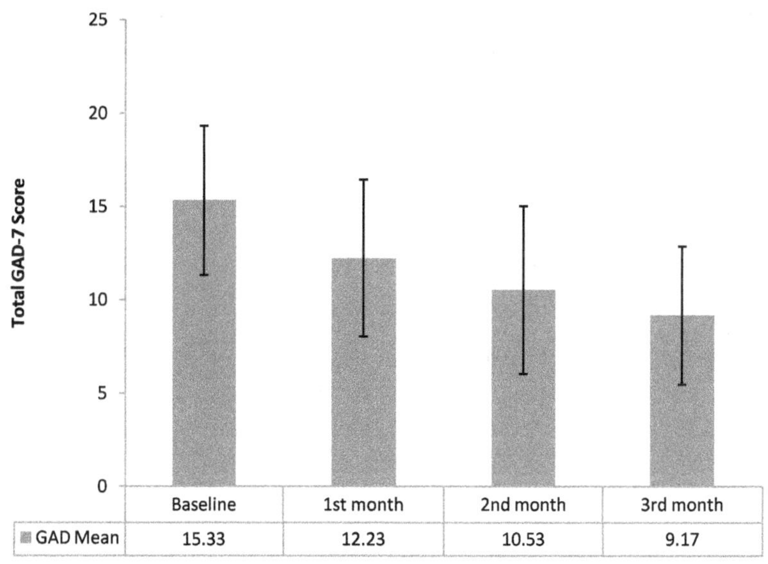

Figure 4.3.4: The Mean and SD of General Anxiety Disorder Score from baseline to third month

Table 4.3.4.1: Pair-wise comparison of General Anxiety Disorder (GAD-7) variable from Baseline to Third month at different time frame

Time frame	n	Mean difference	Standard Error	P	95% CI [b]	
					Lower bound	Upper bound
Baseline – 1 month		3.10[*]	0.35	< 0.01	2.37	3.83
1 month – 2 month	30	4.80[*]	0.65	< 0.01	3.45	6.14
2 month – 3 month		6.16[*]	0.64	< 0.01	4.85	7.48

n = number of participants, CI = Confidence Interval; [*] The mean difference is significant at the 0.05 level; b. Adjustment for multiple comparisons: Least Significant Difference (equivalent to no adjustments).

Table 4.3.4.1 showing the pair-wise comparison of Mean Difference (MD) and Standard Error (SE) on different time frame at baseline to 1st month (MD = 3.10; SE = 0.35; p = < 0.01), 1st month – 2nd month (MD = 4.80; SE = 0.65; $p \leq 0.01$), and 2nd – 3rd month (MD = 6.16; SE = 0.64; $P \leq 0.01$) the result showing statistical significance ($p \leq 0.01$).

131

Table 4.3.5: Comparison of Short Form-36 Physical Component Summary (SF-36 PCS) variable within the group-2 from Baseline to Third month

Variable	n	Mean ± SD	SE	df	F	P
SF - 36 PCS (B)		28.06 ± 15.49	2.83			
SF - 36 PCS (1)	30	47.09 ± 21.34	3.89	3	94.80	< 0.01*
SF - 36 PCS (2)		64.21 ± 18.16	3.31			
SF - 36 PCS (3)		72.73 ± 17.85	3.25			

SF - 36 PCS = Short Form – 36 Physical Component Summary; **n** = Number of participants; **SD** = Standard Deviation; **SE** = Standard Error; **df** = differential frequency; **F** = Mean of the within group variances. * = The Mean score is significant at the 0.05 level.

Table 4.3.5 depicts the mean and standard deviation for Short Form-36 Physical Component Summary at baseline (28.06 ± 15.49), 1st month (47.09 ± 21.34), 2nd month (64.21 ± 18.16), and 3rd month (72.73 ± 17.85) in CBTAIPT group. The result showed significant difference (F = 94.80, p ≤ 0.01).

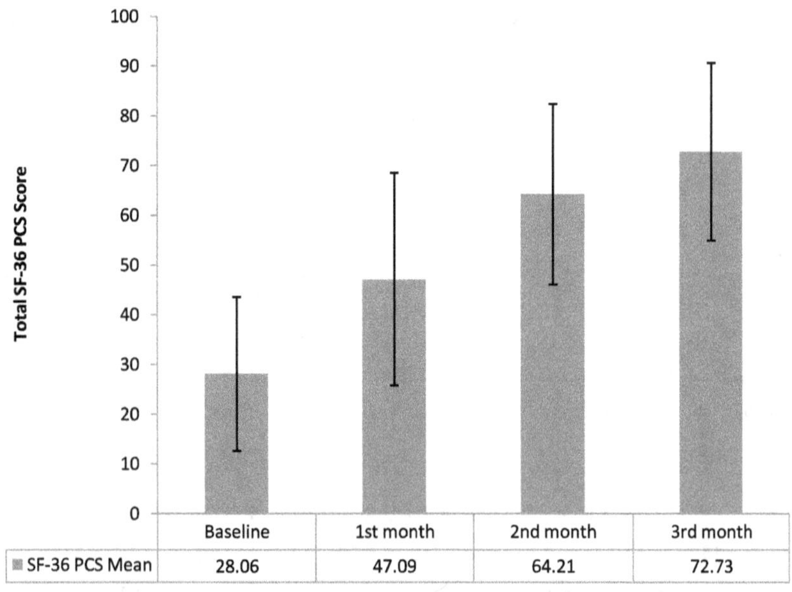

Figure 4.3.5: The Mean and SD of Short Form-36 Physical Component Summary score from baseline to third month

Table 4.3.5.1: Pair-wise comparison of Short Form-36 Physical Component Summary (SF-36 PCS) variable from Baseline to Third month at different time frame

Time frame	n	Mean difference	Standard Error	P	95% CI [b]	
					Lower bound	Upper bound
Baseline – 1 month		19.03*	2.78	< 0.01	24.73	13.33
1 month – 2 month	30	36.15*	3.21	< 0.01	42.72	29.58
2 month – 3 month		44.66*	3.30	< 0.01	51.43	37.90

n = number of participants, CI = Confidence Interval

*= The mean difference is significant at the 0.05 level.

b. Adjustment for multiple comparisons: Least Significant Difference (equivalent to no adjustments).

Table 4.3.5.1 showing the pair-wise comparison of Mean Difference (MD) and Standard Error (SE) on different time frame at baseline to 1st month (MD = 19.03; SE = 2.78; $p \leq 0.01$), 1st month – 2nd month (MD = 36.15; SE = 3.21; $p \leq 0.01$), and 2nd – 3rd month (MD = 44.66; SE = 3.30; $P \leq 0.01$) the result showing statistical significance ($p \leq 0.01$).

Table 4.3.6: Comparison of Short Form-36 Mental Component Summary (SF-36 MCS) variable within the group-2 from Baseline to Third month

Variable	n	Mean ± SD	SE	df	F	P
SF - 36 MCS (B)		28.06 ± 18.50	3.37			
SF - 36 MCS (1)	30	47.09 ± 20.53	3.74	3	65.24	< 0.01*
SF - 36 MCS (2)		64.21 ± 17.83	3.25			
SF - 36 MCS (3)		72.73 ± 15.37	2.80			

SF - 36 MCS = Short Form – 36 Mental Component Summary; **n** = Number of participants; **SD** = Standard Deviation; **SE** = Standard Error; **df** = differential frequency; **F** = Mean of the within group variances. * = The Mean score is Non-significant at the 0.05 level.

Table 4.3.6 depicts the mean and standard deviation for Short Form-36 Mental Component Summary at baseline (28.06 ± 18.50), 1st month (47.09 ± 20.53), 2nd month (64.21 ± 17.83), and 3rd month (72.73 ± 15.37) in CBTAIPT group. The result showed significant difference (F = 65.24, $p \leq 0.01$).

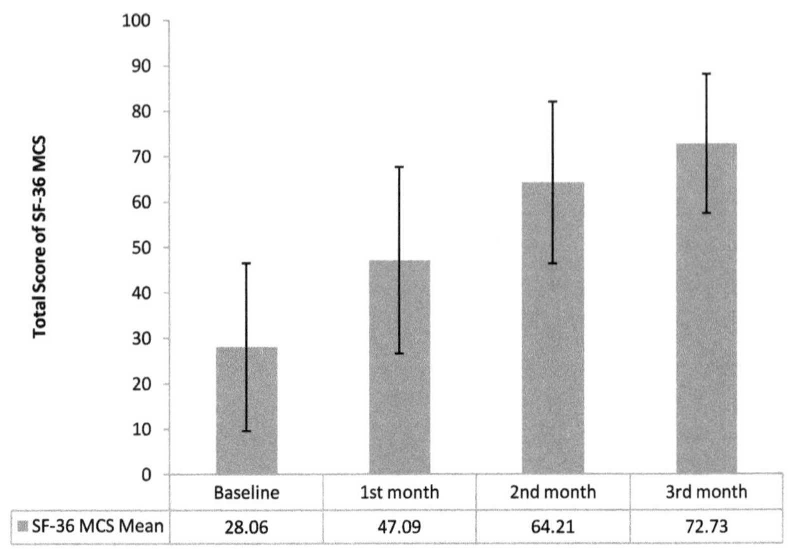

Figure 4.3.6: The Mean and SD of Short Form-36 Mental Component Summary score from baseline to third month

Table 4.3.6.1: Pair-wise comparison of Short Form-36 Mental Component Summary (SF-36 MCS) variable from Baseline to Third month at different time frame

Time frame	n	Mean difference	Standard Error	P	95% CI [b]	
					Lower bound	Upper bound
Baseline – 1 month		14.78[*]	2.25	< 0.01	19.40	10.17
1 month – 2 month	30	30.84[*]	3.50	< 0.01	38.01	23.66
2 month – 3 month		38.13[*]	3.51	< 0.01	45.32	30.93

n = number of participants, CI = Confidence Interval; [*] = The mean difference is significant at the 0.05 level. b. Adjustment for multiple comparisons: Least Significant Difference (equivalent to no adjustments).

Table 4.3.6.1 showing the pair-wise comparison of Mean Difference (MD) and Standard Error (SE) on different time frame at baseline to 1st month (MD = 14.78; SE = 2.25; $p \leq 0.01$), 1st month – 2nd month (MD = 30.84; SE = 3.50; $p \leq 0.01$), and 2nd – 3rd month (MD = 38.13; SE = 3.51; $P \leq 0.01$) the result showing statistical significance ($p \leq 0.01$).

Table 4.3.7: Comparison of Shoulder Girdle Left (SGL) variable within the group-2 from Baseline to Third month

Variable	n	Mean ± SD	SE	df	F	P
SGL (B)		1.15 ± 0.67	0.12			
SGL (1)	30	1.59 ± 0.85	0.15	3	80.32	< 0.01*
SGL (2)		1.98 ± 0.96	0.17			
SGL (3)		2.40 ± 1.13	0.20			

SGL = Shoulder Girdle Left; **n** = Number of participants; **SD** = Standard Deviation; **SE** = Standard Error; **df** = differential frequency; **F** = Mean of the within group variances; * = The Mean score is significant at the 0.05 level.

Table 4.3.7 depicts the comparison of Mean and standard deviation within the group for pain pressure threshold of shoulder girdle left side point on algometer at Baseline (1.15 ± 0.67), 1st month (1.59 ± 0.85), 2nd Month (1.98 ± 0.96), and 3rd month (2.40 ± 1.13) in CBTAIPT group. The result showed significant difference (F = 80.32, $p \leq 0.01$).

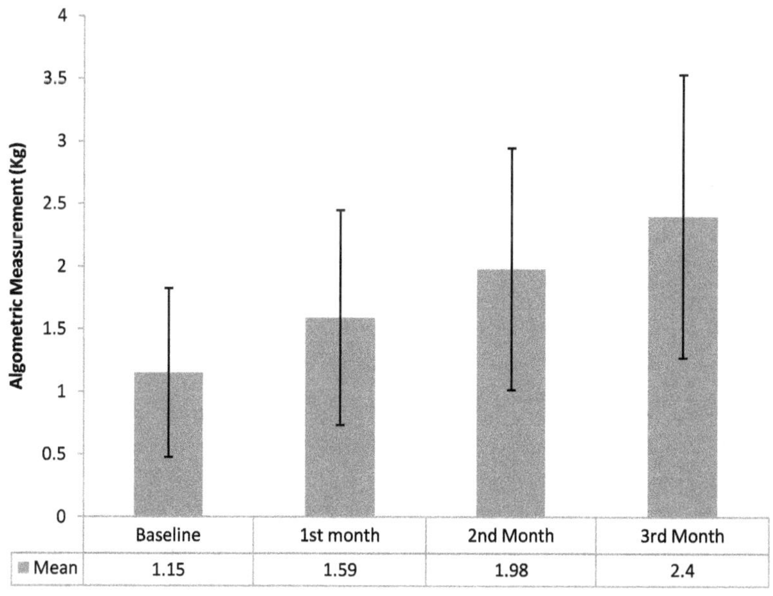

Figure 4.3.7: The Mean and SD of Shoulder Girdle Left from baseline to third month

Table 4.3.7.1: Pair-wise comparison of Shoulder Girdle Left (SGL) variable from Baseline to Third month at different time frame

Time frame	n	Mean difference	Standard Error	P	95% CI [b]	
					Lower bound	Upper bound
Baseline – 1 month		0.43[*]	0.07	< 0.01	0.58	0.29
1 month – 2 month	30	0.82[*]	0.09	< 0.01	1.02	0.63
2 month – 3 month		1.24[*]	0.12	< 0.01	1.50	0.99

Based on estimated marginal means

n = number of participants, CI = Confidence Interval

* = The mean difference is significant at the 0.05 level.

b. Adjustment for multiple comparisons: Least Significant Difference (equivalent to no adjustments).

Table 4.3.7.1 showing the pair-wise comparison of Mean Difference (MD) and Standard Error (SE) on different time frame at baseline to 1st month (MD = 0.43; SE = 0.07; $p \leq 0.01$), 1st month – 2nd month (MD = 0.82; SE = 0.09; $p \leq 0.01$), and 2nd – 3rd month (MD = 1.24; SE = 0.12; $p \leq 0.01$) the result showing statistical significance ($p \leq 0.01$). Same findings are presented in Figure.

Table 4.3.8: Comparison of Shoulder Girdle Right (SGR) variable within the group-2 from Baseline to Third month

Variable	n	Mean ± SD	SE	df	F	P
SGR (B)		1.07 ± 0.73	0.13			
SGR (1)	30	1.49 ± 0.81	0.15	3	70.02	< 0.01*
SGR (2)		1.86 ± 0.94	0.17			
SGR (3)		2.29 ± 1.14	0.21			

SGR = Shoulder Girdle Right; n = Number of participants; SD = Standard Deviation; SE = Standard Error; df = differential frequency; F = Mean of the within group variances. * = The Mean score is significant at the 0.05 level.

Table 4.3.8 depicts the Mean and standard deviation for pain pressure threshold of shoulder girdle right side point on algometer at Baseline (1.07 ± 0.73), 1st month (1.49 ± 0.81), 2nd Month (1.86 ± 0.94), and 3rd month (2.29 ± 1.14) in CBTAIPT group. The result showed significant difference (F = 70.02, $p \leq 0.01$).

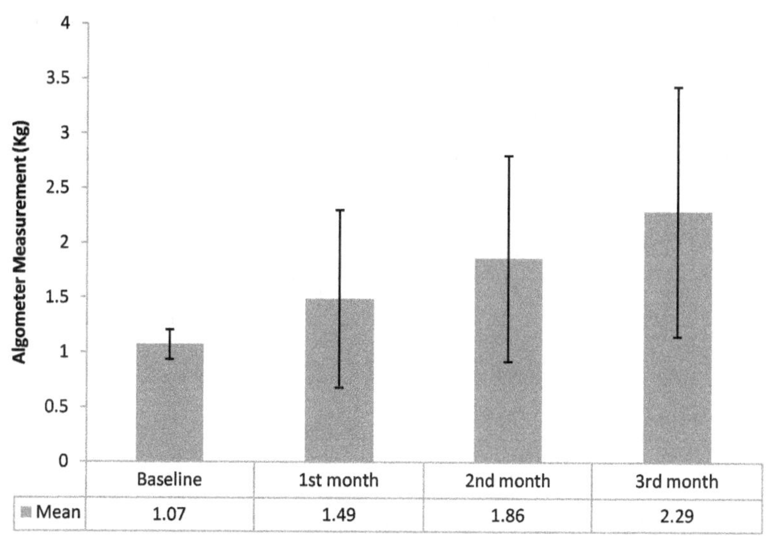

Figure 4.3.8: The Mean and SD of Shoulder Girdle Right from baseline to third month

Table 4.3.8.1: Pair-wise comparison of Shoulder Girdle Right (SGR) variable from Baseline to Third month at different time frame

Time frame	n	Mean difference	Standard Error	P	95% CI [b]	
					Lower bound	Upper bound
Baseline – 1 month		0.43[*]	0.07	< 0.01	0.58	0 .29
1 month – 2 month	30	0.82[*]	0.09	< 0.01	1.02	0 .63
2 month – 3 month		1.24[*]	0.12	< 0.01	1.50	0 .99

Based on estimated marginal means

n = number of participants, CI = Confidence Interval

* = The mean difference is significant at the 0.05 level.

b. Adjustment for multiple comparisons: Least Significant Difference (equivalent to no adjustments).

Table 4.3.8.1 showing the pair-wise comparison of Mean Difference (MD) and Standard Error (SE) on different time frame at baseline to 1st month (MD = 0.49; SE = 0.05; p $\leq$ 0.01), 1st month – 2nd month (MD = 0.97; SE = 0.08; p $\leq$ 0.01), and 2nd – 3rd month (MD = 1.38; SE = 0.09; p $\leq$ 0.01) the result showing statistical significance (p $\leq$ 0.01). Same findings are presented in Figure.

Table 4.3.9: Comparison of Upper Arm Left (UAL) variable within the group-2 from Baseline to Third month

Variable	n	Mean ± SD	SE	df	F	P
UAL (B)		0.23 ± 0.62	0.11			
UAL (1)	30	0.29 ± 0.76	0.14	3	4.29	< 0.05*
UAL (2)		0.35 ± 0.93	0.17			
UAL (3)		0.39 ± 1.02	0.18			
UAL = Upper Arm Left; n = Number of participants; SD = Standard Deviation; SE = Standard Error; df = differential frequency; F = Mean of the within group variances. * = The Mean score is significant at the 0.05 level.						

Table 4.3.9 depicts the Mean and standard deviation for pain pressure threshold of upper arm leftt side point on algometer at Baseline (0.23 ± 0.62), 1st month (0.29 ± 0.76), 2nd Month (0.35 ± 0.93), and 3rd month (0.39 ± 1.02) in CBTAIPT group. The result showed significant difference (F = 4.29, p $\leq$ 0.05).

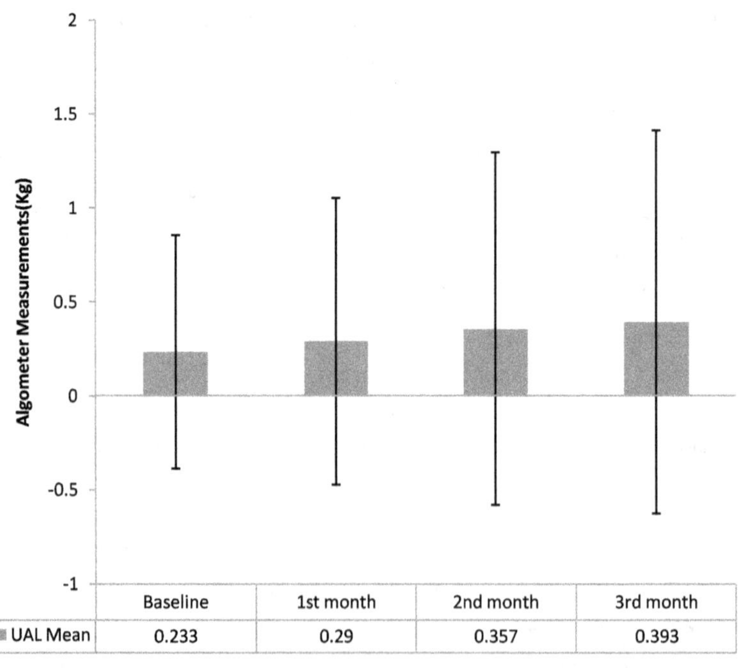

Figure 4.3.9: The Mean and SD of Upper Arm Left from baseline to third month

Table 4.3.9.1: Pair-wise comparison of Upper Arm Left (UAL) variable from Baseline to Third month at different time frame

Time frame	n	Mean difference	Standard Error	P	95% CI [b]	
					Lower bound	Upper bound
Baseline – 1 month		0.05[#]	0.02	0.06	0.11	0.00
1 month – 2 month	30	0.12[*]	0.05	0.04	0.24	0.00
2 month – 3 month		0.16[*]	0.07	0.04	0.31	0.00
Based on estimated marginal means						
n = number of participants, CI = Confidence Interval						
* = The mean difference is significant at the 0.05 level and [#] = Non- Significant.						
b. Adjustment for multiple comparisons: Least Significant Difference (equivalent to no adjustments).						

Table 4.3.9.1 showing the pair-wise comparison of Mean Difference (MD) and Standard Error (SE) on different time frame at baseline to 1st month (MD = 0.05; SE = 0.02; p = 0.06), 1st month – 2nd month (MD = 0.12; SE = 0.05; p = 0.04), and 2nd – 3rd month (MD = 0.16; SE = 0.07; P = 0.04) the result showing statistical significance ($p \leq 0.05$).

Table 4.3.10: Comparison of Upper Arm Right (UAR) variable within the group-2 from Baseline to Third month

Variable	n	Mean ± SD	SE	df	F	P
UAR (B)		0.32 ± 0.80	0.11			
UAR (1)		0.39 ± 0.93	0.14			
UAR (2)	30	0.49 ± 1.20	0.17	3	4.36	< 0.05*
UAR (3)		0.59 ± 1.44	0.18			
UAR = Upper Arm Right; n = Number of participants; SD = Standard Deviation; SE = Standard Error; df = differential frequency; F = Mean of the within group variances. * = The Mean score is significant at the 0.05 level.						

Table 4.3.10 depicts the Mean and standard deviation for pain pressure threshold of upper arm right side point on algometer at Baseline (0.32 ± 0.80), 1st month (0.39 ± 0.93), 2nd Month (0.49 ± 1.20), and 3rd month (0.59 ± 1.44) in CBTAIPT group. The result showed significant difference (F = 4.36, $p \leq 0.05$).

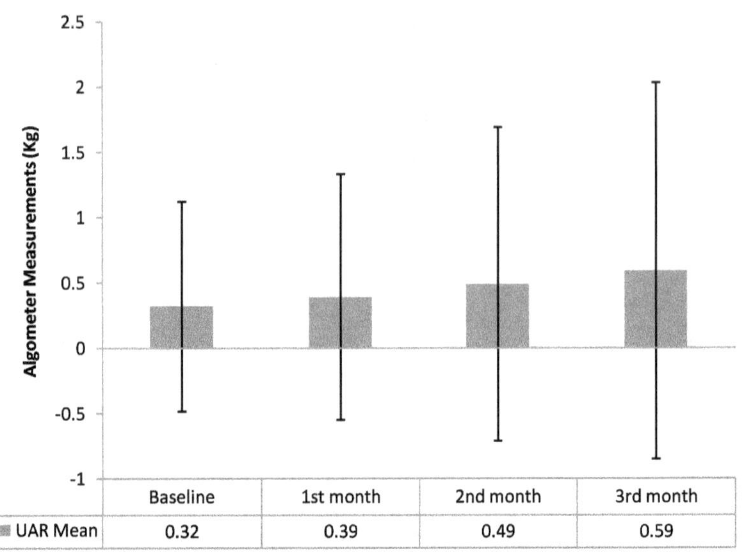

	Baseline	1st month	2nd month	3rd month
▦ UAR Mean	0.32	0.39	0.49	0.59

Figure 4.3.10: The Mean and SD of Upper Arm Right from baseline to third month

Table 4.3.10.1: Pair-wise comparison of Upper Arm Right (UAR) variable from Baseline to Third month at different time frame

Time frame	n	Mean difference	Standard Error	P	95% CI [b]	
					Lower bound	Upper bound
Baseline – 1 month		0.06[*]	0.02	0.03	0.12	0.00
1 month – 2 month	30	0.16[*]	0.07	0.03	0.31	0.00
2 month – 3 month		0.26[*]	0.12	0.03	0.51	0.01

Based on estimated marginal means

n = number of participants, CI = Confidence Interval

* = The mean difference is significant at the 0.05 level.

b. Adjustment for multiple comparisons: Least Significant Difference (equivalent to no adjustments).

Table 4.3.10.1 showing the pair-wise comparison of Mean Difference (MD) and Standard Error (SE) on different time frame at baseline to 1st month (MD = 0.06; SE = 0.02; p = 0.03), 1st month – 2nd month (MD = 0.16; SE = 0.07; p = 0.03), and 2nd – 3rd month (MD = -0.263; SE = 0.121; P = 0.038) the result showing statistical significance ($p \leq 0.05$).

Table 4.3.11: Comparison of Lower Arm Left (LAL) variable within the group-2 from Baseline to Third month

Variable	n	Mean ± SD	SE	df	F	P
LAL (B)		0.26 ± 0.81	0.14			
LAL (1)	30	0.35 ± 0.08	0.19	3	2.87	> 0.05[#]
LAL (2)		0.38 ± 1.18	0.21			
LAL (3)		0.41 ± 1.27	0.23			
LAL = Lower Arm Left; n = Number of participants; SD = Standard Deviation; SE = Standard Error; df = differential frequency; F = Mean of the within group variances. # NS = The Mean score is Non-significant at the 0.05 level.						

Table 4.3.11 depicts the Mean and standard deviation for pain pressure threshold of lower arm left side point on algometer at Baseline (0.26 ± 0.81), 1st month (0.35 ± 0.08), 2nd Month (0.38 ± 1.18), and 3rd month (0.41 ± 1.27) in CBTAIPT group. The result showed significant difference (F = 2.87, p > 0.05).

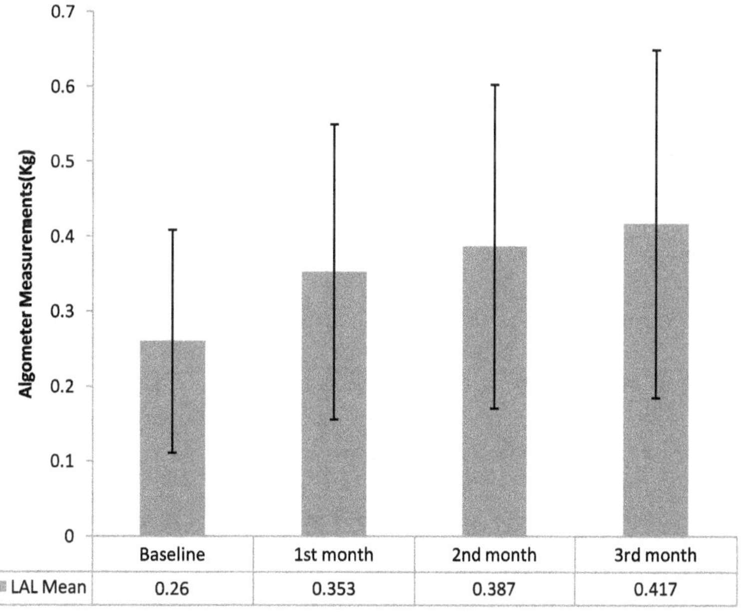

Figure 4.3.11: The Mean and SD of Lower Arm Left from baseline to third month

Table 4.3.11.1: Pair-wise comparison of Lower Arm Left (LAL) variable from Baseline to Third month at different time frame

Time frame	n	Mean difference	Standard Error	P	95% CI [b]	
					Lower bound	Upper bound
Baseline – 1 month		0.09[#]	0.05	0.10	0.20	0.02
1 month – 2 month	30	0.12[#]	0.07	0.10	0.28	0.02
2 month – 3 month		0.15[#]	0.09	0.09	0.34	0.03

Based on estimated marginal means

n = number of participants, CI = Confidence Interval

[#]. The mean difference is non-significant at the 0.05 level.

b. Adjustment for multiple comparisons: Least Significant Difference (equivalent to no adjustments).

Table 4.3.11.1 showing the pair-wise comparison of Mean Difference (MD) and Standard Error (SE) on different time frame at baseline to 1st month (MD = 0.09; SE = 0.05; p = 0.10), 1st month – 2nd month (MD = 0.12; SE = 0.07; p = 0.10), and 2nd – 3rd month (MD = 0.15; SE = 0.09; P = 0.09) the result showing statistical significance ($p > 0.05$).

Table 4.3.12: Comparison of Lower Arm Right (LAR) variable within the group-2 from Baseline to Third month

Variable	n	Mean ± SD	SE	df	F	P
LAR (B)		0.20 ± 0.59	0.10			
LAR (1)		0.29 ± 0.83	0.15			
LAR (2)	30	0.35 ± 0.99	0.18	3	3.76	> 0.05[#]
LAR (3)		0.43 ± 1.20	0.22			

LAR = Lower Arm Right; n = Number of participants; SD = Standard Deviation; SE = Standard Error; df = differential frequency; F = Mean of the within group variances. # NS = The Mean score is Non-significant at the 0.05 level.

Table 4.3.12 depicts the Mean and standard deviation for pain pressure threshold of lower arm right side point on algometer at Baseline (0.20 ± 0.59), 1st month (0.29 ± 0.83), 2nd Month (0.35 ± 0.99), and 3rd month (0.43 ± 1.20) in CBTAIPT group. The result showed significant difference (F = 3.76, $p > 0.05$).

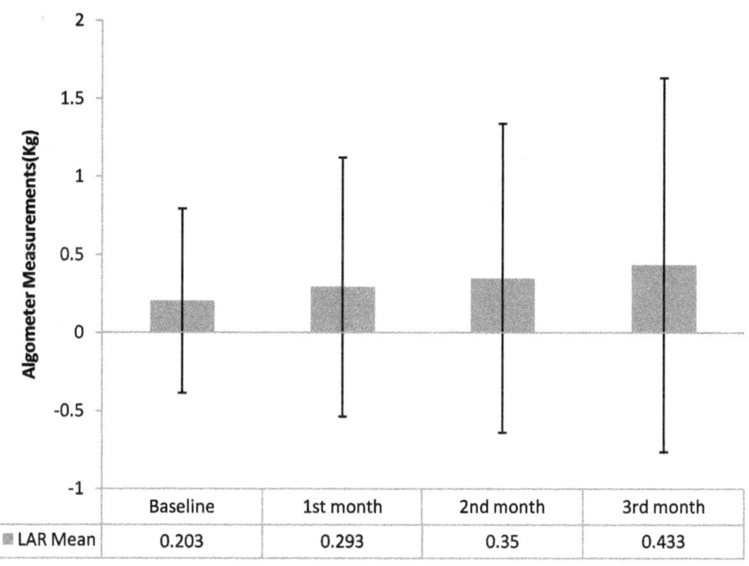

Figure 4.3.12: The Mean and SD of Lower Arm Right from baseline to third month

Table 4.3.12.1: Pair-wise comparison of Lower Arm Right (LAR) variable from Baseline to Third month at different time frame

Time frame	n	Mean difference	Standard Error	P	95% CI [b]	
					Lower bound	Upper bound
Baseline – 1 month		0.09[#]	0.04	0.06	0.18	0.00
1 month – 2 month	30	0.14*	0.07	0.05	0.29	0.00
2 month – 3 month		0.23*	0.11	0.05	0.46	0.00

n = number of participants, CI = Confidence Interval

[#]. The mean difference is non-significant at the 0.05 level; b. Adjustment for multiple comparisons: Least Significant Difference (equivalent to no adjustments).

Table 4.3.12.1 showing the pair-wise comparison of Mean Difference (MD) and Standard Error (SE) on different time frame at baseline to 1st month (MD = 0.09; SE = 0.04; p = 0.06), 1st month – 2nd month (MD = 0.14; SE = 0.07; p = 0.05), and 2nd – 3rd month (MD = 0.23; SE = 0.11; P = 0.05) the result showing statistical significance (p = 0.05).

Table 4.3.13: Comparison of Hip Buttock Left [H (B) L] variable within the group-2 from Baseline to Third month

Variable	N	Mean ± SD	SE	df	F	P
HBL (B)		1.39 ± 1.14	0.20			
HBL (1)	30	1.69 ± 1.38	0.25	3	33.46	< 0.01*
HBL (2)		1.92 ± 1.52	0.27			
HBL (3)		2.16 ± 1.69	0.30			

HBL = Hip Buttock Left; n = Number of participants; SD = Standard Deviation; SE = Standard Error; df = differential frequency; F = Mean of the within group variances; * = The Mean score is significant at the 0.05 level.

Table 4.3.13 depicts the mean and standard deviation for pain pressure threshold of hip buttock left side point on algometer at baseline (1.39 ± 1.14), 1st month (1.69 ± 1.38), 2nd month (1.92 ± 1.52), and 3rd month (2.16 ± 1.69) in CBTAIPT group. The result showed significant difference (F = 33.46, p ≤ 0.01).

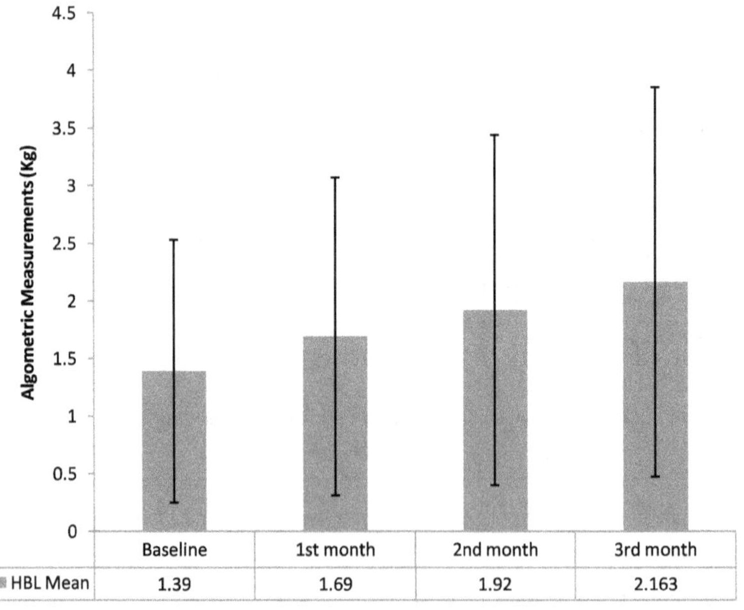

Figure 4.3.13: The Mean and SD of Hip Buttock Left from baseline to third month

Table 4.3.13.1: Pair-wise comparison of Hip Buttock Left (H (B) L) variable from Baseline to Third month at different time frame

Time frame	n	Mean difference	Standard Error	P	95% CI [b]	
					Lower bound	Upper bound
Baseline – 1 month		0.29[*]	0.06	< 0.01	0.42	0.16
1 month – 2 month	30	0.52[*]	0.08	< 0.01	0.70	0.34
2 month – 3 month		0.76[*]	0.11	< 0.01	1.00	0.53

n = number of participants, CI = Confidence Interval

[*] = The mean difference is significant at the 0.05 level.

b. Adjustment for multiple comparisons: Least Significant Difference (equivalent to no adjustments).

Table **4.3.13.1** showing the pair-wise comparison of Mean Difference (MD) and Standard Error (SE) on different time frame at baseline to 1st month (MD = 0.29; SE = 0.06; p = < 0.01), 1st month – 2nd month (MD = 0.52; SE = 0.08; p = < 0.01), and 2nd – 3rd month (MD = 0.76; SE = 0.11; P = < 0.01) the result showing statistical significance (p $\leq$ 0.01).

Table 4.3.14: Comparison of Hip Buttock Right [H (B) R] variable within the group-2 from Baseline to Third month

Variable	n	Mean ± SD	SE	df	F	P
HBR (B)		1.29 ± 1.10	0.20			
HBR (1)	30	1.56 ± 1.28	0.23	3	37.71	< 0.01
HBR (2)		1.82 ± 1.50	0.27			
HBR (3)		2.08 ± 1.67	0.30			

HBR = Hip Buttock Right; n = Number of participants; SD = Standard Deviation; SE = Standard Error; df = differential frequency; F = Mean of the within group variances. * = The Mean score is significant at the 0.05 level.

Table **4.3.14** depicts the mean and standard deviation for pain pressure threshold of hip buttock right side point on algometer at baseline (1.29 ± 1.10), 1st month (1.56 ± 1.28), 2nd month (1.82 ± 1.50), and 3rd month (2.08 ± 1.67) in CBTAIPT group. The result showed significant difference (F = 37.71, p $\leq$ 0.01).

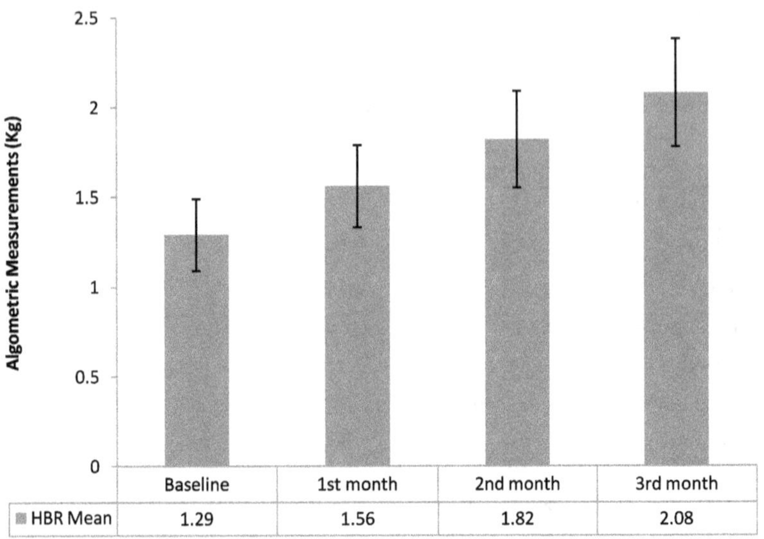

Figure 4.3.14: The Mean and SD of Hip Buttock Right from baseline to third month

Table 4.3.14.1: Pair-wise comparison of Hip Buttock Right (H (B) R) variable from Baseline to Third month at different time frame

Time frame	n	Mean difference	Standard Error	P	95% CI [b]	
					Lower bound	Upper bound
Baseline – 1 month		0.26[*]	0.04	< 0.01	0.36	0.16
1 month – 2 month	30	0.53[*]	0.09	< 0.01	0.71	0.34
2 month – 3 month		0.78[*]	0.12	< 0.01	1.03	0.53

n = number of participants, CI = Confidence Interval

[*] The mean difference is significant at the 0.05 level.

b. Adjustment for multiple comparisons: Least Significant Difference (equivalent to no adjustments).

Table 4.3.14.1 showing the pair-wise comparison of Mean Difference (MD) and Standard Error (SE) on different time frame at baseline to 1st month (MD = 0.26; SE = 0.04; p < 0.01), 1st month – 2nd month (MD = 0.53; SE = 0.09; p < 0.01), and 2nd – 3rd month (MD = 0.78; SE = 0.12; P < 0.01) the result showing statistical significance (p ≤ 0.01).

Table 4.3.15: Comparison of Upper Leg Left (ULL) variable within the group-2 from Baseline to Third month

Variable	n	Mean ± SD	SE	df	F	P
ULL (B)		0.12 ± 0.59	0.10			
ULL (1)	30	0.16 ± 0.66	0.12	3	1.93	> 0.05[#]
ULL (2)		0.20 ± 0.81	0.14			
ULL (3)		0.22 ± 0.87	0.16			

ULL = Upper Leg Left; n = Number of participants; SD = Standard Deviation; SE = Standard Error; df = differential frequency; F = Mean of the within group variances. # = The Mean score is Non-significant at the 0.05 level.

Table 4.3.15 depicts the mean and standard deviation for pain pressure threshold of upper limb left side point on algometer at baseline (0.12 ± 0.59), 1st month (0.16 ± 0.66), 2nd month (0.20 ± 0.81), and 3rd month (0.22 ± 0.87) in CBTAIPT group. The result showed non-significant difference (F = 1.93, p > 0.05).

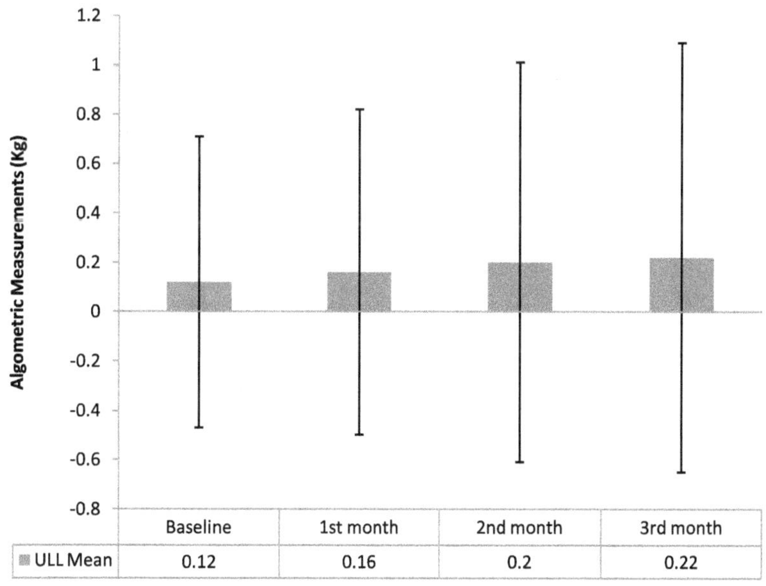

Figure 4.3.15: The Mean and SD of Upper Leg Left from baseline to third month

Table 4.3.15.1: Pair-wise comparison of Upper Leg Left (ULL) variable from Baseline to Third month at different time frame

Time frame	n	Mean difference	Standard Error	P	95% CI [b]	
					Lower bound	Upper bound
Baseline – 1 month		0.03[#]	0.02	0.23	0.08	0.02
1 month – 2 month	30	0.07[#]	0.05	0.18	0.19	0.03
2 month – 3 month		0.09[#]	0.06	0.17	0.22	0.04

n = number of participants, CI = Confidence Interval

[#]. The mean difference is non-significant at the 0.05 level.

b. Adjustment for multiple comparisons: Least Significant Difference (equivalent to no adjustments).

Table 4.3.15.1 showing the pair-wise comparison of Mean Difference (MD) and Standard Error (SE) on different time frame at baseline to 1st month (MD = 0.03; SE = 0.02; p = < 0.23), 1st month – 2nd month (MD = 0.07; SE = 0.05; p = 0.18), and 2nd – 3rd month (MD = 0.09; SE = 0.06; P = 0.17) the result showing statistical non-significance (p > 0.05).

Table 4.3.16: Comparison of Upper Leg Right (ULR) variable within the group-2 from Baseline to Third month

Variable	n	Mean ± SD	SE	df	F	P
ULR (B)		0.13 ± 0.57	0.10			
ULR (1)	30	0.15 ± 0.66	0.12	3	1.99	> 0.05[#]
ULR (2)		0.18 ± 0.74	0.13			
ULR (3)		0.20 ± 0.82	0.15			

ULR = Upper Leg Right; n = Number of participants; SD = Standard Deviation; SE = Standard Error; df = differential frequency; F = Mean of the within group variances. # = The Mean score is Non-significant at the 0.05 level.

Table 4.3.16 depicts the mean and standard deviation for pain pressure threshold of upper limb right side point on algometer at baseline (0.13 ± 0.57), 1st month (0.15 ± 0.66), 2nd month (0.18 ± 0.74), and 3rd month (0.20 ± 0.82) in CBTAIPT group. The result showed significant difference (F = 1.99, p > 0.05).

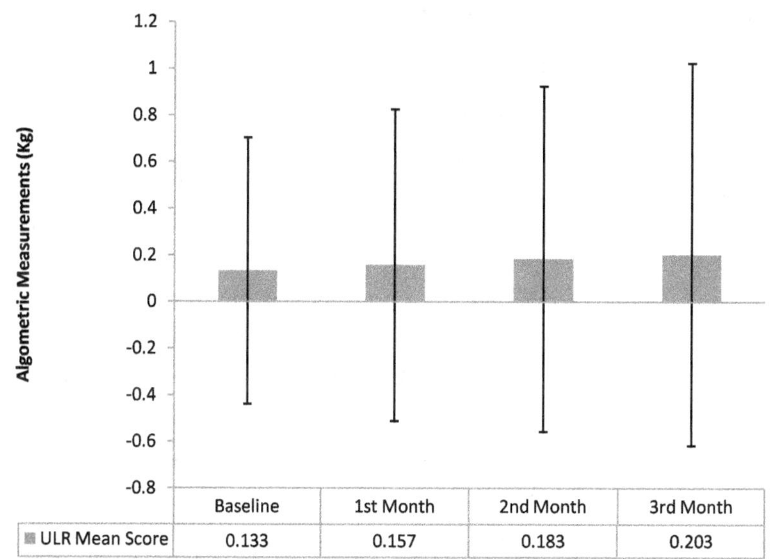

Figure 4.3.16: The Mean and SD of Upper Leg Right from baseline to third month

Table 4.3.16.1: Pair-wise comparison of Upper Leg Right (ULR) variable from Baseline to Third month at different time frame

Time frame	n	Mean difference	Standard Error	P	95% CI [b]	
					Lower bound	Upper bound
Baseline – 1 month		$0.02^{\#}$	0.01	0.19	0.06	0.01
1 month – 2 month	30	$0.05^{\#}$	0.03	0.16	0.12	0.02
2 month – 3 month		$0.07^{\#}$	0.04	0.16	0.17	0.03
Based on estimated marginal means						
n = number of participants, CI = Confidence Interval						
$^{\#}$. The mean difference is non-significant at the 0.05 level.						
b. Adjustment for multiple comparisons: Least Significant Difference (equivalent to no adjustments).						

Table 4.3.16.1 showing the pair-wise comparison of Mean Difference (MD) and Standard Error (SE) on different time frame at baseline to 1st month (MD = 0.02; SE = 0.01; p = 0.19), 1st month – 2nd month (MD = 0.05; SE = 0.03; p = 0.16), and 2nd – 3rd month (MD = 0.07; SE = 0.04; P = 0.16) the result showing statistical non-significance (p > 0.05).

Table 4.3.17: Comparison of Lower Leg Left (LLL) variable within the group-2 from Baseline to Third month

Variable	n	Mean ± SD	SE	df	F	P
LLL (B)		0.52 ± 0.86	0.15			
LLL (1)	30	0.66 ± 1.09	0.19	3	9.50	< 0.05*
LLL (2)		0.76 ± 1.23	0.22			
LLL (3)		0.89 ± 1.42	0.26			

LLL = Lower Leg Left; n = Number of participants; SD = Standard Deviation; SE = Standard Error; df = differential frequency; F = Mean of the within group variances. * = The Mean score is significant at the 0.05 level.

Table 4.3.17 depicts the mean and standard deviation for pain pressure threshold of lower limb left side point on algometer at baseline (0.52 ± 0.86), 1st month (0.66 ± 1.09), 2nd month (0.76 ± 1.23), and 3rd month (0.89 ± 1.42) in CBTAIPT group. The result showed significant difference (F = 9.50, p ≤ 0.05).

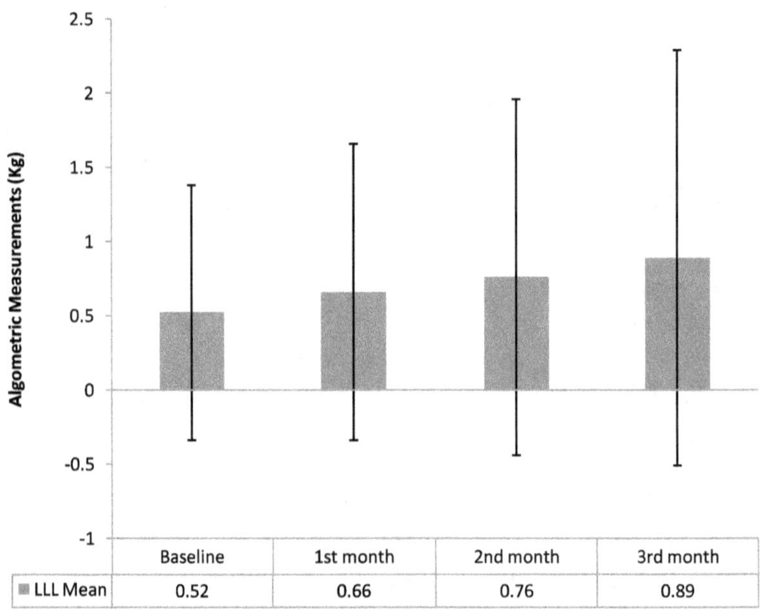

Figure 4.3.17: The Mean and SD of Lower Leg Left from baseline to third month

Table 4.3.17.1: Pair-wise comparison of Lower Leg Left (LLL) variable from Baseline to Third month at different time frame

Time frame	n	Mean difference	Standard Error	P	95% CI [b]	
					Lower bound	Upper bound
Baseline – 1 month		0.13*	0.06	< 0.01	0.25	0.01
1 month – 2 month	30	0.23*	0.08	< 0.01	0.41	0.06
2 month – 3 month		0.37*	0.11	< 0.01	0.60	0.14

n = number of participants, CI = Confidence Interval

*= The mean difference is significant at the 0.05 level.

b. Adjustment for multiple comparisons: Least Significant Difference (equivalent to no adjustments).

Table **4.3.17.1** showing the pair-wise comparison of Mean Difference (MD) and Standard Error (SE) on different time frame at baseline to 1st month (MD = 0.13; SE = 0.06; p = < 0.01), 1st month – 2nd month (MD = 0.23; SE = 0.08; p = < 0.01), and 2nd – 3rd month (MD = 0.37; SE = 0.11; P = < 0.01) the result showing statistical significance (p ≤ 0.05).

Table 4.3.18: Comparison of Lower Leg Right (LLR) variable within the group-2 from Baseline to Third month

Variable	n	Mean ± SD	SE	df	F	P
LLR (B)		0.59 ± 0.97	0.17			
LLR (1)	30	0.70 ± 1.13	0.20	3	10.65	< 0.01*
LLR (2)		0.79 ± 1.26	0.23			
LLR (3)		0.95 ± 1.51	0.27			

LLR = Lower Leg Right; n = Number of participants; SD = Standard Deviation; SE = Standard Error; df = differential frequency; F = Mean of the within group variances. * = The Mean score is significant at the 0.05 level.

Table **4.3.18** depicts the mean and standard deviation for pain pressure threshold of lower limb right side point on algometer at baseline (0.59 ± 0.97), 1st month (0.70 ± 1.13), 2nd month (0.79 ± 1.26), and 3rd month (0.95 ± 1.51) in CBTAIPT group. The result showed significant difference (F = 10.65, p ≤ 0.05).

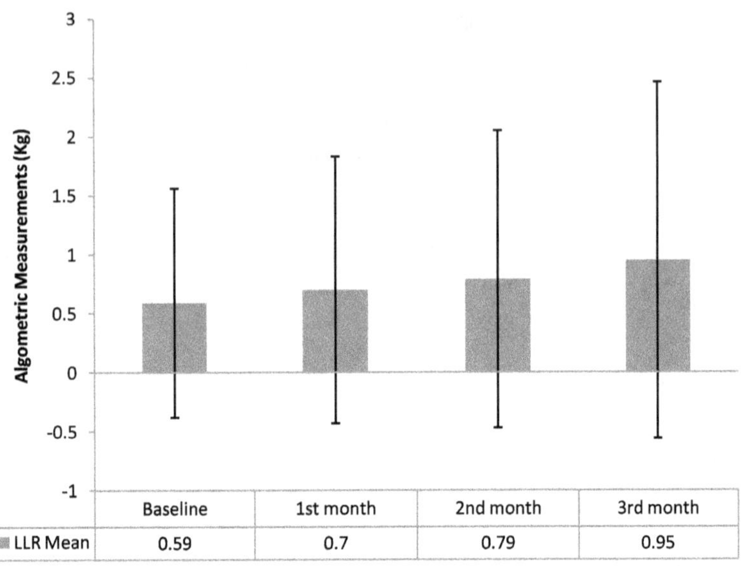

Figure 4.3.18: The Mean and SD of Lower Leg Right from baseline to third month

Table 4.3.18.1: Pair-wise comparison of Lower Leg Right (LLR) variable from Baseline to Third month at different time frame

Time frame	n	Mean difference	Standard Error	P	95% CI [b]	
					Lower bound	Upper bound
Baseline – 1 month		0.11[*]	0.04	0.01	0.19	0.02
1 month – 2 month	30	0.19[*]	0.05	< 0.01	0.31	0.07
2 month – 3 month		0.35[*]	0.10	< 0.01	0.57	0.13

Based on estimated marginal means

n = number of participants, CI = Confidence Interval

[*] = The mean difference is significant at the 0.05 level.

b. Adjustment for multiple comparisons: Least Significant Difference (equivalent to no adjustments).

Table **4.3.18.1** showing the pair-wise comparison of Mean Difference (MD) and Standard Error (SE) on different time frame at baseline to 1st month (MD = 0.11; SE = 0.04; p = < 0.01), 1st month – 2nd month (MD = 0.19; SE = 0.05; p = < 0.01), and 2nd – 3rd month (MD = 0.35; SE = 0.10; P = < 0.01) the result showing statistical significance ($p \leq 0.05$).

Table 4.3.19: Comparison of Jaw Left variable within the group-2 from Baseline to Third month

Variable	n	Mean ± SD	SE	df	F	P
JAWL (B)		0.03 ± 0.14	0.02			
JAWL (1)	30	0.07 ± 0.28	0.05	3	1.67	> 0.05[#]
JAWL (2)		0.09 ± 0.37	0.06			
JAWL (3)		0.10 ± 0.41	0.07			

JAWL = Jaw Left; **n** = Number of participants; **SD** = Standard Deviation; **SE** = Standard Error; **df** = differential frequency; **F** = Mean of the within group variances. # NS = The Mean score is Non-significant at the 0.05 level.

Table 4.3.19 depicts the mean and standard deviation for pain pressure threshold of jaw left side point on algometer at baseline (0.03 ± 0.14), 1st month (0.07 ± 0.28), 2nd month (0.09 ± 0.37), and 3rd month (0.10 ± 0.41) in CBTAIPT group. The result showed non-significant difference (F = 1.67, p > 0.05).

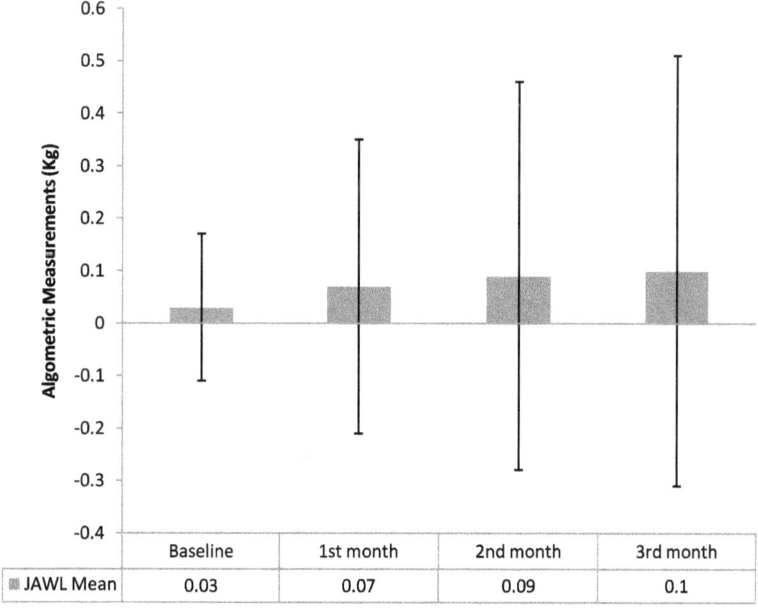

Figure 4.3.19: The Mean and SD of Jaw Left from baseline to third month

Table 4.3.19.1: Pair-wise comparison of Jaw Left (JawL) variable from Baseline to Third month at different time frame

Time frame	n	Mean difference	Standard Error	P	95% CI [b]	
					Lower bound	Upper bound
Baseline – 1 month		$0.03^{\#}$	0.03	0.27	0.09	0.02
1 month – 2 month	30	$0.05^{\#}$	0.04	0.21	0.14	0.03
2 month – 3 month		$0.07^{\#}$	0.05	0.19	0.17	0.03

n = number of participants, CI = Confidence Interval

$^{\#}$. The mean difference is non-significant at the 0.05 level.

b. Adjustment for multiple comparisons: Least Significant Difference (equivalent to no adjustments).

Table 4.3.19.1 showing the pair-wise comparison of Mean Difference (MD) and Standard Error (SE) on different time frame at baseline to 1st month (MD = 0.03; SE = 0.03; p = 0.27), 1st month – 2nd month (MD = 0.05; SE = 0.04; p = 0.21), and 2nd – 3rd month (MD = 0.07; SE = 0.05; P = 0.19) the result showing non-statistical significance (p > 0.05).

Table 4.3.20: Comparison of Jaw Right variable within the group-2 from Baseline to Third month

Variable	n	Mean ± SD	SE	df	F	P
JAWR (B)		0.15 ± 0.50	0.09			
JAWR (1)	30	0.17 ± 0.56	0.10	3	2.71	$> 0.05^{\#}$
JAWR (2)		0.21 ± 0.69	0.12			
JAWR (3)		0.24 ± 0.76	0.13			

JAWR = Jaw Right; **n** = Number of participants; **SD** = Standard Deviation; **SE** = Standard Error; **df** = differential frequency; **F** = Mean of the within group variances. # = The Mean score is Non-significant at the 0.05 level.

Table 4.3.20 depicts the mean and standard deviation for pain pressure threshold of jaw right side point on algometer at baseline (0.15 ± 0.50), 1st month (0.17 ± 0.56), 2nd month (0.21 ± 0.69), and 3rd month (0.24 ± 0.76) in CBTAIPT group. The result showed significant difference (F = 2.71, p > 0.05).

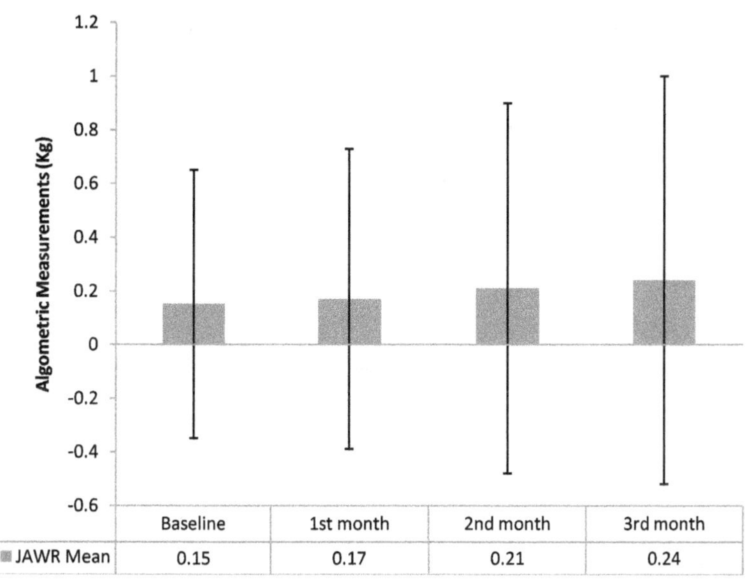

	Baseline	1st month	2nd month	3rd month
JAWR Mean	0.15	0.17	0.21	0.24

Figure 4.3.20: The Mean and SD of Jaw Right from baseline to third month

Table 4.3.20.1: Pair-wise comparison of Jaw Right (JawR) variable from Baseline to Third month at different time frame

Time frame	N	Mean difference	Standard Error	P	95% CI [b]	
					Lower bound	Upper bound
Baseline – 1 month		$0.02^{\#}$	0.01	0.09	0.05	0.00
1 month – 2 month	30	$0.06^{\#}$	0.03	0.09	0.14	0.01
2 month – 3 month		$0.09^{\#}$	0.05	0.10	0.20	0.01

n = number of participants, CI = Confidence Interval

[#]. The mean difference is non-significant at the 0.05 level.

b. Adjustment for multiple comparisons: Least Significant Difference (equivalent to no adjustments).

Table 4.3.20.1 showing the pair-wise comparison of Mean Difference (MD) and Standard Error (SE) on different time frame at baseline to 1st month (MD = 0.02; SE = 0.01; p = 0.09), 1st month – 2nd month (MD = 0.06; SE = 0.03; p = 0.09), and 2nd – 3rd month (MD = 0.09; SE = 0.05; P = 0.10) the result showing statistical non-significance (p > 0.05).

Table 4.3.21: Comparison of Chest variable within the group-2 from Baseline to Third month

Variable	n	Mean ± SD	SE	df	F	P
CHEST (B)		0.33 ± 0.58	0.10			
CHEST (1)	30	0.56 ± 0.90	0.16	3	10.62	< 0.01*
CHEST (2)		0.66 ± 1.05	0.19			
CHEST (3)		0.78 ± 1.22	0.22			

n = Number of participants; **SD** = Standard Deviation; **SE** = Standard Error; **df** = differential frequency; **F** = Mean of the within group variances. * = The Mean score is significant at the 0.05 level.

Table 4.3.21 depicts the mean and standard deviation for pain pressure threshold of chest point on algometer at baseline (0.33 ± 0.58), 1st month (0.56 ± 0.90), 2nd month (0.66 ± 1.05), and 3rd month (0.78 ± 1.22) in CBTAIPT group. The result showed significant difference (F = 10.62, p = 0.05).

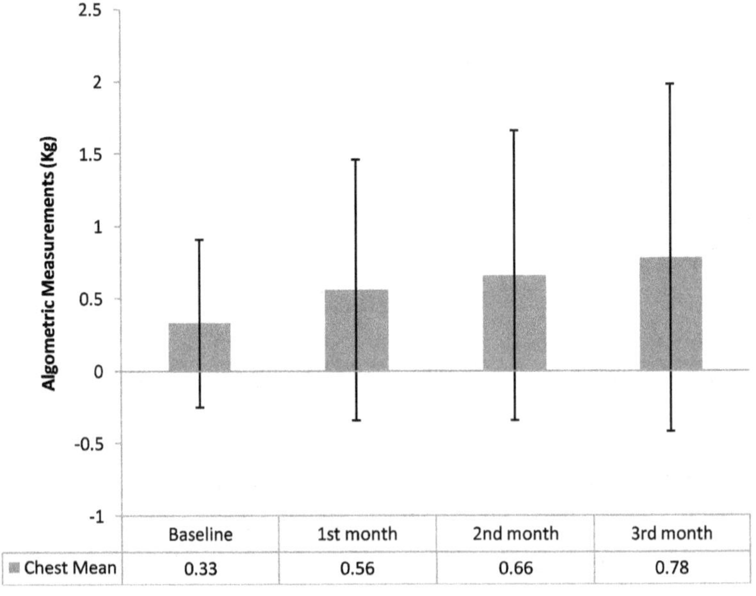

Figure 4.3.21: The Mean and SD of Chest point from baseline to third month

Table 4.3.21.1: Pair-wise comparison of Chest point variable from Baseline to Third month at different time frame

Time frame	n	Mean difference	Standard Error	P	95% CI [b]	
					Lower bound	Upper bound
Baseline – 1 month		0.23*	0.07	< 0.01	0.38	0.07
1 month – 2 month	30	0.33*	0.10	< 0.01	0.53	0.12
2 month – 3 month		0.45*	0.13	< 0.01	0.72	0.17

n = number of participants, CI = Confidence Interval

*= The mean difference is significant at the 0.05 level.

b. Adjustment for multiple comparisons: Least Significant Difference (equivalent to no adjustments).

Table 4.3.21.1 showing the pair-wise comparison of Mean Difference (MD) and Standard Error (SE) on different time frame at baseline to 1st month (MD = 0.23; SE = 0.07; p < 0.01), 1st month – 2nd month (MD = 0.33; SE = 0.10; p < 0.01), and 2nd – 3rd month (MD = 0.45; SE = 0.13; P < 0.01) the result showing statistical significance (p = 0.05).

Table 4.3.22: Comparison of Neck variable within the group-2 from Baseline to Third month

Variable	n	Mean ± SD	SE	df	F	P
NECK (B)		1.10 ± 0.89	0.16			
NECK (1)	30	1.51 ± 1.13	0.20	3	48.57	< 0.01*
NECK (2)		1.87 ± 1.35	0.24			
NECK (3)		2.29 ± 1.58	0.28			

n = Number of participants; SD = Standard Deviation; SE = Standard Error; df = differential frequency; F = Mean of the within group variances. * = The Mean score is significant at the 0.05 level.

Table 4.3.22 depicts the mean and standard deviation for pain pressure threshold of neck point on algometer at baseline (1.10 ± 0.89), 1st month (1.51 ± 1.13), 2nd month (1.87 ± 1.35), and 3rd month (2.29 ± 1.58) in CBTAIPT group. The result showed significant difference (F = 48.57, p ≤ 0.01).

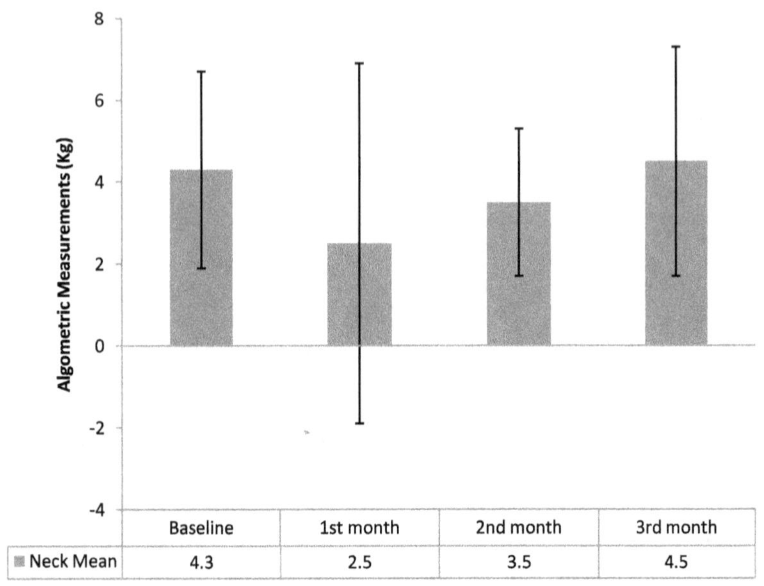

Figure 4.3.22: The Mean and SD of Neck point from baseline to third month

Table 4.3.22.1: Pair-wise comparison of Neck point variable from Baseline to Third month at different time frame

Time frame	n	Mean difference	Standard Error	P	95% CI [b]	
					Lower bound	Upper bound
Baseline – 1 month		0.41[*]	0.06	< 0.01	0.54	0.27
1 month – 2 month	30	0.77[*]	0.11	< 0.01	0.99	0.54
2 month – 3 month		1.19[*]	0.15	< 0.01	1.50	0.87
n = number of participants, CI = Confidence Interval						
[*] = The mean difference is significant at the 0.05 level.						
b. Adjustment for multiple comparisons: Least Significant Difference (equivalent to no adjustments).						

Table 4.3.22.1 showing the pair-wise comparison of Mean Difference (MD) and Standard Error (SE) on different time frame at baseline to 1st month (MD = 0.41; SE = 0.06; $p \leq 0.01$), 1st month – 2nd month (MD = 0.77; SE = 0.11; $p \leq 0.01$), and 2nd – 3rd month (MD = 1.19; SE = 0.15; $P \leq 0.01$) the result showing statistical significance ($p \leq 0.01$).

Table 4.3.23: Comparison of Upper Back (UB) variable within the group-2 from Baseline to Third month

Variable	n	Mean ± SD	SE	df	F	P
UB (B)		1.42 ± 0.92	0.16			
UB (1)	30	1.89 ± 1.15	0.21	3	67.48	< 0.01*
UB (2)		2.32 ± 1.34	0.24			
UB (3)		2.75 ± 1.50	0.27			

UB = Upper Back; **n** = Number of participants; **SD** = Standard Deviation; **SE** = Standard Error; **df** = differential frequency; **F** = Mean of the within group variances. * = The Mean score is Non-significant at the 0.05 level.

Table 4.3.23 depicts the mean and standard deviation for pain pressure threshold of upper back point on algometer at baseline (1.42 ± 0.92), 1st month (1.89 ± 1.15), 2nd month (2.32 ± 1.34), and 3rd month (2.75 ± 1.50) in CBTAIPT group. The result showed significant difference (F = 67.48, p ≤ 0.01).

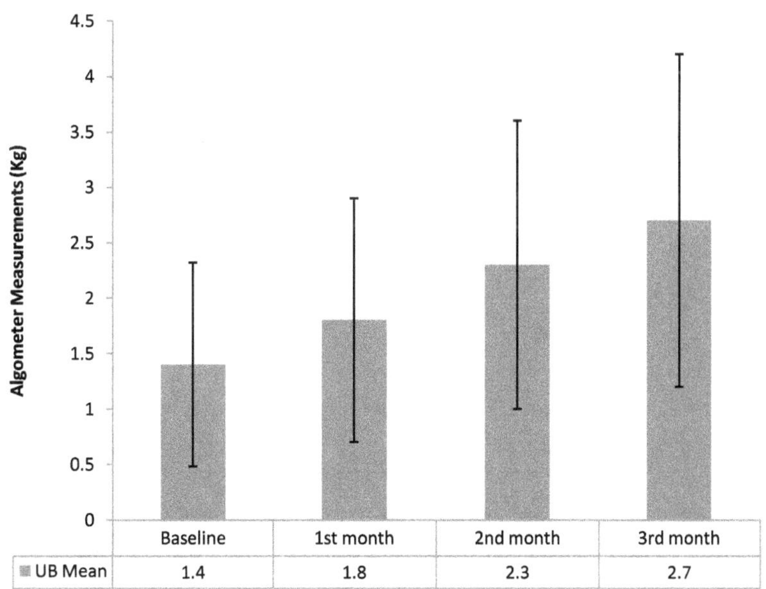

Figure 4.3.23: The Mean and SD of Upper Back point from baseline to third month

Table 4.3.23.1: Pair-wise comparison of Upper Back (UB) variable from Baseline to Third month at different time frame

Time frame	n	Mean difference	Standard Error	P	95% CI [b]	
					Lower bound	Upper bound
Baseline – 1 month		0.46[*]	0.06	< 0.01	0.60	0.32
1 month – 2 month	30	0.89[*]	0.12	< 0.01	1.14	0.65
2 month – 3 month		1.32[*]	0.14	< 0.01	1.62	1.02

n = number of participants, CI = Confidence Interval

[*] = The mean difference is significant at the 0.05 level.

b. Adjustment for multiple comparisons: Least Significant Difference (equivalent to no adjustments).

Table 4.3.23.1 showing the pair-wise comparison of Mean Difference (MD) and Standard Error (SE) on different time frame at baseline to 1st month (MD = 0.46; SE = 0.06; $p \leq 0.01$), 1st month – 2nd month (MD = 0.89; SE = 0.12; $p \leq 0.01$), and 2nd – 3rd month (MD = 1.32; SE = 0.14; $P \leq 0.01$) the result showing statistical significance ($p \leq 0.01$).

Table 4.3.23: Comparison of Lower Back (LB) variable within the group-2 from Baseline to Third month

Variable	N	Mean ± SD	SE	df	F	P
LB (B)		1.14 ± 0.87	0.15			
LB (1)	30	1.60 ± 1.15	0.21	3	47.78	< 0.01*
LB (2)		1.98 ± 1.40	0.25			
LB (3)		2.32 ± 1.57	0.28			

LB = Lower Back; **n** = Number of participants; **SD** = Standard Deviation; SE = Standard Error; **df** = differential frequency; **F** = Mean of the within group variances. * = The Mean score is significant at the 0.05 level.

Table 4.3.24 depicts the mean and standard deviation for pain pressure threshold of lower back point on algometer at baseline (1.14 ± 0.87), 1st month (1.60 ± 1.15), 2nd month (1.98 ± 1.40) and 3rd month (2.32 ± 1.57) in CBTAIPT group. The result showed significant difference (F = 47.78, $p \leq 0.01$).

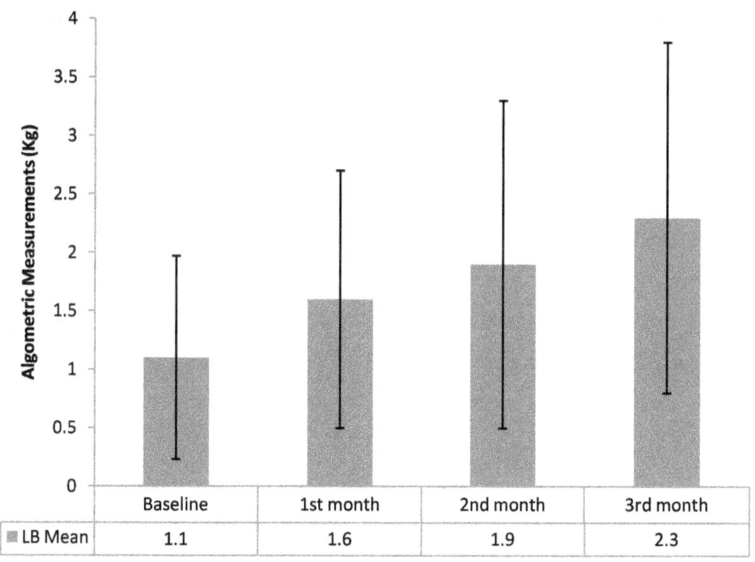

Figure 4.3.24: The Mean and SD of Upper Back point from baseline to third month

Table 4.3.24.1: Pair-wise comparison of Upper Back (UB) variable from Baseline to Third month at different time frame

Time frame	N	Mean difference	Standard Error	P	95% CI [b] Lower bound	Upper bound
Baseline – 1 month		0.46[*]	0.08	< 0.01	0.61	0.30
1 month – 2 month	30	0.83[*]	0.12	< 0.01	1.08	0.58
2 month – 3 month		1.17[*]	0.15	< 0.01	1.49	0.86
n = number of participants, CI = Confidence Interval						
[*] = The mean difference is significant at the 0.05 level.						
b. Adjustment for multiple comparisons: Least Significant Difference (equivalent to no adjustments).						

Table 4.3.24.1 showing the pair-wise comparison of Mean Difference (MD) and Standard Error (SE) on different time frame at baseline to 1st month (MD = 0.46; SE = 0.08; $p \leq 0.01$), 1st month – 2nd month (MD = 0.83; SE = 0.12; $p \leq 0.01$), and 2nd – 3rd month (MD = 1.17; SE = 0.15; $P \leq 0.01$) the result showing statistical significance ($p \leq 0.01$).

Summary of the result of cognitive behavioral therapy along with Integrated Physiotherapy Techniques alone group

The primary outcome measure FIQR revealed significant results within the group cognitive behavioral therapy and integrated physiotherapy techniques ($p \leq 0.01$); also other variables showed significant ($p < 0.05$) results on beck depression index, visual analog scale, general anxiety disorder and short-form – 36 health survey. Furthermore, on most of the variables of widespread pain index measured by algometer for the pain pressure threshold over the shoulder girdle left (SGL), shoulder girdle right, upper arm left, upper arms right, hip buttock left, hip buttock right, lower leg left, lower leg right, chest, neck, upper back, and lower back tender points. However, some of the variables shown non-significant results ($p > 0.05$) viz. lower arm left, lower arm right, upper leg left, upper leg right, jaw left, and right side. Thus, it signifies that CBTAIPT was effective in improving the quality of life, physical and mental health, reduction of pain, anxiety, depression, and the trigger point sensitivity.

4.4 Role of Integrated Physiotherapy Techniques (Group-III) in Fibromyalgia

As per the study protocol, the experimental group-III (n=30) received Integrated Physiotherapy Techniques only. The total duration of intervention was similar to experimental group 2. Analysis of Variance (ANOVA) was used to compare the study variable at different level of intervention. So as to examine the role of Integrated Physiotherapy Techniques alone in patients with fibromyalgia

Table 4.4.1: Comparison of Revised Fibromyalgia Impact Questionnaire (FIQR) variable within the group-3 from Baseline to Third month

Variable	n	Mean ± SD	SE	df	F	P
FIQR (B)		60.60 ± 16.66	3.04			
FIQR (1)	30	45.38 ± 13.87	2.53	3	81.17	< 0.01*
FIQR (2)		34.23 ± 11.76	2.14			
FIQR (3)		24.62 ± 14.05	2.56			

FIQR = Revised Fibromyalgia Impact Questionnaire; **n** = Number of participants; **SD** = Standard Deviation; **SE** = Standard Error; **df** = differential frequency; **F** = Mean of the within group variances. * = The Mean score is significant at the 0.05 level.

Table 4.4.1 depicts the mean and standard deviation for Revised Fibromyalgia Impact Questionnaire at baseline (60.60 ± 16.66), 1st month (45.38 ± 13.87), 2nd month (34.23 ± 11.76), and 3rd month (24.62 ± 14.05) of IPT group. The result showed significant difference (F = 81.17, p ≤ 0.01).

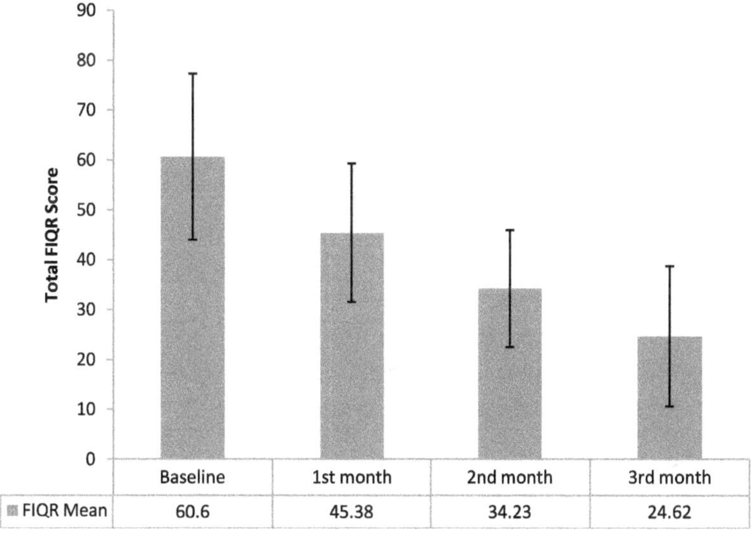

Figure 4.4.1: The Mean and SD of Revised Fibromyalgia Impact Questionnaire score from baseline to third month

Table 4.4.1.1: Pair-wise comparison of Revised Fibromyalgia Impact Questionnaire (FIQR) variable from Baseline to Third month at different time frame

Time frame	n	Mean difference	Standard Error	P	95% CI[b]	
					Lower bound	Upper bound
Baseline – 1 month		15.22[*]	1.90	< 0.01	11.32	19.11
1 month – 2 month	30	26.37[*]	2.39	< 0.01	21.48	31.26
2 month – 3 month		35.97[*]	3.54	< 0.01	28.73	43.21

n = number of participants, CI = Confidence Interval

[*] = The mean difference is significant at the 0.05 level.

b. Adjustment for multiple comparisons: Least Significant Difference (equivalent to no adjustments).

163

Table 4.4.1.1 shows the pair-wise comparison of Mean Difference (MD) and Standard Error (SE) on different time frame at baseline to 1st month (MD = 15.22; SE = 1.90; p ≤ 0.01), 1st month – 2nd month (MD = 26.37; SE = 2.39; p ≤ 0.01), and 2nd – 3rd month (MD = 35.97; SE = 3.54; P ≤ 0.01) the result shows statistical significance (p ≤ 0.01).

Table 4.4.2: Comparison of Beck Depression Index (BDI) variable within the group-1 from Baseline to Third month

Variable	n	Mean ± SD	SE	df	F	P
BDI (B)		22.77 ± 8.74	1.59			
BDI (1)	30	20.83 ± 9.38	1.71	3	19.59	< 0.01*
BDI (2)		18.10 ± 9.50	1.73			
BDI (3)		14.93 ± 10.55	1.92			

BDI = Beck Depression Index; **n** = Number of participants; **SD** = Standard Deviation; **SE** = Standard Error; **df** = differential frequency; **F** = Mean of the within group variances; * = The Mean score is significant at the 0.05 level.

Table 4.4.2 depicts the mean and standard deviation for Beck Depression Index at baseline (22.77 ± 8.74), 1st month (20.83 ± 9.38), 2nd month (18.10 ± 9.50), and 3rd month (14.93 ± 10.55) of IPT group. The result showed significant difference (F = 19.59, p ≤ 0.01).

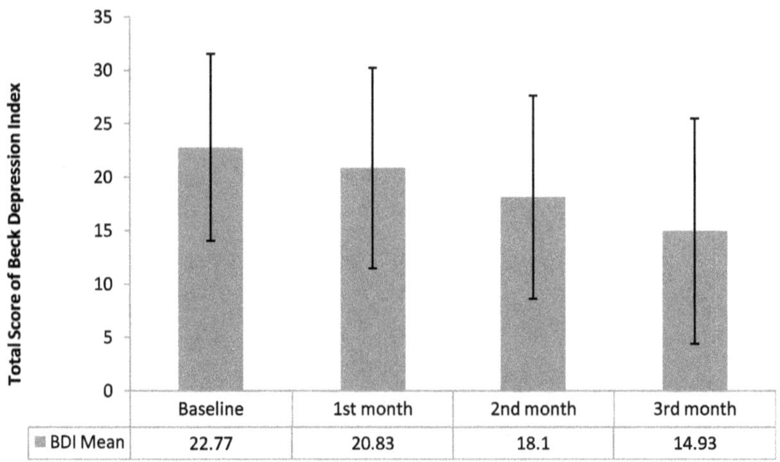

Figure 4.4.2: The Mean and SD of Beck Depression Index score from baseline to third month

Table 4.4.2.1: Pair-wise comparison of Beck Depression Index (BDI) variable from Baseline to Third month at different time frame

Time frame	n	Mean difference	Standard Error	P	95% CI [b]	
					Lower bound	Upper bound
Baseline – 1 month		1.93[#]	1.03	0.07	0.19	4.05
1 month – 2 month	30	4.66[*]	1.08	< 0.01	2.44	6.88
2 month – 3 month		7.83[*]	1.37	< 0.01	5.02	10.64

n = number of participants, CI = Confidence Interval

[*] = The mean difference is significant at the 0.05 level.

b. Adjustment for multiple comparisons: Least Significant Difference (equivalent to no adjustments).

Table 4.4.2.1 shows the pair-wise comparison of Mean Difference (MD) and Standard Error (SE) on different time frame at baseline to 1st month (MD = 1.93; SE = 1.03; p = 0.07), 1st month – 2nd month (MD = 4.66; SE = 1.08; p ≤ 0.01), and 2nd – 3rd month (MD = 7.83; SE = 1.37; P ≤ 0.01) the result shows statistical significance (p ≤ 0.01).

Table 4.4.3: Comparison of Visual Analogue Scale (VAS) variable within the group-3 from Baseline to Third month

Variable	N	Mean ± SD	SE	df	F	P
VAS (B)		8.20 ± 1.60	0.29			
VAS (1)	30	5.80 ± 1.97	0.36	3	113.4	< 0.01*
VAS (2)		4.23 ± 1.96	0.35			
VAS (3)		2.43 ± 1.96	0.35			

VAS = Visual Analogue Scale; n = Number of participants; SD = Standard Deviation; SE = Standard Error; df = differential frequency; F = Mean of the within group variances. * = The Mean score is significant at the 0.05 level.

Table 4.4.3 depicts the mean and standard deviation for Visual Analogue Scale at baseline (8.20 ± 1.60), 1st month (5.80 ± 1.97), 2nd month (4.23 ± 1.96), and 3rd month (2.43 ± 1.96) of IPT group. The result showed significant difference (F = 113.4, p ≤ 0.01).

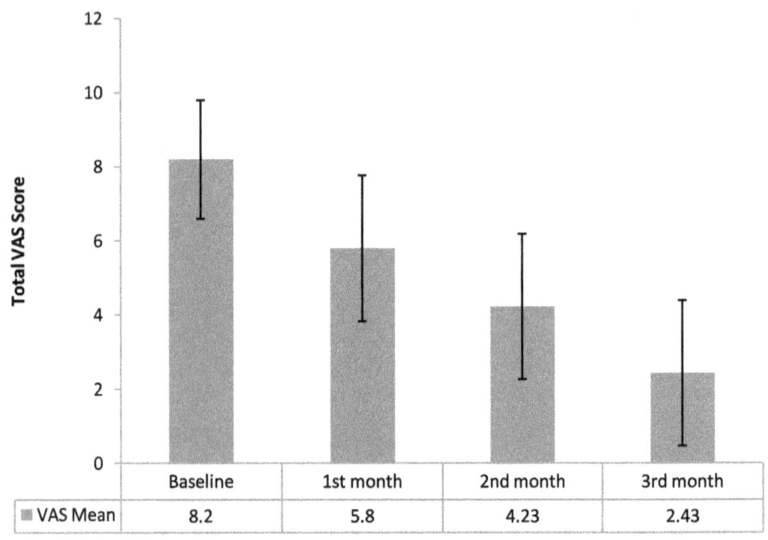

Figure 4.4.3: The Mean and SD of Visual Analogue Scale score from baseline to third month

Table 4.4.3.1: Pair-wise comparison of Visual Analogue Scale (VAS) variable from Baseline to Third month at different time frame

Time frame	n	Mean difference	Standard Error	P	95% CI [b]	
					Lower bound	Upper bound
Baseline – 1 month		2.40[*]	0.31	< 0.01	1.76	3.04
1 month – 2 month	30	3.96[*]	0.31	< 0.01	3.32	4.60
2 month – 3 month		5.76[*]	0.40	< 0.01	4.94	6.59

n = number of participants, CI = Confidence Interval

[*] = The mean difference is significant at the 0.05 level.

b. Adjustment for multiple comparisons: Least Significant Difference (equivalent to no adjustments).

 Table 4.4.3.1 shows the pair-wise comparison of Mean Difference (MD) and Standard Error (SE) on different time frame at baseline to 1st month (MD = 2.40; SE = 0.31; p ≤ 0.01), 1st month – 2nd month (MD = 3.96; SE = 0.31; p ≤ 0.01), and 2nd – 3rd month (MD = 5.76; SE = 0.40; P ≤ 0.01) the result shows statistical significance (p ≤ 0.01).

Table 4.4.4: Comparison of General Anxiety Disorder (GAD) variable within the group-3 from Baseline to Third month

Variable	n	Mean ± SD	SE	df	F	P
GAD - 7 (B)		14.33 ± 3.84	0.70			
GAD - 7 (1)	30	11.97 ± 3.40	0.62	3	18.01	< 0.01*
GAD - 7 (2)		10.67 ± 3.82	0.69			
GAD - 7 (3)		8.57 ± 4.98	0.91			
GAD - 7 = General Anxiety Disorder – 7 Scale; **n** = Number of participants; **SD** = Standard Deviation; **SE** = Standard Error; **df** = differential frequency; **F** = Mean of the within group variances. * = The Mean score is significant at the 0.05 level.							

Table 4.4.4 depicts the mean and standard deviation for General Anxiety Disorder at baseline (14.33 ± 3.84), 1st month (11.97 ± 3.40), 2nd month (10.67 ± 3.82), and 3rd month (8.57 ± 4.98) of IPT group. The result showed significant difference (F = 18.01, p ≤ 0.01).

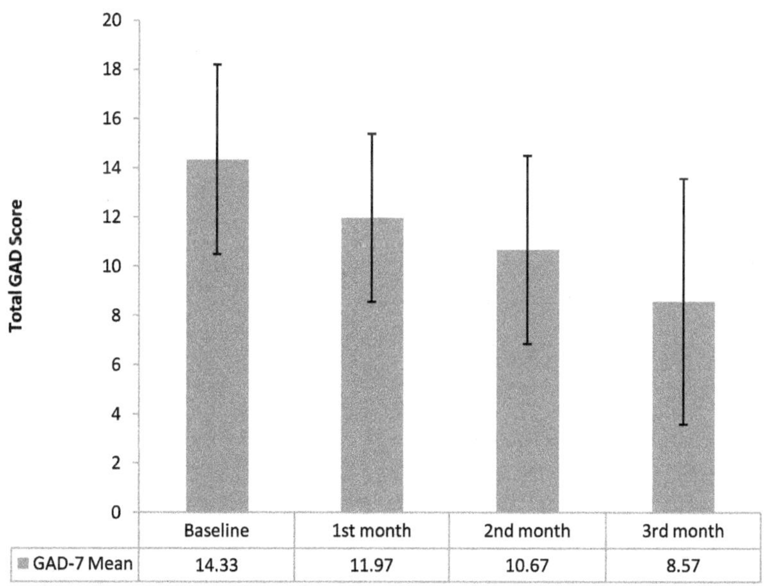

Figure 4.4.4: The Mean and SD of General Anxiety Disorder score from baseline to third month

Table 4.4.4.1: Pair-wise comparison of General Anxiety Disorder (GAD) variable from Baseline to Third month at different time frame

Time frame	N	Mean difference	Standard Error	P	95% CI [b]	
					Lower bound	Upper bound
Baseline – 1 month		2.36[*]	0.60	< 0.01	1.12	3.60
1 month – 2 month	30	3.66[*]	0.92	< 0.01	1.77	5.55
2 month – 3 month		5.76[*]	1.10	< 0.01	3.50	8.02

n = number of participants, CI = Confidence Interval

[*] = The mean difference is significant at the 0.05 level.

b. Adjustment for multiple comparisons: Least Significant Difference (equivalent to no adjustments).

Table 4.4.4.1 shows the pair-wise comparison of Mean Difference (MD) and Standard Error (SE) on different time frame at baseline to 1st month (MD = 2.36; SE = 0.60; p = 0.01), 1st month – 2nd month (MD = 3.66; SE = 0.92; p ≤ 0.01), and 2nd – 3rd month (MD = 5.76; SE = 1.10; P ≤ 0.01) the result shows statistical significance (p ≤ 0.01).

Table 4.4.5: Comparison of Short Form-36 health survey Physical Component Summary (SF-36 PCS) variable within the group-3 from Baseline to Third month

Variable	n	Mean ± SD	SE	Df	F	P
SF - 36 PCS (B)		32.45 ± 7.86	1.43			
SF - 36 PCS (1)	30	41.70 ± 11.06	2.02	3	54.40	< 0.01*
SF - 36 PCS (2)		48.91 ± 12.26	2.23			
SF - 36 PCS (3)		62.33 ± 18.94	3.45			

SF - 36 PCS = Short Form – 36 Physical Component Summary; **n** = Number of participants; **SD** = Standard Deviation; **SE** = Standard Error; **df** = differential frequency; **F** = Mean of the within group variances. * = The Mean score is significant at the 0.05 level.

Table 4.4.5 depicts the mean and standard deviation for Short Form-36 Physical Component Summary at baseline (32.45 ± 7.86), 1st month (41.70 ± 11.06), 2nd month (48.91 ± 12.26), and 3rd month (62.33 ± 18.94) of IPT group. The result showed significant difference (F = 54.40, p ≤ 0.01).

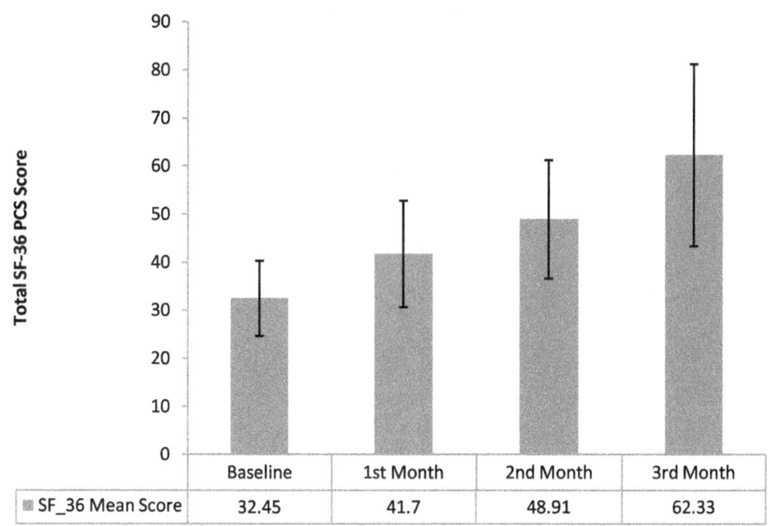

Figure 4.4.5: The Mean and SD of Short Form – 36 Physical Component summary score from baseline to third month

Table 4.4.5.1: Pair-wise comparison of Short Form-36 health survey Physical Component Summary (SF-36 PCS) variable from Baseline to Third month at different time frame

Time frame	n	Mean difference	Standard Error	P	95% CI [b]	
					Lower bound	Upper bound
Baseline – 1 month		9.24[*]	1.43	< 0.01	12.17	6.32
1 month – 2 month	30	16.45[*]	2.00	< 0.01	20.55	12.36
2 month – 3 month		29.88[*]	3.46	< 0.01	36.97	22.79
n = number of participants, CI = Confidence Interval						
[*] = The mean difference is significant at the 0.05 level.						
b. Adjustment for multiple comparisons: Least Significant Difference (equivalent to no adjustments).						

Table 4.4.5.1 shows the pair-wise comparison of Mean Difference (MD) and Standard Error (SE) on different time frame at baseline to 1st month (MD = 9.24; SE = 1.43; p = < 0.01), 1st month – 2nd month (MD = 16.45; SE = 2.00; $p \leq 0.01$), and 2nd – 3rd month (MD = 29.88; SE = 3.46; $P \leq 0.01$) the result shows statistical significance ($p \leq 0.01$).

Table 4.4.6: Comparison of Short Form-36 health survey Mental Component Summary (SF-36 MCS) variable within the group-3 from Baseline to Third month

Variable	n	Mean ± SD	SE	df	F	P
SF - 36 MCS (B)		35.01 ± 10.91	1.99			
SF - 36 MCS (1)	30	39.98 ± 12.48	2.28	3	33.53	< 0.01*
SF - 36 MCS (2)		48.35 ± 13.81	2.52			
SF - 36 MCS (3)		57.11 ± 17.48	3.19			

SF - 36 MCS = Short Form – 36 Mental Component Summary; **n** = Number of participants; **SD** = Standard Deviation; **SE** = Standard Error; **df** = differential frequency; **F** = Mean of the within group variances. * = The Mean score is significant at the 0.05 level.

Table 4.4.6 depicts the mean and standard deviation for Short Form-36 Mental Component Summary at baseline (35.01 ± 10.91), 1st month (39.98 ± 12.48), 2nd month (48.35 ± 13.81) and 3rd month (57.11 ± 17.48) of IPT group. The result showed significant difference (F = 33.532, p ≤ 0.001).

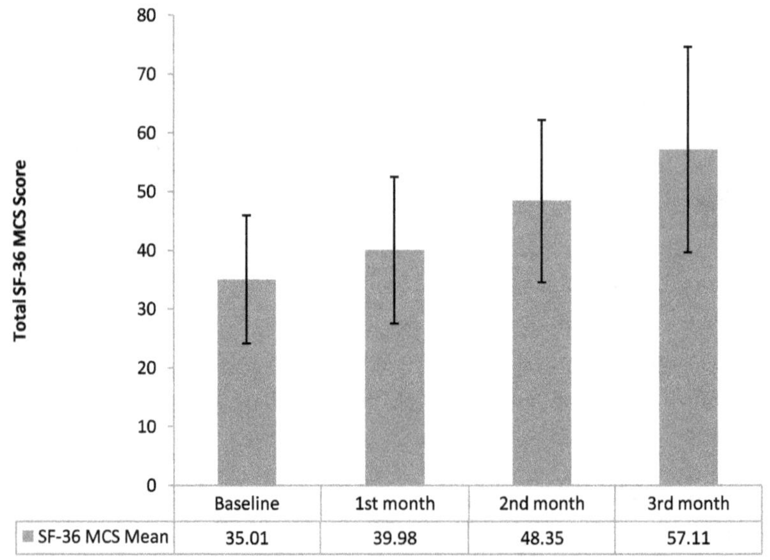

Figure 4.4.6: The Mean and SD of Short Form – 36 Mental Component summary score from baseline to third month

Table 4.4.6.1: Pair-wise comparison of Short Form-36 health survey Mental Component Summary (SF-36 PCS) variable from Baseline to Third month at different time frame

Time frame	n	Mean difference	Standard Error	P	95% CI [b]	
					Lower bound	Upper bound
Baseline – 1 month	30	4.97*	2.14	0.02	9.35	0.59
1 month – 2 month		13.34*	2.41	< 0.01	18.27	8.40
2 month – 3 month		22.10*	2.96	< 0.01	28.17	16.03

Based on estimated marginal means
n = number of participants, CI = Confidence Interval
*= The mean difference is significant at the 0.05 level.
b. Adjustment for multiple comparisons: Least Significant Difference (equivalent to no adjustments).

     Table 4.4.6.1 shows the pair-wise comparison of Mean Difference (MD) and Standard Error (SE) on different time frame at baseline to 1st month (MD = 4.97; SE = 2.14; p = 0.02), 1st month – 2nd month (MD = 13.34; SE = 2.41; $p \leq 0.01$), and 2nd – 3rd month (MD = 22.10; SE = 2.96; $P \leq 0.01$) the result shows statistical significance ($p \leq 0.01$).

Table 4.4.7: Comparison of algometric measurement of widespread pain index points on Shoulder Girdle Left (SGL) variable within the group-3 from Baseline to Third month

Variable	n	Mean ± SD	SE	df	F	P
SGL (B)	30	1.10 + 0.78	0.14	3	32.67	< 0.01*
SGL (1)		1.43 ± 0.84	0.15			
SGL (2)		1.78 ± 1.10	0.20			
SGL (3)		2.16 ± 1.25	0.22			

SGL = Shoulder Girdle Left; **n** = Number of participants; **SD** = Standard Deviation; **SE** = Standard Error; **df** = differential frequency; **F** = Mean of the within group variances; * = The Mean score is significant at the 0.05 level.

     Table 4.4.1 depicts the comparison of Mean and standard deviation within the group for pain pressure threshold of shoulder girdle left side point on algometer at Baseline (1.10 ± 0.78), 1st month (1.43 ± 0.84), 2nd Month (1.78 ± 1.10), and 3rd month (2.16 ± 1.25) in integrated physiotherapy group. The result showed significant difference (F = 32.67, $p \leq 0.01$).

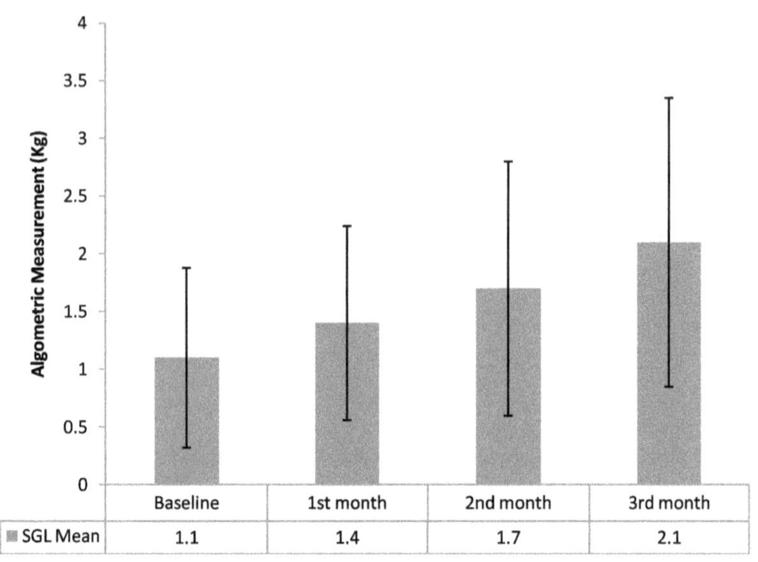

Figure 4.4.7: The Mean and SD on algometer measurement in shoulder girdle left side point from baseline to third month

Table 4.4.7.1: Pair-wise comparison of algometric measurement of widespread pain index points on Shoulder Girdle Left (SGL) variable from Baseline to Third month at different time frame

Time frame	n	Mean difference	Standard Error	P	95% CI [b]	
					Lower bound	Upper bound
Baseline – 1 month		0.33[*]	0.04	< 0.01	0.43	0.23
1 month – 2 month	30	0.68[*]	0.13	< 0.01	0.94	0.41
2 month – 3 month		1.05[*]	0.16	< 0.01	1.39	0.71
n = number of participants, CI = Confidence Interval						
* = The mean difference is significant at the 0.05 level.						
b. Adjustment for multiple comparisons: Least Significant Difference (equivalent to no adjustments).						

Table 4.4.7.1 shows the pair-wise comparison of Mean Difference (MD) and Standard Error (SE) on different time frame at baseline to 1st month (MD = 0.33; SE = 0.04; p ≤ 0.01), 1st month – 2nd month (MD = 0.68; SE = 0.13; p ≤ 0.01), and 2nd – 3rd month (MD = 1.05; SE = 0.16; p ≤ 0.01) the result shows statistical significance (p ≤ 0.01).

Table 4.4.8: Comparison of algometric measurement of widespread pain index points on Shoulder Girdle Right (SGR) variable within the group-3 from Baseline to Third month

Variable	n	Mean ± SD	SE	Df	F	P
SGR (B)		1.28 ± 0.85	0.15			
SGR (1)	30	1.61 ± 0.93	0.17	3	48.93	< 0.01*
SGR (2)		1.93 ± 0.96	0.17			
SGR (3)		2.42 ± 1.22	0.22			
SGR = Shoulder Girdle Right; n = Number of participants; SD = Standard Deviation; SE = Standard Error; df = differential frequency; F = Mean of the within group variances; * = The Mean score is significant at the 0.05 level.						

Table 4.4.8 depicts the Mean and standard deviation for pain pressure threshold of shoulder girdle right side point on algometer at Baseline (1.28 ± 0.85), 1st month (1.61 ± 0.93), 2nd Month (1.93 ± 0.96), and 3rd month (2.42 ± 1.22) in integrated physiotherapy group. The result showed significant difference (F = 48.93, p ≤ 0.01).

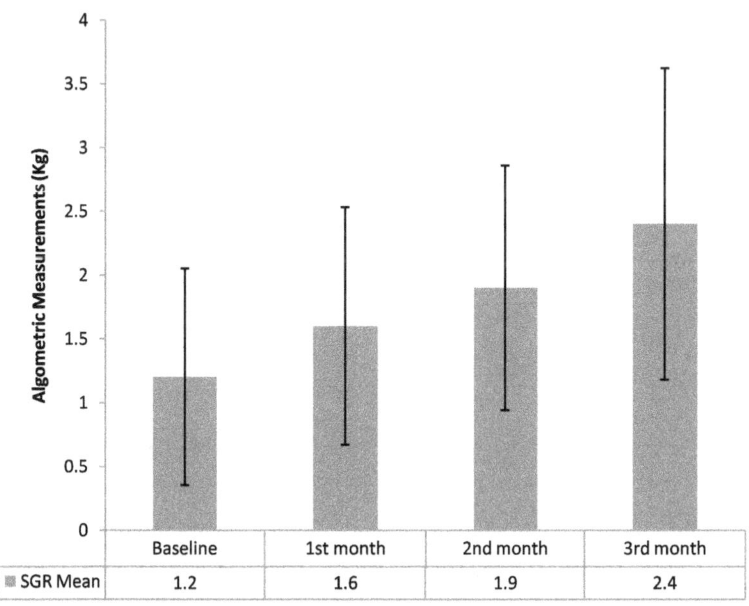

Figure 4.4.8: The Mean and SD on algometer measurement in Shoulder Girdle Right side point from baseline to third month

Table 4.4.8.1: Pair-wise comparison of algometric measurement of widespread pain index points on Shoulder Girdle Right (SGR) variable from Baseline to Third month at different time frame

Time frame	n	Mean difference	Standard Error	P	95% CI [b]	
					Lower bound	Upper bound
Baseline – 1 month		0.32[*]	0.05	< 0.01	0.42	0.21
1 month – 2 month	30	0.64[*]	0.08	< 0.01	0.81	0.48
2 month – 3 month		1.13[*]	0.15	< 0.01	1.45	0.81

n = number of participants, CI = Confidence Interval

* = The mean difference is significant at the 0.05 level.

b. Adjustment for multiple comparisons: Least Significant Difference (equivalent to no adjustments).

Table 4.4.8.1 shows the pair-wise comparison of Mean Difference (MD) and Standard Error (SE) on different time frame at baseline to 1st month (MD = 0.32; SE = 0.05; p ≤ 0.01), 1st month – 2nd month (MD = 0.64; SE = 0.08; p ≤ 0.01), and 2nd – 3rd month (MD = 1.13; SE = 0.15; p ≤ 0.01) the result shows statistical significance (p ≤ 0.01).

Table 4.4.9: Comparison of algometric measurement of widespread pain index points on Upper Arm Left (UAL) variable within the group-3 from Baseline to Third month

Variable	n	Mean ± SD	SE	df	F	P
UAL (B)		0.657 ± 0.8320	0.152			
UAL (1)	30	0.787 ± 0.9544	0.174	3	19.043	< 0.05*
UAL (2)		0.917 ± 1.0876	0.199			
UAL (3)		1.147 ± 1.3051	0.238			

UAL = Upper Arm Left; n = Number of participants; SD = Standard Deviation; SE = Standard Error; df = differential frequency; F = Mean of the within group variances. = * = The Mean score is significant at the 0.05 level.

Table 4.4.9 depicts the Mean and standard deviation for pain pressure threshold of upper arm left side point on algometer at Baseline (0.65 ± 0.83), 1st month (0.78 ± 0.95), 2nd Month (0.91 ± 1.087) and 3rd month (1.14 ± 1.30) in integrated physiotherapy group. The result showed significant difference (F = 19.04, p ≤ 0.05).

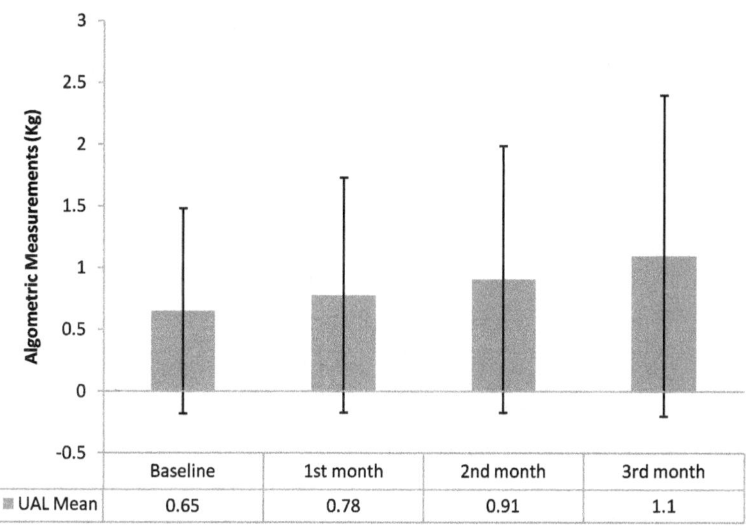

Figure 4.4.9: The Mean and SD on algometer measurement in upper arm left side point from baseline to third month

Table 4.4.9.1: Pair-wise comparison of algometric measurement of widespread pain index points on upper arm left (UAL) variable from Baseline to Third month at different time frame

Time frame	n	Mean difference	Standard Error	P	95% CI [b]	
					Lower bound	Upper bound
Baseline – 1 month		0.13	0.03	0.06	0.19	0.06
1 month – 2 month	30	0.26[*]	0.05	0.04	0.37	0.14
2 month – 3 month		0.49[*]	0.10	0.04	0.71	0.26
Based on estimated marginal means						
n = number of participants, CI = Confidence Interval						
* = The mean difference is significant at the 0.05 level.						
b. Adjustment for multiple comparisons: Least Significant Difference (equivalent to no adjustments).						

Table 4.4.9.1 shows the pair-wise comparison of Mean Difference (MD) and Standard Error (SE) on different time frame at baseline to 1st month (MD = 0.13; SE = 0.03; p = 0.06), 1st month – 2nd month (MD = 0.26; SE = 0.05; p = 0.04), and 2nd – 3rd month (MD = 0.49; SE = 0.10; P = 0.04) the result shows statistical significance (p ≤ 0.05).

Table 4.4.10: Comparison of algometric measurement of widespread pain index points on Upper Arm Right (UAR) variable within the group-3 from Baseline to Third month

Variable	n	Mean ± SD	SE	df	F	P
UAR (B)		0.86 ± 1.00	0.18			
UAR (1)	30	1.12 ± 1.23	0.23	3	13.05	< 0.01*
UAR (2)		1.34 ± 1.47	0.27			
UAR (3)		1.62 ± 1.77	0.33			
UAR = Upper Arm Right; **n** = Number of participants; **SD** = Standard Deviation; **SE** = Standard Error; **df** = differential frequency; **F** = Mean of the within group variances. * = The Mean score is significant at the 0.05 level.							

Table 4.4.10 depicts the Mean and standard deviation for pain pressure threshold of upper arm right side point on algometer at Baseline (0.86 ± 1.00), 1st month (1.12 ± 1.23), 2nd Month (1.34 ± 1.47), and 3rd month (1.62 ± 1.77) in integrated physiotherapy group. The result showed significant difference (F = 13.05, p ≤ 0.05).

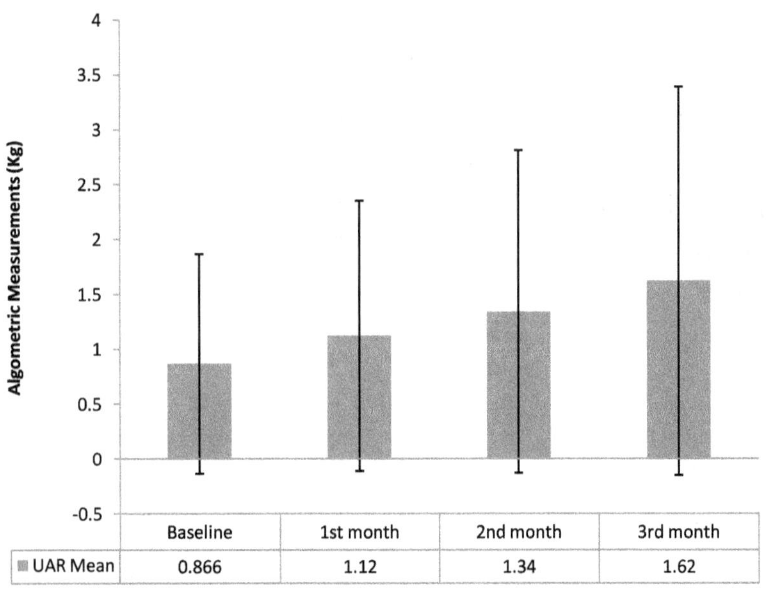

Figure 4.4.10: The Mean and SD on algometer measurement in Upper Arm Right side point from baseline to third month

Table 4.4.10.1: Pair-wise comparison of algometric measurement of widespread pain index points on Upper Arm Right (UAR) variable from Baseline to Third month at different time frame

Time frame	n	Mean difference	Standard Error	P	95% CI [b]	
					Lower bound	Upper bound
Baseline – 1 month		0.25[*]	0.08	< 0.01	0.43	0.08
1 month – 2 month	30	0.48[*]	0.14	< 0.01	0.77	0.18
2 month – 3 month		0.76[*]	0.20	< 0.01	1.18	0.33

n = number of participants, CI = Confidence Interval

* = The mean difference is significant at the 0.05 level.

b. Adjustment for multiple comparisons: Least Significant Difference (equivalent to no adjustments).

Table 4.4.10.1 shows the pair-wise comparison of Mean Difference (MD) and Standard Error (SE) on different time frame at baseline to 1st month (MD = 0.25; SE = 0.08; p < 0.01), 1st month – 2nd month (MD = 0.48; SE = 0.14; p < 0.00), and 2nd – 3rd month (MD = 0.76; SE = 0.20; P < 0.01) the result shows statistical significance ($p \leq 0.05$).

Table 4.4.11: Comparison of algometric measurement of widespread pain index points on Lower Arm Left (LAL) variable within the group-3 from Baseline to Third month

Variable	n	Mean ± SD	SE	df	F	P
LAL (B)		0.09 ± 0.32	0.05			
LAL (1)	30	0.13 ± 0.40	0.07	3	2.69	> 0.05[#]
LAL (2)		0.15 ± 0.46	0.08			
LAL (3)		0.20 ± 0.64	0.11			

LAL = Lower Arm Left; **n** = Number of participants; **SD** = Standard Deviation; **SE** = Standard Error; **df** = differential frequency; **F** = Mean of the within group variances. # = The Mean score is Non-significant at the 0.05 level.

Table 4.4.11 depicts the Mean and standard deviation for pain pressure threshold of lower arm left side point on algometer at Baseline (0.09 ± 0.32), 1st month (0.13 ± 0.40), 2nd Month (0.15 ± 0.46), and 3rd month (0.20 ± 0.64) in integrated physiotherapy group. The result showed non-significant difference (F = 2.69, p > 0.05).

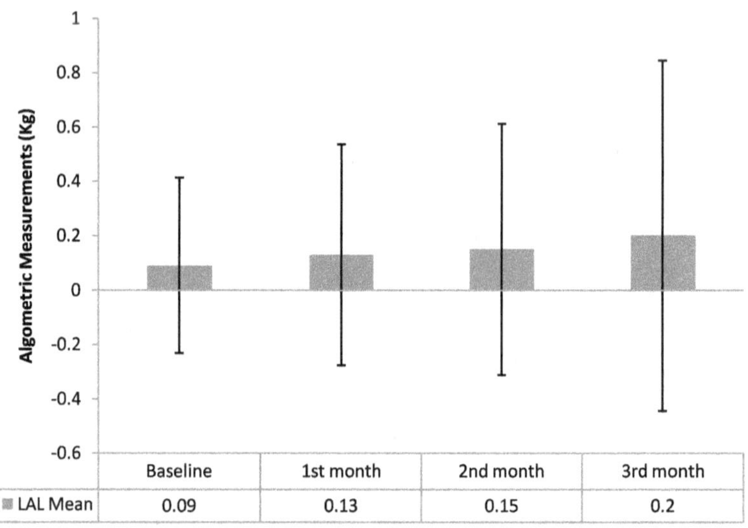

Figure 4.4.11: The Mean and SD on algometer measurement in Lower Arm Left side point from baseline to third month

Table 4.4.11.1: Pair-wise comparison of algometric measurement of widespread pain index points on Lower Arm Left (LAL) variable from Baseline to Third month at different time frame

Time frame	n	Mean difference	Standard Error	P	95% CI [b]	
					Lower bound	Upper bound
Baseline – 1 month		0.03[#]	0.02	0.20	0.09	0.021
1 month – 2 month	30	0.05[#]	0.03	0.11	0.12	0.01
2 month – 3 month		0.11[#]	0.06	0.08	0.24	0.01

Based on estimated marginal means

n = number of participants, CI = Confidence Interval

[#]. The mean difference is non-significant at the 0.05 level.

b. Adjustment for multiple comparisons: Least Significant Difference (equivalent to no adjustments).

    Table 4.4.11.1 shows the pair-wise comparison of Mean Difference (MD) and Standard Error (SE) on different time frame at baseline to 1st month (MD = 0.03; SE = 0.02; p = 0.20), 1st month – 2nd month (MD = 0.05; SE = 0.03; p = 0.11), and 2nd – 3rd month (MD = 0.11; SE = 0.06; P = 0.08) the result shows statistical non-significance (p > 0.05).

Table 4.4.12: Comparison of algometric measurement of widespread pain index points on Lower Arm Right (LAR) variable within the group-3 from Baseline to Third month

Variable	n	Mean ± SD	SE	df	F	P
LAR (B)		0.27 ± 0.73	0.13			
LAR (1)	30	0.31 ± 0.83	0.15	3	4.07	0.05*
LAR (2)		0.34 ± 0.90	0.16			
LAR (3)		0.41 ± 1.10	0.20			

LAR = Lower Arm Right; **n** = Number of participants; **SD** = Standard Deviation; **SE** = Standard Error; **df** = differential frequency; **F** = Mean of the within group variances; * = The Mean score is significant at the 0.05 level.

Table 4.4.12 depicts the Mean and standard deviation for pain pressure threshold of lower arm right side point on algometer at Baseline (0.27 ± 0.73), 1st month (0.31 ± 0.83), 2nd Month (0.34 ± 0.90), and 3rd month (0.41 ± 1.10) in integrated physiotherapy group. The result showed significant difference (F = 4.07, p = 0.05).

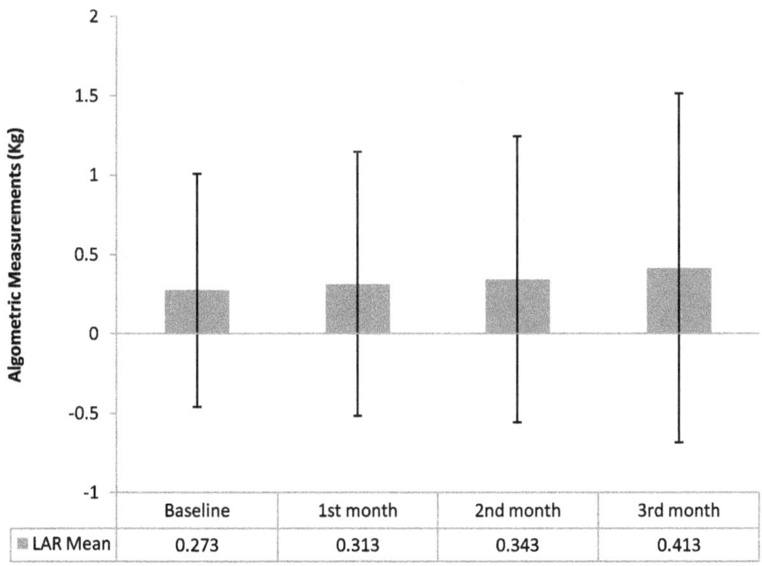

Figure 4.4.12: Figure showings the mean and SD on algometer measurement in Lower Arm Right side point from baseline to third month

Table 4.4.12.1: Pair-wise comparison of algometric measurement of widespread pain index points on Lower Arm Right (LAR) variable from Baseline to Third month at different time frame

Time frame	n	Mean difference	Standard Error	P	95% CI [b]	
					Lower bound	Upper bound
Baseline – 1 month		0.04[*]	0.02	0.05	0.08	4.68
1 month – 2 month	30	0.07[*]	0.03	0.04	0.13	0.00
2 month – 3 month		0.14[*]	0.06	0.04	0.27	0.00

n = number of participants, CI = Confidence Interval
[*]. The mean difference is significant at the 0.05 level.
b. Adjustment for multiple comparisons: Least Significant Difference (equivalent to no adjustments).

Table 4.4.12.1 shows the pair-wise comparison of Mean Difference (MD) and Standard Error (SE) on different time frame at baseline to 1st month (MD = 0.04; SE = 0.02; p = 0.05), 1st month – 2nd month (MD = 0.07; SE = 0.03; p = 0.04), and 2nd – 3rd month (MD = 0.14; SE = 0.06; P = 0.04) the result shows statistical significance (p < 0.05).

Table 4.4.13: Comparison of algometric measurement of widespread pain index points on Hip Buttock Left [H (B) L] variable within the group-3 from Baseline to Third month

Variable	n	Mean ± SD	SE	Df	F	P
HBL (B)		1.24 ± 0.99	0.18			
HBL (1)	30	1.50 ± 1.09	0.20	3	51.69	< 0.01*
HBL (2)		1.77 ± 1.21	0.22			
HBL (3)		2.10 ± 1.37	0.25			

HBL = Hip Buttock Left; **n** = Number of participants; **SD** = Standard Deviation; **SE** = Standard Error; **df** = differential frequency; **F** = Mean of the within group variances: * = The Mean score is significant at the 0.05 level.

Table 4.4.13 depicts the mean and standard deviation for pain pressure threshold of hip buttock left side point on algometer at baseline (1.24 ± 0.99), 1st month (1.50 ± 1.09), 2nd month (1.77 ± 1.21), and 3rd month (2.10 ± 1.37) of IPT group. The result showed significant difference (F = 51.69, p ≤ 0.01).

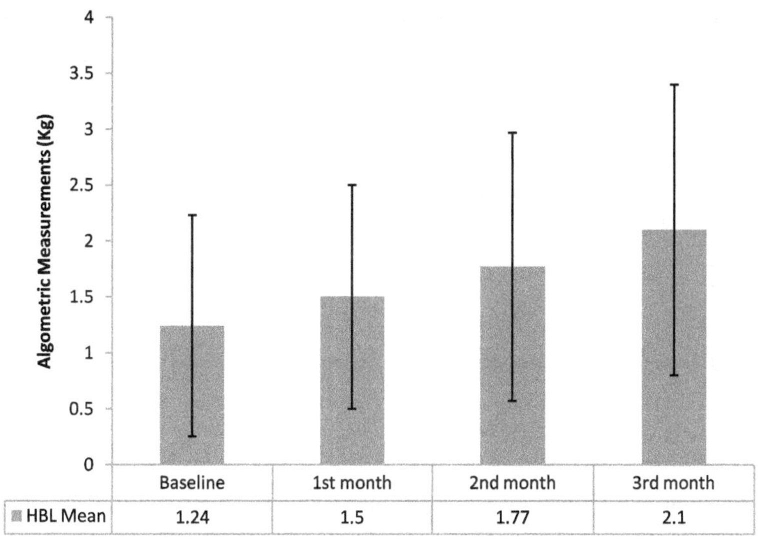

Figure 4.4.13: The Mean and SD on algometer measurement in Hip Buttock Left [H (B) L] point from baseline to third month

Table 4.4.13.1: Pair-wise comparison of algometric measurement of widespread pain index points on Hip Buttock Left [H (B) L] variable from Baseline to Third month at different time frame

Time frame	N	Mean difference	Standard Error	P	95% CI [b] Lower bound	Upper bound
Baseline – 1 month		0.26[*]	0.03	< 0.01	0.33	0.18
1 month – 2 month	30	0.53[*]	0.07	< 0.01	0.68	0.38
2 month – 3 month		0.86[*]	0.11	< 0.01	1.09	0.63
n = number of participants, CI = Confidence Interval						
[*] = The mean difference is significant at the 0.05 level.						
b. Adjustment for multiple comparisons: Least Significant Difference (equivalent to no adjustments).						

    Table 4.4.13.1 shows the pair-wise comparison of Mean Difference (MD) and Standard Error (SE) on different time frame at baseline to 1st month (MD = 0.26; SE = 0.03; p = < 0.01), 1st month – 2nd month (MD = 0.53; SE = 0.075; p = < 0.01), and 2nd – 3rd month (MD = 0.86; SE = 0.11; P = < 0.01) the result shows statistical significance ($p \leq 0.01$).

Table 4.4.14: Comparison of algometric measurement of widespread pain index points on Hip Buttock Right [H (B) R] variable within the group-3 from Baseline to Third month

Variable	n	Mean ± SD	SE	df	F	P
HBR (B)		1.12 ± 0.92	0.16			
HBR (1)	30	1.37 ± 1.01	0.18	3	42.13	< 0.01*
HBR (2)		1.61 ± 1.15	0.21			
HBR (3)		1.93 ± 1.31	0.24			
HBR = Hip Buttock Right; **n** = Number of participants; **SD** = Standard Deviation; **SE** = Standard Error; **df** = differential frequency; **F** = Mean of the within group variances; * = The Mean score is significant at the 0.05 level.						

Table 4.4.14 depicts the mean and standard deviation for pain pressure threshold of hip buttock right side point on algometer at baseline (1.12 ± 0.92), 1st month (1.37 ± 1.01), 2nd month (1.61 ± 1.15), and 3rd month (1.93 ± 1.31) of IPT group. The result showed significant difference (F = 42.13, p ≤ 0.01).

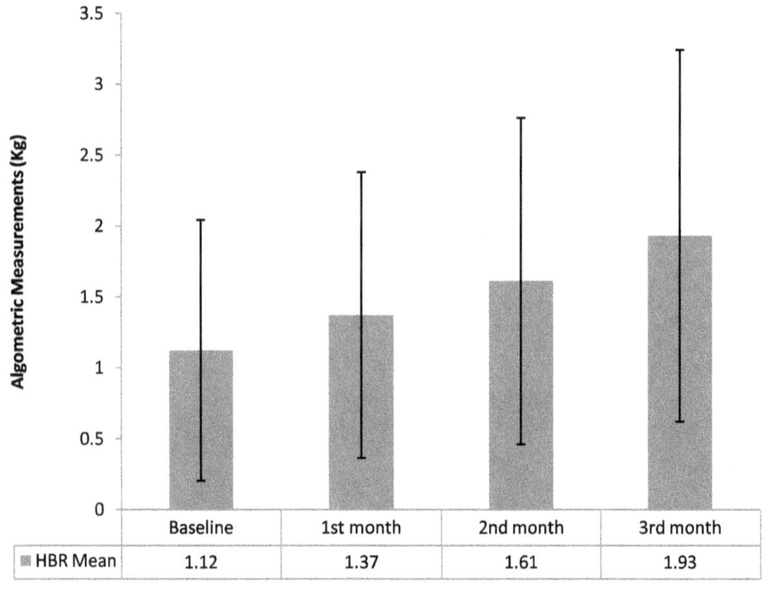

Figure 4.4.14: The Mean and SD on algometer measurement in Hip Buttock Right [H (B) R] point from baseline to third month

Table 4.4.14.1: Pair-wise comparison of algometric measurement of widespread pain index points on Hip Buttock Right [H (B) R] variable from Baseline to Third month at different time frame

Time frame	n	Mean difference	Standard Error	P	95% CI [b]	
					Lower bound	Upper bound
Baseline – 1 month		0.25^*	0.05	< 0.01	0.35	0.14
1 month – 2 month	30	0.49^*	0.08	< 0.01	0.67	0.31
2 month – 3 month		0.81^*	0.11	< 0 .01	1.05	0.56

n = number of participants, CI = Confidence Interval
* = The mean difference is significant at the 0.05 level.
b. Adjustment for multiple comparisons: Least Significant Difference (equivalent to no adjustments).

Table 4.4.14.1 shows the pair-wise comparison of Mean Difference (MD) and Standard Error (SE) on different time frame at baseline to 1st month (MD = 0.25; SE = 0.05; p = < 0.01), 1st month – 2nd month (MD = 0.49; SE = 0.08; p = < 0.01), and 2nd – 3rd month (MD = 0.81; SE = 0.11; P = < 0.01) the result shows statistical significance ($p \leq 0.01$).

Table 4.4.15: Comparison of algometric measurement of widespread pain index points on Upper Leg Left (ULL) variable within the group-3 from Baseline to Third month

Variable	n	Mean ± SD	SE	df	F	P
ULL (B)		0.18 ± 0.56	0.10			
ULL (1)	30	0.24 ± 0.69	0.12	3	3.69	$> 0.05^{\#}$
ULL (2)		0.26 ± 0.73	0.13			
ULL (3)		0.31 ± 0.82	0.15			

ULL = Upper Leg Left; **n** = Number of participants; **SD** = Standard Deviation; **SE** = Standard Error; **df** = differential frequency; **F** = Mean of the within group variances. # = The Mean score is Non-significant at the 0.05 level.

Table 4.4.15 depicts the mean and standard deviation for pain pressure threshold of upper leg left side point on algometer at baseline (0.18 ± 0.56), 1st month (0.24 ± 0.69), 2nd month (0.26 ± 0.73), and 3rd month (0.31 ± 0.82) of IPT group. The result showed significant difference (F = 3.69, p > 0.05).

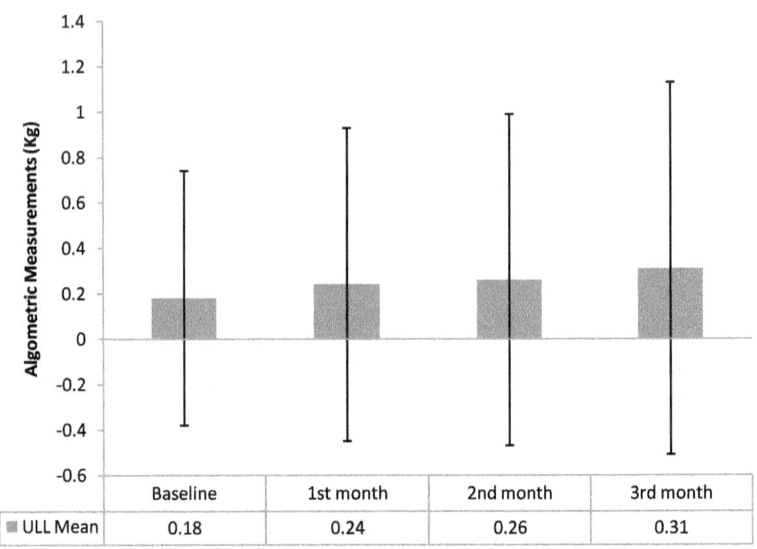

Figure 4.4.15: The Mean and SD on algometer measurement in Upper Leg Left (ULL) point from baseline to third month

Table 4.4.15.1: Pair-wise comparison of algometric measurement of widespread pain index points on Upper Leg Left (ULL) variable from Baseline to Third month at different time frame

Time frame	n	Mean difference	Standard Error	P	95% CI [b]	
					Lower bound	Upper bound
Baseline – 1 month		0.06[#]	0.03	0.06	0.13	0.00
1 month – 2 month	30	0.08[*]	0.04	0.05	0.16	0.00
2 month – 3 month		0.13[#]	0.06	0.06	0.26	0.00

n = number of participants, CI = Confidence Interval
[#]. The mean difference is non-significant at the 0.05 level and * = Significant.
b. Adjustment for multiple comparisons: Least Significant Difference (equivalent to no adjustments).

Table 4.4.15.1 shows the pair-wise comparison of Mean Difference (MD) and Standard Error (SE) on different time frame at baseline to 1st month (MD = 0.06; SE = 0.03; p = 0.06), 1st month – 2nd month (MD = 0.04; SE = 0.03; p = 0.05), and 2nd – 3rd month (MD = 0.13; SE = 0.06; P = 0.06) the result shows statistical non-significance (p > 0.05).

Table 4.4.16: Comparison of algometric measurement of widespread pain index points on Upper Leg Right (ULR) variable within the group-3 from Baseline to Third month

Variable	n	Mean ± SD	SE	df	F	P
ULR (B)		0.12 ± 0.35	0.06			
ULR (1)	30	0.18 ± 0.49	0.09	3	3.62	> 0.05[#]
ULR (2)		0.24 ± 0.68	0.12			
ULR (3)		0.30 ± 0.82	0.15			
ULR = Upper Leg Right; **n** = Number of participants; **SD** = Standard Deviation; **SE** = Standard Error; **df** = differential frequency; **F** = Mean of the within group variances. * = The Mean score is significant at the 0.05 level.						

Table **4.4.16** depicts the mean and standard deviation for pain pressure threshold of upper limb right side point on algometer at baseline (0.12 ± 0.35), 1st month (0.18 ± 0.49), 2nd month (0.24 ± 0.68), and 3rd month (0.30 ± 0.82) of IPT group. The result showed significant difference (F = 3.62, p > 0.05).

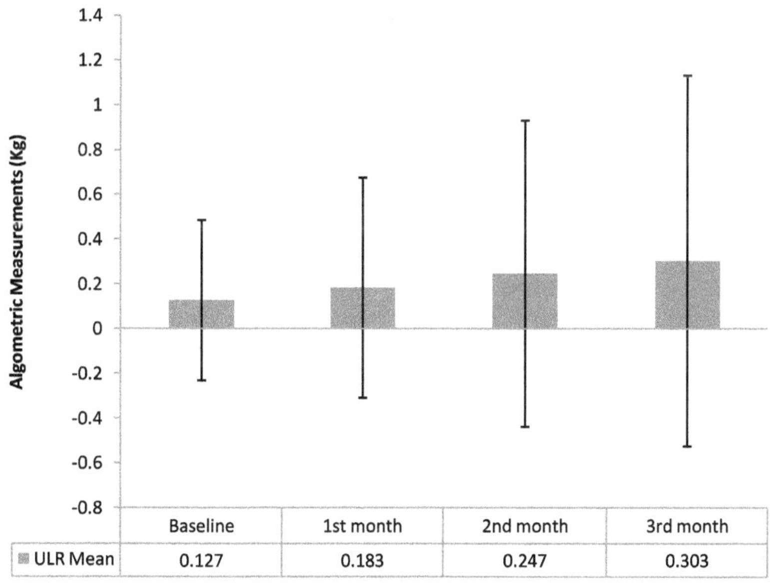

Figure 4.4.16: The Mean and SD on algometer measurement in Upper Leg Right (ULR) point from baseline to third month

Table 4.4.16.1: Pair-wise comparison of algometric measurement of widespread pain index points on Upper Leg Right (ULR) variable from Baseline to Third month at different time frame

Time frame	n	Mean difference	Standard Error	P	95% CI [b]	
					Lower bound	Upper bound
Baseline – 1 month		$0.05^{\#}$	0.03	0.09	0.12	0.01
1 month – 2 month	30	$0.12^{\#}$	0.06	0.06	0.25	0.01
2 month – 3 month		$0.17^{\#}$	0.09	0.06	0.36	0.00

Based on estimated marginal means

n = number of participants, CI = Confidence Interval

[#]. The mean difference is non-significant at the 0.05 level.

b. Adjustment for multiple comparisons: Least Significant Difference (equivalent to no adjustments).

Table 4.4.16.1 shows the pair-wise comparison of Mean Difference (MD) and Standard Error (SE) on different time frame at baseline to 1st month (MD = 0.05; SE = 0.03; p = 0.09), 1st month – 2nd month (MD = 0.12; SE = 0.06; p = 0.06), and 2nd – 3rd month (MD = 0.17; SE = 0.09; P = 0.06) the result shows statistical non-significance (p > 0.05).

Table 4.4.17: Comparison of algometric measurement of widespread pain index points on Lower Leg Left (LLL) variable within the group-3 from Baseline to Third month

Variable	n	Mean ± SD	SE	df	F	P
LLL (B)		0.26 ± 0.71	0.13			
LLL (1)	30	0.29 ± 0.72	0.13	3	4.71	$< 0.05^{\#}$
LLL (2)		0.37 ± 0.90	0.16			
LLL (3)		0.44 ± 1.08	0.19			

LLL = Lower Leg Left; **n** = Number of participants; **SD** = Standard Deviation; **SE** = Standard Error; **df** = differential frequency; **F** = Mean of the within group variances. # = The Mean score is Non-significant at the 0.05 level.

Table 4.4.17 depicts the mean and standard deviation for pain pressure threshold of lower limb left side point on algometer at baseline (0.26 ± 0.71), 1st month (0.29 ± 0.72), 2nd month (0.37 ± 0.90), and 3rd month (0.44 ± 1.08) of IPT group. The result showed significant difference (F = 4.71, p ≤ 0.05).

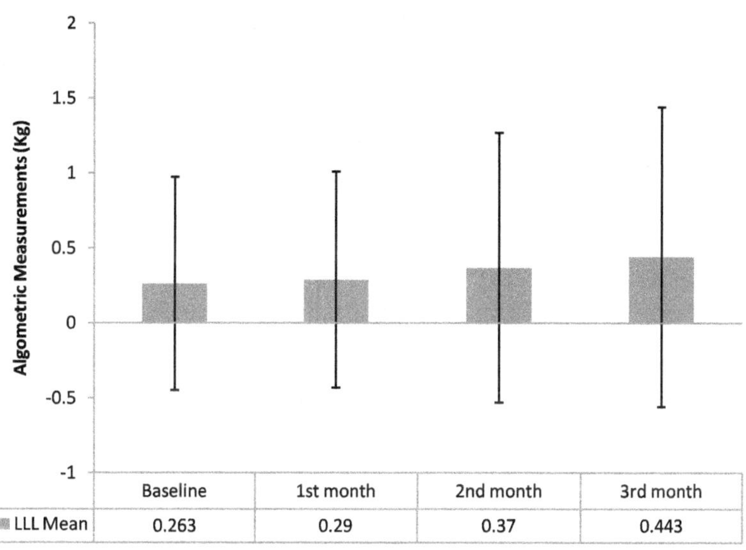

Figure 4.4.17: The Mean and SD on algometer measurement in Lower Leg Left (LLL) point from baseline to third month

Table 4.4.17.1: Pair-wise comparison of algometric measurement of widespread pain index points on Lower Leg Left (LLL) variable from Baseline to Third month at different time frame

Time frame	n	Mean difference	Standard Error	P	95% CI [b]	
					Lower bound	Upper bound
Baseline – 1 month		$0.02^{\#}$	0.02	0.31	0.08	0.02
1 month – 2 month	30	0.10^{*}	0.04	0.03	0.20	0.00
2 month – 3 month		0.18^{*}	0.08	0.03	0.34	0.01

n = number of participants, CI = Confidence Interval

[*] = The mean difference is significant at the 0.05 level and [#] = Non-Significant

b. Adjustment for multiple comparisons: Least Significant Difference (equivalent to no adjustments).

Table 4.4.17.1 shows the pair-wise comparison of Mean Difference (MD) and Standard Error (SE) on different time frame at baseline to 1st month (MD = 0.02; SE = 0.02; p = 0.31), 1st month – 2nd month (MD = 0.10; SE = 0.04; p = 0.03), and 2nd – 3rd month (MD = 0.18; SE = 0.08; P = < 0.03) the result shows statistical significance (p = 0.05).

Table 4.4.18: Comparison of algometric measurement of widespread pain index points on Lower Leg Right (LLR) variable within the group-3 from Baseline to Third month

Variable	n	Mean ± SD	SE	df	F	P
LLR (B)		0.16 ± 0.46	0.08			
LLR (1)	30	0.16 ± 0.46	0.10	3	3.89	> 0.05[#]
LLR (2)		0.25 ± 0.70	0.12			
LLR (3)		0.28 ± 0.77	0.14			
LLR = Lower Leg Right; n = Number of participants; SD = Standard Deviation; SE = Standard Error; df = differential frequency; F = Mean of the within group variances. # = The Mean score is Non-significant at the 0.05 level.						

Table 4.4.18.1 depicts the mean and standard deviation for pain pressure threshold of lower limb right side point on algometer at baseline (0.16 ± 0.46), 1st month (0.16 ± 0.46), 2nd month (0.25 ± 0.70), and 3rd month (0.28 ± 0.77) of IPT group. The result showed significant difference (F = 3.89, p > 0.05).

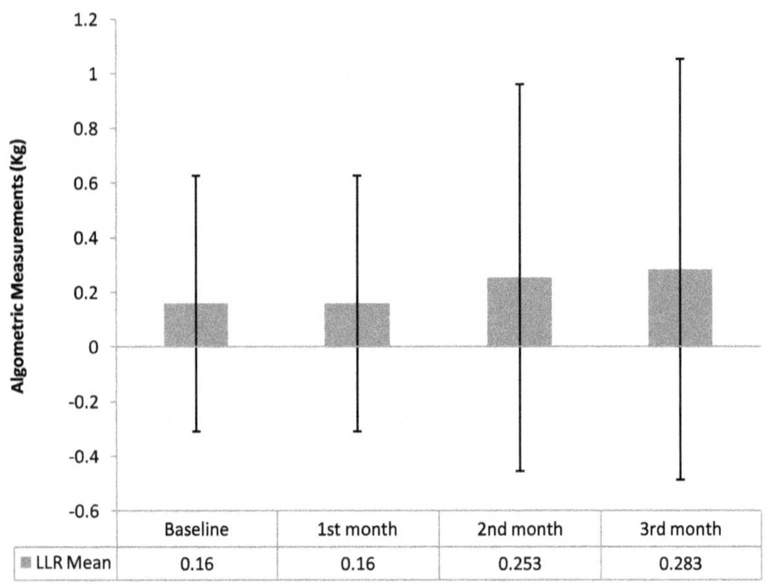

Figure 4.4.18: The Mean and SD on algometer measurement in Lower Leg Right (LLR) point from baseline to third month

Table 4.4.18.1: **Pair-wise comparison of algometric measurement of widespread pain index points on Lower Leg Right (LLR) variable from Baseline to Third month at different time frame**

Time frame	n	Mean difference	Standard Error	P	95% CI [b]	
					Lower bound	Upper bound
Baseline – 1 month		0.05[*]	0.02	0.05	0.10	0.00
1 month – 2 month	30	0.09[#]	0.04	0.06	0.19	0.00
2 month – 3 month		0.12[*]	0.06	0.04	0.24	0.00

n = number of participants, CI = Confidence Interval
[*] = The mean difference is significant at the 0.05 level and [#] = Non-Significant
b. Adjustment for multiple comparisons: Least Significant Difference (equivalent to no adjustments).

Table 4.4.18.1 shows the pair-wise comparison of Mean Difference (MD) and Standard Error (SE) on different time frame at baseline to 1st month (MD = 0.05; SE = 0.02; p = 0.05), 1st month – 2nd month (MD = 0.09; SE = 0.04; p = 0.06), and 2nd – 3rd month (MD = 0.12; SE = 0.06; P = 0.04) the result shows statistical significance ($p \leq 0.05$).

Table 4.4.19: **Comparison of algometric measurement of widespread pain index points on Jaw Left (JAWL) variable within the group-3 from Baseline to Third month**

Variable	n	Mean ± SD	SE	df	F	P
JAWL (B)		0.07 ± 0.30	0.05			
JAWL (1)	30	0.10 ± 0.38	0.07	3	1.82	> 0.05[#]
JAWL (2)		0.12 ± 0.49	0.09			
JAWL (3)		0.14 ± 0.56	0.10			

JAWL = Jaw Left; n = Number of participants; SD = Standard Deviation; SE = Standard Error; df = differential frequency; F = Mean of the within group variances. # = The Mean score is Non-significant at the 0.05 level.

Table 4.4.19 depicts the mean and standard deviation for pain pressure threshold of jaw left side point on algometer at baseline (0.07 ± 0.30), 1st month (0.10 ± 0.38), 2nd month (0.12 ± 0.49), and 3rd month (0.14 ± 0.56) of IPT group. The result showed significant difference (F = 1.82, p > 0.05).

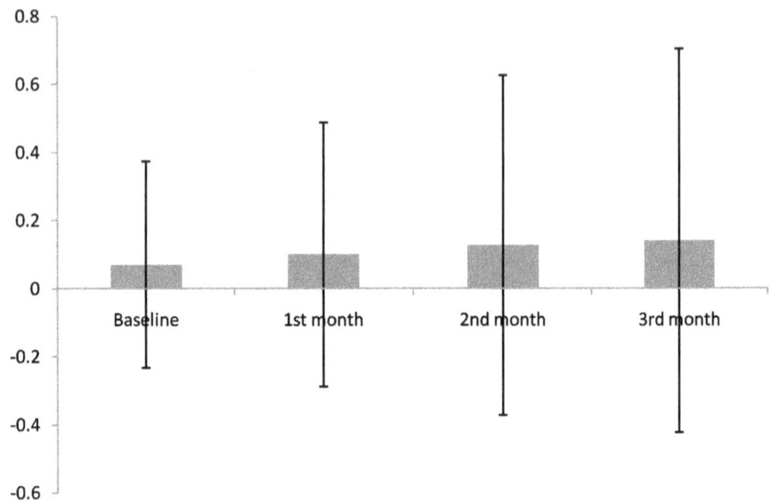

Figure 4.4.19: The Mean and SD on algometer measurement in Jaw Left (JAWL) point from baseline to third month

Table 4.4.19.1: Pair-wise comparison of algometric measurement of widespread pain index points on Jaw Left (JAWL) variable from Baseline to Third month at different time frame

Time frame	n	Mean difference	Standard Error	P	95% CI [b]	
					Lower bound	Upper bound
Baseline – 1 month		0.03[#]	0.02	0.22	0.07	0.01
1 month – 2 month	30	0.05[#]	0.03	0.16	0.13	0.02
2 month – 3 month		0.07[#]	0.04	0.16	0.17	0.03

Based on estimated marginal means

n = number of participants, CI = Confidence Interval

[#]. The mean difference is non-significant at the 0.05 level.

b. Adjustment for multiple comparisons: Least Significant Difference (equivalent to no adjustments).

Table 4.4.19.1 shows the pair-wise comparison of Mean Difference (MD) and Standard Error (SE) on different time frame at baseline to 1st month (MD = 0.03; SE = 0.02; p = 0.22), 1st month – 2nd month (MD = 0.05; SE = 0.03; p = 0.16), and 2nd – 3rd month (MD = 0.07; SE = 0.04; P = 0.16) the result shows statistical significance (p > 0.05).

Table 4.4.20: Comparison of algometric measurement of widespread pain index points on Jaw Right (JAWR) variable within the group-3 from Baseline to Third month

Variable	n	Mean ± SD	SE	df	F	P
JAWR (B)		0.12 ± 0.41	0.07			
JAWR (1)	30	0.17 ± 0.56	0.10	3	2.48	> 0.05[#]
JAWR (2)		0.29 ± 0.64	0.11			
JAWR (3)		0.22 ± 0.68	0.12			

JAWR = Jaw Right; **n** = Number of participants; **SD** = Standard Deviation; **SE** = Standard Error; **df** = differential frequency; **F** = Mean of the within group variances. # = The Mean score is Non-significant at the 0.05 level.

Table 4.4.20 depicts the mean and standard deviation for pain pressure threshold of jaw right side point on algometer at baseline (0.120 ± 0.41), 1st month (0.17 ± 0.56), 2nd month (0.29 ± 0.64), and 3rd month (0.22 ± 0.68) of IPT group. The result showed significant difference (F = 2.48, p > 0.05).

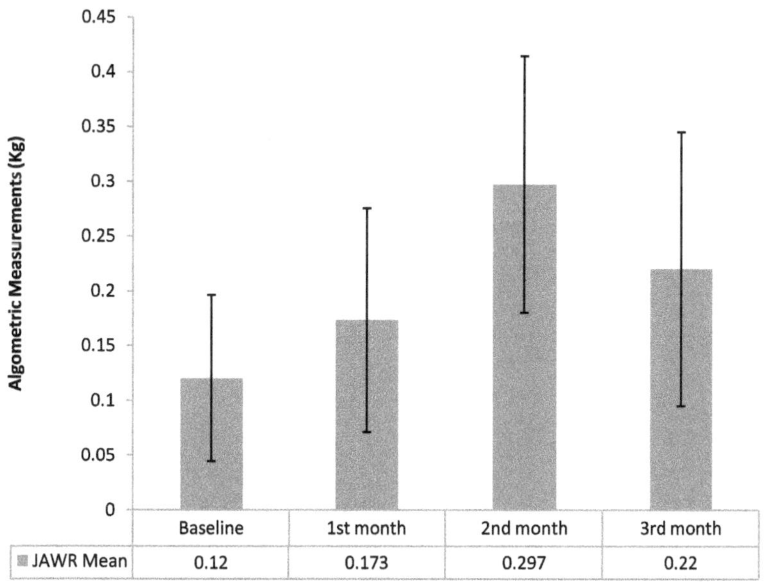

Figure 4.4.20: The Mean and SD on algometer measurement in Jaw Right (JAWR) point from baseline to third month

Table 4.4.20.1: Pair-wise comparison of algometric measurement of widespread pain index points on Jaw Right (JAWR) variable from Baseline to Third month at different time frame

Time frame	n	Mean difference	Standard Error	P	95% CI [b]	
					Lower bound	Upper bound
Baseline – 1 month		$0.05^{\#}$	0.03	0.09	0.11	0.00
1 month – 2 month	30	$0.07^{\#}$	0.04	0.10	0.17	0.01
2 month – 3 month		$0.10^{\#}$	0.06	0.11	0.22	0.02

n = number of participants, CI = Confidence Interval

#. The mean difference is non-significant at the 0.05 level.

b. Adjustment for multiple comparisons: Least Significant Difference (equivalent to no adjustments).

Table 4.4.20.1 shows the pair-wise comparison of Mean Difference (MD) and Standard Error (SE) on different time frame at baseline to 1st month (MD = 0.05; SE = 0.03; p = 0.09), 1st month – 2nd month (MD = 0.07; SE = 0.04; p = 0.10), and 2nd – 3rd month (MD = 0.10; SE = 0.06; P = 0.11) the result shows statistical significance (p > 0.05).

Table 4.4.21: Comparison of algometric measurement of widespread pain index points on Chest variable within the group-3 from Baseline to Third month

Variable	n	Mean ± SD	SE	df	F	P
CHEST (B)		0.35 ± 0.90	0.16			
CHEST (1)	30	0.46 ± 1.09	0.20	3	6.13	< 0.05*
CHEST (2)		0.57 ± 1.34	0.24			
CHEST (3)		0.67 ± 1.48	0.27			

n = Number of participants; SD = Standard Deviation; SE = Standard Error; df = differential frequency; F = Mean of the within group variances. * = The Mean score is significant at the 0.05 level.

Table 4.4.21 depicts the mean and standard deviation for pain pressure threshold of chest point on algometer at baseline (0.350 ± 0.9039), 1st month (0.467 ± 1.0999), 2nd month (0.570 ± 1.3430) and 3rd month (0.673 ± 1.4842) of IPT group. The result showed significant difference (F = 6.132, p = 0.05).

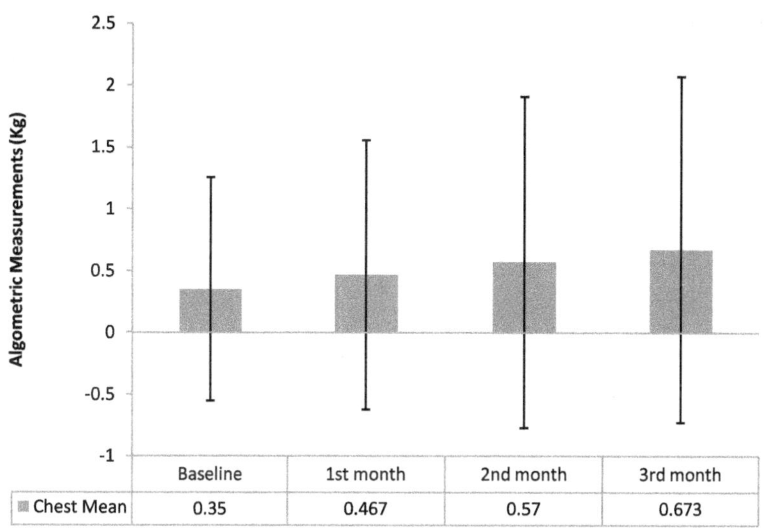

Figure 4.4.21: The Mean and SD on algometer measurement in Chest point from baseline to third month

Table 4.4.21.1: Pair-wise comparison of algometric measurement of widespread pain index points on Chest variable from Baseline to Third month at different time frame

Time frame	n	Mean difference	Standard Error	P	95% CI [b]	
					Lower bound	Upper bound
Baseline – 1 month		0.11[*]	0.05	0.03	0.22	0.01
1 month – 2 month	30	0.22[*]	0.09	0.02	0.41	0.02
2 month – 3 month		0.32[*]	0.12	0.01	0.58	0.06
n = number of participants, CI = Confidence Interval						
[*] = The mean difference is significant at the 0.05 level.						
b. Adjustment for multiple comparisons: Least Significant Difference (equivalent to no adjustments).						

Table 4.4.21.1 shows the pair-wise comparison of Mean Difference (MD) and Standard Error (SE) on different time frame at baseline to 1st month (MD = 0.11; SE = 0.05; p = 0.03), 1st month – 2nd month (MD = 0.22; SE = 0.09; p = 0.02), and 2nd – 3rd month (MD = 0.32; SE = 0.12; P = 0.01) the result shows statistical significance (p = 0.05).

Table 4.4.22: Comparison of algometric measurement of widespread pain index points on Abdomen variable within the group-3 from Baseline to Third month

Variable	n	Mean ± SD	SE	df	F	P
ABDOMEN (B)		0.19 ± 0.61	0.11			
ABDOMEN (1)	30	0.21 ± 0.67	0.12	3	2.93	$> 0.05^{\#}$
ABDOMEN (2)		0.26 ± 0.80	0.14			
ABDOMEN (3)		0.29 ± 0.89	0.16			

n = Number of participants; **SD** = Standard Deviation; **SE** = Standard Error; **df** = differential frequency; **F** = Mean of the within group variances. # = The Mean score is Non-significant at the 0.05 level.

Table 4.4.22 depicts the mean and standard deviation for pain pressure threshold of abdomen point on algometer at baseline (0.19 ± 0.61), 1st month (0.21 ± 0.67), 2nd month (0.26 ± 0.80), and 3rd month (0.29 ± 0.89) of IPT group. The result showed significant difference (F = 2.93, p > 0.05).

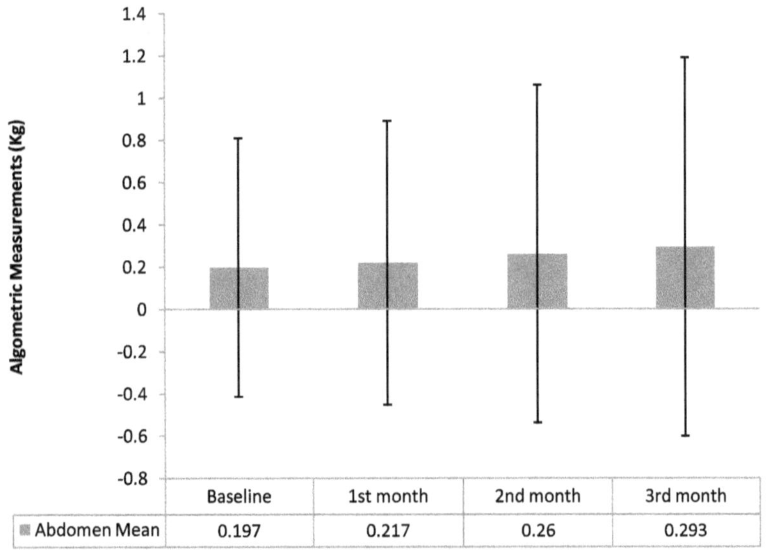

	Baseline	1st month	2nd month	3rd month
Abdomen Mean	0.197	0.217	0.26	0.293

Figure 4.4.22: The Mean and SD on algometer measurement in abdomen point from baseline to third month

194

Table 4.4.22.1: Pair-wise comparison of algometric measurement of widespread pain index points on abdomen variable from Baseline to Third month at different time frame

Time frame	n	Mean difference	Standard Error	P	95% CI [b]	
					Lower bound	Upper bound
Baseline – 1 month		$0.02^{\#}$	0.01	0.08	0.04	0.01
1 month – 2 month	30	$0.06^{\#}$	0.03	0.08	0.13	0.01
2 month – 3 month		$0.09^{\#}$	0.05	0.09	0.21	0.01

Based on estimated marginal means

n = number of participants, CI = Confidence Interval

*= The mean difference is significant at the 0.05 level.

b. Adjustment for multiple comparisons: Least Significant Difference (equivalent to no adjustments).

Table 4.4.22 shows the pair-wise comparison of Mean Difference (MD) and Standard Error (SE) on different time frame at baseline to 1st month (MD = 0.02; SE = 0.01; p = 0.08), 1st month – 2nd month (MD = 0.06; SE = 0.03; p = 0.08), and 2nd – 3rd month (MD = 0.09; SE = 0.05; P = 0.09) the result shows non-statistical significance (p > 0.05).

Table 4.4.23: Comparison of algometric measurement of widespread pain index points on Neck variable within the group-3 from Baseline to Third month

Variable	n	Mean ± SD	SE	df	F	P
NECK (B)		1.35 ± 1.25	0.22			
NECK (1)	30	1.76 ± 1.41	0.25	3	86.77	< 0.01*
NECK (2)		2.15 ± 1.51	0.27			
NECK (3)		2.57 ± 1.57	0.28			

n = Number of participants; **SD** = Standard Deviation; **SE** = Standard Error; **df** = differential frequency; **F** = Mean of the within group variances. * = The Mean score is significant at the 0.05 level.

Table 4.4.23 depicts the mean and standard deviation for pain pressure threshold of neck point on algometer at baseline (1.35 ± 1.25), 1st month (1.76 ± 1.41), 2nd month (2.15 ± 1.51), and 3rd month (2.57 ± 1.57) of IPT group. The result showed significant difference (F = 86.77, p ≤ 0.01).

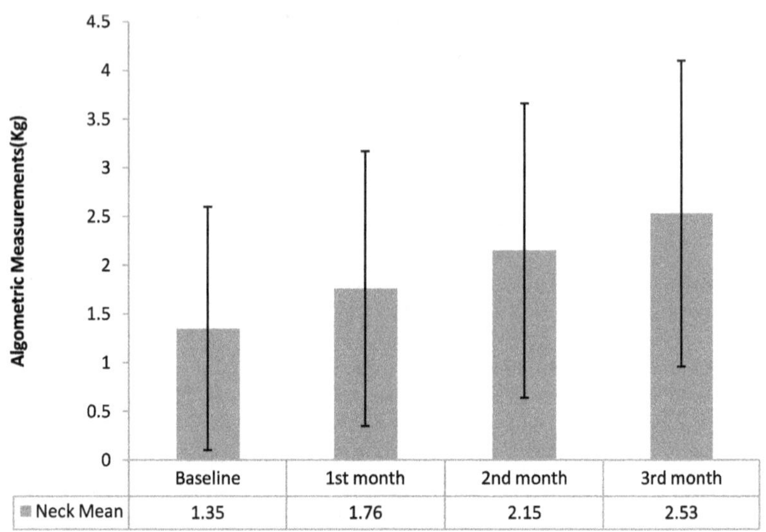

Figure 4.4.23: Figure shows the Mean and SD on algometer measurement in Neck point from baseline to third month

Table 4.4.23.1: Pair-wise comparison of algometric measurement of widespread pain index points on Neck variable from Baseline to Third month at different time frame

Time frame	n	Mean difference	Standard Error	P	95% CI [b]	
					Lower bound	Upper bound
Baseline – 1 month		0.41[*]	0.05	< 0.01	0.52	0.29
1 month – 2 month	30	0.80[*]	0.09	< 0.01	0.984	0.61
2 month – 3 month		1.22[*]	0.11	< 0.01	1.457	0.98

n = number of participants, CI = Confidence Interval

[*] = The mean difference is significant at the 0.05 level.

b. Adjustment for multiple comparisons: Least Significant Difference (equivalent to no adjustments).

Table 4.4.23.1 shows the pair-wise comparison of Mean Difference (MD) and Standard Error (SE) on different time frame at baseline to 1st month (MD = -0.410; SE = 0.05; p ≤ 0.01), 1st month – 2nd month (MD = 0.80; SE = 0.09; p ≤ 0.01), and 2nd – 3rd month (MD = 1.22; SE = 0.11; P ≤ 0.01) the result shows statistical significance (p ≤ 0.01).

Table 4.4.24: Comparison of algometric measurement of widespread pain index points on Upper Back (UB) variable within the group-3 from Baseline to Third month

Variable	n	Mean ± SD	SE	df	F	P
UB (B)		1.65 ± 1.63	0.29			
UB (1)	30	2.00 ± 1.70	0.31	3	54.29	< 0.01*
UB (2)		2.33 ± 1.70	0.31			
UB (3)		2.67 ± 1.77	0.32			

UB = Upper Back; **n** = Number of participants; **SD** = Standard Deviation; **SE** = Standard Error; **df** = differential frequency; **F** = Mean of the within group variances. * = The Mean score is significant at the 0.05 level.

Table 4.4.24 depicts the mean and standard deviation for pain pressure threshold of upper back point on algometer at baseline (1.65 ± 1.63), 1st month (2.00 ± 1.70), 2nd month (2.33 ± 1.70), and 3rd month (2.67 ± 1.77) of IPT group. The result showed significant difference (F = 54.29, p ≤ 0.01).

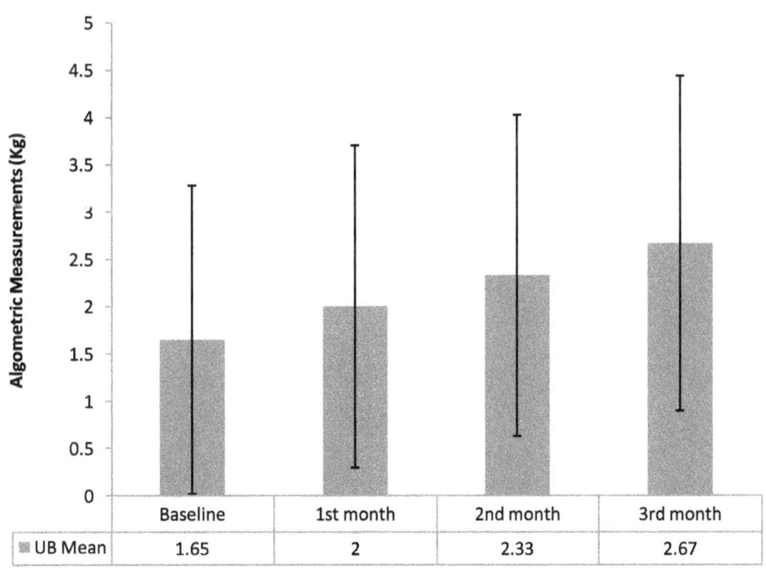

Figure 4.4.24: The Mean and SD on algometer measurement in upper back point from baseline to third month

Table 4.4.24.1: Pair-wise comparison of algometric measurement of widespread pain index points on upper back variable from Baseline to Third month at different time frame

Time frame	n	Mean difference	Standard Error	P	95% CI [b]	
					Lower bound	Upper bound
Baseline – 1 month		0.35[*]	0.04	< 0.01	0.44	0.25
1 month – 2 month	30	0.67[*]	0.08	< 0.01	0.83	0.51
2 month – 3 month		1.02[*]	0.12	< 0.01	1.28	0.76

n = number of participants, CI = Confidence Interval
[*] The mean difference is significant at the 0.05 level.
b. Adjustment for multiple comparisons: Least Significant Difference (equivalent to no adjustments).

Table 4.4.24.1 showed the pair-wise comparison of Mean Difference (MD) and Standard Error (SE) on different time frame at baseline to 1st month (MD = 0.35; SE = 0.04; $p \leq 0.01$), 1st month – 2nd month (MD = 0.67; SE = 0.08; $p \leq 0.01$), and 2nd – 3rd month (MD = 1.02; SE = 0.12; $P \leq 0.01$) the result shows statistical significance ($p \leq 0.01$).

Table 4.4.25: Comparison of algometric measurement of widespread pain index points on Lower Back (LB) variable within the group-3 from Baseline to Third month

Variable	n	Mean ± SD	SE	df	F	P
LB (B)		1.17 ± 1.02	0.18			
LB (1)	30	1.43 ± 1.14	0.20	3	39.22	< 0.01*
LB (2)		1.72 ± 1.29	0.23			
LB (3)		2.05 ± 1.44	0.26			

LB = Lower Back; n = Number of participants; SD = Standard Deviation; SE = Standard Error; df = differential frequency; F = Mean of the within group variances. * = The Mean score is significant at the 0.05 level.

Table 4.4.25 depicts the mean and standard deviation for pain pressure threshold of lower back point on algometer at baseline (1.17 ± 1.02), 1st month (1.43 ± 1.14), 2nd month (1.72 ± 1.29), and 3rd month (2.05 ± 1.44) of IPT group. The result showed significant difference (F = 39.22, $p \leq 0.01$).

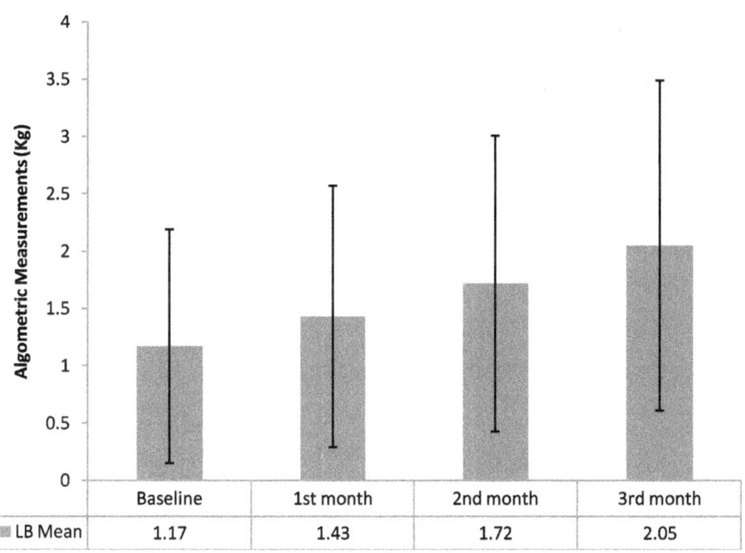

Figure 4.4.25: The Mean and SD on algometer measurement in lower back point from baseline to third month

Table 4.4.25.1: Pair-wise comparison of algometric measurement of widespread pain index points on lower back variable from Baseline to Third month at different time frame

Time frame	n	Mean difference	Standard Error	P	95% CI [b]	
					Lower bound	Upper bound
Baseline – 1 month		0.25[*]	0.05	< 0.01	0.36	0.15
1 month – 2 month	30	0.54[*]	0.09	< 0.01	0.73	0.34
2 month – 3 month		0.87[*]	0.12	< 0.01	1.13	0.62

n = number of participants, CI = Confidence Interval

[*] = The mean difference is significant at the 0.05 level.

b. Adjustment for multiple comparisons: Least Significant Difference (equivalent to no adjustments).

Table 4.4.25.1 shows the pair-wise comparison of Mean Difference (MD) and Standard Error (SE) on different time frame at baseline to 1st month (MD = 0.25; SE = 0.05; $p \leq 0.01$), 1st month – 2nd month (MD = 0.543; SE = 0.095; $p \leq 0.001$), and 2nd – 3rd month (MD = 0.87; SE = 0.12; $P \leq 0.01$) the result shows statistical significance ($p \leq 0.01$).

Summary of the result of Integrated Physiotherapy Techniques alone group

The primary outcome measure FIQR revealed significant results within the group IPT ($p \leq 0.01$); also, other variables showed that significant results ($p < 0.05$) on beck depression index, visual analog scale, general anxiety disorder, and short-form – 36 health survey. Furthermore, on most of the variables of widespread pain index measured by algometer for the pain pressure threshold over the SGL, shoulder girdle right, upper arm left, upper arm right, lower arm right, hip buttock left, hip buttock right, lower leg left, chest, neck, upper back, and lower back tender points shown statistical significance ($p < 0.05$). However, some of the variables demonstrated non-significant results ($p > 0.05$) viz. lower arm left, upper leg left, upper leg right, lower leg right, jaw left, jaw right, and abdomen. Thus, it signifies that IPT alone was effective in improving the quality of life, physical and mental health, reduction of pain, anxiety, depression, and the trigger point sensitivity.

4.5 Identifying individual differences between all the three groups

The main objective of the present study was to investigate the role of individual and combined effects of integrated Physiotherapy techniques along with pregabalin drug and cognitive behavioral therapy on FM patients. The total duration of the intervention was 3 months. The evaluation of FM was carried out at different time period. The role of treatment techniques was evaluated by comparison of outcomes at pre-intervention, in between intervention and at completion of intervention (3 months). Analysis of variance was used for this purpose.

Table 4.5.1: Comparison of difference in means (MD) of Revised Fibromyalgia Impact Questionnaire (FIQR) variable between the groups at different time frame from Baseline to Third month

Variable (Time frame)	Groups	Mean ± SD	SOS Between Groups	SOS Within Group	F	P
FIQR **(Baseline – 1ˢᵗ Month)**	PHAIPT	8.98 ± 7.61	759.4	5748	5.74	<0.01*
	CBTAIPT	15.05 ± 5.63				
	IPT Only	15.22 ± 10.4				
FIQR **(1ˢᵗ – 2ⁿᵈ Month)**	PHAIPT	7.54 ± 7.97	195.2	4517	1.88	0.15
	CBTAIPT	9.39 ± 6.50				
	IPT Only	11.15 ± 7.08				
FIQR **(2ⁿᵈ 3ʳᵈ Month)**	PHAIPT	5.13 ± 4.81	352.6	5303	2.89	0.06
	CBTAIPT	5.74 ± 5.56				
	IPT Only	9.60 ± 11.35				
FIQR **(Baseline 3ʳᵈ Month)**	PHAIPT	21.65 ± 11.33	3113	1796	7.54	<0.01*
	CBTAIPT	30.18 ± 10.73				
	IPT Only	35.97 ± 19.39				

FIQR = Revised Fibromyalgia Impact Questionnaire; SD = Standard Deviation; CBT = Cognitive Behavioral Therapy; IPT = Integrated Physiotherapy Techniques; SOS = Sum of Squares

Table 4.5.1 depicts the Mean and standard deviation of revised fibromyalgia impact questionnaire at baseline to first month (8.98 ± 7.61; 15.05 ± 5.63; 15.22 ± 10.4 with F = 5.74 and the p = 0.00), first to second month (7.54 ±7.97; 9.39 ± 6.50; 11.15 ± 7.08 with F = 1.88, p = 0.15), second to third month (5.13 ± 4.81; 5.74 ± 5.56; 9.60 ± 11.35 with F = 2.89, p = 0.06), baseline to third month (21.65 ±11.33; 30.18 ±10.73; 35.97 ± 19.39 with F = 7.54, p < 0.01), for Group 1, Group 2 and Group 3 respectively at the level of significance with p value ≤ 0.05. This signifies that the experimental groups role in reducing the disability and improve the functional ability of participants between groups in fibromyalgia patients.

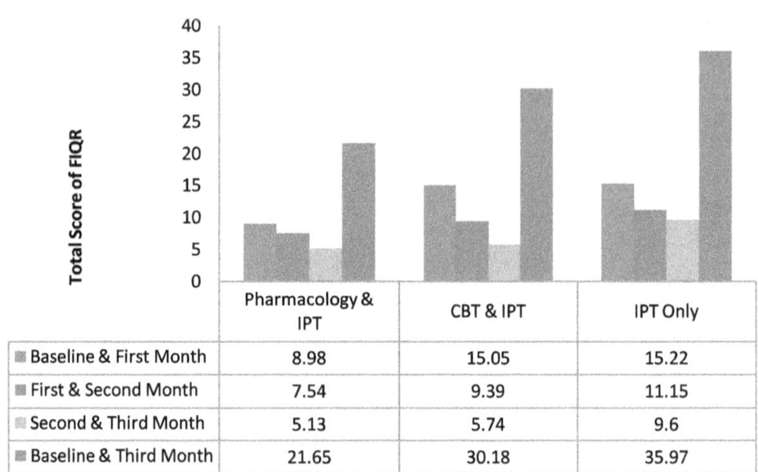

	Pharmacology & IPT	CBT & IPT	IPT Only
Baseline & First Month	8.98	15.05	15.22
First & Second Month	7.54	9.39	11.15
Second & Third Month	5.13	5.74	9.6
Baseline & Third Month	21.65	30.18	35.97

Figure 4.5.1: The Difference in means (MD) of Revised Fibromyalgia Impact Questionnaire from baseline to third month between group 1, 2 and 3

Table 4.5.1.1: Multiple comparison of difference in means (MD) of improvement on Revised Fibromyalgia Impact Questionnaire among different interventional group

Time frame between	Interventional group		MD	Standard Error	P value	95% Confidence Interval	
						Lower Bound	Upper Bound
Baseline - 1st Month	PHAIPT group	CBTAIPT group	6.08*	2.10	0.00	1.91	10.25
		IPT Group	6.24*	2.10	0.00	2.07	10.42
	CBTAIPT group	IPT Group	0.17#	2.10	0.94	4.01	4.34
1st Month - 2nd Month	PHAIPT group	CBTAIPT group	1.84#	1.86	0.32	1.85	5.54
		IPT Group	3.61#	1.86	0.06	0.09	7.31
	CBTAIPT group	IPT Group	1.76#	1.86	0.35	1.93	5.46
2nd Month - 3rd Month	PHAIPT group	CBTAIPT group	0.61#	2.02	0.76	3.40	4.61
		IPT Group	4.47*	2.02	0.03	0.46	8.48
	CBTAIPT group	IPT Group	3.86#	2.02	0.06	0.14	7.87
Baseline - 3rd Month	PHAIPT group	CBTAIPT group	8.53*	3.71	0.02	1.15	15.90
		IPT Group	14.32*	3.71	0.00	6.95	21.69
	CBTAIPT group	IPT Group	5.79#	3.71	0.12	1.58	13.17

CBT = Cognitive Behavioral Therapy; IPT = Integrated Physiotherapy Group; MD = Difference in means (MD); * = Significant; # = Non-Significant

Table 4.5.1.1 summarized the comparisons of differences in mean improvement in FIQR using post hoc Least Significant difference (LSD). The result specifies that level of improvement was greater in experimental group I & III at baseline to first month and baseline to third month (p ≤ 0.05) as compared to experimental group II.

Also, the improvement was greater in experimental group III at second to third month and baseline to third month as compared to experimental group I. however; it does not show the statistically significant difference (p > 0.05) in experimental group I & II at the remaining time frame as compared to experimental group III. This signifies that the role of PHAIPT and IPT in improving the health status of fibromyalgia patients.

Table 4.5.2: Comparison of difference in means (MD) of Beck Depression Index (BDI) variable between the groups at different time frame from Baseline to Third month

Variable (Time frame)	Groups	Mean ± SD	SOS Between Groups	SOS Within Group	F	P
BDI (Baseline – 1st Month)	PHAIPT	4.70 ± 7.22	176.4	37.60	4.69	0.01*
	CBTAIPT	6.77 ± 5.32				
	IPT Only	1.93 ± 5.69				
BDI (1st – 2nd Month)	PHAIPT	5.43 ± 6.42	252.7	35.22	7.17	<0.01*
	CBTAIPT	8.53 ± 6.98				
	IPT Only	2.73 ± 3.97				
BDI (2nd – 3 Month)	PHAIPT	3.57 ± 4.83	4.044	21.88	0.18	0.83[#]
	CBTAIPT	3.90 ± 4.22				
	IPT Only	3.17 ± 4.96				
BDI (Baseline – 3rd Month)	PHAIPT	13.7 ± 10.3	969.3	86.42	11.2	<0.01*
	CBTAIPT	19.2 ± 9.78				
	IPT Only	7.83 ± 7.53				

BDI = Beck Depression Index; SD = Standard Deviation; CBT = Cognitive Behavioral Therapy; IPT = Integrated Physiotherapy Techniques; SOS = Sum Of Squares.

Table 4.5.2 Depicts the Mean and standard deviation of Beck Depression Index at baseline to first month (4.70 ± 7.22; 6.77 ± 5.32; 1.93 ± 5.69 with F = 4.69 and the p = 0.01), first to second month (5.43 ± 6.42; 8.53 ± 6.98; 2.73 ± 3.97 with F = 7.174 and the p < 0.01), second to third month (3.57 ± 4.83; 3.90 ± 4.22; 3.17 ± 4.96 with F = 0.18 and the p = 0.83), baseline to third month (13.7 ± 10.3; 19.2 ± 9.78; 7.83 ± 7.53 with F = 11.21, p < 0.01), for Group 1, Group 2 and Group 3 respectively at the level of significance with p value ≤ 0.05. This signifies that the experimental groups role in reducing the depression of fibromyalgia patients.

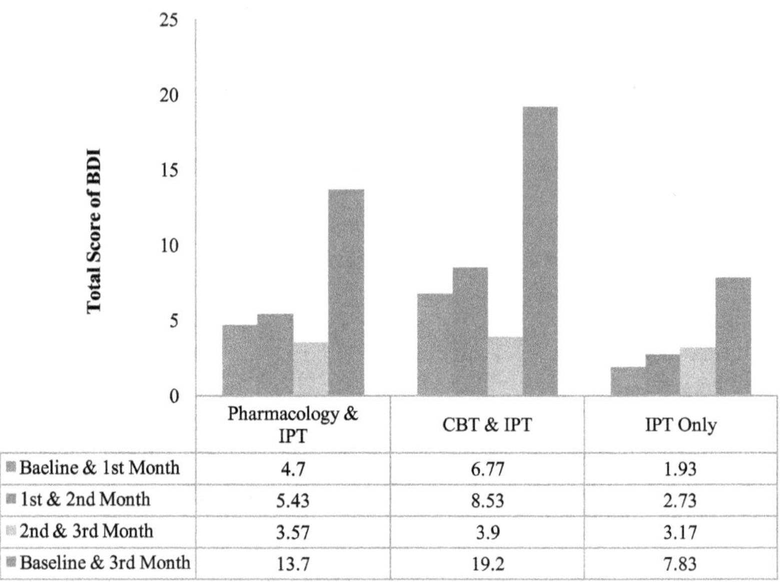

	Pharmacology & IPT	CBT & IPT	IPT Only
Baeline & 1st Month	4.7	6.77	1.93
1st & 2nd Month	5.43	8.53	2.73
2nd & 3rd Month	3.57	3.9	3.17
Baseline & 3rd Month	13.7	19.2	7.83

Figure 4.5.2: The Difference in means (MD) of Beck Depression Index from baseline to third month between group 1, 2 and 3

Table 4.5.2.1: Multiple comparison of difference in means (MD) of improvement on Beck Depression Index among different interventional group

Time frame between	Interventional group		MD	Standard Error	P value	95% Confidence Interval	
						Lower Bound	Upper Bound
Baseline -	PHAIPT group	CBTAIPT group	$2.07^{\#}$	1.58	0.20	1.08	5.21
		IPT Group	$2.77^{\#}$	1.58	0.08	0.38	5.91
1st Month	CBTAIPT group	IPT Group	4.83^{*}	1.58	<0.01	1.69	7.98
1st Month -	PHAIPT group	CBTAIPT group	3.10^{*}	1.53	0.05	0.05	6.15
		IPT Group	$2.70^{\#}$	1.53	0.08	0.35	5.75
2nd Month	CBTAIPT group	IPT Group	5.80^{*}	1.53	<0.01	2.75	8.85
2nd Month -	PHAIPT group	CBTAIPT group	$0.33^{\#}$	1.21	0.78	2.07	2.73
		IPT Group	$0.40^{\#}$	1.21	0.74	2.00	2.80
3rd Month	CBTAIPT group	IPT Group	$0.73^{\#}$	1.21	0.55	1.67	3.13
Baseline -	PHAIPT group	CBTAIPT group	5.50^{*}	2.40	0.02	0.73	10.27
		IPT Group	5.87^{*}	2.40	0.02	1.10	10.64
3rd Month	CBTAIPT group	IPT Group	11.37^{*}	2.40	< 0.01	6.60	16.14

CBT = Cognitive Behavioral Therapy; IPT = Integrated Physiotherapy Group; MD = Difference in means (MD) * = Significant

Table 4.5.2.1 summarized the comparisons of differences in mean improvement in VAS using post hoc Least Significant difference (LSD). The result specifies that level of improvement was greater in experimental group II at baseline to first month, first to second month as well as baseline to third month ($p \leq 0.05$) as compared to experimental group III. Also, the improvement was greater in experimental group I at first to second month and baseline to third month as compared to experimental group II. However; it does not show the statistically significant difference ($p > 0.05$) in experimental group I & II at the remaining time frame as compared to experimental group III. This signifies that the role of IPT and CBTAIPT in improving the depression status of fibromyalgia patients.

Table 4.5.3: Comparison of difference in means (MD) of Visual Analogue Scale (VAS) variable between the groups at different time frame from Baseline to Third month

Variable (Time frame)	Groups	Mean ± SD	SOS Between Groups	SOS Within Group	F	P
VAS (Baseline – 1st Month)	PHAIPT	2.63 ± 1.27	6.03	2.00	3.01	0.05*
	CBTAIPT	3.27 ± 1.20				
	IPT Only	2.40 ± 1.71				
VAS (1st – 2nd Month)	PHAIPT	1.43 ± 1.17	3.34	1.15	2.89	0.06[#]
	CBTAIPT	2.07 ± 1.08				
	IPT Only	1.57 ± 0.97				
VAS (2nd – 3rd Month)	PHAIPT	0.73 ± 0.83	9.07	1.72	5.27	<0.01*
	CBTAIPT	1.03 ± 1.07				
	IPT Only	1.80 ± 1.83				
VAS (Baseline – 3rd Month)	PHAIPT	4.80 ± 1.65	18.74	2.97	6.29	<0.01*
	CBTAIPT	6.37 ± 1.16				
	IPT Only	5.77 ± 2.21				

VAS = Visual Analogue Scale; SD = Standard Deviation; CBT = Cognitive Behavioral Therapy; IPT = Integrated Physiotherapy Techniques; SOS = Sum Of Squares.

Table 4.5.3 depicts the Mean and standard deviation of Visual Analogue Scale at baseline to first month (2.63 ± 1.27; 3.27 ± 1.20; 2.40 ± 1.71 with F = 3.01 and the p = 0.05), first to second month (1.43 ± 1.17; 2.07 ± 1.08; 1.57 ± .97 with F = 2.89 and the p = 0.06), second to third month (0.73 ± .83; 1.03 ± 1.07; 1.80 ± 1.83 with F = 5.27

and the p < 0.01), baseline to third month (4.80 ± 1.65; 6.37 ± 1.16; 5.77 ± 2.21 with F = 6.29, p < 0.01), for Group 1, Group 2 and Group 3 respectively at the level of significance with p value ≤ 0.05. This signifies that the experimental groups role in reducing the pain of participants between groups in fibromyalgia patients.

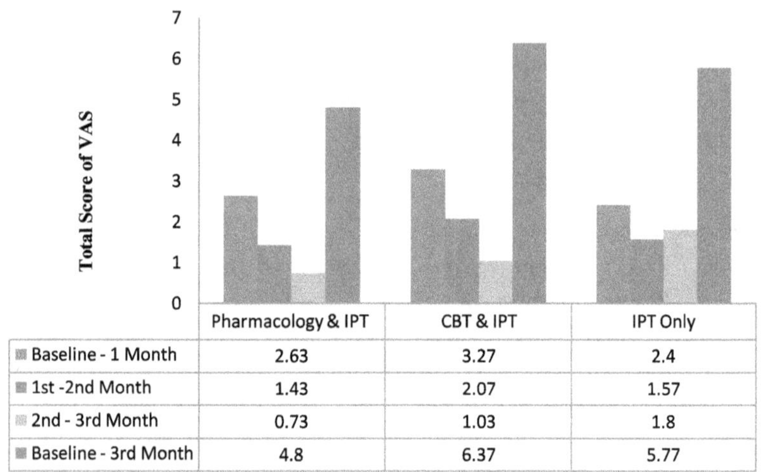

	Pharmacology & IPT	CBT & IPT	IPT Only
Baseline - 1 Month	2.63	3.27	2.4
1st -2nd Month	1.43	2.07	1.57
2nd - 3rd Month	0.73	1.03	1.8
Baseline - 3rd Month	4.8	6.37	5.77

Figure 4.5.3: The Difference inmeans (MD) of Visual Analogue Scale from baseline to third month between group 1, 2 and 3

Table 4.5.3.1: Multiple comparison of difference in means (MD) of improvement on Visual Analogue Scale among different interventional group

Time frame between	Interventional group		MD	Standard Error	P value	95% Confidence Interval	
						Lower Bound	Upper Bound
Baseline - 1st Month	PHAIPT group	CBTAIPT group	0.63[#]	0.37	0.09	0.09	1.36
		IPT Group	0.23[#]	0.37	0.52	0.49	0.96
	CBTAIPT group	IPT Group	0.87[*]	0.37	0.02	0.14	1.59
1st Month - 2nd Month	PHAIPT group	CBTAIPT group	0.63[*]	0.28	0.02	0.08	1.19
		IPT Group	0.13[#]	0.28	0.63	0.42	0.69
	CBTAIPT group	IPT Group	0.50[#]	0.28	0.08	0.05	1.05
2nd Month - 3rd Month	PHAIPT group	CBTAIPT group	0.30[#]	0.34	0.38	0.37	0.97
		IPT Group	1.07[*]	0.34	0.00	0.39	1.74
	CBTAIPT group	IPT Group	0.77[*]	0.34	0.03	0.09	1.44
Baseline - 3rd Month	PHAIPT group	CBTAIPT group	1.57[*]	0.45	0.00	0.68	2.45
		IPT Group	0.97[*]	0.45	0.03	0.08	1.85
	CBTAIPT group	IPT Group	0.60[#]	0.45	0.18	0.29	1.49

CBT = Cognitive Behavioral Therapy; IPT = Integrated Physiotherapy Group; MD = Difference in means (MD) * = Significant; [#] = Non-Significant

Table 4.5.3.1 summarized the comparisons of differences in mean improvement in VAS using post hoc Least Significant difference (LSD). The result specifies that level of improvement was greater in experimental group I & II at second to third month and baseline to third month ($p \leq 0.05$) as compared to experimental group III. Also, the improvement was greater in experimental group II at baseline to first month and second to third month as compared to experimental group III. Additionally, group I show significant effect at first to second month and baseline to third month as compared to group II and the group III shown the improvement between baselines to first month and second to third month as compared to group III. However; it does not show the statistically significant difference ($p > 0.05$) in experimental group I & II at the remaining time frame as compared to experimental group III. This signifies that the role of PHAIPT and CBTAIPT in decreasing the pain status of fibromyalgia patients.

Table 4.5.4: Comparison of difference in means (MD) of General Anxiety Disorder 7 (GAD7) variables between the groups at different time frame from Baseline to Third month.

Variable (Time frame)	Groups	Mean ± SD	SOS Between Groups	SOS Within Group	F	P
GAD 7 (Baseline – 1st Month)	PHAIPT	1.90 ± 3.09	21.95	708.3	1.34	0.26[#]
	CBTAIPT	3.10 ± 1.95				
	IPT Only	2.37 ± 3.33				
GAD 7 (1st – 2nd Month)	PHAIPT	2.03 ± 3.55	8.08	1113	0.31	0.73[#]
	CBTAIPT	1.70 ± 3.76				
	IPT Only	1.30 ± 3.42				
GAD 7 (2nd – 3rd Month)	PHAIPT	1.23 ± 2.50	13.06	623.0	0.91	0.40[#]
	CBTAIPT	1.37 ± 2.04				
	IPT Only	2.10 ± 3.33				
GAD 7 (Baseline – 3rd Month)	PHAIPT	5.17 ± 3.82	15.20	1845	0.35	0.70[#]
	CBTAIPT	6.17 ± 3.52				
	IPT Only	5.77 ± 6.06				
GAD 7 = General Anxiety Disorder – 7 Scale; SD = Standard Deviation; CBT = Cognitive Behavioral Therapy; IPT = Integrated Physiotherapy Techniques; SOS = Sum Of Squares.						

Table 4.5.4 depicts the Mean and standard deviation of General Anxiety Disorder – 7 Scale at baseline to first month (1.90 ± 3.09; 3.10 ± 1.95; 2.37 ± 3.33 with F = 1.34 and the p = 0.26), first to second month (2.03 ± 3.55; 1.70 ± 3.76; 1.30 ± 3.42 with F = 0.31 and the p = 0.73), second to third month (1.23 ± 2.50; 1.37 ± 2.04; 2.10 ± 3.33 with F = 0.91 and the p = 0.40), baseline to third month (5.17 ± 3.82; 6.17 ± 3.52; 5.77 ± 6.06 with F = 0.35, p = 0.70), for Group 1, Group 2 and Group 3 respectively at the   level of significance with   p   value ≤ 0.05. This signifies that the experimental groups have no role in reducing the anxiety of fibromyalgia patients.

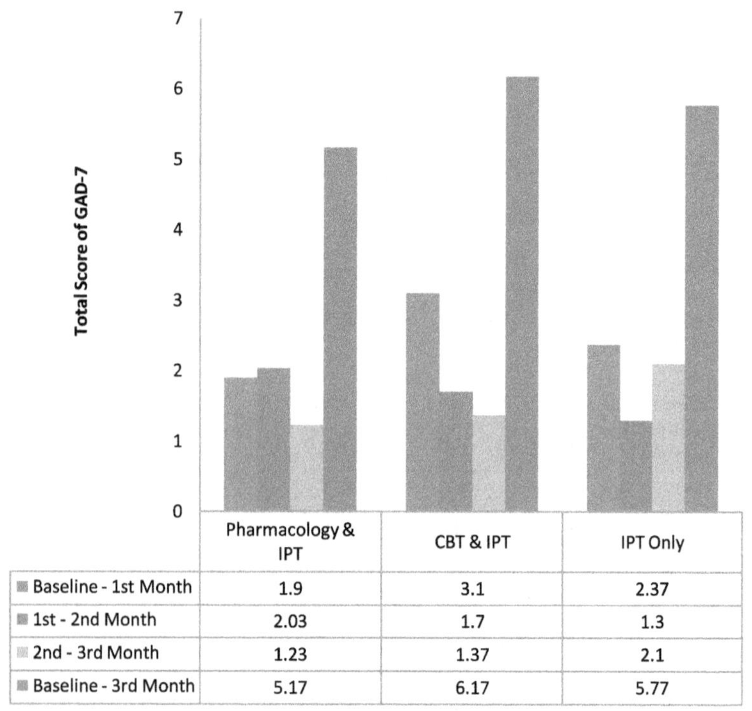

	Pharmacology & IPT	CBT & IPT	IPT Only
Baseline - 1st Month	1.9	3.1	2.37
1st - 2nd Month	2.03	1.7	1.3
2nd - 3rd Month	1.23	1.37	2.1
Baseline - 3rd Month	5.17	6.17	5.77

Figure 4.5.4: The Difference inmeans (MD) of General Anxiety Disorder – 7 scale from baseline to third month between group 1, 2 and 3

Table 4.5.4.1: Multiple comparison of difference in means (MD) of improvement in General Anxiety Disorder – 7 Scale among different interventional group

Time frame Between	Interventional group		MD	Standard Error	P value	95% Confidence Interval	
						Lower Bound	Upper Bound
Baseline - 1st Month	PHAIPT group	CBTAIPT group	1.20[#]	0.74	0.11	2.66	.26
		IPT Group	0.47[#]	0.74	0.53	1.93	1.00
	CBTAIPT group	IPT Group	0.73[#]	0.74	0.32	0.73	2.20
1st Month - 2nd Month	PHAIPT group	CBTAIPT group	0.33[#]	0.92	0.72	1.50	2.17
		IPT Group	0.73[#]	0.92	0.43	1.10	2.57
	CBTAIPT group	IPT Group	0.40[#]	0.92	0.67	1.44	2.24
2nd Month - 3rd Month	PHAIPT group	CBTAIPT group	0.13[#]	0.69	0.85	1.24	1.51
		IPT Group	0.87[#]	0.69	0.21	0.51	2.24
	CBTAIPT group	IPT Group	0.73[#]	0.69	0.29	0.64	2.11
Baseline - 3rd Month	PHAIPT group	CBTAIPT group	1.00[#]	1.19	0.40	3.36	1.36
		IPT Group	0.60[#]	1.19	0.62	1.76	2.96
	CBTAIPT group	IPT Group	0.40[#]	1.19	0.74	1.96	2.76
CBT = Cognitive Behavioral Therapy; IPT = Integrated Physiotherapy Group; MD = Difference in means (MD) [#] = Non-Significant							

Table 4.5.4.1 summarized the comparisons of differences in mean improvement in General Anxiety Disorder – 7 Scale using post hoc Least Significant difference (LSD). The difference in means (MD) between groups showed a non-significant improvement on anxiety. This signifies that the role of PHAIPT and CBTAIPTare not effective in decreasing the anxiety status of fibromyalgia patients.

Table 4.5.5: Comparison of difference in means (MD) of Short Form– 36 Health Survey Scale Physical Component Summary (SF-36 PCS) variable between the groups at different time frame from Baseline to Third month

Variable (Time frame)	Groups	Mean ± SD	SOS Between Groups	SOS Within Group	F	P
SF36 PCS (Baseline – 1st Month)	PHAIPT	10.81 ± 17.51	1659	1741	4.14	0.01*
	CBTAIPT	19.04 ± 15.25				
	IPT Only	9.25 ± 7.83				
SF36 PCS (1st – 2nd Month)	PHAIPT	11.58 ± 18.11	1478	1792	3.58	0.03*
	CBTAIPT	17.12 ± 14.03				
	IPT Only	7.21 ± 9.66				
SF36 PCS (2nd – 3rd Month)	PHAIPT	8.14 ± 8.89	521.8	1070	2.12	0.12[#]
	CBTAIPT	8.52 ± 11.63				
	IPT Only	13.43 ± 12.45				
SF36 PCS (Baseline – 3rd Month)	PHAIPT	30.53 ± 22.47	4187	3461	5.26	< 0.01*
	CBTAIPT	44.67 ± 18.12				
	IPT Only	29.88 ± 18.98				

SF36 = Short Form– 36 Health Survey Scale Physical Component Summary; SD = Standard Deviation; CBT = Cognitive Behavioral Therapy; IPT = Integrated Physiotherapy Techniques; SOS = Sum Of Squares.

Table 4.5.5 depicts the Mean and standard deviation of Short Form– 36 Health Survey Scale Physical Component Summary at baseline to first month (10.81 ± 17.51; 19.04 ± 15.25; 9.25 ± 7.83 with F = 4.14 and the p = 0.01), first to second month (11.58 ± 18.11; 17.12 ± 14.03; 7.21 ± 9.66 with F = 3.58 and the p = 0.03), second to third month (8.14 ± 8.89; 8.52 ± 11.63; 13.43 ± 12.45 with F = 2.12 and the p = 0.12), baseline to third month (30.53 ± 22.47; 44.67 ± 18.12; 29.88 ± 18.98 with F = 5.26, p = < 0.01), for Group 1, Group 2 and Group 3 respectively at the level of significance with p value ≤ 0.05. This signifies that the experimental groups role in improving the physical status fibromyalgia patients on the short form 36 health survey.

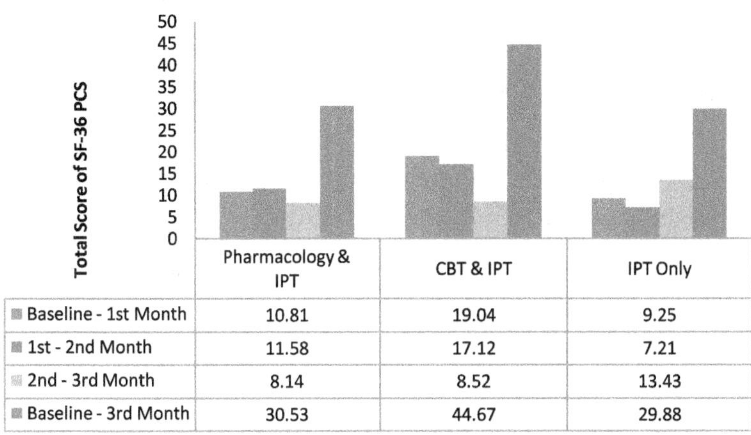

	Pharmacology & IPT	CBT & IPT	IPT Only
Baseline - 1st Month	10.81	19.04	9.25
1st - 2nd Month	11.58	17.12	7.21
2nd - 3rd Month	8.14	8.52	13.43
Baseline - 3rd Month	30.53	44.67	29.88

Figure 4.5.5: The Difference in means (MD) of Short Form 36 Physical Component Summary from baseline to third month between group 1, 2 and 3

Table 4.5.5.1: Multiple comparison of difference in means (MD) of improvement in Short Form 36 Health survey Physical Component summary among different interventional group

Time frame Between	Interventional group		MD	Standard Error	P value	95% Confidence Interval	
						Lower Bound	Upper Bound
Baseline – 1st Month	PHAIPT group	CBTAIPT group	8.23*	3.65	0.03	0.97	15.49
		IPT Group	1.56#	3.65	0.67	8.82	5.70
	CBTAIPT group	IPT Group	9.79*	3.65	0.01	2.53	17.05
1st – 2nd Month	PHAIPT group	CBTAIPT group	5.53#	3.71	0.14	1.83	12.90
		IPT Group	4.37#	3.71	0.24	2.99	11.74
	CBTAIPT group	IPT Group	9.91*	3.71	0.01	2.54	17.27
2nd – 3rd Month	PHAIPT group	CBTAIPT group	0.37#	2.86	0.90	5.32	6.07
		IPT Group	5.29#	2.86	0.07	0.41	10.98
	CBTAIPT group	IPT Group	4.91#	2.86	0.09	0.78	10.60
Baseline – 3rd Month	PHAIPT group	CBTAIPT group	14.13*	5.15	0.01	3.90	24.37
		IPT Group	0.65#	5.15	0.90	9.59	10.89
	CBTAIPT group	IPT Group	14.78*	5.15	0.01	25.02	4.55
CBT = Cognitive Behavioral Therapy; IPT = Integrated Physiotherapy Group; MD = Difference in means (MD); * = Significant, # non-significant							

Table 4.5.5.1 summarized the comparisons of differences in mean improvement in Short form – 36 physical component summaries using post hoc Least Significant difference (LSD). The result specifies that level of improvement was greater in experimental group I at baseline to first month and baseline to third month ($p \leq 0.05$) as compared to experimental group II. Also, the improvement was greater in experimental

211

group II at baseline to first month, first to second month and baseline to third month as compared to experimental group III. However; it does not show the statistically significant difference (p > 0.05) in experimental group I at baseline to first, second and third month, also in group II it is non-significant between second to third month as compared to experimental group III. This signifies that the role of IPT and CBTAIPT in improving the physical health status of fibromyalgia patients.

Table 4.5.6: Comparison of difference in means (MD) of Short Form– 36 Health Survey Mental Component Summary (SF36 MCS) variable between the groups at different time frame from Baseline to Third month

Variable (Time frame)	Groups	Mean ± SD	SOS Between Groups	SOS Within Group	F	P
SF36 MCS (Baseline – 1ˢᵗ Month)	PHAIPT	10.72 ± 16.39	1458	1620	3.91	0.02*
	CBTAIPT	14.79 ± 12.37				
	IPT Only	4.98 ± 11.73				
SF36 MCS (1ˢᵗ - 2ⁿᵈ Month)	PHAIPT	8.44 ± 13.98	1169	1554	3.27	0.04*
	CBTAIPT	16.05 ± 16.06				
	IPT Only	8.36 ± 9.10				
SF36 MCS (2ⁿᵈ – 3ʳᵈ Month)	PHAIPT	7.73 ± 11.42	34.13	1210	0.12	0.88#
	CBTAIPT	7.29 ± 11.73				
	IPT Only	8.76 ± 12.23				
SF36 MCS (Baseline – 3ʳᵈ Month)	PHAIPT	26.90 ± 17.81	4062	2763	6.39	< 0.01*
	CBTAIPT	38.13 ± 19.27				
	IPT Only	22.10 ± 16.25				

SF36 = Short Form– 36 Health Survey Scale Mental Component Summary; SD = Standard Deviation; CBT = Cognitive Behavioral Therapy; IPT = Integrated Physiotherapy Techniques; SOS = Sum Of Squares; * = Significant; # = Non-Significant

Table 4.5.6 depicts the Mean and standard deviation of Short Form– 36 Health Survey Scale Mental Component Summary at baseline to first month (10.72 ± 16.39; 14.79 ± 12.37; 4.98 ± 11.73 with F = 3.91 and the p = 0.02), first to second month (8.44 ± 13.98; 16.05 ± 16.06; 8.36 ± 9.10 with F = 3.27 and the p = 0.04), second to third month (7.73 ± 11.42; 7.29 ± 11.73; 8.76 ± 12.23 with F = 0.12 and the p = 0.88), baseline to third month (26.90 ± 17.81; 38.13 ± 19.27; 22.10 ± 16.25 with F = 6.39, p = 0.00), for Group 1, Group 2 and Group 3 respectively at the level of significance with p value ≤ 0.05. This signifies that the experimental group's role in improving the mental health of fibromyalgia patients on the short form36 health survey scale.

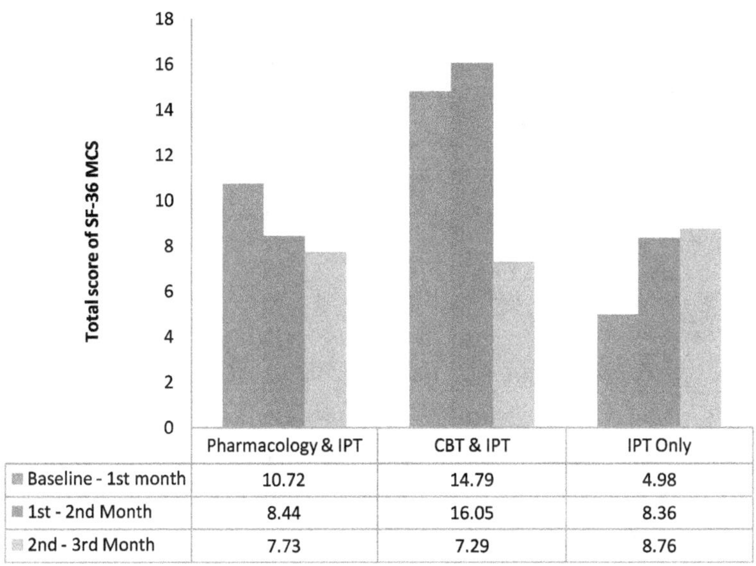

	Pharmacology & IPT	CBT & IPT	IPT Only
Baseline - 1st month	10.72	14.79	4.98
1st - 2nd Month	8.44	16.05	8.36
2nd - 3rd Month	7.73	7.29	8.76

Figure 4.5.6: The Difference in means (MD) of Short Form 36 Mental Component Summary from baseline to third month between group 1, 2 and 3

Table 4.5.6.1: Multiple comparison of difference in means (MD) of improvement in Short Form 36 Health survey Mental Component summary among different interventional group

Time frame Between	Interventional group		MD	Standard Error	P value	95% Confidence Interval	
						Lower Bound	Upper Bound
Baseline – 1st Month	PHAIPT group	CBTAIPT group	4.06#	3.52	0.25	2.94	11.07
		IPT Group	5.75#	3.52	0.11	1.26	12.75
	CBTAIPT group	IPT Group	9.81*	3.52	0.01	2.81	16.82
1st Month – 2nd Month	PHAIPT group	CBTAIPT group	7.61*	3.45	0.03	14.47	0.75
		IPT Group	0.08#	3.45	0.98	6.78	6.94
	CBTAIPT group	IPT Group	7.69*	3.45	0.03	0.83	14.55
2nd Month – 3rd Month	PHAIPT group	CBTAIPT group	0.43#	3.05	0.89	5.62	6.49
		IPT Group	1.03#	3.05	0.74	5.02	7.09
	CBTAIPT group	IPT Group	1.47#	3.05	0.63	4.59	7.52
Baseline – 3rd Month	PHAIPT group	CBTAIPT group	11.24*	4.60	0.02	2.09	20.38
		IPT Group	4.79#	4.60	0.30	4.35	13.94
	CBTAIPT group	IPT Group	16.03*	4.60	0.00	6.89	25.18
CBT = Cognitive Behavioral Therapy; IPT = Integrated Physiotherapy Group; MD = Difference in means (MD) * = Significant							

Table 4.5.6.1 summarized the comparisons of differences in mean improvement in Short form – 36 physical component summaries using post hoc Least Significant difference (LSD). The result specifies that level of improvement was greater in experimental group I at first to second month and baseline to third month ($p \leq 0.05$) as compared to experimental group II. Also, the improvement was greater in experimental group II at baseline to first month, first to second month and baseline to third month as compared to experimental group III. However; it does not show the statistically significant difference ($p > 0.05$) in experimental group I at baseline to first month, second and third month, also in group II it is non-significant between second to third months as compared to experimental group III. This signifies that the role of IPT and CBTAIPT in improving the mental health status of fibromyalgia patients.

Table 4.5.7: Comparison of difference in means (MD) of Shoulder Girdle Left (SGL) variable on algometer between the groups at different time frame from Baseline to Third month

Variable (Time frame)	Groups	Mean ± SD	SOS Between Groups	SOS Within Group	F	P
SGL (Baseline – 1st Month)	PHAIPT	0.48 ± 0.28	0.34	8.78	1.70	0.18[#]
	CBTAIPT	0.44 ± 0.39				
	IPT Only	0.33 ± 0.27				
SGL (1st – 2nd Month)	PHAIPT	0.51 ± 0.23	0.38	11.50	1.45	0.23[#]
	CBTAIPT	0.39 ± 0.25				
	IPT Only	0.35 ± 0.53				
SGL (2nd – 3rd Month)	PHAIPT	0.51 ± 0.38	0.29	9.67	1.30	0.27[#]
	CBTAIPT	0.42 ± 0.31				
	IPT Only	0.37 ± 0.31				
SGL (Baseline – 3rd Month)	PHAIPT	1.49 ± 0.50	2.87	44.84	2.79	0.06[#]
	CBTAIPT	1.25 ± 0.69				
	IPT Only	1.06 ± 0.91				

SGL = Shoulder Girdle Left; SD = Standard Deviation; CBT = Cognitive Behavioral Therapy; IPT = Integrated Physiotherapy Techniques; SOS = Sum Of Squares. [#] = Non-Significant

Table 4.5.7 depicts the Mean and standard deviation of shoulder girdle left on algometer at baseline to first month (0.48 ± 0.28; 0.44 ± 0.39; 0.33 ± 0.27 with F = 1.70 and the p = 0.18), first to second month (0.51 ± 0.23; 0.39 ± 0.25; 0.35 ± 0.53 with F = 1.45 and the p = 0.23), second to third month (0.51 ± .38; 0.42 ± .31; 0.37 ± .31 with F = 1.30 and the p = 0.27), baseline to third month (1.49 ± 0.50; 1.25 ± 0.69;

1.06 ± 0.91 with F = 2.79, p = 0.06), for Group 1, Group 2 and Group 3 respectively at the level of significance with p value ≤ 0.05. This signifies that the experimental groups have no role in reducing the pain of participants on shoulder girdle left point between groups in fibromyalgia patients.

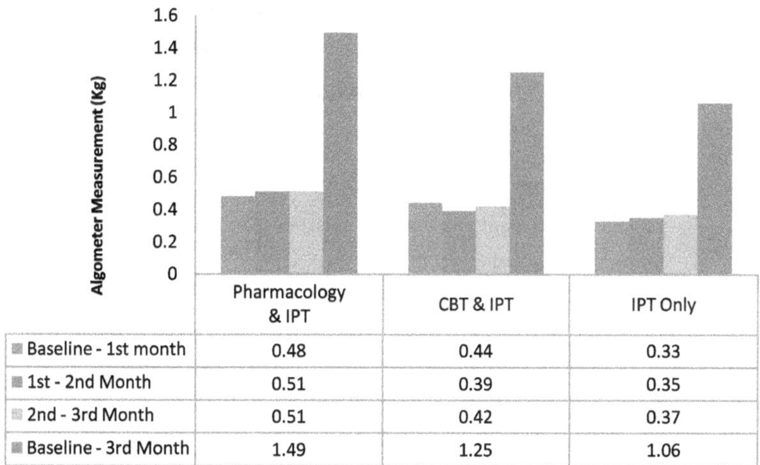

	Pharmacology & IPT	CBT & IPT	IPT Only
Baseline - 1st month	0.48	0.44	0.33
1st - 2nd Month	0.51	0.39	0.35
2nd - 3rd Month	0.51	0.42	0.37
Baseline - 3rd Month	1.49	1.25	1.06

Figure 4.5.7: The Difference in means (MD) of Shoulder Girdle Left point on pain pressure algometer from baseline to third month between group 1, 2 and 3

Table 4.5.7.1: Multiple comparison of difference in means (MD) of improvement in Shoulder Girdle Left point on Pain Pressure Threshold among different interventional group

Time frame Between	Interventional group		MD	Standard Error	P value	95% Confidence Interval	
						Lower Bound	Upper Bound
Baseline - 1st Month	PHAIPT group	CBTAIPT group	0.04#	0.08	0.63	0.12	0.20
		IPT Group	0.15#	0.08	0.08	0.02	0.31
	CBTAIPT group	IPT Group	0.11#	0.08	0.20	0.06	0.27
1st Month - 2nd Month	PHAIPT group	CBTAIPT group	0.12#	0.09	0.22	0.07	0.30
		IPT Group	0.15#	0.09	0.11	0.03	0.34
	CBTAIPT group	IPT Group	0.04#	0.09	0.70	0.15	0.22
2nd Month - 3rd Month	PHAIPT group	CBTAIPT group	0.09#	0.09	0.30	0.08	0.26
		IPT Group	0.14#	0.09	0.12	0.03	0.31
	CBTAIPT group	IPT Group	0.05#	0.09	0.59	0.12	0.22
Baseline - 3rd Month	PHAIPT group	CBTAIPT group	0.25#	0.19	0.19	0.12	0.62
		IPT Group	0.44*	0.19	0.02	0.07	0.81
	CBTAIPT group	IPT Group	0.19#	0.19	0.31	0.18	0.56

CBT = Cognitive Behavioral Therapy; IPT = Integrated Physiotherapy Group; MD = Difference in means (MD) * = Significant; # = Non-significant.

Table 4.5.7.1 summarized the comparisons of differences in mean improvement in shoulder girdle left side painful point using post hoc Least Significant difference (LSD). The result specifies that level of improvement was greater in experimental group I at baseline to third month ($p \leq 0.05$) as compared to experimental group III. However; it does not show the statistically significant difference ($p > 0.05$) in experimental group I and II from other time frames as compared to experimental group III. This signifies that the role of Pharmacotherapy along with integrated physiotherapy techniques in decreasing the pain pressure threshold level of fibromyalgia patients.

Table 4.5.8: Comparison of difference in means (MD) of Shoulder Girdle Right (SGR) variable on algometer between the groups at different time frame from Baseline to Third month

Variable (Time frame)	Groups	Mean ± SD	SOS Between Groups	SOS Within Group	F	P
SGR (Baseline 1ˢᵗ Month)	PHAIPT	0.49 ± 0.32	0.43	9.52	1.99	0.14[#]
	CBTAIPT	0.42 ± 0.38				
	IPT Only	0.32 ± 0.28				
SGR (1ˢᵗ – 2ⁿᵈ Month)	PHAIPT	0.48 ± 0.27	0.39	6.62	2.57	0.08[#]
	CBTAIPT	0.37 ± 0.29				
	IPT Only	0.32 ± 0.27				
SGR (2ⁿᵈ – 3ʳᵈ Month)	PHAIPT	0.41 ± 0.20	0.10	12.37	0.36	0.69[#]
	CBTAIPT	0.43 ± 0.37				
	IPT Only	0.49 ± 0.50				
SGR (Baseline – 3ʳᵈ Month)	PHAIPT	1.38 ± 0.49	0.95	42.57	0.97	0.38[#]
	CBTAIPT	1.22 ± 0.70				
	IPT Only	1.14 ± 0.86				

SGR = Shoulder Girdle Right; SD = Standard Deviation; CBT = Cognitive Behavioral Therapy; IPT = Integrated Physiotherapy Techniques; SOS = Sum Of Squares. [#] = Non-Significant

Table 4.5.8 depicts the Mean and standard deviation of shoulder girdle right on algometer at baseline to first month (0.49 ± 0.32; 0.42 ± 0.38; 0.32 ± 0.28 with F = 1.99 and the p = 0.14), first to second month (0.48 ± 0.27; 0.37 ± 0.29; 0.32 ± 0.27 with F = 2.57 and the p = 0.08), second to third month (0.41 ± 0.20; 0.43 ± 0.37; 0.49 ± 0.50 with F = 0.36 and the p = 0.69), baseline to third month (1.38 ± 0.49; 1.22 ± 0.70; 1.14 ± 0.86 with F = 0.97, p = 0.38), for Group 1, Group 2 and Group 3 respectively at the level of significance with p value ≤ 0.05. This signifies that the experimental groups role in reducing the pain of participants between groups in fibromyalgia patients.

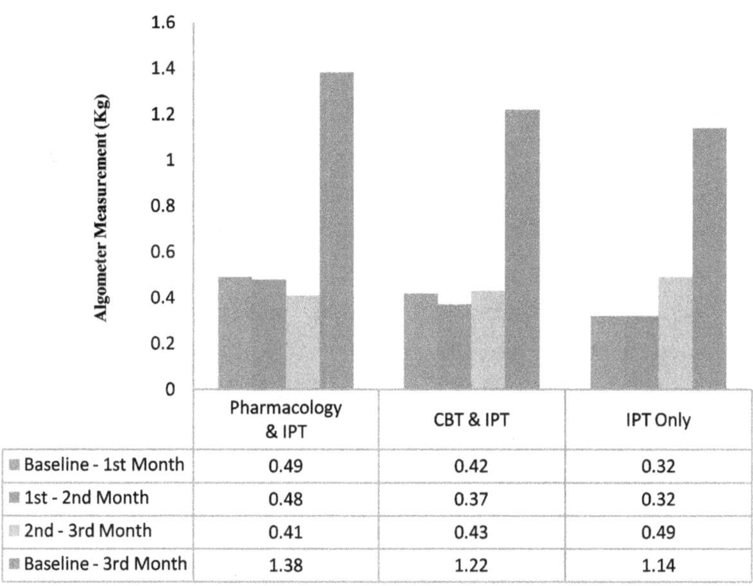

	Pharmacology & IPT	CBT & IPT	IPT Only
Baseline - 1st Month	0.49	0.42	0.32
1st - 2nd Month	0.48	0.37	0.32
2nd - 3rd Month	0.41	0.43	0.49
Baseline - 3rd Month	1.38	1.22	1.14

Figure 4.5.8: The Difference in means (MD) of Shoulder Girdle Right point on pain pressure algometer from baseline to third month between group 1, 2 and 3

Table 4.5.8.1: Multiple comparison of difference in means (MD) of improvement in Shoulder Girdle Right point on Pain Pressure Threshold among different interventional group

Time frame between	Interventional group		MD	Standard Error	P value	95% Confidence Interval	
						Lower Bound	Upper Bound
Baseline –	PHAIPT group	CBTAIPT group	$0.07^{\#}$	0.09	0.39	0.10	0.24
		IPT Group	0.17^{*}	0.09	0.05	0.00	0.34
1st Month	CBTAIPT group	IPT Group	$0.10^{\#}$	0.09	0.26	0.07	0.27
1st Month –	PHAIPT group	CBTAIPT group	$0.11^{\#}$	0.07	0.12	0.03	0.25
		IPT Group	0.16^{*}	0.07	0.03	0.02	0.30
2nd Month	CBTAIPT group	IPT Group	$0.04^{\#}$	0.07	0.54	0.10	0.18
2nd Month –	PHAIPT group	CBTAIPT group	$0.02^{\#}$	0.10	0.84	0.17	0.21
		IPT Group	$0.08^{\#}$	0.10	0.41	0.11	0.27
3rd Month	CBTAIPT group	IPT Group	$0.06^{\#}$	0.10	0.54	0.13	0.25
Baseline –	PHAIPT group	CBTAIPT group	$0.17^{\#}$	0.18	0.36	0.19	0.53
		IPT Group	$0.25^{\#}$	0.18	0.18	0.11	0.61
3rd Month	CBTAIPT group	IPT Group	$0.08^{\#}$	0.18	0.66	0.28	0.44

CBT = Cognitive Behavioral Therapy; IPT = Integrated Physiotherapy Group; MD = Difference in means (MD) * = Significant

Table 4.5.8.1 summarized the comparisons of differences in mean improvement in shoulder girdle right side painful point using post hoc Least Significant difference (LSD). The result specifies that level of improvement was greater in experimental group I at baseline to first month ($p \leq 0.05$) and at first to second month as compared to experimental group III. However; it does not show the statistically significant difference ($p > 0.05$) in experimental group I and II from other time frames as compared to experimental group III. This signifies that the role of Pharmacotherapy along with integrated physiotherapy techniques in decreasing the pain pressure threshold level of fibromyalgia patients.

Table 4.5.9: Comparison of difference in means (MD) of Upper Arm Left (UAL) variable on algometer between the groups at different time frame from Baseline to Third month

Variable (Time frame)	Groups	Mean ± SD	SOS Between Groups	SOS Within Group	F	P
UAL (Baseline – 1st Month)	PHAIPT	0.14 ± 0.24	0.12	3.30	1.63	0.20[#]
	CBTAIPT	0.06 ± 0.16				
	IPT Only	0.13 ± 0.17				
UAL (1st – 2nd Month)	PHAIPT	0.16 ± 0.36	0.13	5.72	1.03	0.35[#]
	CBTAIPT	0.07 ± 0.18				
	IPT Only	0.13 ± 0.18				
UAL (2nd – 3rd Month)	PHAIPT	0.12 ± 0.23	0.56	5.09	4.83	0.01*
	CBTAIPT	0.04 ± 0.11				
	IPT Only	0.23 ± 0.33				
UAL (Baseline – 3rd Month)	PHAIPT	0.42 ± 0.75	1.80	31.64	2.47	0.09[#]
	CBTAIPT	0.16 ± 0.42				
	IPT Only	0.49 ± 0.59				

UAL = Upper Arm Left; SD = Standard Deviation; CBT = Cognitive Behavioral Therapy; IPT = Integrated Physiotherapy Techniques; SOS = Sum Of Squares.

Table 4.5.9 depicts the Mean and standard deviation of upper arm left on algometer at baseline to first month (0.14 ± 0.24; 0.06 ± 0.16; 0.13 ± 0.17 with F = 1.63 and the p = 0.20), first to second month (0.16 ± 0.36; 0.07 ± 0.18; 0.13 ± 0.18 with F = 1.03 and the p = 0.35), second to third month (0.12 ± 0.23; 0.04 ± 0.11; 0.23 ± 0.33 with F = 4.83 and the p = 0.01), baseline to third month (0.42 ± 0.75; 0.16 ± 0.42; 0.49 ± 0.59 with F = 2.47, p = 0.09), for Group 1, Group 2 and Group 3 respectively at the level of significance with p value ≤ 0.05. This signifies that the experimental groups role in reducing the pain of participants between groups in fibromyalgia patients.

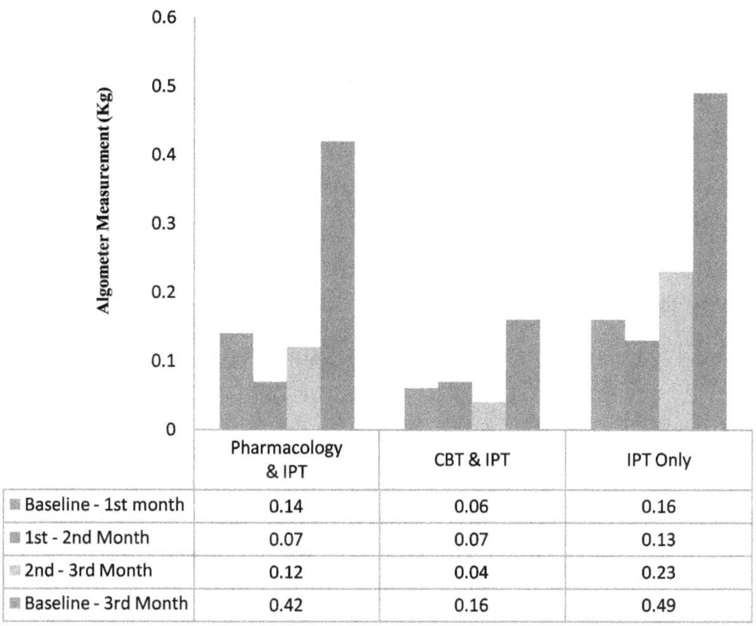

	Pharmacology & IPT	CBT & IPT	IPT Only
Baseline - 1st month	0.14	0.06	0.16
1st - 2nd Month	0.07	0.07	0.13
2nd - 3rd Month	0.12	0.04	0.23
Baseline - 3rd Month	0.42	0.16	0.49

Figure 4.5.9: The Difference in means (MD) of Upper Arm Left point on pain pressure algometer from baseline to third month between group 1, 2 and 3

Table 4.5.9.1: Multiple comparison of difference in means (MD) of improvement in Upper Arm Left point on Pain Pressure Threshold among different interventional group

Time frame between	Interventional group		MD	Standard Error	P value	95% Confidence Interval	
						Lower Bound	Upper Bound
Baseline –	PHAIPT group	CBTAIPT group	0.08	0.05	0.10	0.02	0.18
		IPT Group	0.01	0.05	0.84	0.09	0.11
1st Month	CBTAIPT group	IPT Group	0.07	0.05	0.15	0.03	0.17
1st Month –	PHAIPT group	CBTAIPT group	0.09	0.07	0.16	0.04	0.22
		IPT Group	0.03	0.07	0.65	0.10	0.16
2nd Month	CBTAIPT group	IPT Group	0.06	0.07	0.34	0.07	0.19
2nd Month –	PHAIPT group	CBTAIPT group	0.08	0.06	0.20	0.04	0.20
		IPT Group	0.11	0.06	0.07	0.01	0.24
3rd Month	CBTAIPT group	IPT Group	0.19*	0.06	0.00	0.07	0.32
Baseline –	PHAIPT group	CBTAIPT group	0.26	0.16	0.10	0.05	0.57
		IPT Group	0.07	0.16	0.64	0.24	0.38
3rd Month	CBTAIPT group	IPT Group	0.33*	0.16	0.04	0.02	0.64

CBT = Cognitive Behavioral Therapy; IPT = Integrated Physiotherapy Group; MD = Difference in means (MD) * = Significant

Table 4.5.9.1 summarized the comparisons of differences in mean improvement in upper arm left side painful point using post hoc LSD. The result specifies that level of improvement was greater in experimental group II at second to third month and baseline to third month (p ≤ 0.05) as compared to experimental group III. However; it does not show the statistically significant difference (p > 0.05) in experimental group I and II from the other time frames as compared to experimental group III. Thus, it is not signifies the role of Pharmacotherapy along with integrated physiotherapy techniques in decreasing the pain pressure threshold level of fibromyalgia patients.

Table 4.5.10: Comparison of difference in means (MD) of Upper Arm Right (UAR) variable on algometer between the groups at different time frame from Baseline to Third month

Variable (Time frame)	Groups	Mean ± SD	SOS Between Groups	SOS Within Group	F	P
UAR (Baseline 1st Month)	PHAIPT	0.10 ± 0.21	0.59	7.91	3.26	0.04*
	CBTAIPT	0.06 ± 0.15				
	IPT Only	0.25 ± 0.45				
UAR (1st – 2nd Month)	PHAIPT	0.13 ± 0.28	0.19	8.46	1.01	0.36[#]
	CBTAIPT	0.10 ± 0.30				
	IPT Only	0.21 ± 0.36				
UAR (2nd – 3rd Month)	PHAIPT	0.08 ± 0.21	0.68	7.51	3.98	0.02*
	CBTAIPT	0.10 ± 0.28				
	IPT Only	0.28 ± 0.37				
UAR (Baseline – 3rd Month)	PHAIPT	0.31 ± 0.64	4.47	59.52	3.27	0.04*
	CBTAIPT	0.26 ± 0.66				
	IPT Only	0.76 ± 1.10				

UAR = Upper Arm Right; SD = Standard Deviation; CBT = Cognitive Behavioral Therapy; IPT = Integrated Physiotherapy Techniques; SOS = Sum Of Squares. [#] = Non-Significant

Table 4.5.10 depicts the Mean and standard deviation of upper arm right on algometer at baseline to first month (0.10 ± 0.21; 0.06 ± 0.15; 0.25 ± 0.45 with F = 3.26 and the p = 0.04), first to second month (0.13 ± 0.28; 0.10 ± 0.30; 0.21 ± 0.36 with F = 1.01 and the p = 0.36), second to third month (0.08 ± 0.21; 0.10 ± 0.28; 0.28 ± 0.37 with F = 3.98 and the p = 0.02), baseline to third month (0.31 ± 0.64; 0.26 ± 0.66; 0.76 ± 1.10 with F = 3.27, p = 0.04), for Group 1, Group 2 and Group 3 respectively at the level of significance with p value ≤ 0.05. This signifies that the experimental groups role in reducing the pain of participants between groups in fibromyalgia patients.

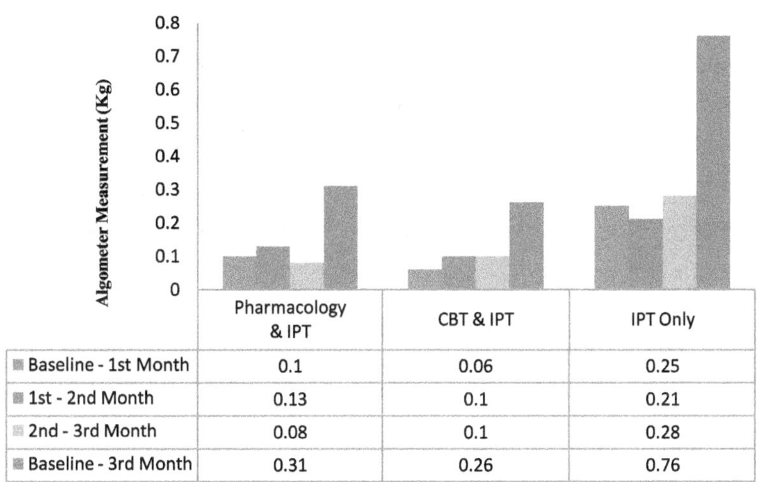

	Pharmacology & IPT	CBT & IPT	IPT Only
Baseline - 1st Month	0.1	0.06	0.25
1st - 2nd Month	0.13	0.1	0.21
2nd - 3rd Month	0.08	0.1	0.28
Baseline - 3rd Month	0.31	0.26	0.76

Figure 4.5.10: The Difference in means (MD) of Upper Arm Right point on pain pressure algometer from baseline to third month between group 1, 2 and 3

Table 4.5.10.1: Multiple comparison of difference in means (MD) of improvement in Upper Arm Right point on Pain Pressure Threshold among different interventional group

Time frame Between	Interventional group		MD	Standard Error	P value	95% Confidence Interval	
						Lower Bound	Upper Bound
Baseline – 1st Month	PHAIPT group	CBTAIPT group	0.03[#]	0.08	0.67	0.12	0.19
		IPT Group	0.15[#]	0.08	0.05	0.00	0.31
	CBTAIPT group	IPT Group	0.19[*]	0.08	0.02	0.03	0.34
1st Month – 2nd Month	PHAIPT group	CBTAIPT group	0.03[#]	0.08	0.74	0.13	0.19
		IPT Group	0.08[#]	0.08	0.30	0.08	0.24
	CBTAIPT group	IPT Group	0.11[#]	0.08	0.18	0.05	0.27
2nd Month – 3rd Month	PHAIPT group	CBTAIPT group	0.02[#]	0.08	0.83	0.13	0.17
		IPT Group	0.19[*]	0.08	0.01	0.04	0.34
	CBTAIPT group	IPT Group	0.18[*]	0.08	0.02	0.03	0.33
Baseline – 3rd Month	PHAIPT group	CBTAIPT group	0.04[#]	0.21	0.84	0.38	0.47
		IPT Group	0.45[*]	0.21	0.04	0.03	0.87
	CBTAIPT group	IPT Group	0.49[*]	0.21	0.02	0.07	0.92
CBT = Cognitive Behavioral Therapy; IPT = Integrated Physiotherapy Group; MD = Difference in means (MD); * = Significant; [#]= Non-Significant.							

Table 4.5.10.1 summarized the comparisons of differences in mean improvement in upper arm right side painful point using post hoc LSD. The result specifies that level of improvement was greater in experimental group I at second to third month and baseline to third month ($p \leq 0.05$) as compared to experimental group

III. Also, this is significant in experimental group II at baseline to first month, second to third month and baseline to third month (p ≤ 0.05) as compared to experimental group III. However; it does not show the statistically significant difference (p > 0.05) in experimental group I and II from the other time frames as compared to experimental group III. Thus, it signifies that the role of Pharmacotherapy along with integrated physiotherapy techniques in decreasing the pain pressure threshold level of fibromyalgia patients.

Table 4.5.11: Comparison of difference in means (MD) of Lower Arm Left (LAL) variable on algometer between the groups at different time frame from Baseline to Third month

Variable (Time frame)	Groups	Mean ± SD	SOS Between Groups	SOS Within Group	F	P
LAL (Baseline – 1st Month)	PHAIPT	0.03 ± 0.08	0.07	3.66	0.92	0.40[#]
	CBTAIPT	0.09 ± 0.31				
	IPT Only	0.04 ± 0.15				
LAL (1st – 2nd Month)	PHAIPT	0.04 ± 0.15	0.00	1.14	0.31	0.73[#]
	CBTAIPT	0.03 ± 0.11				
	IPT Only	0.02 ± 0.08				
LAL (2nd – 3rd Month)	PHAIPT	0.05 ± 0.15	0.01	2.01	0.25	0.77[#]
	CBTAIPT	0.03 ± 0.09				
	IPT Only	0.06 ± 0.19				
LAL (Baseline – 3rd Month)	PHAIPT	0.12 ± 0.37	0.03	14.81	0.09	0.90[#]
	CBTAIPT	0.16 ± 0.50				
	IPT Only	0.11 ± 0.35				

LAL = Lower Arm Left; SD = Standard Deviation; CBT = Cognitive Behavioral Therapy; IPT = Integrated Physiotherapy Techniques; SOS = Sum Of Squares. [#] = Non-Significant

Table 4.5.11 depicts the Mean and standard deviation of Lower arm left on algometer at baseline to first month (0.03 ± 0.08; 0.09 ± 0.31; 0.04 ± 0.15 with F = 0.92 and the p = 0.40), first to second month (0.04 ± 0.15; 0.03 ± 0.11; 0.02 ± 0.08 with F = 0.31 and the p = 0.73), second to third month (0.05 ± 0.15; 0.03 ± 0.09; 0.06 ± 0.19with F = 0.25 and the p = 0.77), baseline to third month (0.12 ± 0.37; 0.16 ± 0.50; 0.11 ± 0.35 with F = 0.09, p = 0.90), for Group 1, Group 2 and Group 3 respectively at the level of significance with p value ≤ 0.05. This signifies that the experimental groups have no role in reducing the pain of fibromyalgia patients on the left side lower arm painful area.

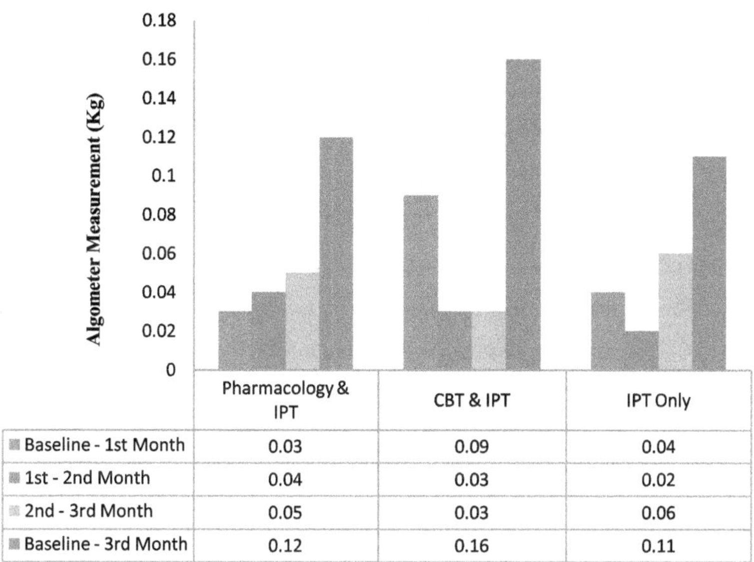

	Pharmacology & IPT	CBT & IPT	IPT Only
Baseline - 1st Month	0.03	0.09	0.04
1st - 2nd Month	0.04	0.03	0.02
2nd - 3rd Month	0.05	0.03	0.06
Baseline - 3rd Month	0.12	0.16	0.11

Figure 4.5.11: The Difference in means (MD) of Lower Arm Left point on pain pressure algometer from baseline to third month between group 1, 2 and 3

Table 4.5.11.1: Multiple comparison of difference in means (MD) of improvement in Lower Arm Left point on Pain Pressure Threshold among different interventional group

Time frame Between	Interventional group		MD	Standard Error	P value	95% Confidence Interval	
						Lower Bound	Upper Bound
Baseline –	PHAIPT group	CBTAIPT group	0.07[#]	0.05	0.21	0.04	0.17
		IPT Group	0.01[#]	0.05	0.85	0.10	0.12
1st Month	CBTAIPT group	IPT Group	0.06[#]	0.05	0.29	0.05	0.16
1st Month –	PHAIPT group	CBTAIPT group	0.01[#]	0.03	0.74	0.05	0.07
		IPT Group	0.02[#]	0.03	0.43	0.04	0.08
2nd Month	CBTAIPT group	IPT Group	0.01[#]	0.03	0.65	0.05	0.07
2nd Month –	PHAIPT group	CBTAIPT group	0.02[#]	0.04	0.61	0.06	0.10
		IPT Group	0.01[#]	0.04	0.87	0.07	0.08
3rd Month	CBTAIPT group	IPT Group	0.03[#]	0.04	0.50	0.05	0.10
Baseline –	PHAIPT group	CBTAIPT group	0.04[#]	0.11	0.73	0.18	0.25
		IPT Group	0.01[#]	0.11	0.95	0.21	0.22
3rd Month	CBTAIPT group	IPT Group	0.04[#]	0.11	0.69	0.17	0.26
CBT = Cognitive Behavioral Therapy; IPT = Integrated Physiotherapy Group; MD = Difference in means (MD) [#] = Non Significant							

Table 4.5.11.1 summarized the comparisons of differences in mean improvement in lower arm left point using post hoc LSD. The difference in means (MD) between groups showed a nonsignificant improvement on the pain pressure threshold reading by algometer. This signifies that the role of PHAIPT and CBTAIPTare not effective in increasing the pain pressure threshold level of fibromyalgia patients.

Table 4.5.12: Comparison of difference in means (MD) of Lower Arm Right (LAR) variable on algometer between the groups at different time frame from Baseline to Third month

Variable (Time frame)	Groups	Mean ± SD	SOS Between Groups	SOS Within Group	F	P
LAR (Baseline – 1ˢᵗ Month)	PHAIPT	0.04 ± 0.18	0.04	3.17	0.64	$0.52^{\#}$
	CBTAIPT	0.09 ± 0.26				
	IPT Only	0.04 ± 0.11				
LAR (1ˢᵗ – 2ⁿᵈ Month)	PHAIPT	0.03 ± 0.10	0.01	1.39	0.50	$0.60^{\#}$
	CBTAIPT	0.06 ± 0.17				
	IPT Only	0.03 ± 0.08				
LAR (2ⁿᵈ 3ʳᵈ Month)	PHAIPT	0.05 ± 0.22	0.01	4.53	0.13	$0.87^{\#}$
	CBTAIPT	0.08 ± 0.26				
	IPT Only	0.07 ± 0.20				
LAR (Baseline & 3ʳᵈ Month)	PHAIPT	0.12 ± 0.47	0.19	21.58	0.39	$0.67^{\#}$
	CBTAIPT	0.23 ± 0.62				
	IPT Only	0.14 ± 0.37				

LAR = Lower Arm Right; SD = Standard Deviation; CBT = Cognitive Behavioral Therapy; IPT = Integrated Physiotherapy Techniques; SOS = Sum Of Squares; [#]Non-significant.

Table 4.5.12 depicts the Mean and standard deviation of Lower arm right on algometer at baseline to first month (0.04 ± 0.18; 0.09 ± 0.26; 0.04 ± 0.11 with F = 0.64 and the p = 0.52), first to second month (0.03 ± 0.10; 0.06 ± 0.17; 0.03 ± 0.08 with F = 0.50 and the p = 0.60), second to third month (0.05 ± 0.22; 0.08 ± 0.26; 0.07 ± 0.20 with F = 0.13 and the p = 0.87), baseline to third month (0.12 ± 0.47; 0.23 ± 0.62; 0.14 ± 0.37 with F = 0.39, p = 0.67), for Group 1, Group 2 and Group 3 respectively at the level of significance with p value ≤ 0.05. This Figure showing that the experimental groups have no role in reducing the pain of participants between groups in fibromyalgia patients on the right side lower arm painful area.

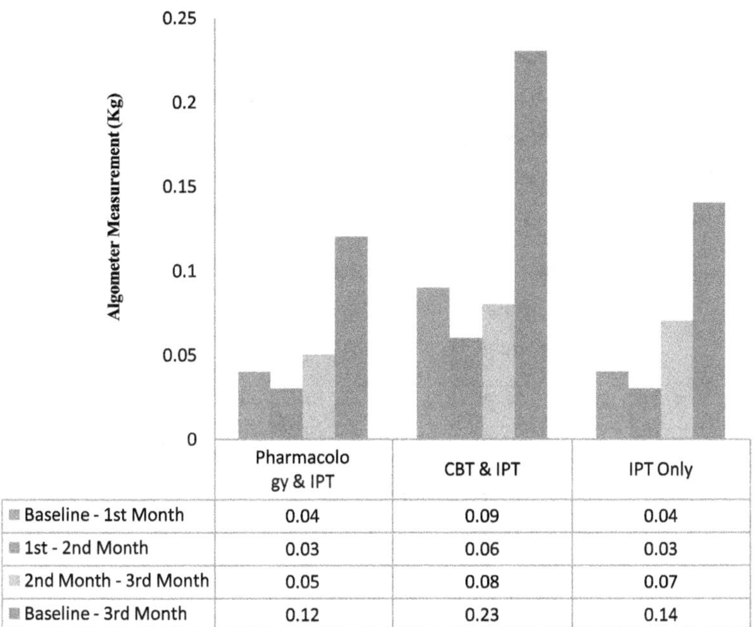

	Pharmacology & IPT	CBT & IPT	IPT Only
Baseline - 1st Month	0.04	0.09	0.04
1st - 2nd Month	0.03	0.06	0.03
2nd Month - 3rd Month	0.05	0.08	0.07
Baseline - 3rd Month	0.12	0.23	0.14

Figure 4.5.12: The Difference in means (MD) of Lower Arm Right point on pain pressure algometer from baseline to third month between group 1, 2 and 3

Table 4.5.12.1: Multiple comparison of difference in means (MD) of improvement in Lower Arm Right point on Pain Pressure Threshold among different interventional group

Time frame between	Interventional group		MD	Standard Error	P value	95% Confidence Interval	
						Lower Bound	Upper Bound
Baseline –	PHAIPT group	CBTAIPT group	$0.05^{\#}$	0.05	0.35	0.05	0.14
		IPT Group	$0.00^{\#}$	0.05	0.95	0.09	0.10
1st Month	CBTAIPT group	IPT Group	$0.05^{\#}$	0.05	0.31	0.05	0.15
1st Month –	PHAIPT group	CBTAIPT group	$0.03^{\#}$	0.03	0.36	0.03	0.09
		IPT Group	$0.00^{\#}$	0.03	0.92	0.06	0.07
2nd Month	CBTAIPT group	IPT Group	$0.03^{\#}$	0.03	0.42	0.04	0.09
2nd Month –	PHAIPT group	CBTAIPT group	$0.03^{\#}$	0.06	0.61	0.09	0.15
		IPT Group	$0.02^{\#}$	0.06	0.78	0.10	0.13
3rd Month	CBTAIPT group	IPT Group	$0.01^{\#}$	0.06	0.82	0.10	0.13
Baseline –	PHAIPT group	CBTAIPT group	$0.11^{\#}$	0.13	0.41	0.15	0.36
		IPT Group	$0.02^{\#}$	0.13	0.90	0.24	0.27
3rd Month	CBTAIPT group	IPT Group	$0.09^{\#}$	0.13	0.49	0.17	0.35

CBT = Cognitive Behavioral Therapy; IPT = Integrated Physiotherapy Group; MD = Difference in means (MD) [#] = Non-Significant

Table 4.5.12.1 summarized the comparisons of differences in mean improvement in lower arm right point using post hoc LSD. The difference in means (MD) between groups showed a non-significant improvement on the pain pressure threshold reading by algometer. This signifies that the role of PHAIPT and CBTAIPTare not effective in increasing the pain pressure threshold level of fibromyalgia patients.

Table 4.5.13: Comparison of difference in means (MD) of Hip Buttock Left (HBL) variable on algometer between the groups at different time frame from Baseline to Third month

Variable (Time frame)	Groups	Mean ± SD	SOS Between Groups	SOS Within Group	F	P
HBL (Baseline – 1st Month)	PHAIPT	0.41 ± 0.36	0.38	8.59	1.94	0.14[#]
	CBTAIPT	0.30 ± 0.35				
	IPT Only	0.26 ± 0.21				
HBL (1st 2nd Month)	PHAIPT	0.31 ± 0.25	0.08	7.00	0.55	0.57[#]
	CBTAIPT	0.23 ± 0.33				
	IPT Only	0.27 ± 0.26				
HBL (2nd 3rd Month)	PHAIPT	0.35 ± 0.30	0.20	6.89	1.27	0.28[#]
	CBTAIPT	0.24 ± 0.23				
	IPT Only	0.33 ± 0.31				
HBL (Baseline 3rd Month)	PHAIPT	1.07 ± 0.66	1.40	35.36	1.72	0.18[#]
	CBTAIPT	0.77 ± 0.63				
	IPT Only	0.87 ± 0.62				

HBL = Hip Buttock Left; SD = Standard Deviation; CBT = Cognitive Behavioral Therapy; IPT = Integrated Physiotherapy Techniques; SOS = Sum Of Squares. [#] = Non-Significant

Table 4.5.13 depicts the Mean and standard deviation of hip buttock left on algometer at baseline to first month (0.41 ± 0.36; 0.30 ± 0.35; 0.26 ± 0.21 with F = 1.94 and the p = 0.14), first to second month (0.31 ± 0.25; 0.23 ± 0.33; 0.27 ± 0.26 with F = 0.55 and the p = 0.57), second to third month (0.35 ± 0.30; 0.24 ± 0.23; 0.33 ± 0.31 with F = 1.27 and the p = 0.28), baseline to third month (1.07 ± 0.66; 0.77 ± 0.63; 0.87 ± 0.62 with F = 1.72, p = 0.18), for Group 1, Group 2 and Group 3 respectively at the level of significance with p value ≤ 0.05. This Figure showing that the experimental groups have no role in reducing the pain of fibromyalgia patients on the left side hip and buttock painful area.

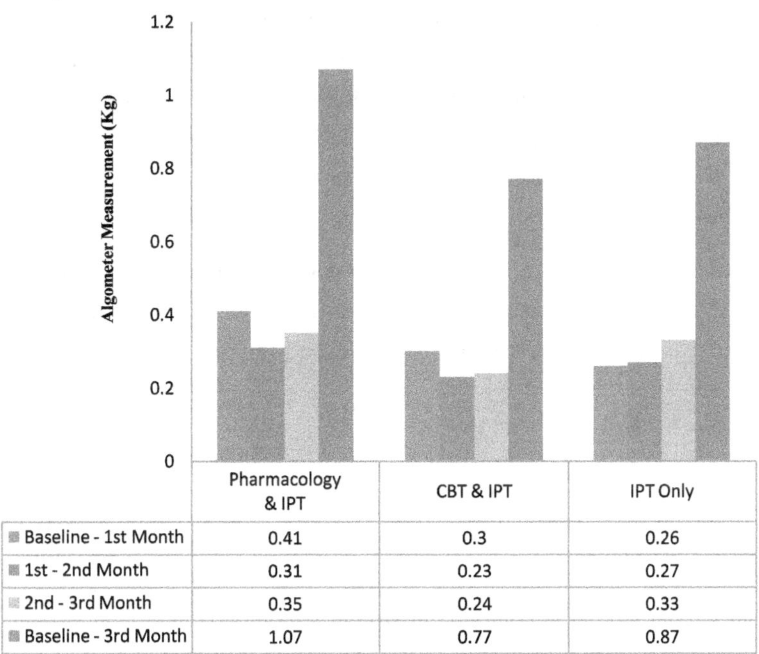

	Pharmacology & IPT	CBT & IPT	IPT Only
Baseline - 1st Month	0.41	0.3	0.26
1st - 2nd Month	0.31	0.23	0.27
2nd - 3rd Month	0.35	0.24	0.33
Baseline - 3rd Month	1.07	0.77	0.87

Figure 4.5.13: The Difference in means (MD) of Hip Buttock Left point on pain pressure algometer from baseline to third month between group 1, 2 and 3

Table 4.5.13.1: Multiple comparison of difference in means (MD) of improvement in Hip Buttock Left point on Pain Pressure Threshold among different interventional group

Time frame Between	Interventional group		MD	Standard Error	P value	95% Confidence Interval	
						Lower Bound	Upper Bound
Baseline –	Pharmacotherapy + IPT Group	CBTAIPT group	$0.12^{\#}$	0.08	0.15	0.04	0.28
		IPT Group	$0.15^{\#}$	0.08	0.06	0.13	0.31
1st Month	CBTAIPT group	IPT Group	$0.04^{\#}$	0.08	0.65	0.12	0.20
1st Month –	Pharmacotherapy + IPT Group	CBTAIPT group	$0.08^{\#}$	0.07	0.30	0.07	0.22
		IPT Group	$0.03^{\#}$	0.07	0.65	0.11	0.18
2nd Month	CBTAIPT group	IPT Group	$0.04^{\#}$	0.07	0.56	0.10	0.19
2nd Month –	Pharmacotherapy + IPT Group	CBTAIPT group	$0.11^{\#}$	0.07	0.15	0.04	0.25
		IPT Group	$0.01^{\#}$	0.07	0.85	0.13	0.16
3rd Month	CBTAIPT group	IPT Group	$0.09^{\#}$	0.07	0.20	0.05	0.24
Baseline –	Pharmacotherapy + IPT Group	CBTAIPT group	$0.30^{\#}$	0.16	0.07	0.03	0.63
		IPT Group	$0.20^{\#}$	0.16	0.23	0.13	0.53
3rd Month	CBTAIPT group	IPT Group	$0.10^{\#}$	0.16	0.55	0.23	0.43
CBT = Cognitive Behavioral Therapy; IPT = Integrated Physiotherapy Group; MD = Difference in means (MD) $^{\#}$ = Non-Significant							

Table 4.5.13.1 summarized the comparisons of differences in mean improvement in hip buttock left point using post hoc LSD. The difference in means (MD) between groups showed a non-significant improvement on the pain pressure threshold reading by algometer. This signifies that the role of PHAIPT and CBTAIPTare not effective in increasing the pain pressure threshold level of fibromyalgia patients.

Table 4.5.14: Comparison of difference in means (MD) of Hip Buttock Right (HBR) variable on algometer between the groups at different time frame from Baseline to Third month

Variable (Time frame)	Groups	Mean ± SD	SOS Between Group	SOS Within Group	F	P
HBR (Baseline – 1st Month)	PHAIPT	0.36 ± 0.30	0.22	7.11	1.37	0.25[#]
	CBTAIPT	0.27 ± 0.27				
	IPT Only	0.25 ± 0.29				
HBR (1st & 2nd Month)	PHAIPT	0.28 ± 0.23	0.01	5.59	0.13	0.87[#]
	CBTAIPT	0.26 ± 0.30				
	IPT Only	0.24 ± 0.23				
HBR (2nd & 3rd Month)	PHAIPT	0.32 ± 0.33	0.07	6.59	0.47	0.64[#]
	CBTAIPT	0.26 ± 0.24				
	IPT Only	0.32 ± 0.25				
HBR (Baseline 3rd Month)	PHAIPT	0.96 ± 0.70	0.51	39.19	0.56	0.57[#]
	CBTAIPT	0.79 ± 0.66				
	IPT Only	0.81 ± 0.65				

HBR = Hip Buttock Right; SD = Standard Deviation; CBT = Cognitive Behavioral Therapy; IPT = Integrated Physiotherapy Techniques; SOS = Sum Of Squares. [#] = Non-Significant

Table 4.5.14 depicts the Mean and standard deviation of hip buttock right on algometer at baseline to first month (0.36 ± 0.30; 0.27 ± 0.27; 0.25 ± 0.29 with F = 1.37 and the p = 0.25), first to second month (0.28 ± 0.23; 0.26 ± 0.30; 0.24 ± 0.23 with F = 0.13 and the p = 0.87), second to third month (0.32 ± 0.33; 0.26 ± 0.24; 0.32 ± 0.25 with F = 0.47 and the p = 0.64), baseline to third month (0.96 ± 0.70; 0.79 ± 0.66; 0.81 ± 0.65 with F = 0.56, p = 0.57), for Group 1, Group 2 and Group 3 respectively at the level of significance with p value ≤ 0.05. This Figure showing that the experimental groups have no role in reducing the pain of fibromyalgia patients on the right side hip and buttock painful area.

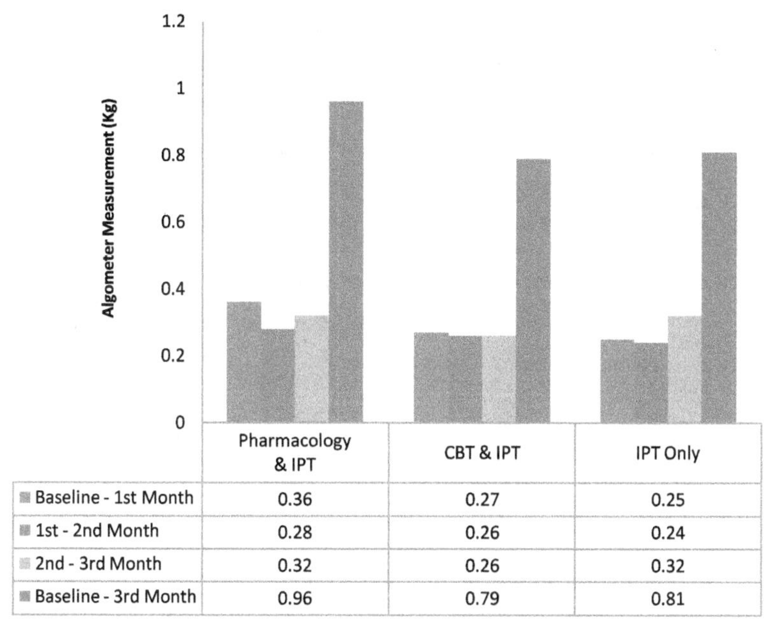

	Pharmacology & IPT	CBT & IPT	IPT Only
Baseline - 1st Month	0.36	0.27	0.25
1st - 2nd Month	0.28	0.26	0.24
2nd - 3rd Month	0.32	0.26	0.32
Baseline - 3rd Month	0.96	0.79	0.81

Figure 4.5.14: The Difference in means (MD) of Hip Buttock Right point on pain pressure algometer from baseline to third month between group 1, 2 and 3

Table 4.5.14.1: Multiple comparison of difference in means (MD) of improvement in Hip Buttock Right point on Pain Pressure Threshold among different interventional group

Time frame between	Interventional group		MD	Standard Error	P value	95% Confidence Interval	
						Lower Bound	Upper Bound
Baseline –	PHAIPT group	CBTAIPT group	0.10[#]	0.07	0.19	0.05	0.24
		IPT Group	0.11[#]	0.07	0.13	0.26	0.03
1st Month	CBTAIPT group	IPT Group	0.02[#]	0.07	0.82	0.13	0.16
1st Month –	PHAIPT group	CBTAIPT group	0.01[#]	0.07	0.84	0.12	0.14
		IPT Group	0.03[#]	0.07	0.61	0.10	0.16
2nd Month	CBTAIPT group	IPT Group	0.02[#]	0.07	0.76	0.15	0.11
2nd Month –	PHAIPT group	CBTAIPT group	0.06[#]	0.07	0.40	0.08	0.20
		IPT Group	0.00[#]	0.07	1.00	0.14	0.14
3rd Month	CBTAIPT group	IPT Group	0.06[#]	0.07	0.40	0.08	0.20
Baseline –	PHAIPT group	CBTAIPT group	0.17[#]	0.17	0.33	0.17	0.51
		IPT Group	0.15[#]	0.17	0.40	0.20	0.49
3rd Month	CBTAIPT group	IPT Group	0.02[#]	0.17	0.89	0.32	0.37

CBT = Cognitive Behavioral Therapy; IPT = Integrated Physiotherapy Group; MD = Difference in means (MD) [#] = Non-Significant

Table 4.5.14.1 summarized the comparisons of differences in mean improvement in hip buttock left point using post hoc LSD. The difference in means (MD) between groups showed a non-significant improvement on the pain pressure threshold reading by algometer. This signifies that the role of PHAIPT and CBTAIPTare not effective in increasing the pain pressure threshold level of fibromyalgia patients.

Table 4.5.15: Comparison of difference in means (MD) of Upper Leg Left (ULL) variable on algometer between the groups at different time frame from Baseline to Third month

Variable (Time frame)	Groups	Mean ± SD	SOS Between Groups	SOS Within Group	F	P
ULL (Baseline – 1st Month)	PHAIPT	0.02 ± 0.06	0.03	1.81	0.93	0.39[#]
	CBTAIPT	0.03 ± 0.15				
	IPT Only	0.07 ± 0.19				
ULL (1st – 2nd Month)	PHAIPT	0.03 ± 0.11	0.01	1.25	0.36	0.69[#]
	CBTAIPT	0.04 ± 0.17				
	IPT Only	0.02 ± 0.05				
ULL (2nd – 3rd Month)	PHAIPT	0.01 ± 0.04	0.02	0.80	1.23	0.29[#]
	CBTAIPT	0.02 ± 0.06				
	IPT Only	0.05 ± 0.15				
ULL (Baseline – 3rd Month)	PHAIPT	0.06 ± 0.22	0.08	9.09	0.38	0.68[#]
	CBTAIPT	0.09 ± 0.36				
	IPT Only	0.13 ± 0.37				
ULL = Upper Leg Left; SD = Standard Deviation; CBT = Cognitive Behavioral Therapy; IPT = Integrated Physiotherapy Techniques; SOS = Sum Of Squares. [#] = Non-Significant						

Table 4.5.15 depicts the Mean and standard deviation of upper leg left on algometer at baseline to first month (0.02 ± 0.06; 0.03 ± 0.15; 0.07 ± 0.19 with F = 0.93 and the p = 0.39), first to second month (0.03 ± 0.11; 0.04 ± 0.17; 0.02 ± 0.05 with F = 0.36 and the p = 0.69), second to third month (0.01 ± 0.04; 0.02 ± 0.06; 0.05 ± 0.15 with F = 1.23 and the p = 0.29), baseline to third month (0.06 ± 0.22; 0.09 ± 0.36; 0.13 ± 0.37 with F = 0.38, p = 0.68), for Group 1, Group 2 and Group 3 respectively at the level of significance with p value ≤ 0.05. This Figure showing that the experimental groups have no role in reducing the pain of fibromyalgia patients on the left side upper leg pain pressure threshold.

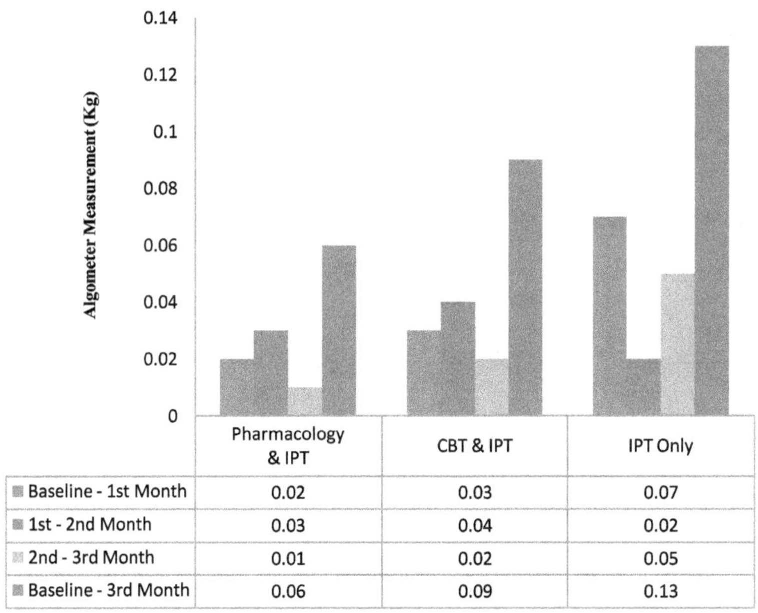

	Pharmacology & IPT	CBT & IPT	IPT Only
Baseline - 1st Month	0.02	0.03	0.07
1st - 2nd Month	0.03	0.04	0.02
2nd - 3rd Month	0.01	0.02	0.05
Baseline - 3rd Month	0.06	0.09	0.13

Figure 4.5.15: The Difference in means (MD) of Upper Leg Left point on pain pressure algometer from baseline to third month between group 1, 2 and 3

Table 4.5.15.1: Multiple comparison of difference in means (MD) of improvement in Upper Leg Left point on Pain Pressure Threshold among different interventional group

Time frame Between	Interventional group		MD	Standard Error	P value	95% Confidence Interval	
						Lower Bound	Upper Bound
Baseline –	PHAIPT group	CBTAIPT group	$0.02^{\#}$	0.04	0.66	0.06	0.09
		IPT Group	$0.05^{\#}$	0.04	0.18	0.02	0.12
1st Month	CBTAIPT group	IPT Group	$0.03^{\#}$	0.04	0.37	0.04	0.11
1st Month –	PHAIPT group	CBTAIPT group	$0.01^{\#}$	0.03	0.67	0.05	0.08
		IPT Group	$0.01^{\#}$	0.03	0.67	0.05	0.08
2nd Month	CBTAIPT group	IPT Group	$0.03^{\#}$	0.03	0.39	0.04	0.09
2nd Month –	PHAIPT group	CBTAIPT group	$0.01^{\#}$	0.02	0.79	0.04	0.06
		IPT Group	$0.04^{\#}$	0.02	0.14	0.01	0.09
3rd Month	CBTAIPT group	IPT Group	$0.03^{\#}$	0.02	0.23	0.02	0.08
Baseline –	PHAIPT group	CBTAIPT group	$0.04^{\#}$	0.08	0.66	0.13	0.20
		IPT Group	$0.07^{\#}$	0.08	0.38	0.09	0.24
3rd Month	CBTAIPT group	IPT Group	$0.04^{\#}$	0.08	0.66	0.13	0.20

CBT = Cognitive Behavioral Therapy; IPT = Integrated Physiotherapy Group; MD = Difference in means (MD) $^{\#}$ = Non-Significant

Table 4.5.15.1 summarized the comparisons of differences in mean improvement in upper leg left point using post hoc LSD. The difference in means (MD) between groups showed a non-significant improvement on the pain pressure threshold reading by algometer. This signifies that the role of PHAIPT and CBTAIPTare not effective in increasing the pain pressure threshold level of fibromyalgia patients.

Table 4.5.16: Comparison of difference in means (MD) of Upper Leg Right (ULR) variable on algometer between the groups at different time frame from Baseline to Third month

Variable (Time frame)	Groups	Mean ± SD	SOS Between Groups	SOS Within Group	F	P
ULR (Baseline 1st Month)	PHAIPT	0.02 ± 0.09	0.02	1.46	0.66	0.51[#]
	CBTAIPT	0.02 ± 0.10				
	IPT Only	0.06 ± 0.18				
ULR (1st – 2nd Month)	PHAIPT	0.02 ± 0.10	0.03	1.92	0.66	0.51[#]
	CBTAIPT	0.03 ± 0.11				
	IPT Only	0.06 ± 0.21				
ULR (2nd – 3rd Month)	PHAIPT	0.03 ± 0.15	0.02	1.56	0.57	0.56[#]
	CBTAIPT	0.02 ± 0.08				
	IPT Only	0.06 ± 0.16				
ULR (Baseline – 3rd Month)	PHAIPT	0.08 ± 0.31	0.20	11.84	0.76	0.46[#]
	CBTAIPT	0.07 ± 0.27				
	IPT Only	0.18 ± 0.49				

ULR = Upper Leg Right; SD = Standard Deviation; CBT = Cognitive Behavioral Therapy; IPT = Integrated Physiotherapy Techniques; SOS = Sum Of Squares. [#] = Non-Significant

Table 4.5.16 depicts the Mean and standard deviation of upper leg right on algometer at baseline to first month (0.02 ± 0.09; 0.02 ± 0.10; 0.06 ± 0.18 with F = 0.66 and the p = 0.51), first to second month (0.02 ± 0.10; 0.03 ± 0.11; 0.06 ± 0.21 with F = 0.66 and the p = 0.51), second to third month (0.03 ± 0.15; 0.02 ± 0.08; 0.06 ± 0.16 with F = 0.57 and the p = 0.56), baseline to third month (0.08 ± 0.31; 0.07 ± 0.27; 0.18 ± 0.49 with F = 0.76, p = 0.46), for Group 1, Group 2 and Group 3 respectively at the level of significance with p value ≤ 0.05. This Figure showing that the experimental groups role in reducing the pain of fibromyalgia patients on the right side upper leg pain pressure threshold.

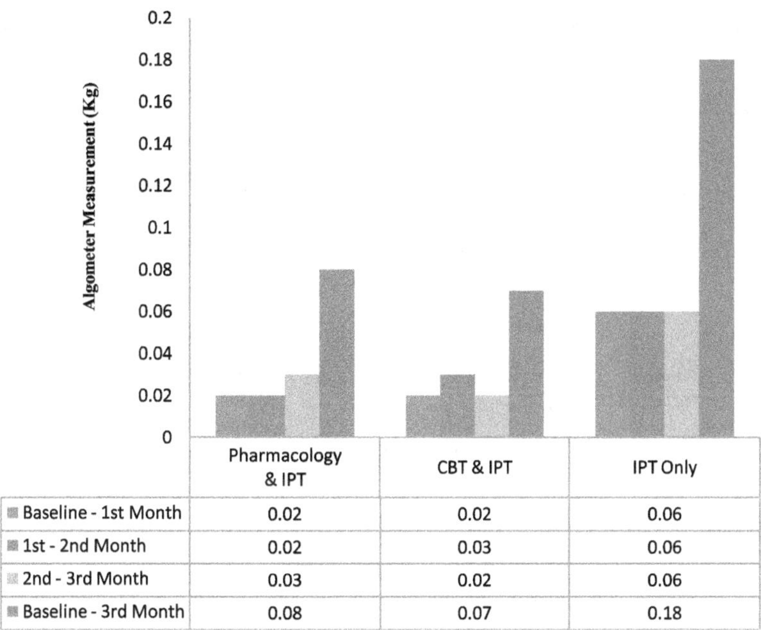

	Pharmacology & IPT	CBT & IPT	IPT Only
Baseline - 1st Month	0.02	0.02	0.06
1st - 2nd Month	0.02	0.03	0.06
2nd - 3rd Month	0.03	0.02	0.06
Baseline - 3rd Month	0.08	0.07	0.18

Figure 4.5.16: The Difference in means (MD) of Upper Leg Right point on pain pressure algometer from baseline to third month between group 1, 2 and 3

Table 4.5.16.1: Multiple comparison of difference in means (MD) of improvement in Upper Leg Right point on Pain Pressure Threshold among different interventional group

Time frame between	Interventional group		MD	Standard Error	P value	95% Confidence Interval	
						Lower Bound	Upper Bound
Baseline –	PHAIPT group	CBTAIPT group	$0.00^{\#}$	0.03	1.00	0.07	0.07
		IPT Group	$0.03^{\#}$	0.03	0.32	0.03	0.10
1st Month	CBTAIPT group	IPT Group	$0.03^{\#}$	0.03	0.32	0.03	0.10
1st Month –	PHAIPT group	CBTAIPT group	$0.00^{\#}$	0.04	0.93	0.07	0.08
		IPT Group	$0.04^{\#}$	0.04	0.30	0.04	0.12
2nd Month	CBTAIPT group	IPT Group	$0.04^{\#}$	0.04	0.34	0.04	0.11
2nd Month –	PHAIPT group	CBTAIPT group	$0.01^{\#}$	0.03	0.70	0.06	0.08
		IPT Group	$0.02^{\#}$	0.03	0.50	0.05	0.09
3rd Month	CBTAIPT group	IPT Group	$0.04^{\#}$	0.03	0.29	0.03	0.11
Baseline –	PHAIPT group	CBTAIPT group	$0.01^{\#}$	0.10	0.92	0.18	0.20
		IPT Group	$0.10^{\#}$	0.10	0.31	0.09	0.29
3rd Month	CBTAIPT group	IPT Group	$0.11^{\#}$	0.10	0.27	0.08	0.30

CBT = Cognitive Behavioral Therapy; IPT = Integrated Physiotherapy Group; MD = Difference in means (MD) [#] = Non-Significant

Table 4.5.16.1 summarized the comparisons of differences in mean improvement in upper leg left point using post hoc LSD. The difference in means (MD) between groups showed a non-significant improvement on the pain pressure threshold reading by algometer. This signifies that the role of PHAIPT and CBTAIPTare not effective in increasing the pain pressure threshold level of fibromyalgia patients.

Table 4.5.17: Comparison of difference in means (MD) of Lower Leg Left (LLL) variable on algometer between the groups at different time frame from Baseline to Third month

Variable (Time frame)	Groups	Mean ± SD	SOS Between Groups	SOS Within Group	F	P
LLL **(Baseline – 1st Month)**	PHAIPT	0.09 ± 0.18	0.18	4.60	1.72	0.18[#]
	CBTAIPT	0.14 ± 0.33				
	IPT Only	0.03 ± 0.14				
LLL **(1st – 2nd Month)**	PHAIPT	0.12 ± 0.29	0.02	4.69	0.22	0.80[#]
	CBTAIPT	0.10 ± 0.19				
	IPT Only	0.08 ± 0.20				
LLL **(2nd – 3rd Month)**	PHAIPT	0.07 ± 0.19	0.08	3.84	0.90	0.40[#]
	CBTAIPT	0.14 ± 0.25				
	IPT Only	0.07 ± 0.19				
LLL **(Baseline – 3rd Month)**	PHAIPT	0.28 ± 0.54	0.56	25.23	0.96	0.38[#]
	CBTAIPT	0.37 ± 0.62				
	IPT Only	0.18 ± 0.44				

LLL = Lower Leg Left; SD = Standard Deviation; CBT = Cognitive Behavioral Therapy; IPT = Integrated Physiotherapy Techniques; SOS = Sum Of Squares. [#] = Non-Significant

Table 4.5.17 depicts the Mean and standard deviation of Lower leg left on algometer at baseline to first month (0.09 ± 0.18; 0.14 ± 0.33; 0.03 ± 0.14 with F = 1.72 and the p = 0.18), first to second month (0.12 ± 0.29; 0.10 ± 0.19; 0.08 ± 0.20 with F = 0.222 and the p = 0.80), second to third month (0.17 ± 0.19; 0.14 ± 0.25; 0.07 ± 0.19 with F = 0.90 and the p = 0.40), baseline to third month (0.28 ± 0.54; 0.37 ± 0.62; 0.18 ± 0.44 with F = 0.96, p = 0.38), for Group 1, Group 2 and Group 3 respectively at the level of significance with p value ≤ 0.05. This Figure showing that the experimental groups have no role in reducing the pain of fibromyalgia patients on the left side lower leg pain pressure threshold.

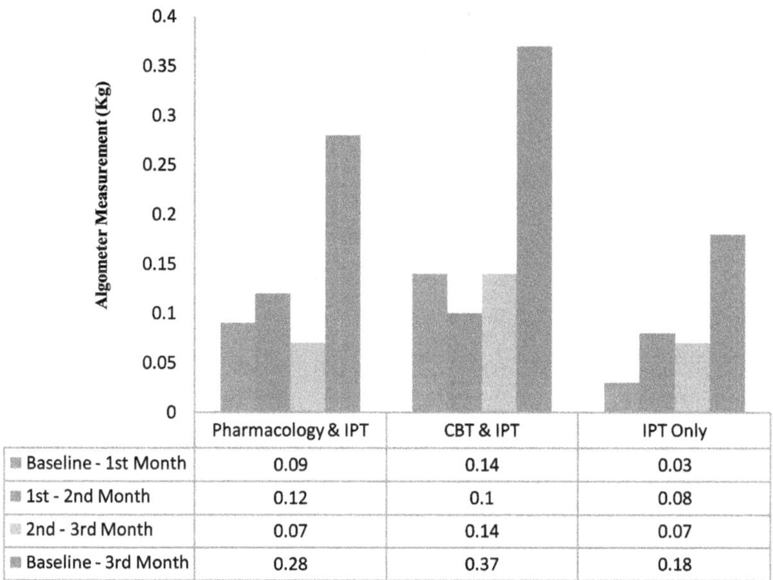

	Pharmacology & IPT	CBT & IPT	IPT Only
Baseline - 1st Month	0.09	0.14	0.03
1st - 2nd Month	0.12	0.1	0.08
2nd - 3rd Month	0.07	0.14	0.07
Baseline - 3rd Month	0.28	0.37	0.18

Figure 4.5.17: The Difference in means (MD) of Lower Leg Left point on pain pressure algometer from baseline to third month between group 1, 2 and 3

Table 4.5.17.1: Multiple comparison of difference in means (MD) of improvement in Lower Leg Left point on Pain Pressure Threshold among different interventional group

Time frame Between	Interventional group		MD	Standard Error	P value	95% Confidence Interval	
						Lower Bound	Upper Bound
Baseline –	PHAIPT group	CBTAIPT group	$0.05^{\#}$	0.06	0.40	0.07	0.17
		IPT Group	$0.06^{\#}$	0.06	0.32	0.06	0.18
1st Month	CBTAIPT group	IPT Group	$0.11^{\#}$	0.06	0.07	0.01	0.23
1st Month –	PHAIPT group	CBTAIPT group	$0.02^{\#}$	0.06	0.74	0.10	0.14
		IPT Group	$0.04^{\#}$	0.06	0.51	0.08	0.16
2nd Month	CBTAIPT group	IPT Group	$0.02^{\#}$	0.06	0.74	0.10	0.14
2nd Month –	PHAIPT group	CBTAIPT group	$0.06^{\#}$	0.05	0.25	0.04	0.17
		IPT Group	$0.00^{\#}$	0.05	1.00	0.11	0.11
3rd Month	CBTAIPT group	IPT Group	$0.06^{\#}$	0.05	0.25	0.04	0.17
Baseline –	PHAIPT group	CBTAIPT group	$0.09^{\#}$	0.14	0.50	0.18	0.37
		IPT Group	$0.10^{\#}$	0.14	0.47	0.18	0.38
3rd Month	CBTAIPT group	IPT Group	$0.19^{\#}$	0.14	0.17	0.08	0.47

CBT = Cognitive Behavioral Therapy; IPT = Integrated Physiotherapy Group; MD = Difference in means (MD); * = Significant; # = Non-significant

Table **4.5.17.1** summarized the comparisons of differences in mean improvement in lower leg left point using post hoc LSD. The difference in means (MD) between groups showed a non-significant improvement on the pain pressure threshold reading by algometer. This signifies that the role of PHAIPT and CBTAIPTare not effective in increasing the pain pressure threshold level of fibromyalgia patients.

Table 4.5.18: Comparison of difference in means (MD) of Lower Leg Right (LLR) variable on algometer between the groups at different time frame from Baseline to Third month

Variable (Time frame)	Groups	Mean ± SD	SOS Between Groups	SOS Within Group	F	P
LLR (Baseline – 1st Month)	PHAIPT	0.11 ± 0.24	0.06	3.68	0.75	0.47[#]
	CBTAIPT	0.11 ± 0.22				
	IPT Only	0.05 ± 0.15				
LLR (1st – 2nd Month)	PHAIPT	0.09 ± 0.19	0.04	2.02	0.95	0.39[#]
	CBTAIPT	0.08 ± 0.14				
	IPT Only	0.04 ± 0.12				
LLR (2nd – 3rd Month)	PHAIPT	0.05 ± 0.12	0.30	3.01	4.33	0.01*
	CBTAIPT	0.16 ± 0.28				
	IPT Only	0.03 ± 0.11				
LLR (Baseline – 3rd Month)	PHAIPT	0.25 ± 0.54	0.79	21.48	1.61	0.20[#]
	CBTAIPT	0.35 ± 0.58				
	IPT Only	0.12 ± 0.33				

LLR = Lower Leg Right; SD = Standard Deviation; CBT = Cognitive Behavioral Therapy; IPT = Integrated Physiotherapy Techniques; SOS = Sum Of Squares. [#] = Non-Significant

Table 4.5.18 depicts the Mean and standard deviation of Lower leg right on algometer at baseline to first month (0.11 ± 0.24; 0.11 ± 0.22; 0.05 ± 0.15 with F = 0.75 and the p = 0.47), first to second month (0.09 ± 0.19; 0.08 ± 0.14; 0.04 ± 0.12 with F = 0.95 and the p = 0.39), second to third month (0.05 ± 0.12; 0.16 ± 0.28; 0.03 ± 0.11 with F = 4.33 and the p = 0.01), baseline to third month (0.25 ± 0.54; 0.35 ± 0.58; 0.12 ± 0.33 with F = 1.61, p = 0.20), for Group 1, Group 2 and Group 3 respectively at the level of significance with p value ≤ 0.05. This signifies that the experimental groups role in reducing the pain on the right side lower leg point in fibromyalgia patients.

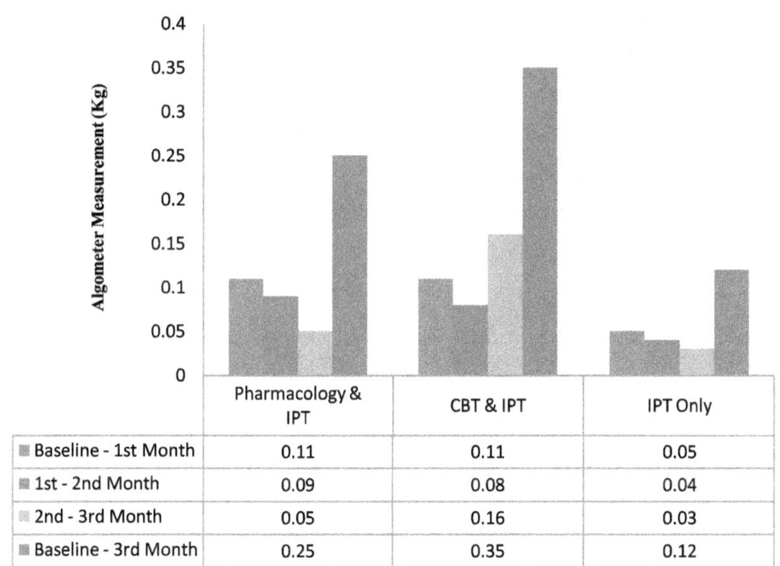

	Pharmacology & IPT	CBT & IPT	IPT Only
Baseline - 1st Month	0.11	0.11	0.05
1st - 2nd Month	0.09	0.08	0.04
2nd - 3rd Month	0.05	0.16	0.03
Baseline - 3rd Month	0.25	0.35	0.12

Figure 4.5.18: The Difference in means (MD) of Lower Leg Right point on pain pressure algometer from baseline to third month between group 1, 2 and 3

Table 4.5.18.1: Multiple comparison of difference in means (MD) of improvement in Lower Leg Right point on Pain Pressure Threshold among different interventional group

Time frame Between	Interventional group		MD	Standard Error	P value	95% Confidence Interval	
						Lower Bound	Upper Bound
Baseline – 1st Month	PHAIPT group	CBTAIPT group	$0.00^{\#}$	0.05	1.00	0.11	0.11
		IPT Group	$0.06^{\#}$	0.05	0.29	0.05	0.16
	CBTAIPT group	IPT Group	$0.06^{\#}$	0.05	0.29	0.05	0.16
1st Month – 2nd Month	PHAIPT group	CBTAIPT group	$0.01^{\#}$	0.04	0.87	0.07	0.08
		IPT Group	$0.05^{\#}$	0.04	0.21	0.03	0.13
	CBTAIPT group	IPT Group	$0.04^{\#}$	0.04	0.27	0.03	0.12
2nd Month – 3rd Month	PHAIPT group	CBTAIPT group	0.11^{*}	0.05	0.02	0.02	0.21
		IPT Group	$0.02^{\#}$	0.05	0.73	0.08	0.11
	CBTAIPT group	IPT Group	0.13^{*}	0.05	0.01	0.03	0.23
Baseline – 3rd Month	PHAIPT group	CBTAIPT group	$0.11^{\#}$	0.13	0.41	0.15	0.36
		IPT Group	$0.12^{\#}$	0.13	0.34	0.13	0.38
	CBTAIPT group	IPT Group	$0.23^{\#}$	0.13	0.08	0.03	0.49

CBT = Cognitive Behavioral Therapy; IPT = Integrated Physiotherapy Group; MD = Difference in means (MD); * = Significant; # = Non-Significant.

Table 4.5.18.1 summarized the comparisons of differences in mean improvement in lower leg right side painful point using post hoc LSD. The result specifies that level of improvement was greater in experimental group I at second to third month (p ≤ 0.05) as compared to experimental group II. However; it does not show the statistically significant difference (p > 0.05) in experimental group I and II from the other time frames as compared to experimental group III. This signifies that the role of Pharmacotherapy along with integrated physiotherapy techniques in decreasing the pain pressure threshold level of fibromyalgia patients.

Table 4.5.19: Comparison of difference in means (MD) of Jaw Left variable on algometer between the groups at different time frame from Baseline to Third month

Variable (Time frame)	Groups	Mean ± SD	SOS Between Groups	SOS Within Group	F	P
Jaw Left (Baseline – 1st Month)	PHAIPT	0.02 ± 0.09	0.00	1.53	0.13	0.87[#]
	CBTAIPT	0.03 ± 0.16				
	IPT Only	0.03 ± 0.13				
Jaw Left (1st – 2nd Month)	PHAIPT	0.02 ± 0.13	0.00	1.08	0.00	0.99[#]
	CBTAIPT	0.02 ± 0.09				
	IPT Only	0.03 ± 0.11				
Jaw Left (2nd – 3rd Month)	PHAIPT	0.01 ±0 .07	0.00	0.38	0.00	1.00[#]
	CBTAIPT	0.01 ± 0.05				
	IPT Only	0.01 ± 0.07				
Jaw Left (Baseline – 3rd Month)	PHAIPT	0.05 ± 0.29	0.00	7.04	0.03	0.96[#]
	CBTAIPT	0.07 ± 0.29				
	IPT Only	0.07 ± 0.27				

SD = Standard Deviation; CBT = Cognitive Behavioral Therapy; IPT = Integrated Physiotherapy Techniques; SOS = Sum Of Squares. [#] = Non-Significant

Table 4.5.19 depicts the Mean and standard deviation of jaw left on algometer at baseline to first month (0.02 ± 0.09; 0.03 ± 0.16; 0.03 ± 0.13 with F = 0.13 and the p = 0.87), first to second month (0.02 ± 0.13; 0.02 ± 0.09; 0.03 ± 0.11 with F = 0.00 and the p = 0.99), second to third month (0.01 ± 0.07; 0.01 ± 0.05; 0.01 ± 0.07 with F = 0.00 and the p = 1.00), baseline to third month (0.05 ± 0.29; 0.07 ± 0.29; 0.07 ± 0.27 with F = 0.03, p = 0.96), for Group 1, Group 2 and Group 3 respectively at the level of significance with p value ≤ 0.05. This Figure showing that the experimental groups have no role in reducing the pain of fibromyalgia patients on left side jaw painful area.

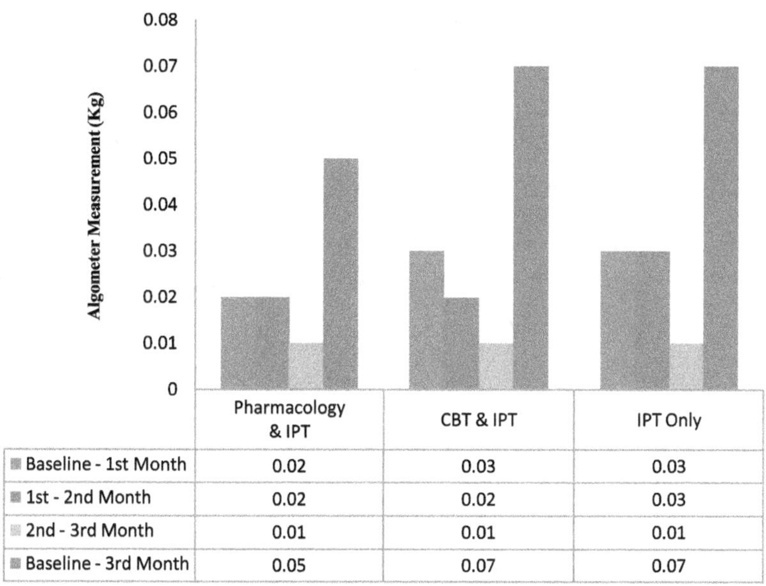

Figure 4.5.19: The Difference in means (MD) of Jaw Left point on pain pressure algometer from baseline to third month between group 1, 2 and 3

Table 4.5.19.1: Multiple comparison of difference in means (MD) of improvement in Jaw Left point on Pain Pressure Threshold among different interventional group

Time frame Between	Interventional group		MD	Standard Error	P value	95% Confidence Interval	
						Lower Bound	Upper Bound
Baseline – 1st Month	PHAIPT group	CBTAIPT group	0.02#	0.03	0.63	0.05	0.08
		IPT Group	0.01#	0.03	0.70	0.05	0.08
	CBTAIPT group	IPT Group	0.00#	0.03	0.92	0.06	0.07
1st Month – 2nd Month	PHAIPT group	CBTAIPT group	0.00#	0.03	1.00	0.06	0.06
		IPT Group	0.00#	0.03	0.91	0.05	0.06
	CBTAIPT group	IPT Group	0.00#	0.03	0.91	0.05	0.06
2nd Month – 3rd Month	PHAIPT group	CBTAIPT group	0.00#	0.02	1.00	0.03	0.03
		IPT Group	0.00#	0.02	1.00	0.03	0.03
	CBTAIPT group	IPT Group	0.00#	0.02	1.00	0.03	0.03
Baseline – 3rd Month	PHAIPT group	CBTAIPT group	0.02#	0.07	0.82	0.13	0.16
		IPT Group	0.02#	0.07	0.82	0.13	0.16
	CBTAIPT group	IPT Group	0.00#	0.07	1.00	0.15	0.15

CBT = Cognitive Behavioral Therapy; IPT = Integrated Physiotherapy Group; MD = Difference in means (MD) # = Non-Significant

Table **4.5.19.1** summarized the comparisons of differences in mean improvement in jaw left point using post hoc LSD. The difference in means (MD) between groups showed a nonsignificant improvement on the pain pressure threshold reading by algometer. This signifies that the role of PHAIPT and CBTAIPTare not effective in increasing the pain pressure threshold level of fibromyalgia patients.

Table 4.5.20: Comparison of difference in means (MD) of Jaw Right variable on algometer between the groups at different time frame from Baseline to Third month

Variable (Time frame)	Groups	Mean ± SD	SOS Between Groups	SOS Within Group	F	P
Jaw Right **(Baseline – 1st Month)**	PHAIPT	0.00 ± 0.00	0.04	0.96	1.92	0.15[#]
	CBTAIPT	0.02 ± 0.07				
	IPT Only	0.05 ± 0.17				
Jaw Right **(1st – 2nd Month)**	PHAIPT	0.00 ± 0.00	0.02	0.96	1.26	0.28[#]
	CBTAIPT	0.04 ± 0.15				
	IPT Only	0.02 ± 0.10				
Jaw Right **(2nd – 3rd Month)**	PHAIPT	0.00 ± 0.00	0.01	0.75	0.73	0.48[#]
	CBTAIPT	0.03 ± 0.10				
	IPT Only	0.02 ± 0.13				
Jaw Right (Baseline – 3rd Month)	PHAIPT	0.00 ± 0.00	0.18	5.95	1.36	0.26[#]
	CBTAIPT	0.09 ± 0.30				
	IPT Only	0.10 ± 0.34				

SD = Standard Deviation; CBT = Cognitive Behavioral Therapy; IPT = Integrated Physiotherapy Techniques; SOS = Sum Of Squares. [#] = Non-Significant

Table 4.5.20 depicts the Mean and standard deviation of jaw right on algometer at baseline to first month (0.00 ± 0.00; 0.02 ± 0.07; 0.05 ± 0.17 with F = 1.92 and the p = 0.15), first to second month (0.00 ± 0.00; 0.04 ± 0.15; 0.02 ± 0.10 with F = 1.26 and the p = 0.28), second to third month (0.00 ± 0.00; 0.03 ± 0.10; 0.02 ± 0.13 with F = 0.73 and the p = 0.48), baseline to third month (0.00 ± 0.00; 0.09 ± 0.30; 0.10 ± 0.34 with F = 1.36, p = 0.26), for Group 1, Group 2 and Group 3 respectively at the level of significance with p value ≤ 0.05. This Figure showing that the experimental groups have no role in reducing the pain of fibromyalgia patients on right side jaw pain.

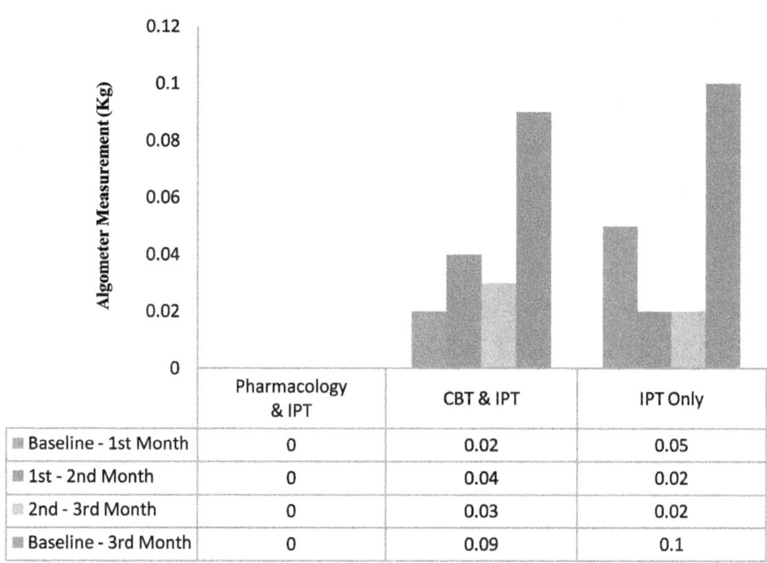

	Pharmacology & IPT	CBT & IPT	IPT Only
Baseline - 1st Month	0	0.02	0.05
1st - 2nd Month	0	0.04	0.02
2nd - 3rd Month	0	0.03	0.02
Baseline - 3rd Month	0	0.09	0.1

Figure 4.5.20: The Difference in means (MD) of Jaw Right point on pain pressure algometer from baseline to third month between group 1, 2 and 3

Table 4.5.20.1: Multiple comparison of difference in means (MD) of improvement in Jaw Right point on Pain Pressure Threshold among different interventional group

Time frame Between	Interventional group		MD	Standard Error	P value	95% Confidence Interval	
						Lower Bound	Upper Bound
Baseline – 1st Month	PHAIPT group	CBTAIPT group	$0.02^{\#}$	0.03	0.39	0.03	0.08
		IPT Group	0.05^{*}	0.03	0.05	0.00	0.11
	CBTAIPT group	IPT Group	$0.03^{\#}$	0.03	0.27	0.02	0.08
1st Month – 2nd Month	PHAIPT group	CBTAIPT group	$0.04^{\#}$	0.03	0.12	0.01	0.10
		IPT Group	$0.02^{\#}$	0.03	0.39	0.03	0.08
	CBTAIPT group	IPT Group	$0.02^{\#}$	0.03	0.46	0.03	0.07
2nd Month – 3rd Month	PHAIPT group	CBTAIPT group	$0.03^{\#}$	0.02	0.27	0.02	0.07
		IPT Group	$0.02^{\#}$	0.02	0.33	0.02	0.07
	CBTAIPT group	IPT Group	$0.00^{\#}$	0.02	0.89	0.04	0.05
Baseline – 3rd Month	PHAIPT group	CBTAIPT group	$0.09^{\#}$	0.07	0.17	0.04	0.23
		IPT Group	$0.10^{\#}$	0.07	0.14	0.03	0.23
	CBTAIPT group	IPT Group	$0.01^{\#}$	0.07	0.92	0.13	0.14

CBT = Cognitive Behavioral Therapy; IPT = Integrated Physiotherapy Group; MD = Difference in means (MD) [#] = NonSignificant

Table 4.5.20.1 summarized the comparisons of differences in mean improvement in lower leg right side painful point using post hoc LSD. The result specifies that level of improvement was greater in experimental group I at baseline to first month (p ≤ 0.05) as compared to experimental group III. However; it does not show the statistically significant difference (p > 0.05) in experimental group I and II from the other time frames as compared to experimental group III. This signifies that the role of Pharmacotherapy along with integrated physiotherapy techniques in decreasing the pain pressure threshold level of fibromyalgia patients.

Table 4.5.21: Comparison of difference in means (MD) of Chest variable on algometer between the groups at different time frame from Baseline to Third month

Variable (Time frame)	Groups	Mean ± SD	SOS Between Groups	SOS Within Group	F	P
Chest (Baseline – 1st Month)	PHAIPT	0.14 ± 0.38	0.21	11.47	0.81	0.44[#]
	CBTAIPT	0.23 ± 0.41				
	IPT Only	0.12 ± 0.28				
Chest (1st 2nd Month)	PHAIPT	0.08 ± 0.24	0.00	4.87	0.06	0.94[#]
	CBTAIPT	0.10 ± 0.20				
	IPT Only	0.10 ± 0.27				
Chest (2nd – 3rd Month)	PHAIPT	0.07 ± 0.18	0.03	3.56	0.47	0.62[#]
	CBTAIPT	0.12 ± 0.21				
	IPT Only	0.10 ± 0 .22				
Chest (Baseline – 3rd Month)	PHAIPT	0.29 ± 0.68	0.41	42.86	0.42	0.65[#]
	CBTAIPT	0.45 ± 0.70				
	IPT Only	0.32 ± 0.69				

SD = Standard Deviation; CBT = Cognitive Behavioral Therapy; IPT = Integrated Physiotherapy Techniques; SOS = Sum Of Squares. [#] = Non-Significant

Table 4.5.21 depicts the Mean and standard deviation of chest on algometer at baseline to first month (0.14 ± 0.38; 0.23 ± 0.41; 0.12 ± 0.28 with F = 0.81 and the p = 0.44), first to second month (0.08 ± 0.24; 0.10 ± 0.20; 0.10 ± 0.27 with F = 0.06 and the p = 0.94), second to third month (0.07 ± 0.18; 0.12 ± 0.21; 0.10 ± 0 .22 with F = 0.47 and the p = 0.62), baseline to third month (0.29 ± 0.68; 0.45 ± 0.70; 0.32 ± 0.69 with F = 0.42, p = 0.65), for Group 1, Group 2 and Group 3 respectively at the level of significance with p value ≤ 0.05. This Figure showing that the experimental groups have no role in reducing the pain of fibromyalgia patients on chest tender area.

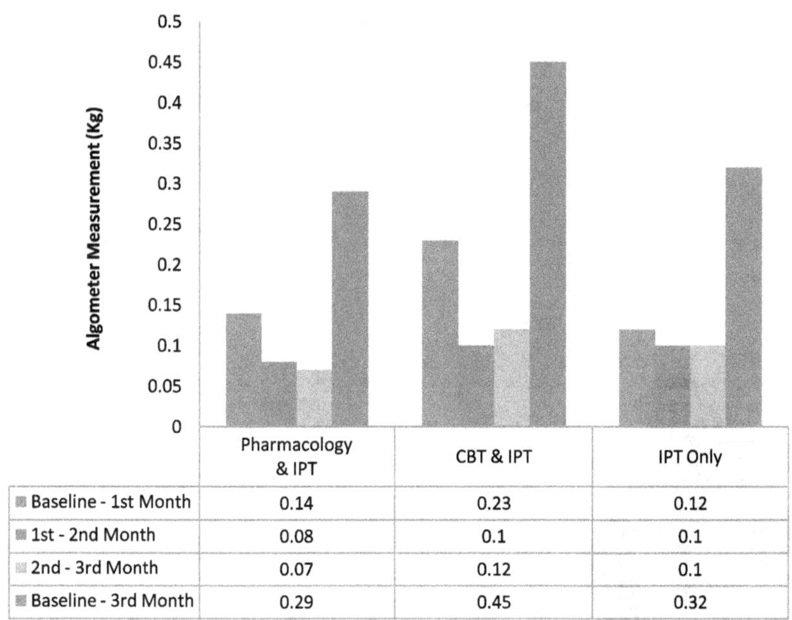

	Pharmacology & IPT	CBT & IPT	IPT Only
Baseline - 1st Month	0.14	0.23	0.12
1st - 2nd Month	0.08	0.1	0.1
2nd - 3rd Month	0.07	0.12	0.1
Baseline - 3rd Month	0.29	0.45	0.32

Figure 4.5.21: The Difference in Means (MD) of Chest point on pain pressure algometer from baseline to third month between group 1, 2 and 3

Table 4.5.21.1: Multiple comparison of difference in means (MD) of improvement in Chest point on Pain Pressure Threshold among different interventional group

Time frame Between	Interventional group		MD	Standard Error	P value	95% Confidence Interval	
						Lower Bound	Upper Bound
Baseline –	PHAIPT group	CBTAIPT group	$0.09^{\#}$	0.09	0.34	0.10	0.28
		IPT Group	$0.02^{\#}$	0.09	0.80	0.12	0.21
1st Month	CBTAIPT group	IPT Group	$0.11^{\#}$	0.09	0.23	0.07	0.30
1st Month –	PHAIPT group	CBTAIPT group	$0.02^{\#}$	0.06	0.79	0.10	0.14
		IPT Group	$0.02^{\#}$	0.06	0.74	0.10	0.14
2nd Month	CBTAIPT group	IPT Group	$0.00^{\#}$	0.06	0.96	0.12	0.12
2nd Month –	PHAIPT group	CBTAIPT group	$0.05^{\#}$	0.05	0.34	0.05	0.15
		IPT Group	$0.03^{\#}$	0.05	0.53	0.07	0.14
3rd Month	CBTAIPT group	IPT Group	$0.02^{\#}$	0.05	0.75	0.12	0.09
Baseline –	PHAIPT group	CBTAIPT group	$0.16^{\#}$	0.18	0.39	0.20	0.52
		IPT Group	$0.03^{\#}$	0.18	0.87	0.33	0.39
3rd Month	CBTAIPT group	IPT Group	$0.13^{\#}$	0.18	0.49	0.23	0.49

CBT = Cognitive Behavioral Therapy; IPT = Integrated Physiotherapy Group; MD = Difference in means (MD) $^{\#}$ = Non-Significant

Table 4.5.21.1 summarized the comparisons of differences in mean improvement in chest point using post hoc LSD. The difference in means (MD) between groups showed a non-significant improvement on the pain pressure threshold reading by algometer. This signifies that the role of PHAIPT and CBTAIPT are not effective in increasing the pain pressure threshold level of fibromyalgia patients.

Table 4.5.22: Comparison of difference in means (MD) of Abdomen variable on algometer between the groups at different time frame from Baseline to Third month

Variable (Time frame)	Groups	Mean ± SD	SOS Between Groups	SOS Within Group	F	P
Abdomen (Baseline – 1st Month)	PHAIPT	0.04 ± 0.12	0.02	0.55	1.57	0.21[#]
	CBTAIPT	0.00 ± 0.00				
	IPT Only	0.02 ± 0.06				
Abdomen (1st – 2nd Month)	PHAIPT	0.05 ± 0.19	0.04	1.60	1.30	0.27[#]
	CBTAIPT	0.00 ± 0.00				
	IPT Only	0.04 ± 0.14				
Abdomen (2nd – 3rd Month)	PHAIPT	0.02 ± 0.08	0.01	0.58	1.31	0.27[#]
	CBTAIPT	0.00 ± 0.00				
	IPT Only	0.03 ± 0.12				
Abdomen (Baseline – 3rd Month)	PHAIPT	0.11 ± 0.37	0.22	6.62	1.47	0.23[#]
	CBTAIPT	0.00 ± 0.00				
	IPT Only	0.10 ± 0.31				

SD = Standard Deviation; CBT = Cognitive Behavioral Therapy; IPT = Integrated Physiotherapy Techniques; SOS = Sum Of Squares. [#] = Non-Significant

Table 4.5.22 depicts the Mean and standard deviation of abdomen on algometer at baseline to first month (0.04 ± 0.12; 0.00 ± 0.00; 0.02 ± 0.06 with F = 1.57 and the p = 0.21), first to second month (0.05 ± 0.19; 0.00 ± 0.00; 0.04 ± 0.14 with F = 1.30 and the p = 0.27), second to third month (0.02 ± 0.08; 0.00 ± 0.00; 0.03 ± 0.12 with F = 1.31 and the p = 0.27), baseline to third month (0.11 ± 0.37; 0.00 ± 0.00; 0.10 ± 0.31 with F = 1.47, p = 0.23), for Group 1, Group 2 and Group 3 respectively at the level of significance with p value ≤ 0.05. This Figure showing that the experimental groups have no role in reducing the pain of fibromyalgia patients on the abdomen area.

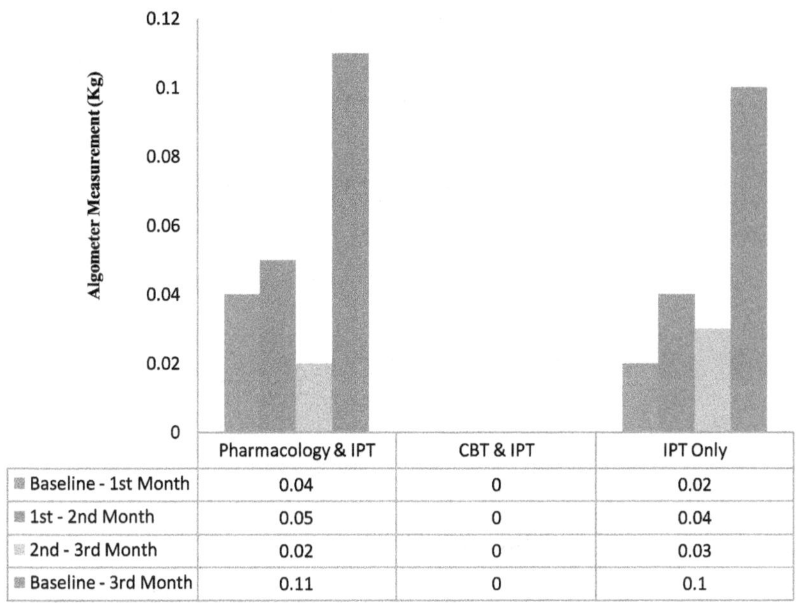

	Pharmacology & IPT	CBT & IPT	IPT Only
Baseline - 1st Month	0.04	0	0.02
1st - 2nd Month	0.05	0	0.04
2nd - 3rd Month	0.02	0	0.03
Baseline - 3rd Month	0.11	0	0.1

Figure 4.5.22: The Difference in Means (MD) of Abdomen point on pain pressure algometer from baseline to third month between group 1, 2 and 3

Table 4.5.22.1: Multiple comparison of difference in means (MD) of improvement in Abdomen point on Pain Pressure Threshold among different interventional group

Time frame Between	Interventional group		MD	Standard Error	P value	95% Confidence Interval	
						Lower Bound	Upper Bound
Baseline –	PHAIPT group	CBTAIPT group	$0.04^{\#}$	0.02	0.08	0.00	0.08
		IPT Group	$0.02^{\#}$	0.02	0.42	0.02	0.06
1st Month	CBTAIPT group	IPT Group	$0.02^{\#}$	0.02	0.34	0.02	0.06
1st Month –	PHAIPT group	CBTAIPT group	$0.05^{\#}$	0.04	0.13	0.02	0.12
		IPT Group	$0.01^{\#}$	0.04	0.78	0.06	0.08
2nd Month	CBTAIPT group	IPT Group	$0.04^{\#}$	0.04	0.22	0.03	0.11
2nd Month –	PHAIPT group	CBTAIPT group	$0.02^{\#}$	0.02	0.27	0.02	0.07
		IPT Group	$0.01^{\#}$	0.02	0.64	0.03	0.05
3rd Month	CBTAIPT group	IPT Group	$0.03^{\#}$	0.02	0.12	0.01	0.08
Baseline –	PHAIPT group	CBTAIPT group	$0.11^{\#}$	0.07	0.12	0.03	0.25
		IPT Group	$0.02^{\#}$	0.07	0.82	0.12	0.16
3rd Month	CBTAIPT group	IPT Group	$0.10^{\#}$	0.07	0.18	0.04	0.24

CBT = Cognitive Behavioral Therapy; IPT = Integrated Physiotherapy Group; MD = Difference in means (MD) $^{\#}$ = Non-Significant

Table 4.5.22.1 summarized the comparisons of differences in mean improvement in abdomen point using post hoc LSD. The difference in means (MD) between groups showed a non-significant improvement on the pain pressure threshold reading by algometer. This signifies that the role of PHAIPT and CBTAIPTare not effective in increasing the pain pressure threshold level of fibromyalgia patients.

Table 4.5.23: Comparison of difference in means (MD) of Neck variable on algometer between the groups at different time frame from Baseline to Third month

Variable (Time frame)	Groups	Mean ± SD	SOS Between Groups	SOS Within Group	F	P
Neck (Baseline – 1st Month)	PHAIPT	0.53 ± 0.38	0.28	10.69	1.17	0.31[#]
	CBTAIPT	0.41 ± 0.37				
	IPT Only	0.41 ± 0.30				
Neck (1st – 2nd Month)	PHAIPT	0.39 ± 0.27	0.01	9.05	0.06	0.94[#]
	CBTAIPT	0.36 ± 0.38				
	IPT Only	0.39 ± 0.31				
Neck (2nd – 3rd Month)	PHAIPT	0.50 ± 0.29	0.13	8.71	0.66	0.51[#]
	CBTAIPT	0.42 ± 0.34				
	IPT Only	0.42 ± 0.31				
Neck (Baseline – 3rd Month)	PHAIPT	1.42 ± 0.72	0.91	47.59	0.83	0.43[#]
	CBTAIPT	1.19 ± 0.85				
	IPT Only	1.22 ± 0.63				

SD = Standard Deviation; CBT = Cognitive Behavioral Therapy; IPT = Integrated Physiotherapy Techniques; SOS = Sum Of Squares. [#] = Non-Significant

Table 4.5.23 depicts the Mean and standard deviation of neck tender point on algometer at baseline to first month (0.53 ± 0.38; 0.41 ± 0.37; 0.41 ± 0.30 with F = 1.17 and the p = 0.31), first to second month (0.39 ± 0.27; 0.36 ± 0.38; 0.39 ± 0.31 with F = 0.06 and the p = 0.94), second to third month (0.50 ± 0.29; 0.42 ± 0.34; 0.42 ± 0.31 with F = 0.66 and the p = 0.51), baseline to third month (1.42 ± 0.72; 1.19 ± 0.85; 1.22 ± 0.63 with F = 0.83, p = 0.43), for Group 1, Group 2 and Group 3 respectively at the level of significance with p value ≤ 0.05. This Figure showing that the experimental groups have no role in reducing the pain of fibromyalgia patient's neck painful area.

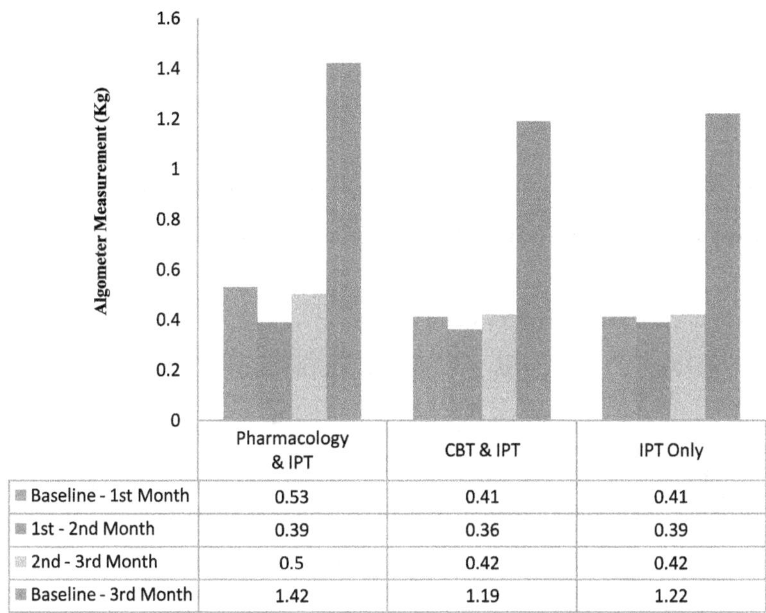

	Pharmacology & IPT	CBT & IPT	IPT Only
Baseline - 1st Month	0.53	0.41	0.41
1st - 2nd Month	0.39	0.36	0.39
2nd - 3rd Month	0.5	0.42	0.42
Baseline - 3rd Month	1.42	1.19	1.22

Figure 4.5.23: The Difference in Means (MD) of Neck point on pain pressure algometer from baseline to third month between group 1, 2 and 3

Table 4.5.23.1: Multiple comparison of difference in means (MD) of improvement in Neck point on Pain Pressure Threshold among different interventional group

Time frame Between	Interventional group		MD	Standard Error	P value	95% Confidence Interval	
						Lower Bound	Upper Bound
Baseline –	PHAIPT group	CBTAIPT group	0.12$^{\#}$	0.09	0.19	0.06	0.30
		IPT Group	0.12$^{\#}$	0.09	0.19	0.06	0.30
1st Month	CBTAIPT group	IPT Group	0.00$^{\#}$	0.09	1.00	0.18	0.18
1st Month –	PHAIPT group	CBTAIPT group	0.02$^{\#}$	0.08	0.78	0.14	0.19
		IPT Group	0.00$^{\#}$	0.08	0.97	0.16	0.17
2nd Month	CBTAIPT group	IPT Group	0.03$^{\#}$	0.08	0.75	0.14	0.19
2nd Month –	PHAIPT group	CBTAIPT group	0.08$^{\#}$	0.08	0.31	0.08	0.25
		IPT Group	0.08$^{\#}$	0.08	0.33	0.08	0.24
3rd Month	CBTAIPT group	IPT Group	0.00$^{\#}$	0.08	0.97	0.16	0.17
Baseline –	PHAIPT group	CBTAIPT group	0.23$^{\#}$	0.19	0.24	0.15	0.61
		IPT Group	0.20$^{\#}$	0.19	0.31	0.18	0.58
3rd Month	CBTAIPT group	IPT Group	0.03$^{\#}$	0.19	0.88	0.35	0.41

CBT = Cognitive Behavioral Therapy; IPT = Integrated Physiotherapy Group; MD = Difference in means (MD) $^{\#}$ = Non-Significant

Table 4.5.23.1 summarized the comparisons of differences in mean improvement in neck point using post hoc LSD. The difference in means (MD) between groups showed a non-significant improvement on the pain pressure threshold reading by algometer. This signifies that the role of PHAIPT and CBTAIPTare not effective in increasing the pain pressure threshold level of fibromyalgia patients.

Table 4.5.24: Comparison of difference in means (MD) of Upper Back (UB) variable on algometer between the groups at different time frame from Baseline to Third month

Variable (Time frame)	Groups	Mean ± SD	SOS Between Groups	SOS Within Group	F	P
Upper Back (Baseline – 1ˢᵗ Month)	PHAIPT	0.49 ± 0.39	0.31	10.45	1.31	0.27[#]
	CBTAIPT	0.46 ± 0.37				
	IPT Only	0.35 ± 0.25				
Upper Back (1ˢᵗ – 2ⁿᵈ Month)	PHAIPT	0.37 ± 0.31	0.18	9.50	0.83	0.43[#]
	CBTAIPT	0.43 ± 0.38				
	IPT Only	0.32 ± 0.27				
Upper Back (2ⁿᵈ – 3ʳᵈ Month)	PHAIPT	0.37 ± 0.33	0.09	9.08	0.46	0.62[#]
	CBTAIPT	0.42 ± 0.27				
	IPT Only	0.34 ± 0.35				
Upper Back (Baseline – 3ʳᵈ Month)	PHAIPT	1.2 ± 0.76	1.43	49.71	1.25	0.29[#]
	CBTAIPT	1.3 ± 0.80				
	IPT Only	1.0 ± 0.69				

SD = Standard Deviation; CBT = Cognitive Behavioral Therapy; IPT = Integrated Physiotherapy Techniques; SOS = Sum Of Squares. [#] = Non-Significant

Table 4.5.24 depicts the Mean and standard deviation of upper back on algometer at baseline to first month (0.49 ± 0.39; 0.46 ± 0.37; 0.35 ± 0.25 with F = 1.31 and the p = 0.27), first to second month (0.37 ± 0.31; 0.43 ± 0.38; 0.32 ± 0.27 with F = 0.83 and the p = 0.43), second to third month (0.37 ± 0.33; 0.42 ± 0.27; 0.34 ± 0.35 with F = 0.46 and the p = 0.62), baseline to third month (1.2 ± 0.76; 1.3 ± 0.80; 1.00 ± 0.69 with F = 1.25, p = 0.29), for Group 1, Group 2 and Group 3 respectively at the level of significance with p value ≤ 0.05. This Figure showing that the experimental groups have no role in reducing the pain of fibromyalgia patients on upper back painful area.

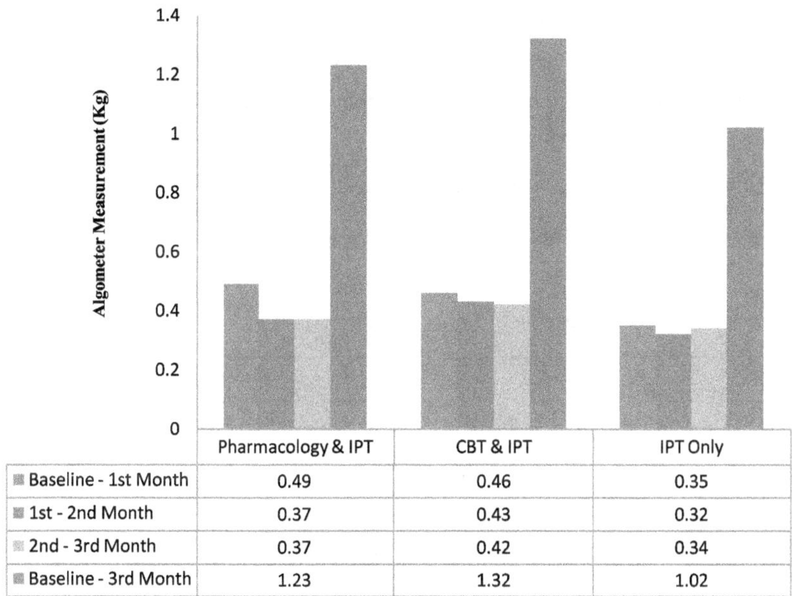

	Pharmacology & IPT	CBT & IPT	IPT Only
Baseline - 1st Month	0.49	0.46	0.35
1st - 2nd Month	0.37	0.43	0.32
2nd - 3rd Month	0.37	0.42	0.34
Baseline - 3rd Month	1.23	1.32	1.02

Figure 4.5.24: The Difference in means (MD) of Upper back point on pain pressure algometer from baseline to third month between group 1, 2 and 3

Table 4.5.24.1: Multiple comparison of difference in means (MD) of improvement in Upper Back point on Pain Pressure Threshold among different interventional group

Time frame Between	Interventional group		MD	Standard Error	P value	95% Confidence Interval	
						Lower Bound	Upper Bound
Baseline –	PHAIPT group	CBTAIPT group	$0.02^{\#}$	0.08	0.76	0.15	0.20
		IPT Group	$0.13^{\#}$	0.08	0.13	0.04	0.31
1st Month	CBTAIPT group	IPT Group	$0.11^{\#}$	0.08	0.22	0.06	0.28
1st Month –	PHAIPT group	CBTAIPT group	$0.06^{\#}$	0.08	0.46	0.10	0.23
		IPT Group	$0.04^{\#}$	0.08	0.58	0.12	0.21
2nd Month	CBTAIPT group	IPT Group	$0.11^{\#}$	0.08	0.20	0.05	0.27
2nd Month –	PHAIPT group	CBTAIPT group	$0.05^{\#}$	0.08	0.55	0.11	0.21
		IPT Group	$0.03^{\#}$	0.08	0.72	0.13	0.19
3rd Month	CBTAIPT group	IPT Group	$0.08^{\#}$	0.08	0.34	0.08	0.24
Baseline –	PHAIPT group	CBTAIPT group	$0.08^{\#}$	0.19	0.65	0.30	0.47
		IPT Group	$0.21^{\#}$	0.19	0.27	0.17	0.60
3rd Month	CBTAIPT group	IPT Group	$0.30^{\#}$	0.19	0.12	0.08	0.68

CBT = Cognitive Behavioral Therapy; IPT = Integrated Physiotherapy Group; MD = Difference in means (MD) $^{\#}$ = Non-Significant

Table 4.5.24.1 summarized the comparisons of differences in mean improvement in upper back point using post hoc LSD. The difference in means (MD) between groups showed a non-significant improvement on the pain pressure threshold reading by algometer. This signifies that the role of PHAIPT and CBTAIPTare not effective in increasing the pain pressure threshold level of fibromyalgia patients.

Table 4.5.25: Comparison of difference in means (MD) of Lower Back (LB) variable on algometer between the groups at different time frame from Baseline to Third month

Variable (Time frame)	Groups	Mean ± SD	SOS Between Groups	SOS Within Group	F	P
Lower Back (Baseline – 1st Month)	PHAIPT	0.45 ± 0.46	0.81	13.49	2.62	0.07[#]
	CBTAIPT	0.46 ± 0.41				
	IPT Only	0.25 ± 0.28				
Lower Back (1st – 2nd Month)	PHAIPT	0.31 ± 0.27	0.12	10.39	0.52	0.59[#]
	CBTAIPT	0.37 ± 0.39				
	IPT Only	0.28 ± 0.35				
Lower Back (2nd – 3rd Month)	PHAIPT	0.25 ± 0.21	0.14	6.29	0.96	0.38[#]
	CBTAIPT	0.34 ± 0.30				
	IPT Only	0.33 ± 0.27				
Lower Back (Baseline – 3rd Month)	PHAIPT	1.02 ± 0.81	1.35	53.70	1.09	0.34[#]
	CBTAIPT	1.17 ± 0.84				
	IPT Only	0.87 ± 0.68				

SD = Standard Deviation; CBT = Cognitive Behavioral Therapy; IPT = Integrated Physiotherapy Techniques; SOS = Sum Of Squares. [#] = Non-Significant

Table 4.5.25 depicts the Mean and standard deviation of Lower back on algometer at baseline to first month (0.45 ± 0.46; 0.46 ± 0.41; 0.25 ± 0.28 with F = 2.62 and the p = 0.07), first to second month (0.31 ± 0.27; 0.37 ± 0.39; 0.28 ± 0.35 with F = 0.52 and the p = 0.59), second to third month (0.25 ± 0.21; 0.34 ± 0.30; 0.33 ± 0.27 with F = 0.96 and the p = 0.38), baseline to third month (1.02 ± 0.81; 1.17 ± 0.84; 0.87 ± 0.68 with F = 1.09, p = 0.34), for Group 1, Group 2 and Group 3 respectively at the level of significance with p value ≤ 0.05. This Figure showing that the experimental groups have no role in reducing the pain of fibromyalgia patients over the lower back painful area.

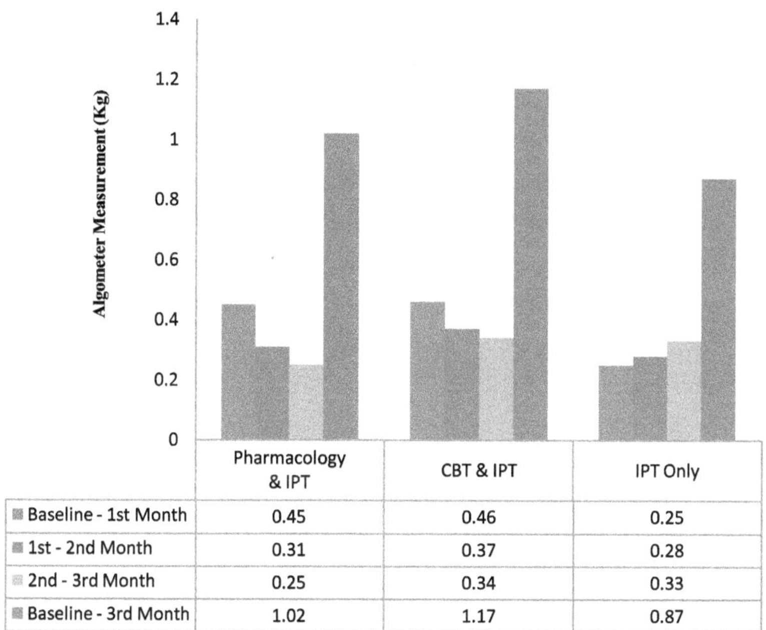

	Pharmacology & IPT	CBT & IPT	IPT Only
Baseline - 1st Month	0.45	0.46	0.25
1st - 2nd Month	0.31	0.37	0.28
2nd - 3rd Month	0.25	0.34	0.33
Baseline - 3rd Month	1.02	1.17	0.87

Figure 4.5.25: The Difference in Means (MD) of Lower back point on pain pressure algometer from baseline to third month between group 1, 2 and 3

Table 4.5.25.1: Multiple comparison of difference in means (MD) of improvement in Lower Back point on Pain Pressure Threshold among different interventional group

Time frame Between	Interventional group		MD	Standard Error	P value	95% Confidence Interval	
						Lower Bound	Upper Bound
Baseline – 1st Month	PHAIPT group	CBTAIPT group	0.00	0.10	0.97	0.19	0.20
		IPT Group	0.20	0.10	0.05	0.00	0.40
	CBTAIPT group	IPT Group	0.20*	0.10	0.04	0.00	0.40
1st Month – 2nd Month	PHAIPT group	CBTAIPT group	0.06	0.08	0.50	0.11	0.23
		IPT Group	0.03	0.08	0.73	0.14	0.20
	CBTAIPT group	IPT Group	0.09	0.08	0.31	0.08	0.26
2nd Month – 3rd Month	PHAIPT group	CBTAIPT group	0.08	0.06	0.21	0.05	0.22
		IPT Group	0.08	0.06	0.25	0.05	0.21
	CBTAIPT group	IPT Group	0.00	0.06	0.92	0.14	0.13
Baseline – 3rd Month	PHAIPT group	CBTAIPT group	0.15	0.20	0.46	0.25	0.55
		IPT Group	0.15	0.20	0.46	0.25	0.55
	CBTAIPT group	IPT Group	0.30	0.20	0.14	0.10	0.70

CBT = Cognitive Behavioral Therapy; IPT = Integrated Physiotherapy Group; MD = Difference in means (MD); * = Significant

Table 4.5.25.1 summarized the comparisons of differences in mean improvement in lower back painful point using post hoc LSD. The result specifies that level of improvement was greater in experimental group II at baseline to first month (p ≤ 0.05) as compared to experimental group III. However; it does not show the statistically significant difference (p > 0.05) in experimental group I and II from the other time frames as compared to experimental group III. This signifies that the role of cognitive behavioral therapy along with integrated physiotherapy techniques in decreasing the pain pressure threshold level of fibromyalgia patients.

Fibromyalgia (FM) is a chronic musculoskeletal disorder characterized by widespread pain and depressed mood (Wolf, 1997). About 40.7% of population indicates a high prevalence of FM in India (Jilumudi *et al.*, 2018) as well as the prevalence estimates varied from 3.4% to 7.1% in western countries (Wolfe *et al.*, 1995). The exact incidence of the disorder is yet to get worked out in India, thus the epidemiological studies in developing countries are scarce. The symptoms of FM syndrome are assorted and unbearable.

The commonest symptom in FM is chronic widespread pain. FM patients repeatedly experience a number of other symptoms include local tenderness, hardness, mood disturbances (e.g. Depression and/or anxiety), and cognitive difficulties (e.g. Trouble concentrating, forgetfulness and disorganized thinking). Tension type headache/ migraine, interstitial cystitis or painful bladder syndrome, chronic prostitis or prostodynia, temporomandibular disorder, chronic pelvic pain and vulvodynia (Williams & Clauw, 2009; Ablin & Clauw, 2009). In general, it is difficult to diagnose the FM condition due to the multi-dimensional aspects of the symptoms. Most of the symptoms are similar to other conditions, such as ankylosing spondylitis, rheumatoid arthritis and systemic lupus erythematosis. None of the diagnostic tests are sensitive to the symptoms to establish a correct diagnosis of FM syndrome.

In 1990, the American college of Rheumatology formed the criteria for the diagnosis of FM syndrome; however they fail to emphasis in extra pain symptoms. Thus in 2010 and 2016, guidelines are revised for diagnosis that replacing the tender point's exam with two separate tests that characterize the overall symptomatic experience (Wolfe *et al.*, 2016) such as i) generalized pain, defined as pain in at least 4 of 5 regions; ii) symptoms have been present at a similar level for at least 3 months; iii) Widespread Pain Index (WPI) ≥ 7 and symptom severity scale (SSS) score ≥ 5 or WPI of 4-6 and SSS score ≥ 9; iv) a diagnosis of FM is valid irrespective of other diagnoses. A diagnosis of FM does not include the presence of other clinically important illnesses. In the present study, the author's utilized 2010 criteria for the diagnosis, if a patient doesn't meet the criteria other treatment has been assigned.

The treatment approaches towards the management of FM has been divided into Pharmacological and non-pharmacological therapies. Arnold *et al.* (2012) reported that the US food and drug administration (FDA) recommended three drugs (Pregabalin, Duloxetine and Milnacipran) and the non-pharmacological therapies for the management of FM includes Exercises, Hydrotherapy, Myofascial release, Guided imagery, Craniosacral therapy, Cognitive behavioral therapy, acupuncture, reiki, whole body vibration, electrotherapy, music therapy thoracic mobilization, tai chi, osteopathic manipulation, hydrokinesiotherapy, complimentary therapy (phytothermotherapy and spa therapy) and Qigong therapy. All the treatment procedures have their individual effects on FM. These individual effects either reduce the widespread pain or the psychosocial aspects of the FM patients. The present study could not locate any study in the literature about the multidisciplinary approach in management of FM.

Therefore the present study has investigated the role of three kinds of interventions (i) Pharmacotherapy along with Integrated Physiotherapy Techniques (PHAIPT) (ii) Cognitive Behavioral Therapy along with Integrated Physiotherapy Techniques (CBTAIPT) (iii) and Integrated Physiotherapy Techniques (IPT) alone. The IPT consist of administration of hot packs, ultrasound, myofascial release, deep transverse friction followed by an exercise regime.

The demographic characteristics of the study population were described the Age, Gender, Education level, Occupation and Marital status of the population (Table 4.1.1). The study population consisted of total 90 participants with male 22.2% (n = 20) and female 77.8% (n = 70). Most participants were females with an undergraduate degree (Table 4.1.1). To strengthen the current study, some of the previous studies accepted that females are more predominant to FM condition, which affects only about 10% of male patients (Wolfe *et al.*, 1997; Yunus, 2002). Recently in 2018, Arout and his colleagues explained that patients with FM were over three times more likely to be female (25.5%) compared to 7.7% among those with other pain diagnoses.

Almost half of the participants are unemployed in the present study. In line with this, the Australian population also showed that the rate of full-time workers decreased from 54% at the time of diagnosis to 16% at the time of the survey (Palstam & Mannerkorpi., 2017). Also, Fibromyalgia had a substantial negative impact on social and occupational function (Arnold *et al.*, 2008). However, they also compared the health status between working and nonworking women with FM. They found that

254

symptom ratings of pain and fatigue were less severe in working than in nonworking women with FM (Liedberg & Björk, 2013; Reisine, 2003). They demonstrated that women without an occupation affect the income; the household income reduced in patients affected with FM.

Marital status in FM was studied from the demographic perspective in terms of explaining the most affected category of the population. The data denotes that most of the married women with the occupation are affected by this condition (80%). To support the current study, Jilumudi and Ram (2018) also accepted that married women account for a significant group of affection. The married females with occupation have multitasking activities at home and the working place; due to work stress and lack of rest, the females are more prone to develop FM symptoms. The previous researches also explained that patients with FM have the disrupted relationships with family and friends, social isolation, reduced activities of daily living and leisure activities, avoidance of physical activity, and loss of career or inability to advance in careers or education (Arnold *et al.*, 2008). Other predictors of fibromyalgia included being divorced or separated, being obese or a current smoker, and not having a college education (Walit *et al.*, 2015).

To the best of the author's knowledge, this is the first prospective study to report the combination of PHAIPT and CBTAIPT for 12 weeks. For the clear understanding the results of the present study has been discussed under the following headings.

5.1   Role of PHAIPT, CBTAIPT and IPT on the quality of life in FM.

5.2   Role of PHAIPT, CBTAIPT and IPT on depression in FM

5.3   Role of PHAIPT, CBTAIPT and IPT on health status in FM.

5.4   Role of PHAIPT, CBTAIPT and IPT on anxiety in FM.

5.5   Role of PHAIPT, CBTAIPT and IPT on physical and mental health in FM.

5.6   Role of PHAIPT, CBTAIPT and IPT on the pain pressure sensitivity on painful sites in FM.

5.7   Effectiveness of experimental groups and its reasoning.

5.1   Role of PHAIPT, CBTAIPT and IPT on the quality of life in FM

The FIQR comprised of 21 individual questions. All questions were described on an 11 point numeric rating scale of 0-10, with ten being worst. FIQR was divided into three domains: function (9 Questions), the overall impact on functioning and symptom severity (2 Questions), and symptoms (10 Questions). The authors showed significant improvement in the FIQR scores, which is improved by 30.18 and 35.97 in CBTAIPT & IPT alone, respectively, whereas it was increased by 21.65 in PHAIPT. The Quality of life did not improved much in the participants receiving PHAIPT where it was enhanced in both the experimental group II & III with a higher level of improvement in patients receiving CBT and IPT (p = 0.00) and IPT alone (p = 0.00) as compared to the patients receiving Pharmacotherapy and IPT. Previous findings by Bernardy *et al.* (2013) also explained that it is due to adverse events, also dropouts were higher in drugs than in CBTs trials.

The possible explanation for the present findings could be a result of the combined effects of CBT and IPT. The IPT comprised of Moist heat pack, MFR, DTF, Ultrasound and exercises; the CBT may avoid patients those having negative thoughts (Thorn *et al.*, 2007), the Myofascial release discharge fascial restrictions (Le Bauer *et al.* .2008), and the DTF facilitate the proliferation of fibroblasts, increases angiogenesis in ischemic tissues and promotes tissue repair (Doley *et al.*, 2013). So, the combined effects of psychotherapy and the combination of Physical therapy treatment procedures improved the overall function and symptom severity in fibromyalgia patients.

5.2 Role of PHAIPT, CBTAIPT and IPT on depression in FM

The depression level in FM had a higher prevalence of both anxiety and depression (Singh & Kaul., 2018). Due to depression, FM patients repeatedly explain poor sleep or sleep disorders. Sleeplessness is an independent risk factor for increasing the chronic pain after acute injury, and the expansion of suffering from a regional disease to an additional widespread condition. All the patients of chronic pain demonstrated that sleep continuity disruption in healthy participants impairs psychophysical measures of endogenous pain inhibitory capacity. Previous studies accepted that if sleep continuity were improved, patients would experience less pain. Functionally this seems plausible as demonstrated by several sleep deprivation studies of healthy participants reporting that sleep deficiency is hyperalgesic (Smith *et al.*, 2008).

The depression was reduced by 13.7 ± 10.3; 19.2 ± 9.78; 7.83 ± 7.53 in experimental groups I, II, & III, respectively, in the present study. However, the CBTAIPT group score on depression has improved more (from 6.77 ± 5.32 to 19.2 ± 9.78) when compared with Pharmacotherapy along with IPT. One of the retrospective results correlated with sleeplessness induces anxiety and depression. Sleep precedes pain in fibromyalgia and in the long term, which leads to depression. So improving sleep quality would decrease pain, depression, and improve function (Affleck *et al.*, 1996). Though, a similar study found no differences among CBT, pharmacological and treatments as usual because patients with FM already diagnosed with depression are under antidepressants in treating depression Alda *et al.* (2011). Thus, the therapy that neglects Pharmacotherapy had shown genuine improvement to improve the depression.

5.3 Role of PHAIPT, CBTAIPT and IPT on health status in FM

Pain is the precursor of the tender point in FM patients. The baseline to first-month value of the visual analog scale was 2.66 ± 1.27; 3.27 ± 1.20; 2.40 ± 1.71 whereas the mean difference between the baseline to the third month was 4.80 ± 1.65; 6.37 ± 1.16; 5.77 ± 2.21 in experimental group 1, 2 and 3 respectively suggesting that there was reduction in pain in all the interventional groups reduced the scores of pain. There was more betterment of symptoms in terms of pain in group 2 and 3 than group1. Thus, it supports the previous report that in FM, the CBT reduced pain for a longer duration over 12 months of follow-ups (Thieme *et al.*, 2006). Also, MFR improved pain over 6-month post-intervention over the placebo (Castro-Sanchez., 2011a). The combination of various techniques in IPT probably in MFR, the slow stretching with proper concentration, relaxation, and breathing will inhibit the gamma spindle response that causes the muscle to shorten when rapidly stretched (Mauntel *et al.*, 2014). Ultrasound combined with massage and exercise (Gam *et al.*, 1998) affects placebo in Myofascial pain syndrome treatment. Thus the present study has demonstrated that the combination of CBT and IPT reduced the overall pain and its related tender point sensitivity in FM. Although Fernandes de-las Penas' (2005) results did not demonstrate any rigorous evidence of manual therapies such as active head retraction exercises. Hence, further research on the synergism of CBT and IPT is needed before concluding that CBT and IPT could help in reducing the pain in FM condition.

5.4 Role of PHAIPT, CBTAIPT and IPT on anxiety in FM

The patho-physiology of FM includes some of the predisposing factors like depression, anxiety, posttraumatic stress and somatization. The three-month intervention of FM patients showed a constant decrement score on the GAD scale from baseline to the third month in all interventional groups. The value from baseline to the first month was 1.90 ± 3.09; 3.10 ± 1.95; 2.37 ± 3.33 whereas at baseline to third month was 5.17 ± 3.82; 6.17 ± 3.52; 5.77 ± 6.06 in experimental group 1, 2 and 3 respectively suggesting that patients with FM in all the experimental groups had an improvement on the reduction of anxiety level. The results of present study are supported by the previous study in which patients showed positive effects that the psychiatric co-morbid engaged by mindfulness meditation might improve pain through a cortical-thalamocortical gating mechanism (Adler Neil and Fadel Zeiden, 2017). Indeed, the previous study of anxiety in FM has similar effects on the entire interventional group (Alda *et al.*, 2011). The psychiatric illness in FM may be due to the presence of an increased number of painful areas, and most of the patients have the augmented rates of post-traumatic stress disorder. Some of the studies proven that the hypothalamic-pituitary-adrenal axis in patients with FM is disturbed, including confirmation of elevated cortisol secretion in reaction to stress (Abeles *et al.*, 2007). The authors found a combination of depression and anxiety symptoms in patients with FM. There is a small number of studies concentrated only on anxiety; studies on the anxiety outcome alone in fibromyalgia yet to be conducted.

5.5 Role of PHAIPT, CBTAIPT and IPT on physical and mental health in FM

The health status profiles of male and female FM patients showed that males had poorer health status than females (Neumann, 2000). The physical component value of SF-36 survey from baseline to the first month was 10.81 ± 17.51; 19.04 ± 15.25; 9.25 ± 7.83 whereas at baseline to the third month was 30.53 ± 22.47; 44.67 ± 18.12; 29.88 ± 18.98 in experimental group 1, 2, and 3 respectively suggesting that patients with FM in the experimental group 2 (CBT + IPT) showed a higher improvement on the Physical health of FM patients. The present study was supported by the previous research, the physical exercise and CBT improved their physical health in FM (Pichierri, 2011). About twenty-five percent of the patients who received CBT were able to achieve clinically meaningful levels of long term improvement in physical functioning (Williams *et al.*, 2002). Another study also supported the present study that the combination of CBT and physical exercise demonstrated to be superior to controls in improving the quality of life (Redondo *et al.*, 2004). The hands-on technique like MFR and DTF stimulates the mechanoreceptors and thus increases the level of serotonin in the brain, which leads to decreased release of substance P in the spinal cord, and thus reducing essential pain signaling. The reduced pain signals automatically improve the physical functions of any patients affected with chronic pain.

The Mental component value of SF-36 survey from baseline to the first month was 10.72 ± 16.39; 14.79 ± 12.37; 4.98 ± 11.73 whereas at baseline to the third month was 26.90 ± 17.81; 38.13 ± 19.27; 22.10 ± 16.25 in experimental group 1, 2, and 3 respectively suggesting that patients with FM in the experimental group 2 (CBT + IPT) showed a higher improvement on the mental health of FM patients. Thus, it increased the self-efficacy and sense of control of one's behavior. The synergism of CBT, along with IPT, provided a positive response to the FM patients. The CBT program increased pain acceptance, motor competence, decreased depression complaints, and it promotes the acquisition of diverse skills needed to manage pain (Alda *et al.*, 2011). On the contrary, to our results, the FM groups had mental health summary scores that fell 1 SD below the general population mean, and physical health summary scores that fell 2 SD below the general population mean (Hoffman, 2008).

5.6 Role of PHAIPT, CBTAIPT and IPT on trigger point pain sensitivity in FM

The pressure algometer is a tool to evaluate and document the smallest pressure over the skin on the specific tender point. Some of the previous research already demonstrated the effectiveness of algometer and has found it as a reliable and valid measure of Myofascial Pain Syndrome sensitivity (Fernandez de las Penas, 2005; Reeves *et al.*, 1986). The tender point sensitivity in FM individual showed statistical significance in seven points [Shoulder Girdle Left (SGL), Shoulder Girdle Right (SGR), Upper Arm Left (UAL), Upper Arm Right (UAR), Lower Leg Right (LLR), JAW Right (JAWR), and Lower Back (LB)] only and non-significant results on the other tender area.

The improvement has varied according to the area and the period of treatment. The CBTAIPT and PHAIPT compared with IPT alone shown similar effects from baseline to the third month. The improvements are more or less equal. The Mean Difference (MD) of SGL (Baseline – 3rd Month, $p = 0.02$), SGR (Baseline – 1st Month, $p = 0.05$; Baseline – 3rd Month, $p = 0.03$), UAR (2nd – 3rd Month, $p = 0.01$; Baseline – 3rd Month, $p = 0.04$) and JAWR (Baseline – 1st Month, $p = 0.05$) tender points showed significance at different time frames in the experimental group I (Pharmacotherapy along with IPT). The Mean Difference (MD) of other tender areas like UAL (2nd – 3rd Month, $p = 0.00$; Baseline – 3rd Month, $p = 0.04$), UAR (baseline -1st month, $p = 02$; 2nd

– 3rd Month, p = 0.02; Baseline – 3rd Month, p = 0.02), LLR (from 2nd – 3rd month, p = 0.01), and LB (from baseline -1st month, p = 0.04) showed significant results at different time frames in the experimental group II (CBT along with IPT) compared with IPT alone group. Additionally, the CBT, along with the IPT group, improved the scores of LLR between the time frame 2nd to 3rd month (p = 0.02) when compared with Pharmacotherapy along with the IPT group. Castro- Sanchez (2011b) supported the results of present study by proving that the painful points at the left rib and left gluteal muscle only showed significant improvements in FM Patients. The previous research reported that sleep disturbance was one of the strong reasons which related to tender point counts, poor sleep might give rise to tender points rather than the different explanation that pain interrupts sleep (Croft *et al.*, 1994).

Additionally, MFR therapies also help to restore regular muscular resting electrical activity. Any pressure release therapy decreases spontaneous electrical activity immediately surrounding Myofascial trigger points, as well as improves basal electrical motion. Increased levels of spontaneous electrical activity and basal electrical movement have caused reducltion in decreased ROM, as they cause the muscle to be locally overactive while at rest and result in pain that may cause individuals to compensate by voluntarily reducing ROM (Mauntel *et al.*, 2014). Another reason for the improvements of only seven areas of tender points is due to a common area of affection, and concentrations of treatment over these areas are uncomplicated.

5.7   Effectiveness of experimental groups and its reasoning

Overall the present study has demonstrated a significant improvement in all outcome measures with the three months administration of Pharmacotherapy along with IPT, cognitive behavioral therapy along with IPT and IPT only. The outcome measures continuously improved in the CBTAIPT and IPT only group from baseline to the third month on Quality of life, pain, physical and mental health, and trigger point sensitivity whereas depression and anxiety scores from baseline to the third month has no improvement in all the groups. These results are consistent with many of the previous studies reported.

For monitoring the efficacy of CBT on individual with insomnia symptoms, Jungquist *et al.* (2010) conducted a study on 28 patients with chronic non-malignant pain in the spinal region. They found that nearly 78% of subjects were treatment responders and they improved their sleep by decreased excessive daytime sleepiness.

A six month RCT found the CBT had higher efficacy than the Recommended Pharmacological Treatment (RPT) and Treatment As Usual (TAU) (Alda *et al.*, 2011). Further, they have shown the FIQ (Cohens d = 0.44 and 0.53) for improving global function and EuroQol VAS for the quality of life (Cohens d = 0.11 and 0.40). The improvements were constant until six months of the post-treatment period.

The individual with FM comparatively experiences different pain than healthy individuals; physiologically all the FM patients have lower pain thresholds than those of healthy individuals. Ang and Colleagues (2010) evaluated the effects of CBT on the Nociceptive Flexion Reflex (NFR) using descending inhibition of nociception. The NFR is an objective measure that documented a lower pain threshold in fibromyalgia patients. They found that CBT causes an increase in the NFR threshold, indicating diminished responsibility to noxious stimulation at weeks 6 and 12 of telephone administered CBT.

Group based stress management CBT was conducted by Karlsson and Colleagues (2015) on forty-eight females with fibromyalgia syndrome (FMS). They found significant improvement in interference from pain, affective distress, support from spouses or significant others, distracting responses and depression between baseline and after treatment of 1-year follow-up. Also, Abeles *et al.*, 2007 explained that the hypothalamic-pituitary-adrenal axis is disturbed and to blame for stress in patients with fibromyalgia, including evidence of elevated cortisol levels deficient diurnal fluctuation and blunted cortisol secretion in response to stress and corticotropin-releasing hormone stimulation testing. The vital exhaustion, stress behavior, and pain severity were rated higher after the CBT intervention.

Thieme and Colleagues (2006) evaluated the effects of Operant Behavioral Therapy (OBT) and CBT on 125 patients of FMS patients. They described a significant reduction in pain intensity, cognitive, and affective variables in the CBT group. The possible explanation is that positive cognitions were successively improved, and patients educated to enhance their handling strategies to decrease awful thinking with the outcome of affective distress. However, the OBT group demonstrated improvements in healthy behavior and reduction in pain behavior at both six and 12-month follow-ups.

Doley *et al.* (2013) conducted a study in which they used PRT and DTFM for gluteus medius trigger point. The pressure pain threshold was the outcome measure for the trigger point sensitivity, and they highlighted the deep, transverse friction was the better choice of treatment to decrease pain and to increase the pressure pain sensitivity on gluteal area trigger points.

A systematic review conducted by Mauntel and Padua (2014), they explained that the MFR therapies are effective in increasing range of motion. Increased levels of spontaneous electrical activity cause the muscle to be locally overactive at rest and result in pain and reducing the range of motion (ROM). The study indicated that any pressure release therapy have been utilized to decrease spontaneous electrical activity immediately surrounding the myofascial trigger points, as well as improves basal electrical activity.

None of the previous studies have demonstrated the combined effects of treatment on both the physical and psychological improvements of the fibromyalgia patients. The present study was possibly the first experimental study to evaluate the role of integrated physiotherapy techniques along with pharmacotherapy and cognitive-behavioral therapy on patients with fibromyalgia. In comparison, the CBTAIPT and IPT alone demonstrated more considerable improvement in the pain, pain pressure threshold, quality of life and physical and mental health than the integrated physiotherapy techniques along with the pharmacotherapy group. Hence the hypothesis H_2 and H_3 have been accepted. The possible explanation for the present findings could be that the combined effects of CBT and IPT modify maladaptive thinking and behavioral responses to pain, and typically either avoid patient's negative emotional experiences or attempts to reduce negative emotions as directly as possible. (Hsu *et al.*, 2010), release fascial restrictions (Le Bauer *et al.*, 2008), facilitate the proliferation of fibroblasts (Mauntel *et al.*, 2014), increases angiogenesis in ischemic tissues, and promotes tissue repair (Doley *et al.*, 2013).

Thus, the results of the present study may help the clinicians to find a new way of combined use of integrated physiotherapy techniques along with cognitive behavioral therapy or IPT alone, to promote the patients with fibromyalgia in the future.

Fibromyalgia (FM) is recognized as a common chronic musculoskeletal pain disorder along with reduced pain thresholds to palpation, fatigue, sleep alterations and a negative effect on the quality of life. Additionally, FM patient often experience a number of other symptoms include tenderness, stiffness, Depression, anxiety, cognitive difficulties, tension type headache/migraine, interstitial cystitis or painful bladder syndrome, chronic prostitis or prostodynia, temporomandibular disorder, chronic pelvic pain, and vulvodynia have been shown to be associated with FM. The 2010 ACR preliminary classification criteria diagnoses fibromyalgia as the sum of the widespread pain index (WPI) and total symptom severity (SS) being more than a certain score, continuing symptoms for more than 3 months, and all three criteria without disease related to symptoms being satisfied. These criteria do not include a tender point test, and the patients are required to indicate the location and severity of pain as well as the extra-pain symptoms. Several researchers demonstrated the individual effects of their therapeutic techniques, till now there is no single treatment to cure FM patients at present. Each patient has a different constellation of symptoms resulting in different responses to therapeutic interventions. A specific intervention will not work for every patient; though there is no agreement but suggestions exist for the multidisciplinary approach in clinical practice for the management of fibromyalgia. therefore, keeping this in mind, the present study entitled **"Effectiveness of Integrated Physiotherapy Techniques with Pharmacotherapy and Cognitive Behavioral Therapy - A Multimodal Treatment Approach In Fibromyalgia"** was conducted to examine the efficacy of all the interventions on the pain, quality of life, depression, anxiety, physical and mental health and pain pressure threshold in patients of Fibromyalgia.

Total ninety patients with FM were included in the study. They were randomly divided into three groups with thirty subjects in each group i.e. Pharmacotherapy along with integrated physiotherapy techniques, cognitive behavioral therapy along with integrated physiotherapy techniques, and integrated physiotherapy techniques alone. In experimental group 1 the subjects received 150 mg of Pregabalin drugs continuously for three months along with integrated physiotherapy techniques treatment, the experimental group 2 subjects received third group (integrated physiotherapy techniques alone) the subjects received ten weekly 90-minute cognitive Behavioral therapy session, and the experimental group 3 received IPT only. All the experimental groups received IPT for 1hour 30 minutes which has been structured as administration of hot packs, ultrasound, deep transverse friction, Myofascial release and home program exercise regime. All the factors evaluated pre-intervention and post-intervention (baseline, 1st month, 2nd month, and 3rd month) on the outcome of pain (VAS), quality of life (FIQR), depression (BDI), anxiety (GAD-7), physical and mental health (SF-36 health survey) and pain pressure threshold (pressure algometer) in patients of Fibromyalgia. Finally data sheet was formulated and statistical analysis was done by using IBM SPSS v25 software. A p value of 0.05 was considered as level of significance. The following conclusions have been drawn on the basis of the results of our present interventional study.

1. Females of the present study were more predominant than their male counterparts in fibromyalgia.

2. In our study, we found that most of the affected patients with fibromyalgia were educated, employed, and married females.

3. Pharmacotherapy along with integrated physiotherapy techniques revealed improvement in depression scores only.

4. Cognitive behavioral therapy along with integrated physiotherapy techniques was effective in pain, Quality of life, physical and mental health and trigger point sensitivity.

5. Similarly, the integrated physiotherapy techniques alone group revealed improvement in pain, Quality of life, physical and mental health and trigger point sensitivity.

6. Integrated physiotherapy techniques along with Pharmacotherapy and cognitive behavioral therapy, all the three interventional groups shown no improvement in anxiety scores.

   In the present study, the researcher concluded that Cognitive Behavioral Therapy along with Integrated Physiotherapy Techniques group proved better results in Fibromyalgia and suuggesting that this should be included in the clinical practice.

Abeles, A.M., Pillinger, M.H., Solitar, B.M. and Abeles, M., 2007. Narrative review: the patho-physiology of fibromyalgia. *Annals of internal medicine, 146*(10), pp.726-734.

Ablin, K. and Clauw, D.J., 2009. From fibrositis to functional somatic syndromes to a bell shaped curve of pain and sensory sensitivity: evolution of a clinical construct. *Rheumatic Disease Clinics, 35*(2), pp.233-251.

Acet, G., Kaya, A., Akturk, S. and Akgol, G., 2017. A comparison of the effectiveness of amitriptilin and pregabalin treatment in fibromyalgia patients. *Northern clinics of Istanbul, 4*(2), p.151.

Adler-Neal, A.L. and Zeidan, F., 2017. Mindfulness meditation for fibromyalgia: mechanistic and clinical considerations. *Current rheumatology reports, 19*(9), p.59.

Affleck G, Urrows S, Tennen H, Higgins P, Abeles M. Sequential daily relations of sleep, pain intensity, and attention to pain among women with fibromyalgia. Pain. 1996;68:363–368. [PubMed: 9121825]

Ahmed, S. and Lawrence, A., 2018. Anxiety and depression in fibromyalgia: Are we putting the cart before the horse?. *Indian Journal of Rheumatology, 13*(3), p.150.

Alda, M., Luciano, J.V., Andrés, E., Serrano-Blanco, A., Rodero, B., del Hoyo, Y.L., Roca, M., Moreno, S., Magallón, R. and García-Campayo, J., 2011. Effectiveness of cognitive behaviour therapy for the treatment of catastrophisation in patients with fibromyalgia: a randomised controlled trial. *Arthritis research & therapy, 13*(5), p.R173.

Alvarez-Buylla, A., Kohwi, M., Nguyen, T.M. and Merkle, F.T., 2008, January. The heterogeneity of adult neural stem cells and the emerging complexity of their niche. In *Cold Spring Harbor symposia on quantitative biology* (Vol. 73, pp. 357-365). Cold Spring Harbor Laboratory Press.

Anderson, R.J., McCrae, C.S., Staud, R., Berry, R.B. and Robinson, M.E., 2012. Predictors of clinical pain in fibromyalgia: examining the role of sleep. *The Journal of Pain, 13*(4), pp.350-358.

Ang, D.C., Chakr, R., Mazzuca, S., France, C.R., Steiner, J. and Stump, T., 2011. Cognitive–behavioral therapy attenuates nociceptive responding in patients with fibromyalgia: a pilot study. *Arthritis care & research, 62*(5), pp.618-623.

Arnold, L.M., Clauw, D.J., Dunegan, L.J. and Turk, D.C., 2012, May. A framework for fibromyalgia management for primary care providers. In *Mayo Clinic Proceedings* (Vol. 87, No. 5, pp. 488-496). Elsevier.

Arnold, L.M., Clauw, D.J., Wohlreich, M.M., Wang, F., Ahl, J., Gaynor, P.J. and Chappell, A.S., 2009. Efficacy of duloxetine in patients with fibromyalgia: pooled analysis of 4 placebo-controlled clinical trials. *Primary care companion to the Journal of clinical psychiatry, 11*(5), p.237.

Arnold, L.M., Crofford, L.J., Mease, P.J., Burgess, S.M., Palmer, S.C., Abetz, L. and Martin, S.A., 2008. Patient perspectives on the impact of fibromyalgia. *Patient education and counseling, 73*(1), pp.114-120.

Arnold, L.M., Gebke, K.B. and Choy, E.H.S., 2016. Fibromyalgia: management strategies for primary care providers. *International journal of clinical practice, 70*(2), pp.99-112.

Arnold, L.M., Hudson, J.I., Keck Jr, P.E., Auchenbach, M.B., Javaras, K.N. and Hess, E.V., 2006. Comorbidity of fibromyalgia and psychiatric disorders. *The Journal of clinical psychiatry.*

Arnold, L.M., Palmer, R.H., Hufford, M.R. and Chen, W., 2012. Effect of milnacipran on body weight in patients with fibromyalgia. *International journal of general medicine, 5*, p.879.

Arnold, L.M., Schikler, K.N., Bateman, L., Khan, T., Pauer, L., Bhadra-Brown, P., Clair, A., Chew, M.L. and Scavone, J., 2016. Safety and efficacy of pregabalin in adolescents with fibromyalgia: a randomized, double-blind, placebo-controlled trial and a 6-month open-label extension study. *Pediatric Rheumatology, 14*(1), p.46.

Arnold, L.M., Wang, F., Ahl, J., Gaynor, P.J. and Wohlreich, M.M., 2011. Improvement in multiple dimensions of fatigue in patients with fibromyalgia treated with duloxetine: secondary analysis of a randomized, placebo-controlled trial. *Arthritis research & therapy, 13*(3), p.R86.

Arout, C.A., Sofuoglu, M., Bastian, L.A. and Rosenheck, R.A., 2018. Gender differences in the prevalence of fibromyalgia and in concomitant medical and psychiatric disorders: a national veterans health Administration Study. *Journal of Women's Health*, *27*(8), pp.1035-1044.

Ayr, S.M. and Etkinliyi, S.U.T., 2010. Effectiveness of ultrasound therapy in cervical myofascial pain syndrome: a double blind, placebo-controlled study. *Turk J Rheumatol*, *25*, pp.110-5.

Babu, A.S., Mathew, E., Danda, D. and Prankash, H., 2007. Management of patients with fibromyalgia using biofeedback: a randomized control trial. *Indian journal of medical sciences*, *61*(8).

Baraniuk, J.N., Whalen, G., Cunningham, J. and Clauw, D.J., 2004. Cerebrospinal fluid levels of opioid peptides in fibromyalgia and chronic low back pain. *BMC musculoskeletal disorders*, *5*(1), p.48.

Bardal, E.M., Roeleveld, K., Johansen, T.O. and Mork, P.J., 2012. Upper limb position control in fibromyalgia. *BMC musculoskeletal disorders*, *13*(1), p.186.

Barnes, J.F., 1996. Myofascial release for craniomandibular pain and dysfunction. *The International journal of orofacial myology: official publication of the International Association of Orofacial Myology*, *22*, p.20.

Baumgartner, E., Finckh, A., Cedraschi, C. and Vischer, T., 2002. A six year prospective study of a cohort of patients with fibromyalgia. *Annals of the rheumatic diseases*, *61*(7), p.644.

Bazzichi, L., Dini, M., Rossi, A., Corbianco, S., De Feo, F., Giacomelli, C., Zirafa, C., Ferrari, C., Rossi, B. and Bombardieri, S., 2009. Muscle modifications in fibromyalgic patients revealed by surface electromyography (SEMG) analysis. *BMC Musculoskeletal disorders*, *10*(1), p.36.

Behm, F.G., Gavin, I.M., Karpenko, O., Lindgren, V., Gaitonde, S., Gashkoff, P.A. and Gillis, B.S., 2012. Unique immunologic patterns in fibromyalgia. *BMC clinical pathology*, *12*(1), p.25.

Beissner, K., Henderson Jr, C.R., Papaleontiou, M., Olkhovskaya, Y., Wigglesworth, J. and Reid, M.C., 2009. Physical therapists' use of cognitive-behavioral therapy for older adults with chronic pain: a nationwide survey. *Physical therapy*, *89*(5), pp.456-469.

Bennett, R., 2005. Fibromyalgia: present to future. *Current rheumatology reports*, 7(5), pp.371-376.

Bennett, R., 2005a. The Fibromyalgia Impact Questionnaire (FIQ): a review of its development, current version, operating characteristics and uses. *Clinical and experimental rheumatology*, 23(5), p.S154.

Bennett, R.M., Bushmakin, A.G., Capelleri, J.C., Zlateva, G., and Sadosky, A.B., 2009. Minimal clinically importance difference in the fibromyalgia impact questionnairre. Journal og Rheumatology. 36(6), p. 1304-1311.

Bennett, R.M., Friend, R., Jones, K.D., Ward, R., Han, B.K. and Ross, R.L., 2009. The revised fibromyalgia impact questionnaire (FIQR): validation and psychometric properties. *Arthritis research & therapy*, 11(4), p.R120.

Bernardy, K., Füber, N., Klose, P. and Häuser, W., 2011. Efficacy of hypnosis/guided imagery in fibromyalgia syndrome-a systematic review and meta-analysis of controlled trials. *BMC musculoskeletal disorders*, 12(1), p.133.

Bernardy, K., Klose, P., Busch, A.J., Choy, E.H. and Häuser, W., 2013. Cognitive behavioural therapies for fibromyalgia. *Cochrane Database of Systematic Reviews*, (9).

Bhusal, S., Diomampo, S. and Magrey, M.N., 2016. Clinical utility, safety, and efficacy of pregabalin in the treatment of fibromyalgia. *Drug, healthcare and patient safety*, 8, p.13.

Bigatti, S.M., Hernandez, A.M., Cronan, T.A. and Rand, K.L., 2008. Sleep disturbances in fibromyalgia syndrome: relationship to pain and depression. *Arthritis Care & Research: Official Journal of the American College of Rheumatology*, 59(7), pp.961-967.

Bijur, P.E., Silver, W. and Gallagher, E.J., 2001. Reliability of the visual analog scale for measurement of acute pain. *Academic emergency medicine*, 8(12), pp.1153-1157.

Bjersing, J.L., Dehlin, M., Erlandsson, M., Bokarewa, M.I. and Mannerkorpi, K., 2012. Changes in pain and insulin-like growth factor 1 in fibromyalgia during exercise: the involvement of cerebrospinal inflammatory factors and neuropeptides. *Arthritis research & therapy*, 14(4), p.R162.

Bjersing, J.L., Larsson, A., Palstam, A., Ernberg, M., Bileviciute-Ljungar, I., Löfgren, M., Gerdle, B., Kosek, E. and Mannerkorpi, K., 2017. Benefits of resistance exercise in lean women with fibromyalgia: involvement of IGF-1 and leptin. *BMC musculoskeletal disorders*, *18*(1), p.106.

Boehm, K., Ostermann, T., Milazzo, S. and Büssing, A., 2012. Effects of yoga interventions on fatigue: a meta-analysis. *Evidence-Based Complementary and Alternative Medicine*, *2012*.

Bonilla, J., Bernal, G., Santos, A. and Santos, D., 2004. A revised Spanish version of the Beck Depression Inventory: Psychometric properties with a Puerto Rican sample of college students. *Journal of clinical psychology*, *60*(1), pp.119-130.

Boomershine, C.S., 2010. Pregabalin for the management of fibromyalgia syndrome. *Journal of pain research*, *3*, p.81.

Boomershine, C.S., 2012. A comprehensive evaluation of standardized assessment tools in the diagnosis of fibromyalgia and in the assessment of fibromyalgia severity. *Pain Research and Treatment*, *2012*.

Boonen, A., van den Heuvel, R., van Tubergen, A., Goossens, M., Severens, J.L., van der Heijde, D. and van der Linden, S., 2005. Large differences in cost of illness and wellbeing between patients with fibromyalgia, chronic low back pain, or ankylosing spondylitis. *Annals of the rheumatic diseases*, *64*(3), pp.396-402.

Boyling, J.D. and Palastanga, N. eds., 1994. Grieve's modern manual therapy, the vertebral column.

Bradley, L.A., 2009. Patho-physiology of fibromyalgia. *The American journal of medicine*, *122*(12), pp.S22-S30.

Branco, J.C., Bannwarth, B., Failde, I., Carbonell, J.A., Blotman, F., Spaeth, M., Saraiva, F., Nacci, F., Thomas, E., Caubère, J.P. and Le Lay, K., 2010, June. Prevalence of fibromyalgia: a survey in five European countries. In *Seminars in arthritis and rheumatism* (Vol. 39, No. 6, pp. 448-453). WB Saunders.

Busch, A.J., Webber, S.C., Brachaniec, M., Bidonde, J., Dal Bello-Haas, V., Danyliw, A.D., Overend, T.J., Richards, R.S., Sawant, A. and Schachter, C.L., 2011. Exercise therapy for fibromyalgia. *Current pain and headache reports*, *15*(5), p.358.

Buskila, D. and Sarzi-Puttini, P., 2006. Biology and therapy of fibromyalgia. Genetic aspects of fibromyalgia syndrome. *Arthritis research & therapy*, *8*(5), p.218.

Calandre, E.P., Morillas-Arques, P., Molina-Barea, R., Rodriguez-Lopez, C.M. and Rico-Villademoros, F., 2011. Trazodone plus pregabalin combination in the treatment of fibromyalgia: a two-phase, 24-week, open-label uncontrolled study. *BMC musculoskeletal disorders*, *12*(1), p.95.

Campbell, S.M., Clark, S., Tindall, E.A., Forehand, M.E. and Bennett, R.M., 1983. Clinical characteristics of fibrositis. *Arthritis & Rheumatism: Official Journal of the American College of Rheumatology*, *26*(7), pp.817-824.

Carvalho, L.S.C., Correa, H., Silva, G.C., Campos, F.S., Baião, F.R., Ribeiro, L.S., Faria, A.M. and D'Avila Reis, D., 2008. May genetic factors in fibromyalgia help to identify patients with differentially altered frequencies of immune cells?. *Clinical & Experimental Immunology*, *154*(3), pp.346-352.

Castro-Sanchez, A.M., Mataran-Penarrocha, G.A., Arroyo-Morales, M., Saavedra-Hernández, M., Fernández-Sola, C. and Moreno-Lorenzo, C., 2011. Effects of myofascial release techniques on pain, physical function, and postural stability in patients with fibromyalgia: a randomized controlled trial. *Clinical Rehabilitation*, *25*(9), pp.800-813.

Castro-Sanchez, A.M., Mataran-Penarrocha, G.A., Granero-Molina, J., Aguilera-Manrique, G., Quesada-Rubio, J.M. and Moreno-Lorenzo, C., 2011. Benefits of massage-myofascial release therapy on pain, anxiety, quality of sleep, depression, and quality of life in patients with fibromyalgia. *Evidence-Based Complementary and Alternative Medicine, 2011*.

Cedraschi, C., Desmeules, J., Rapiti, E., Baumgartner, E., Cohen, P., Finckh, A., Allaz, A.F. and Vischer, T.L., 2004. Fibromyalgia: a randomised, controlled trial of a treatment programme based on self management. *Annals of the rheumatic diseases*, *63*(3), pp.290-296.

Ceko, M., Bushnell, M.C. and Gracely, R.H., 2012. Neurobiology underlying fibromyalgia symptoms. *Pain research and treatment, 2012*.

Chervin, R.D., Teodorescu, M., Kushwaha, R., Deline, A.M., Brucksch, C.B., Ribbens-Grimm, C., Ruzicka, D.L., Stein, P.K., Clauw, D.J. and Crofford, L.J., 2009. Objective measures of disordered sleep in fibromyalgia. *The Journal of rheumatology*, *36*(9).

Cho, K.I., Lee, J.H., Lee, H.G., Kim, S.M. and Kim, T.I., 2010. Assessment of myocardial function in patients with fibromyalgia and the relationship to chronic emotional and physical stress. *Korean circulation journal*, *40*(2), pp.74-80.

Choi, C.J., Knutsen, R., Oda, K., Fraser, G.E. and Knutsen, S.F., 2010. The association between incident self-reported fibromyalgia and nonpsychiatric factors: 25-years follow-up of the Adventist Health Study. *The Journal of Pain*, *11*(10), pp.994-1003.

Clauw, D., 2003. Fibromyalgia: correcting the misconceptions: not a" phantom illness" but a real condition that can have devastating effects. *The Journal of Musculoskeletal Medicine*, *20*(10), pp.467-473.

Cordero, M.D., Alcocer-Gómez, E., Cano-García, F.J., De Miguel, M., Carrión, A.M., Navas, P. and Alcázar, J.A.S., 2011. Clinical symptoms in fibromyalgia are better associated to lipid peroxidation levels in blood mononuclear cells rather than in plasma. *PLoS One*, *6*(10), p.e26915.

Croft, P., Burt, J., Schollum, J., Thomas, E., Macfarlane, G. and Silman, A., 1996. More pain, more tender points: is fibromyalgia just one end of a continuous spectrum?. *Annals of the rheumatic diseases*, *55*(7), pp.482-485.

Croft, P., Schollum, J. and Silman, A., 1994. Population study of tender point counts and pain as evidence of fibromyalgia. *Bmj*, *309*(6956), pp.696-699.

Cuatrecasas, G., Riudavets, C., Güell, M.A. and Nadal, A., 2007. Growth hormone as concomitant treatment in severe fibromyalgia associated with low IGF-1 serum levels. A pilot study. *BMC Musculoskeletal Disorders*, *8*(1), p.119.

Curtis, K., Osadchuk, A. and Katz, J., 2011. An eight-week yoga intervention is associated with improvements in pain, psychological functioning and mindfulness, and changes in cortisol levels in women with fibromyalgia. *Journal of pain research*, *4*, p.189.

Cymet, T.C., 2003. A practical approach to fibromyalgia. *Journal of the National Medical Association*, *95*(4), p.278.

De Carvalho, P.D.T.C., Leal-Junior, E.C.P., Alves, A.C.A., de Melo Rambo, C.S., Sampaio, L.M.M., Oliveira, C.S., Albertini, R. and de Oliveira, L.V.F., 2012.

Effect of low-level laser therapy on pain, quality of life and sleep in patients with fibromyalgia: study protocol for a double-blinded randomized controlled trial. *Trials*, *13*(1), p.221.

De Tommaso, M., Federici, A., Serpino, C., Vecchio, E., Franco, G., Sardaro, M., Delussi, M. and Livrea, P., 2011. Clinical features of headache patients with fibromyalgia comorbidity. *The journal of headache and pain*, *12*(6), p.629.

Deluze, C., Bosia, L., Zirbs, A., Chantraine, A. and Vischer, T.L., 1992. Electroacupuncture in fibromyalgia: results of a controlled trial. *Bmj*, *305*(6864), pp.1249-1252.

Dogru, A., Balkarli, A., Cobankara, V., Tunc, S.E. and Sahin, M., 2017. Effects of vitamin D therapy on quality of life in patients with fibromyalgia. *The Eurasian journal of medicine*, *49*(2), p.113.

Doley, M., Warikoo, D. and Arunmozhi, R., 2013. Effect of positional release therapy and deep transverse friction massage on gluteus medius trigger point-a Comparative Study. *Journal of Exercise Science and Physiotherapy*, *9*(1), p.40.

Donaldson, M.S., Speight, N. and Loomis, S., 2001. Fibromyalgia syndrome improved using a mostly raw vegetarian diet: an observational study. *BMC complementary and alternative medicine*, *1*(1), p.7.

Eccleston, C. and Crombez, G., 1999. Pain demands attention: A cognitive–affective model of the interruptive function of pain. *Psychological bulletin*, *125*(3), p.356.

Eccleston, C., de C Williams, A.C. and Morley, S., 2009. Psychological therapies for the management of chronic pain (excluding headache) in adults. *Cochrane database of systematic reviews*, (2).

Ellingson, L.D., Shields, M.R., Stegner, A.J. and Cook, D.B., 2012. Physical activity, sustained sedentary behavior, and pain modulation in women with fibromyalgia. *The Journal of Pain*, *13*(2), pp.195-206.

Ericsson, A., Bremell, T. and Mannerkorpi, K., 2013. Usefulness of multiple dimensions of fatigue in fibromyalgia. *Journal of rehabilitation medicine*, *45*(7), pp.685-693.

Farasyn, A., 2010. Release of myofascial pain with deep cross-friction named "roptrotherapy". *International Journal of Therapeutic Massage & Bodywork: Research, Education, & Practice*, *3*(1), pp.36-37.

Feng, J., Zhang, Z., Wu, X., Mao, A., Chang, F., Deng, X., Gao, H., Ouyang, C., Dery, K.J., Le, K. and Longmate, J., 2013. Discovery of potential new gene variants and inflammatory cytokine associations with fibromyalgia syndrome by whole exome sequencing. *PLoS One*, *8*(6), p.e65033.

Fernandez-de-las-Peñas, C., Alonso-Blanco, C., Cuadrado, M.L. and Pareja, J.A., 2006. Myofascial trigger points in the suboccipital muscles in episodic tension-type headache. *Manual therapy*, *11*(3), pp.225-230.

Finan, P.H., Zautra, A.J., Davis, M.C., Lemery-Chalfant, K., Covault, J. and Tennen, H., 2010. Genetic influences on the dynamics of pain and affect in fibromyalgia. *Health Psychology*, *29*(2), p.134.

Fischer, A.A., 1987. Pressure algometry over normal muscles. Standard values, validity and reproducibility of pressure threshold. *Pain*, *30*(1), pp.115-126.

Fontaine, K.R., Conn, L. and Clauw, D.J., 2010. Effects of lifestyle physical activity on perceived symptoms and physical function in adults with fibromyalgia: results of a randomized trial. *Arthritis research & therapy*, *12*(2), p.R55.

Fors, E.A. and Sexton, H., 2002. Weather and the pain in fibromyalgia: are they related?. *Annals of the rheumatic diseases*, *61*(3), pp.247-250.

Fraioli, A., Grassi, M., Mennuni, G., Geraci, A., Petraccia, L., Fontana, M., Conte, S. and Serio, A., 2013. Clinical researches on the efficacy of spa therapy in fibromyalgia: a systematic review. *Annali dell'Istituto superiore di sanita*, *49*, pp.219-229.

Friedberg, F., Williams, D.A. and Collinge, W., 2012. Lifestyle-oriented non-pharmacological treatments for fibromyalgia: a clinical overview and applications with home-based technologies. *Journal of pain research*, *5*, p.425.

Gallagher, A.M., Thomas, J.M., Hamilton, W.T. and White, P.D., 2004. Incidence of fatigue symptoms and diagnoses presenting in UK primary care from 1990 to 2001. *Journal of the Royal Society of Medicine*, *97*(12), pp.571-575.

Gam, A.N., Warming, S., Larsen, L.H., Jensen, B., Høydalsmo, O., Allon, I., Andersen, B., Gøtzsche, N.E., Petersen, M. and Mathiesen, B., 1998. Treatment of myofascial trigger-points with ultrasound combined with massage and exercise– a randomised controlled trial. *Pain, 77*(1), pp.73-79.

Ge, H.Y., Wang, Y., Fernandez-de-Las-Penas, C., Graven-Nielsen, T., Danneskiold-Samsøe, B. and Arendt-Nielsen, L., 2011. Reproduction of overall spontaneous pain pattern by manual stimulation of active myofascial trigger points in fibromyalgia patients. *Arthritis research & therapy, 13*(2), p.R48.

Gedalia, A., Press, J., Klein, M. and Buskila, D., 1993. Joint hypermobility and fibromyalgia in schoolchildren. *Annals of the Rheumatic Diseases, 52*(7), pp.494-496.

Geisser, M.E., Glass, J.M., Rajcevska, L.D., Clauw, D.J., Williams, D.A., Kileny, P.R. and Gracely, R.H., 2008. A psychophysical study of auditory and pressure sensitivity in patients with fibromyalgia and healthy controls. *The Journal of Pain, 9*(5), pp.417-422.

Glass, J.M., Williams, D.A., Fernandez-Sanchez, M.L., Kairys, A., Barjola, P., Heitzeg, M.M., Clauw, D.J. and Schmidt-Wilcke, T., 2011. Executive function in chronic pain patients and healthy controls: different cortical activation during response inhibition in fibromyalgia. *The journal of pain, 12*(12), pp.1219-1229.

Gormsen, L., Rosenberg, R., Bach, F.W. and Jensen, T.S., 2010. Depression, anxiety, health-related quality of life and pain in patients with chronic fibromyalgia and neuropathic pain. *European Journal of Pain, 14*(2), pp.127-e1.

Gracely, R.H., Ceko, M. and Bushnell, M.C., 2012. Fibromyalgia and depression. *Pain research and treatment, 2012.*

Greenman, P.E. and Greenman, P.E., 1996. *Principles of manual medicine* (Vol. 572). Baltimore, MD: Williams & Wilkins.

Grondahl, J.R. and Rosvold, E.O., 2008. Hypnosis as a treatment of chronic widespread pain in general practice: a randomized controlled pilot trial. *BMC musculoskeletal disorders, 9*(1), p.124.

Guedj, D. and Weinberger, A., 1990. Effect of weather conditions on rheumatic patients. *Annals of the rheumatic diseases, 49*(3), pp.158-159.

Gupta, A. and Silman, A.J., 2004. Psychological stress and fibromyalgia: a review of the evidence suggesting a neuroendocrine link. *Arthritis Res Ther*, *6*(3), p.98.

Gur, A., Cevik, R., Sarac, A.J., Colpan, L. and Em, S., 2004. Hypothalamic-pituitary-gonadal axis and cortisol in young women with primary fibromyalgia: the potential roles of depression, fatigue, and sleep disturbance in the occurrence of hypocortisolism. *Annals of the rheumatic diseases*, *63*(11), pp.1504-1506.

Gusi, N. and Tomas-Carus, P., 2008. Cost-utility of an 8-month aquatic training for women with fibromyalgia: a randomized controlled trial. *Arthritis research & therapy*, *10*(1), p.R24.

Hadhazy, V.A., Ezzo, J.E.A.N.E.T.T.E., Creamer, P.A.U.L. and Berman, B.M., 2000. Mind-body therapies for the treatment of fibromyalgia. A systematic review. *The Journal of rheumatology*, *27*(12), pp.2911-2918.

Hagen, K.B., Dagfinrud, H., Moe, R.H., Osterås, N., Kjeken, I., Grotle, M. and Smedslund, G., 2012. Exercise therapy for bone and muscle health: an overview of systematic reviews. *BMC medicine*, *10*(1), p.167.

Hakkinen, A., Hakkinen, K., Hannonen, P. and Alen, M., 2001. Strength training induced adaptations in neuromuscular function of premenopausal women with fibromyalgia: comparison with healthy women. *Annals of the rheumatic diseases*, *60*(1), pp.21-26.

Harris, R.E., 2010. Elevated excitatory neurotransmitter levels in the fibromyalgia brain. *Arthritis Research and Therapy*, 12(4), R134.

Harris, R.E., Sundgren, P.C., Craig, A.D., Kirshenbaum, E., Sen, A., Napadow, V. and Clauw, D.J., 2009. Elevated insular glutamate in fibromyalgia is associated with experimental pain. *Arthritis & Rheumatism: Official Journal of the American College of Rheumatology*, *60*(10), pp.3146-3152.

Henriques, S.G., Fráguas, R., Iosifescu, D.V., Menezes, P.R., Lucia, M.C.S.D., Gattaz, W.F. and Martins, M.A., 2009. Recognition of depressive symptoms by physicians. *Clinics*, *64*(7), pp.629-635.

Hernandez, M.E., Becerril, E., Perez, M., Leff, P., Anton, B., Estrada, S., Estrada, I., Sarasa, M., Serrano, E. and Pavon, L., 2010. Proinflammatory cytokine levels in fibromyalgia patients are independent of body mass index. *BMC research notes*, *3*(1), p.156.

Hoffman, D.L. and Dukes, E.M., 2008. The health status burden of people with fibromyalgia: a review of studies that assessed health status with the SF-36 or the SF-12. *International journal of clinical practice*, *62*(1), pp.115-126.

Hong, C. Z., Chen, Y.C., Pon, C.H., and Yu, J., (1993). 'Immediate effects of various physical medicine modalities on pain threshold of an active myofascial trigger point'. J Musculoskelet Pain, (2), pp.37-53.

Hsiao, M.C., 2007. Effective Treatment of Fibromyalgia Comorbid With Premenstrual Dysphoric Disorder With a Low Dose of Venlafaxine. *Primary care companion to the Journal of clinical psychiatry*, *9*(5), p.398.

Hsu, M.C., Schubiner, H., Lumley, M.A., Stracks, J.S., Clauw, D.J. and Williams, D.A., 2010. Sustained pain reduction through affective self-awareness in fibromyalgia: a randomized controlled trial. *Journal of General Internal Medicine*, *25*(10), pp.1064-1070.

Humphrey, L., Arbuckle, R., Mease, P., Williams, D.A., Samsoe, B.D. and Gilbert, C., 2010. Fatigue in fibromyalgia: a conceptual model informed by patient interviews. *BMC musculoskeletal disorders*, *11*(1), p.216.

Itoh, K. and Kitakoji, H., 2010. Effects of acupuncture to treat fibromyalgia: a preliminary randomised controlled trial. *Chinese Medicine*, *5*(1), p.11.

Jilumudi, A.K. and Ram, G.G., 2018. Is fibromyalgia the most common diagnosis amongst female out-patients?. *International Journal of Research in Orthopaedics*, *4*(1), p.1.

Jones, K.D., Burckhardt, C.S., Deodhar, A.A., Perrin, N.A., Hanson, G.C. and Bennett, R.M., 2008. A six-month randomized controlled trial of exercise and pyridostigmine in the treatment of fibromyalgia. *Arthritis & Rheumatism: Official Journal of the American College of Rheumatology*, *58*(2), pp.612-622.

Jungquist, C.R., O'Brien, C., Matteson-Rusby, S., Smith, M.T., Pigeon, W.R., Xia, Y., Lu, N. and Perlis, M.L., 2010. The efficacy of cognitive-behavioral therapy for insomnia in patients with chronic pain. *Sleep medicine*, *11*(3), pp.302-309.

Karlsson, B., Burell, G., Anderberg, U.M. and Svärdsudd, K., 2015. Cognitive behaviour therapy in women with fibromyalgia: A randomized clinical trial. *Scandinavian journal of pain*, *9*(1), pp.11-21.

Kashikar-Zuck, S., Flowers, S.R., Verkamp, E., Ting, T.V., Lynch-Jordan, A.M., Graham, T.B., Passo, M., Schikler, K.N., Hashkes, P.J., Spalding, S. and Banez, G., 2010. Actigraphy-based physical activity monitoring in adolescents with juvenile primary fibromyalgia syndrome. *The Journal of Pain*, *11*(9), pp.885-893.

Kashikar-Zuck, S., Johnston, M., Ting, T.V., Graham, B.T., Lynch-Jordan, A.M., Verkamp, E., Passo, M., Schikler, K.N., Hashkes, P.J., Spalding, S. and Banez, G., 2010. Relationship between school absenteeism and depressive symptoms among adolescents with juvenile fibromyalgia. *Journal of pediatric psychology*, *35*(9), pp.996-1004.

Kashikar-Zuck, S., Myer, G. and Ting, T.V., 2012. Can behavioral treatments be enhanced by integrative neuromuscular training in the treatment of juvenile fibromyalgia?. *Pain management*, *2*(1), pp.9-12.

Kashikar-Zuck, S., Parkins, I.S., Ting, T.V., Verkamp, E., Lynch-Jordan, A., Passo, M. and Graham, T.B., 2010. Controlled follow-up study of physical and psychosocial functioning of adolescents with juvenile primary fibromyalgia syndrome. *Rheumatology*, *49*(11), pp.2204-2209.

Kashikar-Zuck, S., Ting, T.V., Arnold, L.M., Bean, J., Powers, S.W., Graham, T.B., Passo, M.H., Schikler, K.N., Hashkes, P.J., Spalding, S. and Lynch-Jordan, A.M., 2012. Cognitive behavioral therapy for the treatment of juvenile fibromyalgia: A multisite, single-blind, randomized, controlled clinical trial. *Arthritis & Rheumatism*, *64*(1), pp.297-305.

Kassam, A. and Patten, S.B., 2006. Major depression, fibromyalgia and labour force participation: a population-based cross-sectional study. *BMC Musculoskeletal Disorders*, *7*(1), p.4.

Keefe, F.J., Rumble, M.E., Scipio, C.D., Giordano, L.A. and Perri, L.M., 2004. Psychological aspects of persistent pain: current state of the science. *The journal of pain*, *5*(4), pp.195-211.

Kelley, G.A., Kelley, K.S. and Jones, D.L., 2011. Efficacy and effectiveness of exercise on tender points in adults with fibromyalgia: a meta-analysis of randomized controlled trials. *Arthritis, 2011*. 125485.

Kelley, G.A., Kelley, K.S., Hootman, J.M. and Jones, D.L., 2010. Exercise and global well-being in community-dwelling adults with fibromyalgia: a systematic review with meta-analysis. *BMC Public Health, 10*(1), p.198.

Keskindag, B. and Karaaziz, M., 2017. The association between pain and sleep in fibromyalgia. *Saudi medical journal, 38*(5), p.465.

Kessler, R.C., Chiu, W.T., Demler, O. and Walters, E.E., 2005. Prevalence, severity, and comorbidity of 12-month DSM-IV disorders in the National Comorbidity Survey Replication. *Archives of general psychiatry, 62*(6), pp.617-627.

Kim, S.M., Lee, S.H. and Kim, H.R., 2012. Applying the ACR preliminary diagnostic criteria in the diagnosis and assessment of fibromyalgia. *The Korean journal of pain, 25*(3), p.173.

Kim, Y.S., 2011. Why should gastroenterologists know about fibromyalgia? Common pathogenesis and clinical implications. *Journal of neurogastroenterology and motility, 17*(1), p.1.

Kim, Y.S., Kim, K.M., Lee, D.J., Kim, B.T., Park, S.B., Cho, D.Y., Suh, C.H., Kim, H.A., Park, R.W. and Joo, N.S., 2011. Women with fibromyalgia have lower levels of calcium, magnesium, iron and manganese in hair mineral analysis. *Journal of Korean medical science, 26*(10), pp.1253-1257.

Kivimaki, M., Leino-Arjas, P., Kaila-Kangas, L., Virtanen, M., Elovainio, M., Puttonen, S., Keltikangas-Järvinen, L., Pentti, J. and Vahtera, J., 2007. Increased absence due to sickness among employees with fibromyalgia. *Annals of the rheumatic diseases, 66*(1), pp.65-69.

Knight, T., Schaefer, C., Chandran, A., Zlateva, G., Winkelmann, A. and Perrot, S., 2013. Health-resource use and costs associated with fibromyalgia in France, Germany, and the United States. *ClinicoEconomics and outcomes research: CEOR, 5*, p.171.

Kroese, M., Schulpen, G., Bessems, M., Nijhuis, F., Severens, J. and Landewé, R., 2009. The feasibility and efficacy of a multidisciplinary intervention with aftercare meetings for fibromyalgia. *Clinical rheumatology*, *28*(8), pp.923-929.

Lange, G., Janal, M.N., Maniker, A., FitzGibbons, J., Fobler, M., Cook, D. and Natelson, B.H., 2011. Safety and efficacy of vagus nerve stimulation in fibromyalgia: a phase I/II proof of concept trial. *Pain Medicine*, *12*(9), pp.1406-1413.

Lasa, L., Ayuso-Mateos, J.L., Vazquez-Barquero, J.L., Diez-Manrique, F.J. and Dowrick, C.F., 2000. The use of the Beck Depression Inventory to screen for depression in the general population: a preliminary analysis. *Journal of affective disorders*, *57*(1-3), pp.261-265.

Lawrence, R.C., Felson, D.T., Helmick, C.G., Arnold, L.M., Choi, H., Deyo, R.A., Gabriel, S., Hirsch, R., Hochberg, M.C., Hunder, G.G. and Jordan, J.M., 2008. Estimates of the prevalence of arthritis and other rheumatic conditions in the United States: Part II. *Arthritis & Rheumatism*, *58*(1), pp.26-35.

LeBauer, A., Brtalik, R. and Stowe, K., 2008. The effect of myofascial release (MFR) on an adult with idiopathic scoliosis. *Journal of bodywork and movement therapies*, *12*(4), pp.356-363.

Lee, K.H., Kim, C.H., Shin, H.C. and Sung, E.J., 2011. Clinical characteristics of patients with medically unexplained chronic widespread pain: A primary care center study. *Korean journal of family medicine*, *32*(5), p.277.

Lerma, C., Martinez, A., Ruiz, N., Vargas, A., Infante, O. and Martinez-Lavin, M., 2011. Nocturnal heart rate variability parameters as potential fibromyalgia biomarker: correlation with symptoms severity. *Arthritis research & therapy*, *13*(6), p.R185.

Liedberg, G.M., Björk, M. and Börsbo, B., 2015. Self-reported nonrestorative sleep in fibromyalgia–relationship to impairments of body functions, personal function factors, and quality of life. *Journal of pain research*, *8*, p.499.

Lind, B.K., Lafferty, W.E., Tyree, P.T. and Diehr, P.K., 2010. Comparison of health care expenditures among insured users and nonusers of complementary and alternative medicine in Washington State: a cost minimization analysis. *The Journal of Alternative and Complementary Medicine*, *16*(4), pp.411-417.

Lindell, L., Bergman, S., Petersson, I.F., Jacobsson, L.T. and Herrström, P., 2000. Prevalence of fibromyalgia and chronic widespread pain. *Scandinavian journal of primary health care*, *18*(3), pp.149-153.

Linder, J., Ekholm, K.S., Jansen, G.B., Lundh, G. and Ekholm, J., 2009. Long-term sick leavers with difficulty in resuming work: comparisons between psychiatric–somatic comorbidity and monodiagnosis. *International Journal of Rehabilitation Research*, *32*(1), pp.20-35.

Lofgren, M. and Norrbrink, C., 2009. Pain relief in women with fibromyalgia: a cross-over study of superficial warmth stimulation and transcutaneous electrical nerve stimulation. *Journal of rehabilitation medicine*, *41*(7), pp.557-562.

Lukban, J., 2001. The effect of manual physical therapy in patients diagnosed with interstitial cystitis, high-tone pelvic floor dysfunction, and sacroiliac dysfunction. *Urology*, *57*(1), pp.121-122.

Lynch, M., Sawynok, J., Hiew, C. and Marcon, D., 2012. A randomized controlled trial of qigong for fibromyalgia. *Arthritis research & therapy*, *14*(4), p.R178.

Magrey, M.N., Antonelli, M., James, N. and Khan, M.A., 2013. High frequency of fibromyalgia in patients with psoriatic arthritis: a pilot study. *Arthritis*, *2013*.

Makrani, A.H., Afshari, M., Ghajar, M., Forooghi, Z. and Moosazadeh, M., 2017. Vitamin D and fibromyalgia: a meta-analysis. *The Korean journal of pain*, *30*(4), p.250.

Malin, K. and Littlejohn, G.O., 2012. Neuroticism in young women with fibromyalgia links to key clinical features. *Pain research and treatment*, *2012*.

Malin, K. and Littlejohn, G.O., 2012. Personality and fibromyalgia syndrome. *The Open Rheumatology Journal*, *6*, p.273.

Malin, K. and Littlejohn, G.O., 2012. Psychological control is a key modulator of fibromyalgia symptoms and comorbidities. *Journal of pain research*, *5*, p.463.

Malt, E.A., Olafsson, S., Lund, A. and Ursin, H., 2002. Factors explaining variance in perceived pain in women with fibromyalgia. *BMC Musculoskeletal Disorders*, *3*(1), p.12.

Mannerkorpi, K., Landin-Wilhelmsen, K., Larsson, A., Cider, Å., Arodell, O. and Bjersing, J.L., 2017. Acute effects of physical exercise on the serum insulin-like growth factor system in women with fibromyalgia. *BMC musculoskeletal disorders*, *18*(1), p.37.

Mannerkorpi, K., Nordeman, L., Cider, Å. and Jonsson, G., 2010. Does moderate-to-high intensity Nordic walking improve functional capacity and pain in fibromyalgia? A prospective randomized controlled trial. *Arthritis research & therapy*, *12*(5), p.R189.

Martinez-Lavin, M., Vidal, M., Barbosa, R.E., Pineda, C., Casanova, J.M. and Nava, A., 2002. Norepinephrine-evoked pain in fibromyalgia. A randomized pilot study ISCRTN70707830. *BMC Musculoskeletal Disorders*, *3*(1), p.2.

Mataran-Penarrocha, G.A., Castro-Sanchez, A.M., Garcia, G.C., Moreno-Lorenzo, C., Carreno, T.P. and Zafra, M.D.O., 2011. Influence of craniosacral therapy on anxiety, depression and quality of life in patients with fibromyalgia. *Evidence-Based Complementary and Alternative Medicine*, *2011*.

Mauntel, T.C., Clark, M.A. and Padua, D.A., 2014. Effectiveness of myofascial release therapies on physical performance measurements: A systematic review. *Athletic Training and Sports Health Care*, *6*(4), pp.189-196.

McHorney, C.A., Ware, J.E. and Raczek, A.E., 1993. The MOS 36-Item Short-Form Health Survey (SF-36): II. Psychometric and clinical tests of validity in measuring physical and mental health constructs. *MEDICAL CARE-PHILADELPHIA-*, *31*, pp.247-247.

McLoughlin, M.J., Stegner, A.J. and Cook, D.B., 2011. The relationship between physical activity and brain responses to pain in fibromyalgia. *The journal of pain*, *12*(6), pp.640-651.

Mease, P.J., Farmer, M.V., Palmer, R.H., Gendreau, R.M., Trugman, J.M. and Wang, Y., 2013. Milnacipran combined with pregabalin in fibromyalgia: a randomized, open-label study evaluating the safety and efficacy of adding milnacipran in patients with incomplete response to pregabalin. *Therapeutic advances in musculoskeletal disease*, *5*(3), pp.113-126.

Menzies, V. and Lyon, D.E., 2010. Integrated review of the association of cytokines with fibromyalgia and fibromyalgia core symptoms. *Biological research for nursing*, *11*(4), pp.387-394.

Menzies, V., Taylor, A.G. and Bourguignon, C., 2006. Effects of guided imagery on outcomes of pain, functional status, and self-efficacy in persons diagnosed with fibromyalgia. *Journal of alternative & complementary medicine*, *12*(1), pp.23-30.

Mist, S.D., Firestone, K.A. and Jones, K.D., 2013. Complementary and alternative exercise for fibromyalgia: a meta-analysis. *Journal of pain research*, *6*, p.247.

Morf, S., Amann-Vesti, B., Forster, A., Franzeck, U.K., Koppensteiner, R., Uebelhart, D. and Sprott, H., 2004. Microcirculation abnormalities in patients with fibromyalgia–measured by capillary microscopy and laser fluxmetry. *Arthritis Res Ther*, *7*(2), p.R209.

Morley, S., Eccleston, C. and Williams, A., 1999. Systematic review and meta-analysis of randomized controlled trials of cognitive behaviour therapy and behaviour therapy for chronic pain in adults, excluding headache. *Pain*, *80*(1-2), pp.1-13.

Napadow, V., LaCount, L., Park, K., As-Sanie, S., Clauw, D.J. and Harris, R.E., 2010. Intrinsic brain connectivity in fibromyalgia is associated with chronic pain intensity. *Arthritis & Rheumatism*, *62*(8), pp.2545-2555.

Neumann, L., Berzak, A. and Buskila, D., 2000, June. Measuring health status in Israeli patients with fibromyalgiasyndrome and widespread pain and healthy individuals: Utility of the Short Form 36-item health survey (SF-36). In *Seminars in arthritis and rheumatism* (Vol. 29, No. 6, pp. 400-408). WB Saunders.

Nicholl, B.I., Macfarlane, G.J., Davies, K.A., Morriss, R., Dickens, C. and McBeth, J., 2009. Premorbid psychosocial factors are associated with poor health-related quality of life in subjects with new onset of chronic widespread pain–results from the EPIFUND study. *PAIN®*, *141*(1-2), pp.119-126.

Nishiyori, M., Uchida, H., Nagai, J., Araki, K., Mukae, T., Kishioka, S. and Ueda, H., 2011. Permanent relief from intermittent cold stress-induced fibromyalgia-like abnormal pain by repeated intrathecal administration of antidepressants. *Molecular pain*, *7*(1), p.69.

Noller, V. and Sprott, H., 2003. Prospective epidemiological observations on the course of the disease in fibromyalgia patients. *Journal of negative results in biomedicine*, *2*(1), p.4.

Norregaard, J., Bülow, P.M. and Danneskiold-Samsøe, B., 1994. Muscle strength, voluntary activation, twitch properties, and endurance in patients with fibromyalgia. *Journal of Neurology, Neurosurgery & Psychiatry*, *57*(9), pp.1106-1111.

Ohta, H., Oka, H., Usui, C., Ohkura, M., Suzuki, M. and Nishioka, K., 2012. A randomized, double-blind, multicenter, placebo-controlled phase III trial to evaluate the efficacy and safety of pregabalin in Japanese patients with fibromyalgia. *Arthritis research & therapy*, *14*(5), p.R217.

Okifuji, A., Bradshaw, D.H. and Olson, C., 2009. Evaluating obesity in fibromyalgia: neuroendocrine biomarkers, symptoms, and functions. *Clinical rheumatology*, *28*(4), pp.475-478.

Okifuji, A., Bradshaw, D.H., Donaldson, G.W. and Turk, D.C., 2011. Sequential analyses of daily symptoms in women with fibromyalgia syndrome. *The Journal of Pain*, *12*(1), pp.84-93.

Okifuji, A., Donaldson, G.W., Barck, L. and Fine, P.G., 2010. Relationship between fibromyalgia and obesity in pain, function, mood, and sleep. *The Journal of Pain*, *11*(12), pp.1329-1337.

Palstam, A. and Mannerkorpi, K., 2017. Work ability in fibromyalgia: an update in the 21st Century. *Current rheumatology reviews*, *13*(3), pp.180-187.

Palstam, A., Bjersing, J.L. and Mannerkorpi, K., 2012. Which aspects of health differ between working and nonworking women with fibromyalgia? A cross-sectional study of work status and health. *BMC Public Health*, *12*(1), p.1076.

Patten, S.B., Beck, C.A., Kassam, A., Williams, J.V., Barbui, C. and Metz, L.M., 2005. Long-term medical conditions and major depression: strength of association for specific conditions in the general population. *The Canadian Journal of Psychiatry*, *50*(4), pp.195-202.

Paul-Savoie, E., Marchand, S., Morin, M., Bourgault, P., Brissette, N., Rattanavong, V., Cloutier, C., Bissonnette, A. and Potvin, S., 2012. Is the deficit in pain inhibition in fibromyalgia influenced by sleep impairments?. *The open rheumatology journal*, *6*, p.296.

Perez-de-Heredia-Torres, M., Huertas-Hoyas, E., Martínez-Piédrola, R., Palacios-Ceña, D., Alegre-Ayala, J., Santamaría-Vázquez, M. and Fernández-de-las-Peñas, C., 2017. Balance deficiencies in women with fibromyalgia assessed using computerised dynamic posturography: a cross-sectional study in Spain. *BMJ open*, *7*(7), p.e016239.

Perraton, L., Machotka, Z. and Kumar, S., 2009. Components of effective randomized controlled trials of hydrotherapy programs for fibromyalgia syndrome: A systematic review. *Journal of pain research*, *2*, p.165.

Perrot, S., Vicaut, E., Servant, D. and Ravaud, P., 2011. Prevalence of fibromyalgia in France: a multi-step study research combining national screening and clinical confirmation: The DEFI study (Determination of Epidemiology of FIbromyalgia). *BMC musculoskeletal disorders*, *12*(1), p.224.

Pichierri, G., Wolf, P., Murer, K. and de Bruin, E.D., 2011. Cognitive and cognitive-motor interventions affecting physical functioning: a systematic review. *BMC geriatrics*, *11*(1), p.29.

Pollok, B., Krause, V., Legrain, V., Ploner, M., Freynhagen, R., Melchior, I. and Schnitzler, A., 2010. Differential effects of painful and non-painful stimulation on tactile processing in fibromyalgia syndrome and subjects with masochistic behaviour. *PloS one*, *5*(12), p.e15804.

Prentice, W.E. 'Therapeutic Modalities for Physical Therapist'. Second edition. New York: McGraw Hill Medical publishing division, pp.430-431.

Pujol, J., López-Solà, M., Ortiz, H., Vilanova, J.C., Harrison, B.J., Yücel, M., Soriano-Mas, C., Cardoner, N. and Deus, J., 2009. Mapping brain response to pain in fibromyalgia patients using temporal analysis of FMRI. *PloS one*, *4*(4), p.e5224.

Radjieski, J.M., Lumley, M.A. and Cantieri, M.S., 1998. Effect of osteopathic manipulative treatment of length of stay for pancreatitis: a randomized pilot study. *The Journal of the American Osteopathic Association*, *98*(5), pp.264-272.

Ramsay, C., Moreland, J., Ho, M., Joyce, S., Walker, S. and Pullar, T., 2000. An observer-blinded comparison of supervised and unsupervised aerobic exercise regimens in fibromyalgia. *Rheumatology*, *39*(5), pp.501-505.

Raphael, J.H., Southall, J.L., Treharne, G.J. and Kitas, G.D., 2002. Efficacy and adverse effects of intravenous lignocaine therapy in fibromyalgia syndrome. *BMC musculoskeletal disorders*, *3*(1), p.21.

Redondo, J.R., Justo, C.M., Moraleda, F.V., Velayos, Y.G., Puche, J.J.O., Zubero, J.R., Hernández, T.G., Ortells, L.C. and Pareja, M.Á.V., 2004. Long-term efficacy of therapy in patients with fibromyalgia: A physical exercise-based program and a cognitive-behavioral approach. *Arthritis Care & Research*, *51*(2), pp.184-192.

Reiffenberger, D.H. and Amundson, L.H., 1996. Fibromyalgia syndrome: a review. *American Family Physician*, *53*(5), pp.1698-1712.

Reisine, S., Fifield, J., Walsh, S. and Forrest, D.D., 2008. Employment and health status changes among women with fibromyalgia: A five-year study. *Arthritis Care & Research*, *59*(12), pp.1735-1741.

Remvig, L., Ellis, R.M. and Patijn, J., 2008. Myofascial release: an evidence-based treatment approach?. *International Musculoskeletal Medicine*, *30*(1), pp.29-35.

Riberto, M., Alfieri, F.M., de Benedetto Pacheco, K.M., Leite, V.D., Kaihami, H.N., Fregni, F. and Battistella, L.R., 2011. Efficacy of transcranial direct current stimulation coupled with a multidisciplinary rehabilitation program for the treatment of fibromyalgia. *The open rheumatology journal*, *5*, p.45.

Richards, S.C. and Scott, D.L., 2002. Prescribed exercise in people with fibromyalgia: parallel group randomised controlled trial. *Bmj*, *325*(7357), p.185.

Rios, R. and Zautra, A.J., 2011. Socioeconomic disparities in pain: The role of economic hardship and daily financial worry. *Health Psychology*, *30*(1), p.58.

Robinson, M.E., Craggs, J.G., Price, D.D., Perlstein, W.M. and Staud, R., 2011. Gray matter volumes of pain-related brain areas are decreased in fibromyalgia syndrome. *The journal of pain*, *12*(4), pp.436-443.

Ross, R.L., Jones, K.D., Bennett, R.M., Ward, R.L., Druker, B.J. and Wood, L.J., 2010. Preliminary evidence of increased pain and elevated cytokines in fibromyalgia patients with defective growth hormone response to exercise. *The open immunology journal*, *3*, p.9.

Ross, R.L., Jones, K.D., Ward, R.L., Wood, L.J. and Bennett, R.M., 2010. Atypical depression is more common than melancholic in fibromyalgia: an observational cohort study. *BMC musculoskeletal disorders*, *11*(1), p.120.

Ruiz, J.R., Segura-Jiménez, V., Ortega, F.B., Álvarez-Gallardo, I.C., Camiletti-Moirón, D., Aparicio, V.A., Carbonell-Baeza, A., Femia, P., Munguía-Izquierdo, D. and Delgado-Fernández, M., 2013. Objectively measured sedentary time and physical activity in women with fibromyalgia: a cross-sectional study. *BMJ open*, *3*(6), p.e002722.

Salgueiro, M., García-Leiva, J.M., Ballesteros, J., Hidalgo, J., Molina, R. and Calandre, E.P., 2013. Validation of a Spanish version of the revised fibromyalgia impact questionnaire (FIQR). *Health and quality of life outcomes*, *11*(1), p.132.

Santos, D.D.M., Lage, L.V., Jabur, E.K., Kaziyama, H.H.S., Iosifescu, D.V., Lucia, M.C.S.D. and Fraguas, R., 2011. The association of major depressive episode and personality traits in patients with fibromyalgia. *Clinics*, *66*(6), pp.973-978.

Sarzi-Puttini, P., Buskila, D., Carrabba, M., Doria, A. and Atzeni, F., 2008. Treatment strategy in fibromyalgia syndrome: where are we now?. In *Seminars in arthritis and rheumatism* (Vol. 37, No. 6, pp. 353-365). WB Saunders.

Schaefer, C., Chandran, A., Hufstader, M., Baik, R., McNett, M., Goldenberg, D., Gerwin, R. and Zlateva, G., 2011. The comparative burden of mild, moderate and severe fibromyalgia: results from a cross-sectional survey in the United States. *Health and quality of life outcomes*, *9*(1), p.71.

Seo, J., Kim, S.H., Kim, Y.T., Song, H.J., Lee, J.J., Kim, S.H., Han, S.W., Nam, E.J., Kim, S.K., Lee, H.J. and Lee, S.J., 2012. Working memory impairment in fibromyalgia patients associated with altered frontoparietal memory network. *PloS one*, *7*(6), p.e37808.

Shang, Y., Gurley, K., Symons, B., Long, D., Srikuea, R., Crofford, L.J., Peterson, C.A. and Yu, G., 2012. Noninvasive optical characterization of muscle blood flow, oxygenation, and metabolism in women with fibromyalgia. *Arthritis research & therapy*, *14*(6), p.R236.

Short, E.B., Borckardt, J.J., Anderson, B.S., Frohman, H., Beam, W., Reeves, S.T. and George, M.S., 2011. Ten sessions of adjunctive left prefrontal rTMS significantly reduces fibromyalgia pain: a randomized, controlled pilot study. *Pain*, *152*(11), pp.2477-2484.

Sicras-Mainar, A., Rejas, J., Navarro, R., Blanca, M., Morcillo, Á., Larios, R., Velasco, S. and Villarroya, C., 2009. Treating patients with fibromyalgia in primary care settings under routine medical practice: a claim database cost and burden of illness study. *Arthritis research & therapy*, *11*(2), p.R54.

Silva, A., Queiroz, S.S.D., Andersen, M.L., Mônico-Neto, M., Campos, R.M.D.S., Roizenblatt, S., Tufik, S. and Mello, M.T.D., 2013. Passive body heating improves sleep patterns in female patients with fibromyalgia. *Clinics*, *68*(2), pp.135-140.

Silverman, S., Sadosky, A., Evans, C., Yeh, Y., Alvir, J.M.J. and Zlateva, G., 2010. Toward characterization and definition of fibromyalgia severity. *BMC musculoskeletal disorders*, *11*(1), p.66.

Smith, M.T., Edwards, R.R., McCann, U.D. and Haythornthwaite, J.A., 2007. The effects of sleep deprivation on pain inhibition and spontaneous pain in women. *Sleep*, *30*(4), pp.494-505.

Sosa-Reina, M.D., Nunez-Nagy, S., Gallego-Izquierdo, T., Pecos-Martín, D., Monserrat, J. and Álvarez-Mon, M., 2017. Effectiveness of therapeutic exercise in fibromyalgia syndrome: a systematic review and meta-analysis of randomized clinical trials. *BioMed research international*, *2017*.

Spaeth, M. and Briley, M., 2009. Fibromyalgia: a complex syndrome requiring a multidisciplinary approach. *Human PsychoPharmacotherapy: Clinical and Experimental*, *24*(S1), pp.S3-S10.

Sperber, A.D., Akiva, S., Leshno, M., Halpern, Z. and Buskila, D., 2011. Validation of New Symptom-Based Fibromyalgia Criteria for Irritable Bowel Syndrome Co-morbidity Studies. *Journal of neurogastroenterology and motility*, *17*(1), p.67.

Spitzer, R.L., Kroenke, K., Williams, J.B. and Löwe, B., 2006. A brief measure for assessing generalized anxiety disorder: the GAD-7. *Archives of internal medicine*, *166*(10), pp.1092-1097.

Sprott, H., Salemi, S., Gay, R.E., Bradley, L.A., Alarcon, G.S., Oh, S.J., Michel, B.A. and Gay, S., 2004. Increased DNA fragmentation and ultrastructural changes in fibromyalgic muscle fibres. *Annals of the rheumatic diseases*, *63*(3), pp.245-251.

Stasinopoulos, D. and Johnson, M.I., 2004. Cyriax physiotherapy for tennis elbow/lateral epicondylitis. *British journal of sports medicine*, *38*(6), pp.675-677.

Staud, R. and Price, D.D., 2008. Long-term trials of pregabalin and duloxetine for fibromyalgia symptoms: how study designs can affect placebo factors. *Pain*, *136*(3), p.232.

Staud, R., Craggs, J.G., Perlstein, W.M., Robinson, M.E. and Price, D.D., 2008. Brain activity associated with slow temporal summation of C-fiber evoked pain in fibromyalgia patients and healthy controls. *European Journal of Pain*, *12*(8), pp.1078-1089.

Staud, R., Koo, E., Robinson, M.E. and Price, D.D., 2007. Spatial summation of mechanically evoked muscle pain and painful aftersensations in normal subjects and fibromyalgia patients. *Pain*, *130*(1-2), pp.177-187.

Staud, R., Nagel, S., Robinson, M.E. and Price, D.D., 2009. Enhanced central pain processing of fibromyalgia patients is maintained by muscle afferent input: a randomized, double-blind, placebo-controlled study. *PAIN®*, *145*(1-2), pp.96-104.

Staud, R., Weyl, E.E., Price, D.D. and Robinson, M.E., 2012. Mechanical and heat hyperalgesia highly predict clinical pain intensity in patients with chronic musculoskeletal pain syndromes. *The Journal of Pain*, *13*(8), pp.725-735.

Straube, S., Moore, R.A., Paine, J., Derry, S., Phillips, C.J., Hallier, E. and McQuay, H.J., 2011. Interference with work in fibromyalgia-effect of treatment with pregabalin and relation to pain response. *BMC musculoskeletal disorders*, *12*(1), p.125.

Stutts, L.A., Robinson, M.E., McCulloch, R.C., Banou, E., Gremillion, H.A., Waxenberg, L.B. and Staud, R., 2009. Patient centered outcome criteria for successful treatment of facial pain and fibromyalgia. *Journal of orofacial pain*, *23*(1), p.47.

Sucher, B.M., 1993. Myofascial manipulative release of carpal tunnel syndrome: documentation with magnetic resonance imaging. *The Journal of the American Osteopathic Association*, *93*(12), pp.1273-1278.

Sumpton, J.E. and Moulin, D.E., 2008. Fibromyalgia: presentation and management with a focus on pharmacological treatment. *Pain Research and Management*, *13*(6), pp.477-483.

Tanita, T. (2010) Outcomes and Cost minimization between Siriraj cold hot pack and the innovator product. Siriraj Medical Journal; 62(5): 211-214.

Terhorst, L., Schneider, M.J., Kim, K.H., Goozdich, L.M. and Stilley, C.S., 2011. Complementary and alternative medicine in the treatment of pain in fibromyalgia: a systematic review of randomized controlled trials. *Journal of manipulative and physiological therapeutics*, *34*(7), pp.483-496.

Thieme, K. and Turk, D.C., 2005. Heterogeneity of psychophysiological stress responses in fibromyalgia syndrome patients. *Arthritis research & therapy*, *8*(1), p.R9.

Thieme, K., Flor, H. and Turk, D.C., 2006. Psychological pain treatment in fibromyalgia syndrome: efficacy of operant behavioural and cognitive behavioural treatments. *Arthritis research & therapy*, *8*(4), p.R121.

Thieme, K., Gromnica-Ihle, E. and Flor, H., 2003. Operant behavioral treatment of fibromyalgia: a controlled study. *Arthritis Care & Research*, *49*(3), pp.314-320.

Thorn, B.E., Pence, L.B., Ward, L.C., Kilgo, G., Clements, K.L., Cross, T.H., Davis, A.M. and Tsui, P.W., 2007. A randomized clinical trial of targeted cognitive behavioral treatment to reduce catastrophizing in chronic headache sufferers. *The Journal of Pain*, *8*(12), pp.938-949.

Ting, T.V., Hashkes, P.J., Schikler, K., Desai, A.M., Spalding, S. and Kashikar-Zuck, S., 2012. The role of benign joint hypermobility in the pain experience in Juvenile Fibromyalgia: an observational study. *Pediatric Rheumatology*, *10*(1), p.16.

Togo, F., Natelson, B.H., Cherniack, N.S., FitzGibbons, J., Garcon, C. and Rapoport, D.M., 2008. Sleep structure and sleepiness in chronic fatigue syndrome with or without coexisting fibromyalgia. *Arthritis research & therapy*, *10*(3), p.R56.

Tzabazis, A., Aparici, C.M., Rowbotham, M.C., Schneider, M.B., Etkin, A. and Yeomans, D.C., 2013. Shaped magnetic field pulses by multi-coil repetitive transcranial magnetic stimulation (rTMS) differentially modulate anterior cingulate cortex responses and pain in volunteers and fibromyalgia patients. *Molecular pain*, *9*(1), p.33.

Vas, J., Modesto, M., Aguilar, I., Santos-Rey, K., Benítez-Parejo, N. and Rivas-Ruiz, F., 2011. Effects of acupuncture on patients with fibromyalgia: study protocol of a multicentre randomized controlled trial. *Trials*, *12*(1), p.59.

Velly, A.M., Look, J.O., Schiffman, E., Lenton, P.A., Kang, W., Messner, R.P., Holcroft, C.A. and Fricton, J.R., 2010. The effect of fibromyalgia and widespread pain on the clinically significant temporomandibular muscle and joint pain disorders—a prospective 18-month cohort study. *The Journal of Pain*, *11*(11), pp.1155-1164.

Vierck, C.J., 2012. A mechanism-based approach to prevention of and therapy for fibromyalgia. *Pain research and treatment*, *2012*.

Vincent, A., Whipple, M.O., Luedtke, C.A., Oh, T.H., Sood, R., Smith, R.L. and Jatoi, A., 2011. Pain and other symptom severity in women with fibromyalgia and a previous hysterectomy. *Journal of pain research*, *4*, p.325.

Vinjamury, S., Jones, J., Hsiao, L., Moutappa, M. and Weiss, J., 2012. P02. 66. Efficacy of acupuncture for fibromyalgia-RCT. *BMC Complementary and Alternative Medicine*, *12*(S1), p.P122.

Volz, M.S., Suarez-Contreras, V., Mendonca, M.E., Pinheiro, F.S., Merabet, L.B. and Fregni, F., 2013. Effects of sensory behavioral tasks on pain threshold and cortical excitability. *PLoS One*, *8*(1), p.e52968.

Wagner, J.S., DiBonaventura, M.D., Chandran, A.B. and Cappelleri, J.C., 2012. The association of sleep difficulties with health-related quality of life among patients with fibromyalgia. *BMC musculoskeletal disorders*, *13*(1), p.199.

Wahner-Roedler, D.L., Thompson, J.M., Luedtke, C.A., King, S.M., Cha, S.S., Elkin, P.L., Bruce, B.K., Townsend, C.O., Bergeson, J.R., Eickhoff, A.L. and Loehrer, L.L., 2011. Dietary soy supplement on fibromyalgia symptoms: a randomized, double-blind, placebo-controlled, early phase trial. *Evidence-Based Complementary and Alternative Medicine*, *2011*.

Walitt, B., Nahin, R.L., Katz, R.S., Bergman, M.J. and Wolfe, F., 2015. The prevalence and characteristics of fibromyalgia in the 2012 National Health Interview Survey. *PloS one*, *10*(9), p.e0138024.

Walton, A., 2008. Efficacy of myofascial release techniques in the treatment of primary Raynaud's phenomenon. *Journal of bodywork and movement therapies*, *12*(3), pp.274-280.

Wang, C., Schmid, C.H., Rones, R., Kalish, R., Yinh, J., Goldenberg, D.L., Lee, Y. and McAlindon, T., 2010. A randomized trial of tai chi for fibromyalgia. *New England Journal of Medicine*, *363*(8), pp.743-754.

Wilbarger, J.L. and Cook, D.B., 2011. Multisensory hypersensitivity in women with fibromyalgia: implications for well being and intervention. *Archives of physical medicine and rehabilitation*, *92*(4), pp.653-656.

Williams, D.A. and Clauw, D.J., 2009. Understanding fibromyalgia: lessons from the broader pain research community. *The Journal of Pain*, *10*(8), pp.777-791.

Williams, D.A., Cary, M.A., Groner, K.H., Chaplin, W., Glazer, L.J., Rodriguez, A.M. and Clauw, D.J., 2002. Improving physical functional status in patients with fibromyalgia: a brief cognitive behavioral intervention. *The Journal of Rheumatology*, *29*(6), pp.1280-1286.

Williams, D.A., Kuper, D., Segar, M., Mohan, N., Sheth, M. and Clauw, D.J., 2010. Internet-enhanced management of fibromyalgia: a randomized controlled trial. *PAIN®*, *151*(3), pp.694-702.

Wilson, H.D., Robinson, J.P. and Turk, D.C., 2009. Toward the identification of symptom patterns in people with fibromyalgia. *Arthritis Care & Research: Official Journal of the American College of Rheumatology*, *61*(4), pp.527-534.

Wolfe, F., 1997. The relation between tender points and fibromyalgia symptom variables: evidence that fibromyalgia is not a discrete disorder in the clinic. *Annals of the rheumatic diseases*, *56*(4), pp.268-271.

Wolfe, F., Clauw, D.J., Fitzcharles, M.A., Goldenberg, D.L., Häuser, W., Katz, R.L., Mease, P.J., Russell, A.S., Russell, I.J. and Walitt, B., 2016, December. 2016 Revisions to the 2010/2011 fibromyalgia diagnostic criteria. In *Seminars in arthritis and rheumatism* (Vol. 46, No. 3, pp. 319-329). WB Saunders.

Wolfe, F., Clauw, D.J., Fitzcharles, M.A., Goldenberg, D.L., Katz, R.S., Mease, P., Russell, A.S., Russell, I.J., Winfield, J.B. and Yunus, M.B., 2010. The American College of Rheumatology preliminary diagnostic criteria for fibromyalgia and measurement of symptom severity. *Arthritis care & research, 62*(5), pp.600-610.

Wolfe, F., Ross, K., Anderson, J., Russell, I.J. and Hebert, L., 1995. The prevalence and characteristics of fibromyalgia in the general population. *Arthritis & Rheumatism: Official Journal of the American College of Rheumatology, 38*(1), pp.19-28.

Wolfe, F., Smythe, H.A., Yunus, M.B., Bennett, R.M., Bombardier, C., Goldenberg, D.L., Tugwell, P., Campbell, S.M., Abeles, M., Clark, P. and Fam, A.G., 1990. The American College of Rheumatology 1990 criteria for the classification of fibromyalgia. *Arthritis & Rheumatism: Official Journal of the American College of Rheumatology, 33*(2), pp.160-172.

Woolfolk, R.L., Allen, L.A. and Apter, J.T., 2012. Affective-cognitive behavioral therapy for fibromyalgia: a randomized controlled trial. *Pain research and treatment, 2012.*

Wright, C., Carson, J., Carson, K., Bennett, R., Mist, S. and Jones, K., 2012. P02. 193. Yoga of awareness: a randomized trial in fibromyalgia: post intervention and 3 month follow up results. *BMC complementary and alternative medicine, 12*(S1), p.P249.

Yates, W.R., Mitchell, J., Rush, A.J., Trivedi, M., Wisniewski, S.R., Warden, D., Bryan, C., Fava, M., Husain, M.M. and Gaynes, B.N., 2007. Clinical features of depression in outpatients with and without co-occurring general medical conditions in STAR* D: confirmatory analysis. *Primary care companion to the Journal of clinical psychiatry, 9*(1), p.7.

Yunus, M.B., 2012. The prevalence of fibromyalgia in other chronic pain conditions. *Pain research and treatment, 2012.*

Zamuner, A.R., Porta, A., Andrade, C.P., Forti, M., Marchi, A., Furlan, R., Barbic, F., Catai, A.M. and Silva, E., 2017. The degree of cardiac baroreflex involvement during active standing is associated with the quality of life in fibromyalgia patients. *PloS one, 12*(6), p.e0179500.

Zhao, Y., Sun, P. and Bernauer, M., 2012. Comparing common reasons for inpatient and outpatient visits between commercially-insured duloxetine or pregabalin initiators with fibromyalgia. *Journal of pain research, 5*, p.443.

Appendix

SAMPLING CALCULATION

$$n = \frac{2\left(Z_\alpha + Z_\beta\right)^2 \sigma^2}{\left(\mu_s - \mu_t - \delta\right)^2}$$

- Primary outcome measure is FIQ
- Significance level = 5%
- Power = 80%
- n= required sample size
- σ = Standard Deviation = 8.6 (as mentioned in the ref article by Bennett, et., 2009)
- δ= MCID of FIQ = 14
- z_α = 1.96
- z_β= 0.8416
- $\mu_s - \mu_t$ = 18

Inserting the Required Information in the formula gives

$$n = \frac{2(1.96 + 0.8416)^2 (8.6)^2}{(18-14)^2}$$

$$= \frac{2(2.8016)^2 (73.96)}{(4)^2}$$

$$= \frac{2(7.85)\,(73.96)}{(16)}$$

$$= \frac{1161.172}{16}$$

=72.57 approx. 73 with 5% drop out

$$= 73 \times \frac{5}{100} = 3.65$$

Total sample size = 73 + 4 = 77   (> 26 in each group)

FIBROMYALIGIA IMPACT QUESTIONNAIRE (FIQR)

REVISED FIBROMYALGIA
IMPACT QUESTIONNAIRE (FIQR)

Last Name: ___________________________ Duration of FM symptoms (years): ___________

First Name: ___________________________ Time since FM was first diagnosed (years): ___________

Age: ___________________________

DOMAIN 1: FUNCTION

Directions: For each of the following 9 questions, check the box that best indicates how much your Fibromyalgia made it difficult
to perform each of the following activities during the past 7 days. If you did not perform a particular activity in the last 7 days, rate the
difficulty for the last time you performed the activity. If you can't perform an activity, check the last box.

BRUSH OR COMB YOUR HAIR

No difficulty ☐ ☐ ☐ ☐ ☐ ☐ ☐ ☐ ☐ ☐ ☐ Very difficult
0 1 2 3 4 5 6 7 8 9 10

WALK CONTINUOUSLY FOR 20 MINUTES

No difficulty ☐ ☐ ☐ ☐ ☐ ☐ ☐ ☐ ☐ ☐ ☐ Very difficult
0 1 2 3 4 5 6 7 8 9 10

PREPARE A HOMEMADE MEAL

No difficulty ☐ ☐ ☐ ☐ ☐ ☐ ☐ ☐ ☐ ☐ ☐ Very difficult
0 1 2 3 4 5 6 7 8 9 10

VACUUM, SCRUB, OR SWEEP FLOORS

No difficulty ☐ ☐ ☐ ☐ ☐ ☐ ☐ ☐ ☐ ☐ ☐ Very difficult
0 1 2 3 4 5 6 7 8 9 10

LIFT AND CARRY A BAG FULL OF GROCERIES

No difficulty ☐ ☐ ☐ ☐ ☐ ☐ ☐ ☐ ☐ ☐ ☐ Very difficult
0 1 2 3 4 5 6 7 8 9 10

CLIMB ONE FLIGHT OF STAIRS

No difficulty ☐ ☐ ☐ ☐ ☐ ☐ ☐ ☐ ☐ ☐ ☐ Very difficult
0 1 2 3 4 5 6 7 8 9 10

CHANGE BEDSHEETS

No difficulty ☐ ☐ ☐ ☐ ☐ ☐ ☐ ☐ ☐ ☐ ☐ Very difficult
0 1 2 3 4 5 6 7 8 9 10

SIT IN A CHAIR FOR 45 MINUTES

No difficulty ☐ ☐ ☐ ☐ ☐ ☐ ☐ ☐ ☐ ☐ ☐ Very difficult
0 1 2 3 4 5 6 7 8 9 10

No difficulty ☐ ☐ ☐ ☐ ☐ ☐ ☐ ☐ ☐ ☐ ☐ Very difficult
0 1 2 3 4 5 6 7 8 9 10

DOMAIN 1 SUBTOTAL:_______________

DOMAIN 2: OVERALL

Directions: For each of the following 2 questions, check the box that best describes the overall impact of your
Fibromyalgia over the last 7 days.

Never ☐ ☐ ☐ ☐ ☐ ☐ ☐ ☐ ☐ ☐ ☐ Always
0 1 2 3 4 5 6 7 8 9 10

Never ☐ ☐ ☐ ☐ ☐ ☐ ☐ ☐ ☐ ☐ ☐ Always
0 1 2 3 4 5 6 7 8 9 10

DOMAIN 2 SUBTOTAL:_______________

DOMAIN 3: SYMPTOMS

Directions: For each of the following 10 questions, select the box that best indicates your intensity level of these common
Fibromyalgia symptoms over the past 7 days.

No pain ☐ ☐ ☐ ☐ ☐ ☐ ☐ ☐ ☐ ☐ ☐ Unbearable pain
0 1 2 3 4 5 6 7 8 9 10

Lots of energy ☐ ☐ ☐ ☐ ☐ ☐ ☐ ☐ ☐ ☐ ☐ No energy
0 1 2 3 4 5 6 7 8 9 10

No stiffness ☐ ☐ ☐ ☐ ☐ ☐ ☐ ☐ ☐ ☐ ☐ Severe stiffness
0 1 2 3 4 5 6 7 8 9 10

Awoke well rested ☐ ☐ ☐ ☐ ☐ ☐ ☐ ☐ ☐ ☐ ☐ Awoke very tired
0 1 2 3 4 5 6 7 8 9 10

No depression   0   1   2   3   4   5   6   7   8   9   10   Very depressed

Good memory   0   1   2   3   4   5   6   7   8   9   10   Very poor memory

Not anxious   0   1   2   3   4   5   6   7   8   9   10   Very anxious

No tenderness   0   1   2   3   4   5   6   7   8   9   10   Very tender

No imbalance   0   1   2   3   4   5   6   7   8   9   10   Severe imbalance

No sensitivity   0   1   2   3   4   5   6   7   8   9   10   Extreme sensitivity

DOMAIN 3 SUBTOTAL:________________

SCORING:

1) Sum the scores for each of the 3 domains (function, overall, and symptoms)

2) Divide domain 1 score by 3, leave domain 2 score unchanged, and divide domain 3 score by 2

3) Add the 3 resulting domain scores to obtain the total FIQR score

DOMAIN 1 SUBTOTAL _______	÷ 3	= _______		
DOMAIN 2 SUBTOTAL _______	CARRY OVER SUBTOTAL	= _______	▶	**TOTAL FIQR SCORE**
DOMAIN 3 SUBTOTAL _______	÷ 2	= _______		

Appendix

BECK DEPRESSION INVENTORY –II (BDI)

Name:_________________________________ Marital status________________________

Age: ________Sex: ______   Occupation: _______________________________________

Education: ____

Please read each group of statements carefully, and then pick out the one statement in each group that best describes you have been feeling during the past two weeks, including today. Circle the number beside the statement you have picked. If several statements in the group seem to apply equally well, circle the highest number for that group. Be sure that you do not choose more than one statement for any group, including item 16 (Changes in Sleeping Pattern) or Item 18 (Changes in Appetite).

1. Sadness
- 0 I do not feel sad.
- 1 I feel sad much of the time.
- 2 I am sad all the time.
- 3 I am so sad or unhappy that I can't stand it.

2. Pessimism
- 0 I am not discouraged about my future.
- 1 I feel more discouraged about my future than I used to be.
- 2 I do not expect things to work out for me.
- 3 I feel my future is hopeless and will only get worse.

3. Past Failure
- 0 I do not feel like a failure.
- 1 I have failed more than I should have.
- 2 As I look back, I see a lot of failures.
- 3 I feel I am a total failure as a person.

4. Loss of Pleasure
- 0 I get as much pleasure as I ever did from the things I enjoy.
- 1 I don't enjoy things as much as I used to.
- 2 I get very little pleasure from the things I used to enjoy.
- 3 I can't get any pleasure from the things I used to enjoy.

5. Guilty Feelings
- 0 I don't feel particularly guilty.
- 1 I feel guilty over many things I have done or should have done.
- 2 I feel quite guilty most of the time.
- 3 I feel guilty all of the time.

6. Punishment Feelings
- 0 I don't feel I am being punished.
- 1 I feel I may be punished.
- 2 I expect to be punished.
- 3 I feel I am being punished.

7. Self-Dislike
- 0 I feel the same about myself as ever.
- 1 I have lost confidence in myself.
- 2 I am disappointed in myself.
- 3 I dislike myself.

8. Self-Criticalness
- 0 I don't criticize or blame myself more than usual.
- 1 I am more critical of myself than I used to be.
- 2 I criticize myself for all of my faults.
- 3 I blame myself for everything bad that happens.

9. Suicidal Thoughts or Wishes
- 0 I don't have any thoughts of killing myself.
- 1 I have thoughts of killing myself, but I would not carry them out.
- 2 I would like to kill myself.
- 3 I would kill myself if I had the chance.

10. Crying
- 0 I don't cry anymore than I used to.
- 1 I cry more than I used to.
- 2 I cry over every little thing.
- 3 I feel like crying, but I can't.

11. Agitation

0   I am no more restless or wound up than usual.

1   I feel more restless or wound up than usual.

2   I am so restless or agitated that it's hard to stay still.

3   I am so restless or agitated that I have to keep moving or doing something.

12. Loss of Interest

0   I have not lost interest in other people or activities.

1   I am less interested in other people or things than before.

2   I have lost most of my interest in other people or things.

3   It's hard to get interested in anything.

13. Indecisiveness

0   I make decisions about as well as ever.

1   I find it more difficult to make decisions than usual.

2   I have much greater difficulty in making decisions than I used to.

3   I have trouble making any decisions.

14. Worthlessness

0   I do not feel I am worthless.

1   I don't consider myself as worthwhile and useful as I used to.

2   I feel more worthless as compared to other people.

3   I feel utterly worthless.

15. Loss of Energy

0   I have as much energy as ever.

1   I have less energy than I used to have.

2   I don't have enough energy to do very much.

3   I don't have enough energy to do anything.

16. Changes in Sleeping Pattern

0   I have not experienced any change in my sleeping pattern.

1a   I sleep somewhat more than usual.

1b   I sleep somewhat less than usual.

2a   I sleep a lot more than usual.

2b   I sleep a lot less than usual.

3a   I sleep most of the day.

3b   I wake up 1–2 hours early and can't get back to sleep.

17. Irritability

0   I am no more irritable than usual.

1   I am more irritable than usual.

2   I am much more irritable than usual.

3   I am irritable all the time.

18. Changes in Appetite

0   I have not experienced any change in my appetite.

1a   My appetite is somewhat less than usual.

1b   My appetite is somewhat greater than usual.

2a   My appetite is much less than before.

2b   My appetite is much greater than usual.

3a   I have no appetite at all.

3b   I crave food all the time.

19. Concentration Difficulty

0   I can concentrate as well as ever.

1   I can't concentrate as well as usual.

2   It's hard to keep my mind on anything for very long.

3   I find I can't concentrate on anything.

20. Tiredness or Fatigue

0   I am no more tired or fatigued than usual.

1   I get more tired or fatigued more easily than usual.

2   I am too tired or fatigued to do a lot of the things I used to do.

3   I am too tired or fatigued to do most of the things I used to do.

21. Loss of Interest in Sex

0   I have not noticed any recent change in my interest in sex.

1   I am less interested in sex than I used to be.

2   I am much less interested in sex now.

3   I have lost interest in sex completely.

_____________Subtotal page 2

_____________Subtotal page 1

_____________Total score

Appendix

GENERALIZED ANXIETY DISORDER (GAD) - 7

GAD-7				
Over the <u>last 2 weeks</u>, how often have you been bothered by the following problems? *(Use "✔" to indicate your answer)*	**Not at all**	**Several days**	**More than half the days**	**Nearly every day**
1. Feeling nervous, anxious or on edge	0	1	2	3
2. Not being able to stop or control worrying	0	1	2	3
3. Worrying too much about different things	0	1	2	3
4. Trouble relaxing	0	1	2	3
5. Being so restless that it is hard to sit still	0	1	2	3
6. Becoming easily annoyed or irritable	0	1	2	3
7. Feeling afraid as if something awful might happen	0	1	2	3

(For office coding: Total Score T____ = ____ + ____ + ____)

Appendix

SF-36 HEALTH SURVEY

SF-36 QUESTIONNAIRE

Name:______________________   Ref. Dr:________________   Date: _______

ID#: ______________   Age: _______   Gender: M / F

Please answer the 36 questions of the **Health Survey** completely, honestly, and without interruptions.

GENERAL HEALTH:
In general, would you say your health is:
◯ Excellent   ◯ Very Good   ◯ Good   ◯ Fair   ◯ Poor

Compared to one year ago, how would you rate your health in general now?
◯ Much better now than one year ago
◯ Somewhat better now than one year ago
◯ About the same
◯ Somewhat worse now than one year ago
◯ Much worse than one year ago

LIMITATIONS OF ACTIVITIES:
The following items are about activities you might do during a typical day. Does your health now limit you in these activities? If so, how much?

Vigorous activities, such as running, lifting heavy objects, participating in strenuous sports.
◯ Yes, Limited a lot   ◯ Yes, Limited a Little   ◯ No, Not Limited at all

Moderate activities, such as moving a table, pushing a vacuum cleaner, bowling, or playing golf
◯ Yes, Limited a Lot   ◯ Yes, Limited a Little   ◯ No, Not Limited at all

Lifting or carrying groceries
◯ Yes, Limited a Lot   ◯ Yes, Limited a Little   ◯ No, Not Limited at all

Climbing several flights of stairs
◯ Yes, Limited a Lot   ◯ Yes, Limited a Little   ◯ No, Not Limited at all

Climbing one flight of stairs
◯ Yes, Limited a Lot   ◯ Yes, Limited a Little   ◯ No, Not Limited at all

Bending, kneeling, or stooping
◯ Yes, Limited a Lot   ◯ Yes, Limited a Little   ◯ No, Not Limited at all

Walking more than a mile
◯ Yes, Limited a Lot   ◯ Yes, Limited a Little   ◯ No, Not Limited at all

Walking several blocks
◯ Yes, Limited a Lot   ◯ Yes, Limited a Little   ◯ No, Not Limited at all

Walking one block
◯ Yes, Limited a Lot   ◯ Yes, Limited a Little   ◯ No, Not Limited at all

Bathing or dressing yourself

○ Yes, Limited a Lot   ○ Yes, Limited a Little   ○ No, Not Limited at all

PHYSICAL HEALTH PROBLEMS:
During the past 4 weeks, have you had any of the following problems with your work or other regular daily activities as a result of your physical health?

Cut down the amount of time you spent on work or other activities
○ Yes   ○ No

Accomplished less than you would like
○ Yes   ○ No

Were limited in the kind of work or other activities
○ Yes   ○ No

Had difficulty performing the work or other activities (for example, it took extra effort)
○ Yes   ○ No

EMOTIONAL HEALTH PROBLEMS:
During the past 4 weeks, have you had any of the following problems with your work or other regular daily activities as a result of any emotional problems (such as feeling depressed or anxious)?

Cut down the amount of time you spent on work or other activities
○ Yes   ○ No

Accomplished less than you would like
○ Yes   ○ No

Didn't do work or other activities as carefully as usual
○ Yes   ○ No

SOCIAL ACTIVITIES:
Emotional problems interfered with your normal social activities with family, friends, neighbors, or groups?

○ Not at all   ○ Slightly   ○ Moderately   ○ Severe   ○ Very Severe

PAIN:
How much bodily pain have you had during the past 4 weeks?

○ None   ○ Very Mild   ○ Mild   ○ Moderate   ○ Severe   ○ Very Severe

During the past 4 weeks, how much did pain interfere with your normal work (including both work outside the home and housework)?

○ Not at all   ○ A little bit   ○ Moderately   ○ Quite a bit   ○ Extremely

ENERGY AND EMOTIONS:
These questions are about how you feel and how things have been with you during the last 4 weeks. For each question, please give the answer that comes closest to the way you have been feeling.

Did you feel full of pep?
- All of the time
- Most of the time
- A good Bit of the Time
- Some of the time
- A little bit of the time
- None of the Time

Have you been a very nervous person?
- All of the time
- Most of the time
- A good Bit of the Time
- Some of the time
- A little bit of the time
- None of the Time

Have you felt so down In the dumps that nothing could cheer you up?
- All of the time
- Most of the time
- A good Bit of the Time
- Some of the time
- A little bit of the time
- None of the Time

Have you felt calm and peaceful?
- All of the time
- Most of the time
- A good Bit of the Time
- Some of the time
- A little bit of the time
- None of the Time

Did you have a lot of energy?
- All of the time
- Most of the time
- A good Bit of the Time
- Some of the time
- A little bit of the time
- None of the Time

Have you felt downhearted and blue?
○ All of the time
○ Most of the time
○ A good Bit of the Time
○ Some of the time
○ A little bit of the time
○ None of the Time

Did you feel worn out?
○ All of the time
○ Most of the time
○ A good Bit of the Time
○ Some of the time
○ A little bit of the time
○ None of the Time

Have you been a happy person?
○ All of the time
○ Most of the time
○ A good Bit of the Time
○ Some of the time
○ A little bit of the time
○ None of the Time

Did you feel tired?
○ All of the time
○ Most of the time
○ A good Bit of the Time
○ Some of the time
○ A little bit of the time
○ None of the Time

SOCIAL ACTIVITIES:
During the past 4 weeks, how much of the time has your physical health or emotional problems interfered with your social activities (like visiting with friends, relatives, etc.)?

○ All of the time
○ Most of the time
○ Some of the time
○ A little bit of the time
○ None of the Time

GENERAL HEALTH:
How true or false is each of the following statements for you?

I seem to get sick a little easier than other people
◯ Definitely true   ◯ Mostly true   ◯ Don't know   ◯ Mostly false   ◯ Definitely false

I am as healthy as anybody I know
◯ Definitely true   ◯ Mostly true   ◯ Don't know   ◯ Mostly false   ◯ Definitely false

I expect my health to get worse
◯ Definitely true   ◯ Mostly true   ◯ Don't know   ◯ Mostly false   ◯ Definitely false

My health is excellent
◯ Definitely true   ◯ Mostly true   ◯ Don't know   ◯ Mostly false   ◯ Definitely false

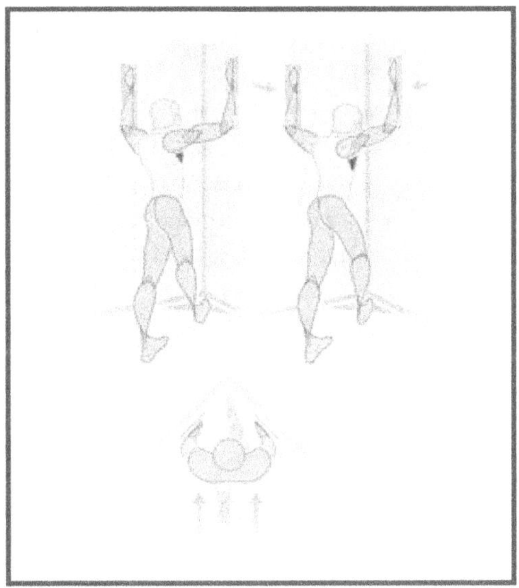

Pectoral stretch: Start: Stand facing a corner of a room, with one foot in the corner and the other foot behind you. Raise your arms so your elbows are slightly higher than your shoulders and pointing forward. Place your hands and forearms against the walls. Keeping your abs engaged, bend your front knee and lean your body into the corner until you feel a slight stretch in the chest. Hold for 30 seconds. Relax for five seconds. Repeat for 5 times.

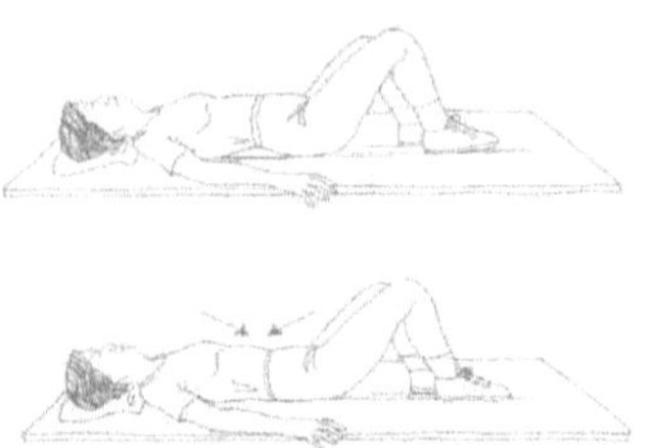

Upper Trap Stretch: Sitting in a chair, upright nice and tall, shoulders back. Reach one arm behind the back. Use the other arm to gently pull your head to the opposite side as if you are trying to bring your ear to your shoulder. Keep your chin level and head back. Once you feel a comfortable stretch, hold for 30 seconds. Relax for five seconds. **Repeat both side 3 times each.**

Abdominal in-drawing / pelvic neutral: lie on your back with knees bent and feet flat on the floor with a small pillow under your head. Tighten your lower abdomen about 20% and bring the lower back towards the floor. **Hold for 10 counts.** Relax for 5 counts. Repeat 5 times twice daily.

Levator scapulae stretch: sit tall and place your hand behind the head diagonally and rotate your head 45 degrees. Bring your head down toward the same side knee. **Once you feel a comfortable stretch, hold for 30 seconds.** Relax for five seconds. **Repeat both side 3 times each.**

Chin tuck exercise: sit tall and place the tips of fingers together behind lower neck. Relax arms and elbows. Look straight, pull chin up and backward. **Hold for 10 counts.** Relax for 5 counts. **Repeat 5 times twice daily.**

Appendix
ETHICAL CONSIDERATION

- The identity of the subjects will be protected throughout the study and in the publication so made.

- Each subject randomly will be allocated a 3-letter secret code number throughout and after the study.

- A decoding note will be made on the subject's first appearance and will be retained by me in full secrecy.

- All subjects will be briefed about this and my legal obligations to observe any act of data protection.

- After briefing only about their rights, I will make them sign the consent form.

- Subjects will be free in any stage of the project to walk out of it, if they feel the need.

- All the potential hazards of the research that can come, are seriously being looked upon by thorough literature review and pilot study.

- All information to be collected shall pertain to the study only.

Appendix

SCREENING FORM

Name   :

Age   :

Sex   :   Male / Female

Address   :

Tel / Mobile No   :

Subjective screening

Do you have general pain all over the body

If yes, how many months / years old problem?

Have you met with accident / trauma / injuries?   Yes / No

If yes, please explain nature of trauma _____________ any fracture _____________
surgeries underwent _____________________.

Do you have any cardiac / respiratory problems _______________________________

If yes, explain _______________________________________.

Do you have any other problems / complaints If yes, explain

☐ Muscle pain	☐ Nervousness	☐ Loss/change in taste
☐ Irritable bowel syndrome	☐ Chest pain	☐ Seizures
☐ Fatigue/tiredness	☐ Blurred vision	☐ Dry eyes
☐ Thinking or remembering problem	☐ Fever	☐ Shortness of breath
☐ Muscle Weakness	☐ Diarrhea	☐ Loss of appetite
☐ Headache	☐ Dry mouth	☐ Rash
☐ Pain/cramps in abdomen	☐ Itching	☐ Sun sensitivity
☐ Numbness/tingling	☐ Wheezing	☐ Hearing difficulties
☐ Dizziness	☐ Raynauld's	☐ Easy bruising
☐ Insomnia	☐ Hives/welts	☐ Hair loss
☐ Depression	☐ Ringing in ears	☐ Frequent urination
☐ Constipation	☐ Vomiting	☐ Painful urination
☐ Pain in upper abdomen	☐ Heartburn	☐ Bladder spasms
☐ Nausea	☐ Oral ulcers	

Appendix – XIV

NEW CLINICAL FIBROMYALGIA DIAGNOSTIC CRITERIA

Part 1

Check each area you have felt pain in over the <u>past week.</u>

- ☐ Shoulder girdle, left
- ☐ Shoulder girdle, right
- ☐ Upper arm, left
- ☐ Upper arm, right
- ☐ Lower arm, left
- ☐ Lower arm, right
- ☐ Hip (buttock) left
- ☐ Hip (buttock) right
- ☐ Upper leg left
- ☐ Upper leg right
- ☐ Lower leg left
- ☐ Lower leg right
- ☐ Jaw left
- ☐ Jaw right
- ☐ Chest
- ☐ Abdomen
- ☐ Neck
- ☐ Upper back
- ☐ Lower back
- ☐ None of these areas

Count up the number of areas checked and enter your Widespread Pain Index or WPI score score here _______.

Symptom Severity Score (SS score) - Part 2a.

Indicate your level of symptom severity over the <u>past week</u> using the following scale.

Fatigue

- ☐ 0 = No problem
- ☐ 1 = Slight or mild problems; generally mild or intermittent
- ☐ 2 = Moderate; considerable problems; often present and/or at a moderate level
- ☐ 3 = Severe: pervasive, continuous, life disturbing problems

Waking unrefreshed

- ☐ 0 = No problem
- ☐ 1 = Slight or mild problems; generally mild or intermittent
- ☐ 2 = Moderate; considerable problems; often present and/or at a moderate level
- ☐ 3 = Severe: pervasive, continuous, life disturbing problems

Cognitive symptoms

- ☐ 0 = No problem
- ☐ 1 = Slight or mild problems; generally mild or intermittent
- ☐ 2 = Moderate; considerable problems; often present and/or at a moderate level
- ☐ 3 = Severe: pervasive, continuous, life disturbing problems

Symptom Severity Score (SS score)- Part 2b

Check each of the following OTHER SYMPTOMS that you have experienced over the <u>past week?</u>

- ☐ Muscle pain
- ☐ Irritable bowel syndrome
- ☐ Fatigue/tiredness
- ☐ Thinking or remembering problem
- ☐ Muscle Weakness
- ☐ Headache
- ☐ Pain/cramps in abdomen
- ☐ Numbness/tingling
- ☐ Dizziness
- ☐ Insomnia
- ☐ Depression
- ☐ Constipation
- ☐ Pain in upper abdomen
- ☐ Nausea
- ☐ Nervousness
- ☐ Chest pain
- ☐ Blurred vision
- ☐ Fever
- ☐ Diarrhea
- ☐ Dry mouth
- ☐ Itching
- ☐ Wheezing
- ☐ Raynauld's
- ☐ Hives/welts
- ☐ Ringing in ears
- ☐ Vomiting
- ☐ Heartburn
- ☐ Oral ulcers
- ☐ Loss/change in taste
- ☐ Seizures
- ☐ Dry eyes
- ☐ Shortness of breath
- ☐ Loss of appetite
- ☐ Rash
- ☐ Sun sensitivity
- ☐ Hearing difficulties
- ☐ Easy bruising
- ☐ Hair loss
- ☐ Frequent urination
- ☐ Painful urination
- ☐ Bladder spasms

Appendix

ASSESSMENT FORM

Name:

Age:

Sex: ☐ Male   Female

Education:

Address and contact number:

Marital Status: ☐ Married   Unmarried

☐ Separated / Divorced   Others

Religion: ☐ Hindu   Muslim

Christian   Others

Community: Tribal   Non-Tribal

Habitat: Rural   Urban

Semi-Urban

Occupation: Employed   Unemployed

Economic Status: Lower   Middle

Higher

Chief complaints:

Other complaints:

1. When the pain has started?

2. Have you had any trauma/injury for the past 6 months?

YES   NO

3. How long the pain remains, is it Continuous   or   intermittent

4. Where is the site of pain? ————————————

        Does it radiate?   YES   NO

5. Is the pain aching, sharp, shooting, pinching, burning or radiating type?

6. If you are given a scale that range from 0-10 .which grade would you mark for your pain.

Visual Analogue Scale:

7. At which part of the day/night the pain is more?

      DAY   NIGHT

8. Does it interfere with your sleep?

      YES   NO

9. What activity/work does your pain increases? and how long it need to subside?

————————————————————————

10. How do you relieve this pain? Explanation?

————————————————————————

11. Tell me the site of pain when it hurts you while applying pressure

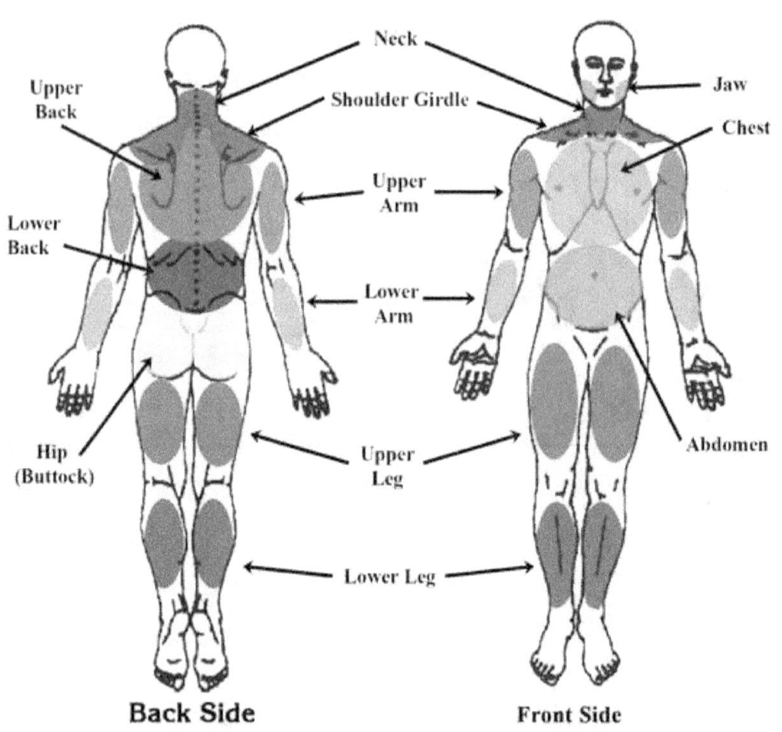

Swelling   Present   Absent

Range of motion (Mark a tick)

Joints	Restriction	Non – restricted	Joints	Restriction	Non – restricted
Cervical			Lumbar		
Upper limb			Hip		
Elbow			Knee		
Wrist			Ankle		

9 782815 491716